Pathways to Career Success
for Minorities

Ferguson
An imprint of ☑®Facts On File

Pathways to Career Success for Minorities

Copyright © 2000 by Facts On File, Inc.

Ferguson
An imprint of Facts On File, Inc.
132 West 31st Street
New York NY 10001

Library of Congress Cataloging-in-Publication Data

Pathways to career success for minorities.
    p. cm.
    Includes index
    ISBN 0-89434-303-3
    1. Minorities—Education (Higher)—United States. 2. Minorities—Employment—
United States. 3. Student aid—United States. 4. Vocational guidance—United States.
I. J. G. Ferguson Publishing Company. II. Title.

LC3727 .P27 2000
378.3—dc21   00-021838

Ferguson books are available at special discounts when purchased in bulk quantities for businesses, associations, institutions, or sales promotions. Please call our Special Sales Department in New York at (212) 967-8800 or (800) 322-8755.

You can find Ferguson on the World Wide Web at http://www.fergpubco.com

Editor: Tim Schaffert
Writers: Sherry Powley, Tim Schaffert
Proofreader: Bonnie Needham
Cover Design: Robert Howard Graphic Design

Printed in the United States of America

10 9 8 7 6 5 4 3 2

This book is printed on acid-free paper.

Table of Contents

INDEXES

Introduction

As the 20th century came to a close, the topic of workplace diversity and minority opportunity was everywhere: Fortune began its annual listing of top companies for minorities; the government, along with the information technology industry, expressed the immediate need for minorities to have access to computers and the Internet; issues of minority representation in the media were addressed by landmark agreements; affirmative action was challenged across the country, just as the Equal Employment Opportunity Commission, and the nation's businesses, developed more efficient methods of addressing workplace discrimination. These issues, and others, are addressed in the 10 essays at the beginning of this book. Whether you're looking to start a business, develop your artistic talents, seek funding for education, or all of the above, these essays will provide you with insight into the issues affecting today's minorities.

Following the essays is a directory of hundreds of financial aid opportunities and organizations. Whether you're just beginning to consider your career and education options, or looking for ways to establish yourself further in your profession, the book will direct you to the necessary resources. The entries are divided into three sections: Financial Aid, Organizations, and Additional Information.

Financial Aid: This section includes fellowships, grants, loans, awards, scholarships, and internships/career guidance opportunities. Though some of these terms are used interchangeably, a fellowship is typically a sum of money awarded to individuals who have demonstrated serious interest in the subject matter, and have possibly earned a degree in the area. A grant is often a cash sum, and is not necessarily awarded to individuals pursuing academic study. A scholarship enables a student to meet the fees and tuition of higher education. In the section on internships/career guidance, you'll find programs that involve individuals in hands-on experience with a profession, usually for a summer between college semesters.

Organizations: This section includes professional organizations, minority colleges, fraternities and sororities, and other groups that assist individuals with the pursuit of career, education, and community. In the section on professional organizations, you'll find nonprofit associations composed of individuals working together to further minorities and students within their particular professions; the section on minority colleges includes those two-year and four-year institutions that have historically demonstrated a commitment to furthering minority students; the section on fraternities and sororities provides a list of some of the national organizations, and their chapters, serving minority college students and alumni; and the section on other organizations includes foundations, Indian tribes, job banks, employment services, and other groups that assist minorities.

Additional Information: This section lists publications (magazines, journals, newspapers) and Web sites of relevance to minorities looking to develop their careers.

The Indexes following the entries can help you locate opportunities by institution and financial aid name, by state, by academic subject, or by minority group (African American, Asian American, Native American, and Hispanic).

Introduction

Each entry is intended to give you a starting point from which to pursue information. You'll find the mailing address, telephone number, and a brief description of the organization or opportunity. Most entries also feature an Internet address. Many of the organizations listed in this book have Web sites with extensive information, including application guidelines, deadlines, and links to other opportunities.

Part I

Essays on Minority Topics

General Minority Work Issues

The U.S. Census Bureau predicts that by 2050, minorities will comprise 47 percent of the population. (In 2000, the number is approximately 30 percent.) The population of Hispanics is expected to increase more than 200 percent by 2050, with a projected population of 96 million. To meet the needs of a much more diverse society, the nation's industries and professions are in the process of great change. Efforts by private businesses, government agencies, and universities are underway to better assist minorities in the workforce. No matter what changes may occur in the political arena, no matter how affirmative action may be altered, career and education opportunities will greatly increase for the minority population. Private industry in particular has recognized the need for multicultural staffing, looking ahead to a more diverse clientele; in order for a company or a profession to progress, it will need to reflect the diversity of the society it serves.

In the essays that follow, you may find some of the information contradictory. In "Information = Success" about the need for minorities in the technology industry, and in "Workplace Diversity" about private companies committing to multiculturalism, you'll read of industries and companies anxious to develop ways to employ and sustain minority professionals and employees. But in "Leveling the Playing Field," you will read how government affirmative action policies are threatened across the nation, limiting special opportunities in education and employment. As a result of lawsuits and government propositions, some of the scholarship opportunities listed in this directory have been changed from minority opportunities to scholarships benefiting only the economically disadvantaged or individuals from urban and rural areas. Colleges and universities are changing their entrance policies, careful to avoid giving special preference to minorities.

However, many of these changes are political in nature, and not practical, and not necessarily reflective of the public interest. Polls have shown that even those who voted against affirmative action in California and Washington actually were in support of programs assisting minorities. And colleges are fighting in the courts for their right to encourage and support a diverse campus, recognizing the educational importance of a multicultural student body. Most colleges and universities have active departments dedicated to the needs of minority students, helping these students to find scholarships and offering career guidance. And scholarship committees are eager to reward talented minority students. Terminology and policies may change, but society will find a way to fill the ranks of its workforce with qualified, educated minorities.

The success of many industries absolutely depends on the training and hiring of minorities. In order to effectively serve diverse communities, the health care industry needs more minority administrators and medical professionals; to effectively cover the news that impacts a multicultural readership, the newspaper industry must have more minority reporters and editors; to meet the increasing demands of technological development, more minority engineers must enter the rapidly growing field of information technology. Practically every professional association in the country is studying the numbers of minorities in its workforce, and devising ways to provide minority students with more educational opportunities, and professionals with more networking opportunities.

Essays on Minority Topics

Whether you are just starting out, or looking to further yourself in your established career, or hoping to change professions, you have every reason to be optimistic about the job market. A *Newsweek* poll conducted in 1999 found that 71 percent of African Americans anticipated their family incomes to increase in the next 10 years. (Only 59 percent of whites were as optimistic about their own incomes.) The future is bright, but obstacles, other than political, still exist. Cases of workplace discrimination still fill the courtrooms, and still impede workplace productivity. Although the employment and home ownership of African Americans is increasing, too many middle class African American students lag behind their white peers. A 1999 article in *The New York Times* focused on this issue, interviewing students and educators. Professionals find a number of reasons for the gap—too few minority teachers and role models, and too low expectations for the success of African American students. Peer pressure and low self-esteem also play a part, according to the article.

But for every troubling statistic about minority career and education, there are many more encouraging ones. Despite obstacles, minorities in the United States are finding more opportunities for success than ever before. To recruit minority students, industries are linking established professionals with high school and college students. The American Psychological Association, for example, has established many projects to interest minorities in psychology doctoral programs. The engineering profession is also active in sending professionals to lecture at historically black colleges and universities, and developing mentorships between professionals and students.

Today's students and job seekers have the added benefit of the Internet. It is difficult for some minorities to get access to the Internet (see "Information = Success"), but government and private programs are working to change this. Hopefully, if you are reading this book in a library, you are only a few feet away from a computer. If Internet access is not available through your library, check with area social service agencies, cultural centers, and schools about reserving time to use the Internet. With the World Wide Web, you can research professions, colleges and universities, scholarship opportunities, and the cities where you would like to live. There are a number of "cyber-communities" for minorities, allowing you to meet others with similar interests and professional goals. Some of these online communities include www.LatinoLink.com and www.click2asia.com. Companies seeking to hire minorities post job listings on the many online employment services (including www.minorities-jb.com and www.diversityemployment.com); most of these services enable you to view listings for free, and to even post your resume for employers. Free email accounts are available from a variety of services, allowing you to communicate directly with college admissions departments, professional organizations, and potential employers. There is also a wealth of career guidance information on the Web, to assist you with writing a resume and searching for jobs. Some people even interview for jobs over the Internet.

A number of publications are also dedicated to professional guidance for minorities. The *Black Collegian* is a free magazine available through the career services department of your college or university, or you can read its articles on the Web at www.blackcollegian.com. *Black Enterprise* and *Hispanic Business* cover the minority business world, and post articles at www.blackenterprise.com and www.hispanicbusiness.com. You should also contact the association dedicated to the profession you are pursuing; most professional associations publish journals and newsletters for their members.

To read more about general minority work and education issues, check out these books:

The Colorblind Career: What Every African American, Hispanic American and Asian American Needs to Know in Today's Tough Job Market by Ollie Stevenson (Peterson's Guides, 1997)

The Minority and Women's Complete Scholarship Book (Sourcebooks Trade, 1998)

How to Build a Career in the New Economy: Guide for Minorities and Women by Anthony Smith (Warwick Publishing, 1999)

Inside Corporate America: A Guide for African Americans by Wilson Simmons III (Perigree, 1996)

Financial Aid for Hispanic Americans by Gail Ann Schlachter (Reference Service Press, 1999)

Best Careers for Bilingual Latinos: Market Your Fluency in Spanish to Get Ahead on the Job by Graciela Kenig (VGM Career Horizons, 1998)

Just Because I'm Latin Doesn't Mean I Mambo: A Success Guide for Hispanic Americans by Juan Roberto Job (Ballantine Books, 1998)

Doing It for Ourselves; Success Stories of African American Women in Business by Donna Ballard (Berkley Publishing Group, 1997)

Where America's Black Leaders Learned to Lead: The Black College Career Guide by Joan Carroll (Zulema Enterprises, 1995)

General Introduction to Financial Aid

The importance of higher education is increasing, and so is the cost of obtaining it. To find the pathway to personal and professional success, minorities must determine the education they need and find a way to get that education. College or graduate school costs can seem overwhelming, but don't lose heart. There are ways to find dollars for college. In fact, there are many options. This article will help you learn how to look for financial aid, where to look, and what kinds of aid are available.

Looking for financial aid can seem confusing, but take it a step at a time, and you'll soon be an expert. The steps outlined below will get you started.

Step 1: Determine Your Financial Need

First, determine whether you actually need financial aid. Use the formula that colleges and funding sources use to determine financial need: the Cost of Attendance minus the Expected Family Contribution (EFC). The cost of attendance includes the cost of schooling (tuition, fees, books, and supplies) plus living expenses (room and board, travel, and incidental expenses). Every school can supply an estimated average cost of attendance. The expected family contribution (EFC) is based on family income and expense information you provide. Subtract the EFC from the cost of attendance at a particular educational institution to determine what your financial need would be if you attended that school.

If the financial need formula shows that you do not need aid, you may just have saved yourself a lot of time and work. Even if you do not need financial aid, read the section below on scholarships and grants (financial aid that you do not have to repay). You may qualify for awards based on particular skills or interests. Read the section on tax credits, too, because you may be able to recover some of the money you spend on education.

Step 2: Contact Financial Aid Offices

If you determine that you do need financial aid, start looking right away. Finding the many kinds of aid that may be available to you takes time and energy. Starting early can improve your chances of obtaining aid. Get off to a good start by contacting the financial aid offices of the schools you are considering. The financial aid packages different colleges offer you may be a determining factor in your final selection. Each college or university has its own requirements, and failing to learn about them could slow down or jeopardize your financial aid. To learn as much as you can about each school's financial aid process, ask a financial aid officer these questions:

What types of financial aid do you offer?

What are your guidelines for requesting financial aid?

What application materials do you require?

What are the deadlines for submitting financial aid requests?

What effect will my request for financial aid have on my admission?

Will your school be able to cover my total financial need?

Will the school cover my financial need for four years?

When will you notify me of my eligibility for financial aid?

What other sources of aid should I know about?

Get to know the aid administrators. Tell them about any unusual circumstances or expenses you have. They may be able to help you. Each school has its own procedures and forms, but most of them also use the Free Application for Federal Student Aid (FAFSA).

Step 3: Complete the FAFSA

The Free Application for Federal Student Aid (FAFSA) is the form you must complete to apply for federal assistance of any kind. Complete the FAFSA first, and complete it as soon after January 1 as possible. Note that you will have to provide tax return information on your FAFSA, so complete your federal and state tax returns before you fill out your FAFSA. Applications are accepted as of January 1 each year, and the earlier you apply, the better your chances of receiving what you need. If you apply late, you will miss out on aid that has already been awarded. The government takes three to four weeks to process the application.

Experts suggest that students submit the FAFSA whether they think they qualify for aid or not. Many colleges and universities use it in their aid decisions. Some forms of private assistance only are available after you have been rejected for federal aid. The FAFSA form is available in high schools and colleges, by telephone (1-800-4-FEDAID), and online (http://www.fafsa.ed.gov).

Step 4: Learn about the Types of Financial Aid

Free information about student aid is available in the reference section of the library. Look under "financial aid" or "student aid." Many books on financial aid are available at the library or in bookstores. The Internet also has a wealth of financial aid information. Some excellent Web sites are mentioned at the end of this article. (If you do not have a computer, go to the library or your school. Most libraries and schools now have computers available at little or no cost.) All of these resources can help you learn more about the three basic kinds of financial aid. Financial aid falls into three general categories:

1. Money you don't have to pay back (grants and scholarships)

2. Money you must pay back (loans)

3. Money you earn as you go (employer tuition reimbursement programs, military tuition assistance programs, work-study programs)

You may need to combine more than one type of financial aid to cover all of the costs of higher education, so learn about, consider, and apply for as many forms of aid as you can.

Money That Does Not Have to Be Paid Back

First, look for sources of funds you do not have to pay back. They fall into two categories: grants and scholarships.

Grants

Grants are monetary awards that do not have to be repaid. There are two kinds: grants based on financial need and grants that support a specific project.

Grants Based on Financial Need. The federal government sponsors two grants that are based entirely on financial need: the Pell Grant and the Federal Supplemental Educational Opportunity Grant (FSEOG). Both require that applicants submit the FAFSA in order to be considered.

Grants That Support a Specific Project. The federal government and other organizations offer funds to support research in specific areas. The sponsor generally requires that applicants submit grant proposals for evaluation. This type of grant is most common in applications for graduate study.

To apply for the Pell and FSEOG grants, consult *The Student Guide* of the US Department of Education. (Ordering information is given on page 13.) The reference desk of the library has books that list grants and fellowships available through government agencies and other organizations throughout the United States. Also check the financial aid Web sites below. Free Internet searches can supply the latest information on available grants.

Scholarships

Scholarships are usually short-term monetary awards. Like grants, they do not have to be repaid. Scholarships are offered by a variety of providers. Each scholarship provider sets the criteria for application. The criteria can range from financial need to special hobbies and interests to academic excellence. This is an area in which creative thinking and research can help you find dollars. Think of all of the kinds of scholarships for which you may be eligible.

First, consider your major and minor subjects. Some organizations offer scholarships especially for minorities who are entering certain fields. Learn about professional associations in your field and find out if they offer scholarships. The Organizations Section of this book contains contact information for many women's associations that may sponsor scholarships, and the Financial Aid Section lists many scholarships that are available to women.

Next think about your hobbies, talents, and interests. Your ability in sports, music, or creative writing or your interest in the environment or in helping others might help finance your education.

Find all the scholarships for which you might qualify and apply for as many as you can. A number of online resources feature free searches to help locate scholarships for which you qualify. Several are listed at the end of this article.

Beware of Scholarship Scams!

While most organizations offer bona fide scholarships, the Federal Trade Commission (FTC) warns that scholarship scams do exist. The FTC recently brought actions against several companies that collectively cheated over 175,000 consumers out of millions of dollars.

Essays on Minority Topics

Keep in mind the old adage, "If it sounds too good to be true, it probably is!" Here are some warning signs of a potential scam:

Offers a scholarship or award for which you did not apply

Guarantees a scholarship in return for advance fees

Asks for credit card or bank account numbers

Charges an advance fee for a loan

Provides only a PO Box

Uses a hard-sell approach

If you suspect a scam, report it to

National Fraud Information Center
PO Box 65868
Washington, DC 20035
Tel: 800-876-7060

or

Federal Trade Commission
Correspondence Branch
Federal Trade Commission, Room 200
6th Street & Pennsylvania Avenue, NW
Washington, DC 20580
Tel: 877-382-4375

Money That Must Be Paid Back

Few individuals who need financial aid can put together enough scholarships to pay for school entirely with "free money." Most students also need loans. Whether loans are federal or private, they must be paid back.

Federal Loans

The largest sources of student financial aid in the United States are the government's Student Financial Assistance Programs. They account for 70 percent of all student financial aid. All federal loans require the completion of the Free Application for Federal Student Aid (FAFSA). The government makes loans to students and to parents.

Loans to Students. Stafford Loans are federal loans to students. Both undergraduate and graduate students may apply. The loan amounts vary. The loan amount can increase, based on years in school, up to as much as $5,500 after two years of study. Interest rates are variable, but they never exceed 8.25 percent.

Perkins Loans are available to both undergraduate and graduate students who have exceptional financial need. These loans are campus-based. Interested students should consult their school financial aid counselors about the availability of and requirements for Perkins Loans.

Loans to Parents. Parent Loan for Undergraduate Students (PLUS) Loans are federal loans available to parents. They must also be repaid. The interest rates are variable, but they never exceed nine percent.

For current rates and application information for federal assistance programs and to complete the FAFSA online, visit FAFSA on the Web and the site of the Office of Student Financial Assistance Programs (OSFAP). The OSFAP also sponsors "Help Lines for Students." Contact information for both organizations is given on page 13.

Private Loans

Many private financial institutions make loans to both students and their parents. Some of the federal financial aid Web sites referenced on page 12 suggest preferred lenders.

Money That Is Paid While Attending School

Many colleges, universities, and other organizations offer alternate forms of financial aid. Some require students to work to earn the financial aid. Others give students credit on different bases.

Tuition Payment Plans

Many colleges and universities offer short-term installment plans. These plans frequently split the costs into equal monthly payments. Many plans are free of interest, but some have finance charges and/or fees. Ask the schools you are considering about the availability of tuition payment plans.

Employer Tuition Support

If you are working, ask whether your employer has an educational assistance program. Many employers recognize the importance of helping employees advance. An added advantage to employer-provided educational assistance is that money received for courses that begin before June 1, 2000, are exempt from taxes. To learn whether that tax credit will be extended beyond that date, see the Internal Revenue Service Web site listed on page 12 for up-to-date information.

Military Service Benefits

Branches of the U.S. military offer a number of tuition assistance programs. The Web addresses for all five branches—Air Force, Army, Coast Guard, Marines, and Navy—are listed at the end of this article.

Work-Study Programs

Work-study programs allow you to earn money by working while you go to school. These programs may involve work on or off campus. Work-study programs are available through colleges and universities, private sources, and the Federal Work-Study Program. Ask financial aid counselors about opportunities at the schools you are considering. For information on the Federal Work-Study Program, see the current volume of *The Student Guide* of the U.S. Department of Education. Details are given at the end of this article.

National Service

The Corporation for National Service sponsors AmeriCorps, a service organization that helps people in need throughout the United States. AmeriCorps projects include tutoring children, building homes, creating health clinics, and hundreds of other projects. AmeriCorps offers living allowances, health insurance, student loans, and education awards to AmeriCorps members.

Corporation for National Service
1201 New York Avenue, NW
Washington, DC 20525
Tel: 202-606-5000
Web: http://www.americorps.org/

Tax Credit

The Taxpayer Relief Act of 1997 and subsequent tax legislation have made a number of tax credits available to students and their parents. These credits can be a great help to most families.

Hope Scholarship Credit. This credit is only available during the first two years of postsecondary education for students who are enrolled at least half time in a program leading to a recognized educational credential, such as a degree or certificate. The maximum credit per tax year is $1,500 per student.

Lifetime Learning Credit. Taxpayers may claim this credit for qualified tuition and related expenses of students of all ages who are enrolled in eligible educational institutions. The program does not have to lead to a degree or certificate. The maximum tax credit per year through 2002 is $1,000. After 2002, the maximum credit will be $2,000.

Student Loan Interest Deduction. Taxpayers who have taken loans to pay for the cost of attending an eligible educational institution may generally deduct the interest on the loans from their income taxes.

Ask the educational institutions that you are considering whether study with them will qualify for these tax deductions. Information on these and other tax credit programs that may help you and/or your family recover some of the costs of financing higher education can be obtained from the Internal Revenue Service. The Internal Revenue Service published "Notice 97-60: Administrative, Procedural, and Miscellaneous Education Tax Incentives" to explain the higher education tax incentives offered by the Taxpayer Relief Act of 1997. The IRS Web site includes up-to-date information on higher education tax incentive programs. To order IRS Notice 97-60, call 1-800-829-3676. http://www.irs.ustreas.gov/hot/not97-60.html. Tax laws change frequently, so keep informed so you can take advantage of any credits that apply to you.

Higher education is indeed expensive, but financial aid is available to nearly everyone. By exploring the many sources of financial aid, you can find a way to finance your pathway to success.

For More Information

College Is Possible (http://www.collegeispossible.com), a Web site produced by a coalition of America's colleges and universities, recommends books, Web sites, and other resources and gives information on preparing for college, choosing a college, and paying for college.

FastWeb (http://www.fastweb.com) is an excellent source of information for planning for college and beyond. It includes admissions, scholarships, financial aid, and tips on college life. It offers a free search of over 400,000 scholarships totaling more than $1 billion in financial aid and a college search to help match colleges to students' interests.

FinAid (http://www.finaid.org) is another excellent Web site that focuses on financial aid. It offers calculators to help determine total school costs and financial need and links to free financial aid searches. It also reviews many books on financial aid for undergraduates and for graduates.

The Student Guide (http://www.ed.gov/prog_info/SFA/StudentGuide/) from the U.S. Department of Education is the most comprehensive resource on all student financial aid available through the federal Student Financial Assistance Programs—grants, loans, and work-study. *The Student Guide* is updated each year. To request a free copy, call: 1-800-4-Fed-AID.

Contact the Office of Student Financial Assistance Programs of the US Department of Education for information on financial assistance and for help applying. The OSFAP sponsors several "Help Lines for Students":

General aid information or help applying for student aid: 800-433-3242

Help with software for applying electronically: 800-801-0576

Help consolidating student loans: 800-557-7394

Help with a defaulted student loan: 800-621-3115

Minorities in Media

According to a *Black Enterprise Magazine* report, entertainment is one of the "Five Hot Business Fields for Women." Of course, this should come as no surprise to anyone familiar with the enormous salaries and prestige of top executives and performers. Careers in the media—such as jobs in television and film, journalism, publishing, recording, and the ever-expanding electronic-based media (such as the Internet)—are some of the most sought after in the nation. Of course, not all jobs in the entertainment industry and the media are lucrative and glamorous, but many do offer the potential for great success. Unfortunately, minorities may not have the same opportunities in the media as non-minorities, according to some professional and minority organizations. Groups such as the National Association for the Advancement of Colored People (NAACP), the National Association of Hispanic Journalists (NAHJ), and Unity (an alliance of minority journalists) are closely examining the media and are offering solutions for how to expand the number of minorities in newsrooms, broadcast stations and networks, and other media workplaces.

The Media "Whitewash"

When the major television networks announced their new schedules for 1999-2000, red was the only color many minorities saw. The casts of the new shows featured too few people of color, prompting Kweisi Mfume, head of the NAACP, and other leaders of minority organizations to call for meetings with network executives, boycotts, and legal action. Ultimately, Mfume purchased 100 shares of the four major networks (ABC, CBS, Fox, and NBC) to allow him to attend shareholders meetings and the opportunity to voice his opinions directly to the network decision-makers. He also brought the issue to the attention of the nation, as major newspapers, magazines, and network news programs featured reports of this "whitewash" of television programming for the many weeks leading up to the new fall season. As a result, the networks quickly made efforts to introduce minority actors to the casts of their new and returning series.

Though a TN Media analysis called "The Diversity Question," released in September 1999, found that the percentage of African Americans in major roles on network television is actually representative of the population, Hispanics and other minorities were found to be greatly underrepresented. Much had been written in the media in 1999 about the increasing influence of Latin culture on America—how Hispanics were showing clout in elections, on the consumer market, and as entertainers—but television executives failed to recognize this when developing new programming.

This exclusion of minority actors and characters is all particularly puzzling when you consider that advertisers encourage the inclusion of programming featuring minority actors so that they can reach a viable market. Another study by TN Media found that African American households watched 70.4 hours a week of television in 1998, which is about 20 hours more per week than non-blacks. So the problem is not a lack of viewers. The problem, according to Mfume and professionals within the entertainment industry, is too few minority executives, resulting in too few minority directors, producers, and performers hired to create original programming.

The Impact

The failure of an industry to hire minorities for powerful positions can have far-reaching consequences—not only can it result in poor minority representation in television and the movies, but also poor representation in the front pages of the newspaper. Without minority reporters and editors making the important decisions in the nation's newsrooms, the issues important to minorities may be ignored, and serious issues in minority communities may go unrecognized.

The American Society of Newspaper Editors (ASNE) responded to the dearth of minority editors by setting a goal for the nation's newspapers—by 2000, news staffs would mirror the general population, with 28 percent minorities. By 1999, however, the minority percentage on news staffs was less than half the proposed percentage. (The percentage of minorities on the staffs of magazines is even lower—according to a 1998 study conducted by the trade magazine *Mediaweek*, minorities comprise only 6.1 percent of the staffs of major magazines.) After failing to meet its goal, the ASNE extended its target date to the year 2025. This extension caused some controversy, leading the National Association of Black Journalists (NABJ) to express serious concern that the ASNE is not committed to diversity in the newsrooms. In a statement to the press, NABJ President Vanessa Williams said, "ASNE's new goal of newsroom parity in 2025—a generation from now—suggests that the organization is trying to distance itself from another potential failure to build newsrooms that reflect the changing face of American society. Parity by 2025 becomes somebody else's problem."

An influential study by Vernon Stone, a professor at the University of Missouri-Columbia, found that minorities lost ground as television and radio news directors between 1990 and 1994, and recent updates to the report predict little change. The Radio-Television News Directors Association (RTNDA) annually release a minorities survey; in 1999, the survey revealed that the percentage of minorities in the television and radio newsrooms dropped from the previous year. However, the survey also showed that the percentage of minorities in management positions in television departments increased in the previous three years. (The percentage of minority executive producers doubled between 1996 and 1999, from 7 percent to 14 percent; the percentage of minority assignment editors rose from 16 percent to 22 percent.)

Despite these increases, other studies show continued dissatisfaction among minorities in the newsroom. A 1999 report by the International Women's Media Foundation (IWMF) focused on opportunities for minority women in the nation's newsrooms. Only 15 percent of the women surveyed were satisfied with the frequency of promotions, and 28 percent were satisfied with their opportunities of career advancement in general. Fifty-one percent believed they were discriminated against in promotions because of their color and ethnic heritage.

The IWMF report also found that only 25 percent of the minority women journalists interviewed believe the news they cover is representative of the markets they serve. This disparity in news coverage has long been a concern, even as far back as 1968 when the Kerner Commission Report criticized the news media for failing to accurately analyze racial problems. Media studies in recent years have found that the desire to end affirmative action, aid to cities, and other benefits to minorities correlate with distorted perspectives of the population: a *Washington Post* study found that those supporting such cuts believed that the average African American had the same advantages (good education, job, health care) as the average white person. However, the U.S. Census and many other studies and statistics dispute such beliefs.

Media scholars and organizations continue to blame the press for these distorted views, and for promoting racism through insensitive, unbalanced reporting. Research has shown that minorities are typically portrayed in news stories as contributing to social problems and conflicts. The Freedom Forum, an organization that sponsors studies of the media, found in 1998 that 92 percent of sound-bites from "experts" were from non-minorities. NAHJ sponsored a study of the 1997 network news stories and found a 25 percent drop from the previous year in the number of Hispanic-focused stories (which comprised only 112 of 12,000 total stories).

Employment opportunities for minorities in broadcasting are also threatened by minorities losing ground as owners of radio and television stations. A 1997-1998 survey by the National Telecommunications and Information Administration (NTIA) showed a small increase (0.1 percent) in minority commercial broadcast ownership; though this represented an increase of 15 stations, minority ownership was found to be falling behind general growth of the industry. Minority owners cited the difficulty of attracting advertisers as one of the problems facing their stations.

Solutions

Some efforts are underway to remedy the problems in today's newsrooms and broadcast stations. In February 1999, President Clinton encouraged the advertising industry to develop guidelines that would take minority-owned outlets and agencies into consideration, and would result in more fair distribution of dollars spent. The American Advertising Federation picked up the gauntlet in May 1999, forming a committee to study the multicultural market and advertising practices.

To encourage more balanced coverage of the news affecting society as a whole, a group called Unity developed as an alliance of minority journalists. Unity hosted a conference in 1999, attended by 6,800 people, including members of the Asian American Journalists Association, NABJ, NAHJ, and the Native American Journalists Association.

Many other media organizations also serve minority media professionals, including the Black Publishers Association, United Minority Media Association, and the National Association of Minority Media Executives.

The Newspaper Association of America offers internships and minority fellowships, as well as diversity training and recruiting kits, for the nation's newsrooms. The Broadcasting Training Program introduces minority students to broadcasting, and a number of job banks direct minorities to jobs in the media: The National Diversity Newspaper Job Bank, the California Chicano News Media Association Job Bank, the Journalism and Women Symposium Job Bank, among them.

Though many of the statistics compiled by the organizations detailing the underrepresentation of minorities in the media are discouraging, and show that much work must be done in the coming years, the fact that such reports are beginning to receive serious attention from the media shows some progress. As media companies and executives give consideration to these facts and figures, talented minority journalists, directors, producers, writers, and actors of the 21st century should find the paths to success better paved.

For More Information

UNITY
P.O. Box 12365
Arlington, VA 22219
Tel: 703-841-9099
Web: http://unity99.org

National Association of Black Journalists
8701-A Adelphi Road
Adelphi, MD 20783
Tel: 301-445-7100
Web: http://www.nabj.org

National Association of Hispanic Journalists
1193 National Press Building
Washington, DC 20045-2100
Tel: 202-662-7145
Web: http://www.nahj.org

Native American Journalists Association
3359 36th Avenue South
Minneapolis, MN 55406
Tel: 612-729-9244
Web: http://naja.com

Asian American Journalists Association
1765 Sutter Street, Suite 1000
San Francisco, CA 94115
Tel: 415-346-2051
Web: http://www.aaja.org

Mentors: Offering Guidance to Minorities in Schools and in the Workplace

Why Do You Need a Mentor?

Whether you're in high school, college, or in your first years of work, you can benefit from a mentor—somebody on the "inside" who has found success within his or her profession and industry, and who is willing to give advice and share experiences. Mentors can help you make informed decisions about your future. For minority students, mentors are even more important—in addition to offering practical advice, they also serve as role models, showing students that, regardless of their background, color, or race, great success is achievable to those who work hard.

And a need for guidance doesn't end once you begin a job. Starting a new job can be exciting, but also can be stressful—you have to learn a whole new set of rules, meet many new people, and figure out all the unique aspects of the workplace. It can take you months to learn all the details of the job, big and small—from which co-workers to trust and which tasks are top priority, to whether it's okay to take breaks outside the building. Minorities often have additional questions—such as whether discrimination exists in the workplace, and if the company regularly promotes minority workers.

Mentors in Schools and Communities

Many corporations, professional associations, colleges, and minority organizations are working together to provide role models to young people through mentoring programs and internships. Mentorships in the community, in which professionals are assigned to grade school and high school students, are often part of a company's diversity initiatives. Wellspring Resources, a company that manages employee benefit plans, initiated a program for the sixth grade students of an area inner-city school. Company employees serve as mentors to the students, and involve the students with regular computer use. These mentors, many of whom are information technology professionals, teach students how to use the Internet as a research tool for school projects, and keep in close contact with their students through email. Through the Wellspring program, students have learned about the business world while developing important computer skills. Another successful mentorship program began in the early 1970s at Northrop Corporation, now called Northrop Grumman, an aviation contractor. Not only has the company's High School Involvement Partnership program linked students in minority communities with workers in a number of departments, but it also has involved students in internships and has hired many of these students after graduation.

Various non-profit organizations have aided corporations in their outreach efforts. INROADS, with its 50 affiliates across the country, is dedicated to placing minority high school and college students into professional and managerial careers. Students with a grade point average of 3.0 or better can apply to this program, which offers access to training workshops, summer employment, and mentors. Many INROADS students take on full-time jobs with their sponsoring companies. More than 8,000 graduates of the INROADS programs have gone on to pursue professional and managerial careers.

A Better Chance is another organization that provides mentors to minority students. Its Business/Professional Partnership Program gives selected high school juniors and seniors access to the organization's corporate partners (which include American Express, Time, Incorporated, and Sears, Roebuck and Company) through internships, seminars, and employment opportunities. The Pathways to College program links A Better Chance students to mentors who assist with college preparation and the admissions process. Nearly all of the graduating high school seniors (more than 99 percent) with A Better Chance enroll in college.

Some colleges and universities have formed their own outreach programs which bring students to campus for special seminars and introduce them to faculty and college students. Mentorship opportunities often become available to students once they have started college as well, through minority assistance programs. The University System of Georgia has initiated an electronic mentoring program for minority students. Using email and the Internet, students can communicate with mentors from participating institutions across the state. As with the Wellspring program, electronic mentoring allows students to develop computer skills while making connections with the students and faculty of various departments.

Colleges and Universities

No matter what college or university you attend, there likely will be a thriving minority organization to assist you with your educational path and career development. You also may choose to attend a college that has traditionally served an African American, Hispanic, or Native American student population. Historically Black Colleges and Universities (HBCU), Hispanic Serving Institutions (HSI) and Tribal Colleges and Universities (TCU) are those institutions devoted particularly to minority students. The U.S. Department of Education maintains a list of accredited postsecondary minority institutions; in 1999, 600 such institutions were listed. As more corporations and professional organizations recognize the importance of a diverse workplace, more mentoring programs have developed for the students of HBCUs, HSIs, and TCUs.

Many organizations are dedicated to promoting minority institutions and to helping them expand. The National Association for Equal Opportunity in Higher Education (NAFEO) represent 118 HBCUs across the country. According to the NAFEO, one-third of all African American college graduates attend HBCUs. The NAFEO sponsors conferences and scholarships, and maintains a Web site listing of schools. Also in support of HBCUs, *Black Enterprise Magazine* has begun to rank the 50 top colleges and universities where African Americans are most likely to succeed.

The Hispanic Association of Colleges and Universities (HACU) represents 179 Hispanic-serving institutions, and aids students through internship programs, scholarships, and college preparation. HACU also maintains a detailed Web site, and publishes the monthly newsletter "The Voice of Hispanic Higher Education." In the last 30 years, tribal colleges have developed to meet the needs of the Native American population. The

American Indian Higher Education Consortium (AIHEC) represents 32 institutions that serve geographically isolated populations.

Mentors in the Workplace

Traditionally, a mentor is someone with experience who plays an almost parental role in guiding a new employee's career, forming both a personal and professional bond with the protégé (the person learning the ropes). A mentor-protégé relationship sometimes forms naturally, when two people take an interest in each other. In the workplace today, these relationships have become more institutionalized, and often are established before mentor and protégé ever meet. Many companies have incorporated mentorships into their diversity plans, giving every new employee access to someone with a great deal of experience and success within the company. These special mentoring programs have proven valuable to minority and non-minority workers alike, allowing new employees to learn about their workplaces from the inside out. A 1998 study of the highest paid minority executives in the country conducted by Korn/Ferry International, an executive placement firm, found that 71 percent of those surveyed had informal mentors, and 22 percent had formal mentors. These executives cited role models as crucial to their careers, and instrumental in helping them set long-term goals.

Though the mentor-protégé relationship is not new, its development as part of company policy has evolved rapidly over the last decade. By the mid-1990s, large corporations such as General Motors, AT&T, and DuPont had established formal mentoring programs, along with about one-third of the nation's largest corporations. By 1998, a special task force of the Equal Employment Opportunity Commission listed mentoring as an important management practice, and today mentoring programs are commonplace. The U.S. military, recognizing the success of mentoring programs in the business sector, has also initiated such programs. Several books published in the last few years—*The Art of Mentoring; Mentoring: How to Develop Successful Mentor Behaviors; Managers as Mentors* among them—aim to teach mentoring skills.

Even if your workplace has no formal mentoring program, you may be able to find a mentor on your own. Once you meet people in the workplace, you can begin to look for someone with a great deal of experience, with whom you also have much in common: maybe you come from similar backgrounds, went to the same college, or participate in some of the same activities outside the workplace. Once you have made a connection with this person, you may be able to rely on him or her for future guidance.

"Networking" also can be an important aspect of establishing productive workplace relationships. This system of meeting people and making connections with others in your profession can lead you to more job opportunities and a better understanding of your profession and the industry in which you work. Professional associations are often the best sources for networking opportunities. For most individual professions, there are associations which allow people to meet and exchange ideas and concerns, as well as direct people toward accredited educational programs, certification, and job opportunities. Many of these associations include minority chapters or councils; some professional associations, such as the National Association of Hispanic Journalists and the National Society of Black Engineers, are devoted entirely to minority members. Many associations sponsor national networking conferences, allowing professionals to meet each other, attend seminars, and speak to corporate recruiters. Online communities also are developing among professionals, allowing you to exchange email addresses, post questions for Web site forums, and reserve Web pages for your resume.

Essays on Minority Topics

Whether you're just starting out, or on your way to becoming well-established in your profession, mentoring and networking may be your most essential tools in finding success. And as more companies and industries stress workplace diversity, opportunities to form strong bonds among other minority professionals will increase.

For More Information

INROADS
10 South Broadway, Suite 700
St. Louis, MO 63102
Tel: 314-241-7488
Web: http://www.inroadsinc.org

A Better Chance
419 Boylston Street
Boston, MA 02116
Tel: 617-421-0950
Web: http://www.abetterchance.org

National Association for Equal Opportunity in Higher Education
8701 Georgia Avenue, Suite 200
Silver Spring, MD 20910
Tel: 301-650-2440
Web: http://www.nafeo.org

Hispanic Association of Colleges and Universities
4204 Gardendale Street, Suite 216
San Antonio, TX 78229
Tel: 210-692-3805
Web: http://www.hacu2000.org

American Indian Higher Education Consortium
121 Oronoco Street
Alexandria, VA 22314
Tel: 703-838-0400
Web: http://www.aihec.org

Information = Success: The Role of Technology in Today's Workplace

It's obvious to some people that knowledge of computers and technology leads to better jobs and better pay in the workplace. To other people, particularly those without computer and Internet access, it's not so obvious. Despite many successful minorities reaping great rewards in the area of "information technology" (IT), many more minorities could be taking advantage of the surplus of jobs within this industry of computer-based careers. But if you don't have a computer, and have never used the Internet, then you probably aren't aware of the significance of computers in the majority of jobs today. Not only are computer skills necessary in technology-based careers such as computer programming and consulting, World Wide Web site development, and electronic engineering, but also in library science, administration, sales, social services, and hundreds of other careers.

The U.S. Bureau of Labor predicts that 1.3 million new IT workers will be needed by 2006. To fill these jobs, the nation will have to work hard to bridge the gap between the "information rich"—those with computers and Internet access—and the "information poor"—a group that too many minorities, particularly African Americans, Hispanics, and Native Americans, fall into.

Minorities Underrepresented in the IT Industry

In June 1999, the Lemelson-MIT program surveyed high school students and their parents about career interests. The survey found that 64 percent of the respondents favor future careers involving the Internet or computing. Lester C. Thurow, Lemelson-MIT board chairman, commented on these findings, saying that this emphasis on technical entrepreneurship will require much from our educational organizations. "Math and science are going to have to be better taught," Thurow said, "and enrollments are going to have to soar."

This necessary emphasis on math and science may be why many young, intelligent minorities are not pursuing careers in technology, and are not taking advantage of the fact that there are more job openings in the IT workplace than there are skilled workers to fill them. Minorities, particularly those living in poor, urban communities, don't have sufficient access to computers and the Internet in their schools and homes. Not only do these students lack computer skills, but many minorities simply aren't aware of the importance of computer skills, and the wide use of computers in the workplace. It's a sad irony that minorities are underrepresented in the information technology workplace simply because they don't have the right tools or information.

"To get into these fields, you need to be on the right track early," said Roscoe Giles, associate professor in the Department of Electrical and Computer Engineering of Boston University, in a December, 1998, interview with the *Boston Globe*, "but for many women and minorities, the necessary math and science is either not available or they're discouraged from pursuing it." As a result, young minorities do not have many role models in the fields of engineering and IT. This finding is reflected in data released by the National Action Council for Minorities in Engineering (NACME). Though general engineering enrollment rose again in 1997-98 (after a peak in 1992-93), enrollment of African Americans declined. Minorities (including African Americans, Latinos, and Native Americans) saw only a 2.8 percent growth in engineering enrollment in 1997-98, compared to a 6.3 percent growth among non-minorities. Despite the fact that engineering is at the heart of IT, as well as at the heart of the current economic growth of the United States, the industry has had to recruit many foreign engineers to fill the vacant positions, and pay starting salaries of over $40,000 a year, with large signing bonuses. "African Americans, Latinos, and Native Americans constitute 29.7 percent of the college-age population in the United States today and a third of the birth rate, but receive fewer than 3 percent of the doctorates annually in all of the natural sciences, mathematics, and engineering," reported Dr. George Campbell Jr., president and CEO of NACME, at a U.S. Department of Labor symposium in October, 1998. He further illustrated the under-representation by pointing out that only 20 African American women have ever received doctorates in physics.

According to a 1999 study by the Computing Research Association (CRA): "If these groups [Hispanics, African Americans, and Native Americans] were represented in the IT workforce in proportion to their representation in the U.S. population, this country would have more than an adequate supply of workers to fill even the most dire estimates of a shortage."

The Digital Divide

Experts have many theories about why this underrepresentation of minorities in technology exists, but the most alarming statistics concern those minorities attending poor schools and living in low-income communities. A significant number of these homes do not even have telephone service. According to the U.S. Department of Commerce report "Falling Through the Net: Defining the Digital Divide," released in July 1999, approximately 95 percent of all white households have phones, regardless of where they live. But only 76.4 percent of Native American, 84.6 percent of Hispanic, and 85.4 percent of African American households have phone service. These percentages are even lower for those minorities with low levels of income. This lack of phone service obviously serves as a barrier to applying and interviewing for jobs. Experts predict that a lack of email access may soon be equally as restrictive, preventing people from finding jobs, receiving public assistance, gaining important community information, and being productive contributors to society.

The Department of Commerce has released three "Falling Through the Net" reports since 1994. The 1999 report showed that Internet and computer use had increased a great deal since 1994, but a gap of six percentage points had grown between the number of white households going online, and the African American and Hispanic households. African American and Hispanic households are only 40 percent as likely as white households to be online. More whites own computers as well: while about 46 percent of all whites have computers, only about 21 percent of African Americans, and only 23 percent of Hispanics do. Recent studies conducted by Computer Intelligence and by Vanderbilt University found similar discrepancies.

Though differences in income between whites and minorities account somewhat for this "digital divide" in computer access, there are additional factors that keep minorities from entering the IT workplace. Grade school and high school teachers may be poorly trained in computer skills themselves, and therefore unable to give students anything more than a basic overview of computer use. Even college programs can fall behind in preparing students for the rapidly changing technology of today's workplace. Minorities also may suffer from having different learning styles than their white peers, and may not gain access to some of the upper-level math and science courses. Intelligent minority students with good learning skills may not score well on the standardized tests that are considered heavily for entrance to such courses and to the highly selective college engineering programs. Affirmative action programs in college admissions have had some success helping minorities graduate from engineering programs. According to Dr. Campbell of NACME, there were only 600 minority graduates in engineering in 1971; in 1997, there were 6,422. However, these improvements are greatly threatened by anti-affirmative action policies (see "Leveling the Playing Field").

There's also reason to believe that some minorities avoid computer-based careers and special computer training. Young people in particular tend to perceive the image of technology professionals as computer "nerds," and may perceive the work as dull and overly technical. And those minorities who don't have access to computers and the Internet, for whom digital technology has little significance, have doubts about its significance in the workplace and the world-at-large. IT careers also may be unappealing to those minorities pursuing work in a social-conscious field; those wanting careers that address the problems in their communities may perceive computer skills to be unnecessary.

Computers in the Schools

President Clinton's Educational Technology Initiative, presented in 1997, has set goals to provide access to computers and educational software for every American student, to assure that these students are connected to the world outside their communities, and to better train teachers in computer use.

In order to better connect students through the Internet, the government initiated special discounts geared toward the development of quality telecommunications services in U.S. grade schools and high schools. Known as the "e-rate," schools and libraries in low-income communities receive the highest discounts. These discounts are intended to help students gain Internet access. But new computers and new services don't necessarily bring students closer to technological proficiency. Many schools, particularly schools in urban areas, need many improvements before computers can be introduced: more desks and classrooms to house the computer units; more outlets and better wiring; and teachers better trained in computer use. And rewiring an old school is often very expensive, because asbestos in the walls makes such tasks difficult.

In a commentary titled "Technology Versus African-Americans" (*The Atlantic Monthly*, January, 1999), writer Anthony Walton asked, "What if ubertechnocrats like Bill Gates and Larry Ellison (the billionaire CEO of Oracle) used their philanthropic millions to fund basic math and science education in elementary schools, to equip the future, instead of giving away merchandise that essentially serves to expand their customer base?" Bill Gates, criticized widely for not being more charitable, recently responded with one of the largest philanthropic donations in history—$1 billion toward the funding of full scholarships for minority students in math, education, science, and engineering. The scholarships will first be offered to high school seniors in the fall of 2000. The Bill and Melinda Gates Foundation is also donating millions of dollars to introducing more computers and Internet services to libraries in poor communities.

Actually, Gates' contributions of this "merchandise"—the computers and software— reflect how important these tools have become in the classroom. Studies show that math and science education can be improved through the use of computers. Computers allow for more individualized teaching of all subjects, and for self-paced instruction, important for minorities with methods of learning different from their white peers. A report by President Clinton's panel on the use of educational technology listed several examples of schools that have greatly benefited from computers in the classroom, and have seen math scores improve. An inner-city school in Union City, New Jersey, with a 91 percent Hispanic student population, provided computer and Internet access to all its seventh grade students. These students, most of them from low-income communities, greatly improved their scores in reading, language arts, and math. They raised their test scores from significantly below the statewide average, to above the average. At East Bakersfield High School in California, the student body (composed of 60 percent Hispanic students, many of whom have limited English skills) has access to a school-to-work program and technology training, resulting in high job placement rates. At the Northbrook Middle School in Texas, where the student body is composed primarily of the children of migrant workers, computers are used to help students develop problem-solving skills, increasing student test scores.

The Department of Commerce report "Falling Through the Net" found that a majority of the African Americans and Hispanics who use the Internet access it outside their homes. Community-based initiatives to bring more computers to more neighborhoods are under way: the U.S. Department of Housing and Urban Development (HUD) has started "Neighborhood Networks," which introduces computer workstations to its HUD-assisted housing; the NAACP is working with AT&T to create technology centers in 20 cities to provide computer training and Internet seminars; Ameritech Corporation and the National Urban League are working together to build new Internet community centers in urban areas such as Detroit and Milwaukee. Other corporations, such as Lucent Technologies, Cisco Systems, and 3Com Corporation, are also dedicated to building technology centers, donating equipment, and providing training across the country.

Other Solutions

Government programs, private institutions, and IT companies have recognized the need to bring more minorities into the digital age. Organizations such as the Computing Research Association (CRA) and the International Technology Association of America (ITAA) are working to expand opportunities for minority workers in computing fields. A study of the workplace by ITAA in 1998 found a shortage of 346,000 programmers, systems analysts, and computer scientists. In 1999, ITAA conducted its first worker availability survey and found that IT companies are suffering from this shortage, and that they believe the lack of skilled workers will be the biggest barrier to future growth. Some companies, therefore, have incorporated new training and recruitment programs and have partnered with colleges and universities to attract more workers. These companies send their representatives to minority student career fairs, to minority colleges, and they advertise in minority publications. Some also offer scholarships and education assistance programs.

But many Silicon Valley companies, leaders of IT industry, have failed to attract minorities, despite the fact that about half of the region's population is composed of minorities. Only two companies based in Silicon Valley—Sun Microsystems and Applied Materials—made *Fortune* magazine's 1999 list of "50 Best Companies For Asians, Blacks, And Hispanics." Asian Americans, well-represented in the industry, do hold 31 percent of the jobs and own nearly a quarter of the start-ups, but even they face a glass ceiling according to industry insiders. The industry may need to incorporate better diversity initiatives (see "Workplace Diversity") in order to reach out to minority engineers and IT professionals. In 1998, the *San Francisco Chronicle* reported that only 4 percent of the Silicon Valley workforce was African American, and only 7 percent Hispanic.

Many organizations are promoting and rewarding success in IT fields in various ways. NACME has initiated the highly successful Engineering Vanguard Program. This program focuses on selecting talented minority students from low-income communities during their junior year of high school, analyzing them on the basis of their school performance and problem-solving skills, and immersing them in mathematics and science courses. These students then receive full scholarships to engineering schools. The Technology Transfer Project, sponsored by the Executive Leadership Council, serves to educate the students and faculty of historically black colleges about the tools of technology. The project provides summer internships that allow students to work with major corporations in order to gain hands-on experience with technology. NAACP sponsors a Diversity and High Tech Job Fair. The Black Engineer of the Year Awards Conference, organized by the Career Communications Group, hosts workshops and seminars that allow students, scientists, engineers, and professionals to meet and network. Professional organizations such as the Society of Hispanic Professional Engineers, the Society for Mexican American Engineers and Scientists, and the National Society for Black Engineers have formed to serve minorities in the IT workforce.

There are also publications geared specifically toward minorities in IT. Equal Opportunity Publications (EOP) publish many titles focusing on the issues of a diverse workplace, including *Minority Engineer* magazine. *Minority Engineer* is distributed free to minority IT students and professionals. The magazine features career articles, job listings, and information about career fairs and recruitment. *Workforce Diversity for Engineering and IT Professionals* is another EOP publication for those in the technology workforce. *Diversity/Careers in Engineering and Information Technology* is also free to IT professionals and students, and features articles, profiles of minority professionals, and updates on technical careers. Twice a year, a special "Minority College Issue" of *Diversity/Careers* focuses on issues of diversity on campus, information about the job market, and profiles of recent graduates. The magazine's Web site (www.diversitycareers.com) posts articles from the current issue, and features an online forum, and links to companies. A quarterly newsletter, *The Conduit,* includes articles on technology and how black professionals use computers and the Internet in their work and recreation.

Though most of the statistics mentioned above are troubling, minorities can take encouragement from the number of opportunities available in the IT industry. For those minorities well-trained in technology, the workplace should prove welcoming. And as companies, and corporate leaders like Bill Gates, slowly but surely recognize the need for minorities to fill their many job openings, better training programs and job placement will bring more minority workers into the fold.

For More Information

National Action Council for Minorities in Engineering
The Empire State Building
350 Fifth Avenue, Suite 2212
New York, NY 10118-2299
Tel: 212-279-2626
Web: http://www.nacme.org

Essays on Minority Topics

International Technology Association of America
1616 North Fort Myer Drive, Suite 1300
Arlington, VA 22209
Tel: 703-522-5055
Web: http://www.itaa.org

National Society of Black Engineers
1454 Duke Street
Alexandria, VA 22314
Tel: 703-549-2207
Web: http://www.nsbe.org

Society of Hispanic Professional Engineers
5400 East Olympic Boulevard, Suite 210
Los Angeles, CA 90022
Tel: 323-725-3970
Web: http://www.shpe.org

Equal Opportunity Publications
1160 East Jericho Turnpike, Suite 200
Huntington, NY 11743
Tel: 516-421-9421
Web: http://www.eop.com

Workplace Diversity: Giving Companies a Competitive Edge in the Business World

A Commitment to Diversity

Just as state and federal affirmative action policies are threatened across the country (see "Leveling the Playing Field"), the private sector is more dedicated than ever to diversity initiatives. Many large companies have long recognized a commitment to diversity as a moral responsibility. These companies recruit and train minority workers, and provide them with clear paths of promotion and a sense of inclusion, helping minorities achieve fair representation in their workforce. Company executives also are beginning to recognize a commitment to diversity as good business sense. Diversely staffed companies have seen greater productivity—by hiring more minority workers and managers, they have increased sales, built better relationships with other companies, and improved public relations. But, critics say that a number of factors can contribute to a company's success, and these factors are difficult to measure. Some critics argue that those companies devoted to diversity initiatives are devoted to their workers in general, providing all employees with more perks and benefits, and thereby creating a happier, more productive staff. Others believe that diversity can introduce serious problems into the workplace, resulting in reverse discrimination and a divided workforce. Despite the controversies, one thing is given: "diversity" will remain a business-world buzzword for years to come.

Considering the number of complaints of workplace discrimination filed annually with the Equal Employment Opportunity Commission (see "Legal Rights and Recourse"), and the continued underrepresentation of minorities in many industries and in college enrollment, U.S. companies are still a long way from true diversity. Altruistic intentions and nearly 40 years of affirmative action haven't been enough to solve the problems facing minorities in the workplace. But the economic boom of recent years has forced company executives to carefully consider the benefits of diversity initiatives. With unemployment figures at their lowest, companies are competing against each other for talented employees, and becoming more concerned about retaining experienced workers. Some industries, particularly high-tech industries such as engineering and information technology (see "Information=Success: The Role of Technology in Today's Workplace"), are faced with severe employment shortages, and must immediately address issues of recruitment and training. But even those industries with more workers than jobs are setting out to improve percentages of minority employment. For example, the American Society of Newspaper Editors has set long-term diversity goals, hoping for the percentage of minorities in the nation's newsrooms to be the same as the percentage in the general population by the year 2025. Also, the American Association of University Professors has instituted mentoring programs and other initiatives to introduce more minority professors to universities across the country. And those are only a few of the many professional associations that have surveyed, studied, and analyzed the minority numbers in their workforces.

The business world's recent commitment to diversity was illustrated in 1998, when *Fortune* magazine introduced its first annual ranking of "Best Companies for Asians, Blacks, and Hispanics." Both the 1998 and 1999 lists featured highly successful companies. The magazine has emphasized the correlation between the success of a company and its commitment to diversity—stocks rose right along with minority employment percentages. Studies by Korn/Ferry International, the world's leading executive search firm, also seem to support these findings—1999 numbers showed that America's largest companies (those with annual revenue of $20 billion or more) had more minority board directors than the average. Though there's no way to directly attribute company growth to diversity, it makes sense to most executives that a cohesive workforce can move a company forward. In addition to better production internally, companies with minority executives and a history of diversity can make better connections with other diversely staffed companies. And with business being conducted on an international level, a company represented by workers from different cultural backgrounds will make stronger impressions globally.

According to Korn/Ferry International, 60 percent of the nation's corporate boards had ethnic minority directors in 1999. Pharmaceutical, energy, and entertainment companies led the pack with the highest percentages of minority directors. In a press release, Craig L. Fuller, chairman of the firm's global board services, emphasized the importance of minorities in corporate board posts: "These are powerful positions," he reported, "and ensure that the process to bring greater diversity to boards is becoming more institutionalized." In a related survey, Korn/Ferry found that 84 percent of senior executives expected more diversity among the top 100 corporate management positions. Fewer than half of these same executives, however, expected more diversity among corporate chief executive officer (CEO) positions. In 2001, Kenneth I. Chenault will break new ground when he assumes the CEO position of American Express Company—a first for an African American executive with a Fortune 100 company. But African Americans and Hispanics combined still make up less than 2 percent of the nation's CEOs.

What Are Diversity Initiatives?

Companies achieve diversity in a variety of ways—these efforts often are referred to as initiatives. To accomplish their initiative, human resource departments often employ trained professionals experienced in promoting diversity, or companies form whole diversity "councils" or equal opportunity departments—groups of professionals dedicated to the many facets of creating a comfortable workplace for all employees regardless of their race, nationality, gender, age, religion, disability, or sexual orientation. Many freelance consultants specialize in diversity and help guide companies in creating initiatives and setting diversity goals.

In their efforts to increase minority employment, companies actively recruit new workers by visiting minority job fairs and placing ads in minority magazines and on Web sites. They also work with job placement firms and programs, such as the Hispanic Alliance for Career Enhancement, which maintains a resume database of Hispanic professionals, or the African American Internetwork online (www.afamnet.com). Some companies recruit college students early on in their education by offering scholarships to those going into the industry. They may form initiatives with minority colleges, forming a link between the company/industry and the school. For example, the Monsanto Company, a biotechnology firm, has formed a program with Howard University, an historically black college. Monsanto wants to increase its number of black chemists, and set out to encourage more black students to complete doctoral degrees. The program supports students with internships and research opportunities, and Monsanto professionals lead seminars and meet with students. As a result of the Monsanto Company/Howard University Initiative, graduates of the Ph.D. program have stepped directly into jobs with the company.

But diversity initiatives can't stop with recruitment—a company must also assure that minorities are allowed to advance, and encouraged to stay. Some companies offer their executives special bonuses for successfully initiating new diversity programs. Such programs would likely include a system of regular feedback and evaluation for workers. One of the most effective methods of introducing minorities to the workplace is mentoring (see "Mentors: Offering Guidance to Minorities in Schools and in the Workplace"). Many companies have begun formal mentoring programs, in which new employees are linked with experienced employees, typically in upper management, who can offer guidance in setting career goals. A minority employee also may be invited to join a group composed of other members of the same minority, in order to network within the company, and to share concerns and ideas.

Some diversity councils also organize multicultural events, such as celebrations of the holidays of other nations, to increase understanding and awareness of the various cultures represented in the workplace. Also, English as a second language (ESL) courses may be instituted to help facilitate communication.

It's important to note that, as with the term "affirmative action," the word "diversity" sparks controversy and confusion. Some believe that a company with diversity initiatives is more committed to hiring minorities than to hiring non-minorities. Though a company with a history of discrimination may be ordered by the court to quickly increase its number of minority workers, quotas and racial preferences are against the law. And even with court orders, a company will hire only qualified minority workers. Diversity initiatives, like all affirmative action programs, are instituted for the sake of equality—to give minorities the same opportunities as non-minorities. However, it's possible for a diversity program, as with any corporate program, to fall short of its ideals, creating the problems it is intended to prevent. If diversity training is not handled sensitively, it can lead to divisiveness within a workplace, heightening hostilities and misunderstandings—non-minority workers may come to believe minorities receive special preferences in hiring, raises, and promotions, and minorities may feel that the company's diversity policies give the impression that the workers are not deserving of their success.

How Do You Know If a Company Is Dedicated to Diversity?

Once you've received your degree and have gained some experience through internships, you'll likely have many job options. When considering a company's job offer, you should carefully examine its relationship with diversity and minority employment. If you have the opportunity to meet with a company's recruiters, ask them about the company's history with minority workers. Is the company only committed to recruiting minorities, or does it also assure that new minority hires feel an important part of the workforce and have clear paths of advancement? You may also be able to learn about a company through a professional organization. Most industries have at least one such organization, and some have organizations devoted entirely to minority professionals in the field. These organizations also can guide you in your career pursuit—they can help you choose a college and pursue scholarships.

You should read trade and professional magazines, and general business magazines— these publications offer insight into the industry, and may feature articles about companies particularly committed to minority employment. If you've chosen a specific city or state where you'd like to work, subscribe to the area's newspapers and read the business pages. Some companies also publish information about minority employment in their annual reports and other publications for stock holders. On the Internet, you can visit a company's Web site, which may feature a career page and email addresses of professionals within the company. Information from the Council on Economic Priorities is also available online; this council rates companies on a variety of criteria, including diversity, and publishes an "honor roll." At the council's site (www.cepnyc.org), you can search for a company by name or industry. Another organization, the Hispanic Association on Corporate Responsibility (HACR) serves as a watchdog group of corporations, recognizing those companies committed to the Hispanic community. *Hispanic Magazine* publishes an annual list of the companies offering the most opportunities for Hispanics.

You may learn a lot about a company's commitment to diversity by contacting its human resources department. A company's human resources professional may be able to direct you to a diversity department. If a company doesn't have a special diversity department or council, it doesn't mean it's without diversity initiatives. A company's human resources department may handle the particulars of minority hiring and promotion, and may be able to give you the percentage of minorities in the workforce and in management positions, as well as information about special diversity initiatives.

You should be careful when examining a company's previous problems with discrimination and racial conflict, and not dismiss the company as uncommitted to diversity; often highly publicized lawsuits and charges of discrimination lead a company to introduce effective new diversity policies and programs. The corporations that own Denny's restaurants and American Airlines have both had to deal with charges of discrimination in recent years, yet made *Fortune* magazine's 1999 list of best companies for minorities.

For More Information

Korn/Ferry International
1800 Century Park East, Suite 900
Los Angeles, CA 90067
Tel: 310-552-1834
Web: http://www.kornferry.com

Hispanic Alliance for Career Enhancement
200 S. Michigan Avenue, Suite 1210
Chicago, IL 60604
Tel: 312-435-0498
Web: http://www.hace-usa.org

Hispanic Association on Corporate Responsibility
1730 Rhode Island, NW, Suite 1008
Washington, DC 20038
Tel: 202-835-9672
Web: http://www.hacr.org

Leveling the Playing Field: Will Minorities Continue to Benefit from Affirmative Action Policies?

What Is Affirmative Action?

We hear the phrase "affirmative action" tossed about in debates, political campaigns, and the media. We're asked to vote on the issue in state elections. But, for many of us, the phrase is unclear. The issue of affirmative action, along with all its controversies, is very complicated. In this essay, you'll read about some of these controversies, as well as the origins of affirmative action programs, the effect of these programs on the colleges and workplaces of the United States, and what experts predict for affirmative action in the future.

The Affirmative Action Review, a White House report written in 1995 in response to President Clinton's questions about the effectiveness of affirmative action, well-defined the issue: "Affirmative action," it reads, "is used first and foremost to remedy specific past and current discrimination or the lingering effects of past discrimination—used sometimes by court order or settlement, but more often used voluntarily by private parties or by governments." This is the basic premise behind the affirmative action programs enforced by the state and federal governments. In addition:

Affirmative action programs can not require "quotas" (policies requiring the hiring of specific numbers or percentages of minority group members). Though courts may order specific institutions that have shown long histories of discrimination to hire a certain number of minorities, these court-ordered "consent decrees" can not be part of affirmative action programs. Consent decrees are mandated only in extreme situations, and on an individual basis. Consent decrees will continue to be issued by judges even if affirmative action is ended.

Affirmative action programs can not promote reverse discrimination. According to opinion polls, some members of the majority feel threatened by the existence of affirmative action programs, fearing that they will be passed up for jobs, promotions, and college entry because institutions are eager to promote minorities. Reverse discrimination, however, is illegal, and victims of such discrimination have won their cases in lower and higher courts.

Affirmative action programs can not promote the hiring of unqualified minorities over qualified white applicants. Affirmative action programs attempt to promote those qualified minorities who might otherwise fail to get job interviews because of discrimination or because they have been unable to make the proper connections and contacts.

Affirmative Action Timeline

The following timeline lists key events in the history of the development and revision of affirmative action:

1961—President Kennedy encourages contractors working for the federal government to "take affirmative action" in employment practices, and to assure that all workers "are treated...without regard to their race, color, religion, sex, or national origin."

1964—The Civil Rights Act is enacted, making it illegal to discriminate in employment. This Act also results in the creation of the Equal Employment Opportunity Commission (EEOC).

1969—The Philadelphia Plan is developed by President Nixon. This plan furthers President Kennedy's call for contractors working for the federal government to actively seek out minorities for employment.

1972—The Equal Opportunity Act expands affirmative action policies to include colleges and universities.

1978—The Supreme Court case "The University of California vs. Bakke" concerns admission policies of the medical school of the University of California at Davis. The school uses a rigid quota system, accepting a pre-determined number of minority students each year. The Court declares this practice unconstitutional, though it does uphold the rights of schools to take such issues as race and ethnicity into consideration when evaluating applicants.

1979—The Supreme Court case "The United Steelworkers vs. Weber" concerns special training programs geared toward minorities. Such temporary programs, even if they give preference to minorities, are deemed constitutional when they are devised to make up for past discrimination within an institution or business.

1991—The 1980s saw more conservatives appointed to the bench of the Supreme Court, and therefore a number of conservative rulings. The Civil Rights Act of 1991 overturns some of these rulings, strengthening anti-discrimination laws.

1995—The Supreme Court case "Adarand Constructors, Inc. vs. Pena" concerns programs using racial/ethnic classifications. The Court declares that affirmative action programs should be carefully scrutinized and "narrowly tailored." As a result, President Clinton calls for the federal government to make changes in its programs. "We should have a simple slogan," Clinton says. "Mend it, but don't end it."

1996—Proposition 209, an act to end affirmative action in the state, is passed by the voters of California, despite the fact that a majority of these voters believe that some forms of affirmative action are necessary.

1998—Initiative 200, a proposition similar to 209, passes in the state of Washington, and other states consider putting such propositions on their own ballots in the near future.

1999—A number of changes in affirmative action policies occur on campuses across the nation: A federal judge finds unconstitutional a University of Georgia admission policy giving preferential treatment to black applicants; the University of Texas at Austin discontinues a special minority professor recruitment program; the University of Washington considers eliminating minority scholarships; the University of Washington Law School experiences a 41 percent drop in black applicants from the previous year when affirmative action policies were still in effect; and the University of California, in an effort to increase enrollment of minority students, decides to admit all high school students in the state graduating in the top 4 percent of their classes.

What's So Controversial About Affirmative Action?

Those in support of affirmative action are of one basic view: that affirmative action is necessary to create a level playing field—to allow minorities the same opportunities for jobs, contracts, promotions, and college acceptances as those allowed the majority. However, those against affirmative action may be of a variety of views: Some believe that affirmative action is unnecessary because discrimination in the workplace no longer exists, and that minority workers have no more challenges than do white workers; some believe that affirmative action results in reverse discrimination and the promotion of unqualified minority workers; some believe that current affirmative action policies are ineffective and need to be reexamined and replaced. Still others object to affirmative action simply because it causes such controversy and dispute, and gives some the impression that minorities are not deserving of their successes.

While some analysts believe that affirmative action has worked in many ways for the benefit of minorities and of the nation as a whole, other critics conceive of affirmative action as a failure, an unfair and outdated practice. Regardless of whatever facts exist, this negative public conception will likely determine the fate of affirmative action. And just what facts do exist?:

—There are thousands of charges of discrimination each year, and few of reverse discrimination. In 1998 alone, there were nearly 30,000 charge filings of racial discrimination filed with the EEOC, and another 6,778 filings of discrimination based on national origin. However, the few cases of reverse discrimination, even when dismissed by courts, often draw the most attention from the media.

—The Glass Ceiling Commission, appointed by President Clinton to examine barriers in the workplace for women and minorities, reported in 1995 that white males comprised 97 percent of the senior management of Fortune 1,000 corporations.

—"Before the Civil Rights Act of 1964," states *The Affirmative Action Review*, "the median black male worker earned only about 60 percent as much as the median white male worker." Though black median income has greatly improved since then, in 1997 it was still around $20,000 less than the average white income (according to a *Newsweek* report published on June 7, 1999).

These facts don't make strong arguments for either side of the affirmative action debate—they show that discrimination and unfair hiring and promotion practices still greatly hurt minorities, requiring special programs and policies. Yet, our current policies of affirmative action, after nearly 40 years in practice, have failed to create equal opportunity for everyone.

Despite affirmative action's opposition across the nation, most Americans believe that special minority programs are important. Americans have expressed in polls, surveys, and interviews, that they are opposed to quotas (which are not legally part of any current state or federal affirmative action policies) and unfair hiring practices. The idea of giving "preferences" bothers Americans of all races and colors. A Washington Post-ABC News national poll conducted in 1995 found that three out of four of the Americans surveyed opposed affirmative action programs giving preferences to minorities. Half of the African Americans surveyed opposed such preferences.

What's to Become of Affirmative Action?

Just as many disagree on the effectiveness of affirmative action, so do many disagree on its future. Some believe that the defeat of affirmative action in California and Washington means that the nation is ready to overturn affirmative action policies. Politicians like John Carlson (who headed the campaign for Washington's Initiative 200) and Ward Connerly (the California businessman behind Proposition 209) are taking their efforts to other states, most notably to Florida. But these efforts to place anti-affirmative action initiatives onto the ballots in other states, particularly in states with high minority populations, have failed. And exit polls showed that the anti-affirmative action initiative in Washington state may have passed because of its vague language. Yvonne Scruggs-Leftwich, the head of the Black Leadership Forum, told the Associated Press, "The exit polls showed the language was so obtuse, people who thought they were voting against it actually voted for it. They [those who drafted the initiative] misled the people."

Even when these anti-affirmative action initiatives pass, it doesn't necessarily mean the end of opportunities for minorities. After the passing of Proposition 209 in California, the private sector began stepping in to improve issues, and the San Francisco Board of Supervisors expanded a program that gave preferences to minorities in city contracting. The University of California (comprised of eight campuses) introduced new policies to assist in the recruitment of minority students (see page 34, Affirmative Action Timeline). Similar policies were introduced in Texas: following the federal court-ordered elimination of affirmative action policies at Texas colleges and universities, minority enrollment dropped by half. The state responded by introducing a "10 percent plan," which automatically admitted to public universities any student in the state who graduated in the top 10 percent of his or her high school class. More minority students have become eligible for enrollment now than with any affirmative action plan of the past.

Affirmative action policies are being most hotly contested in colleges and universities. For decades, minorities were not allowed to attend the same colleges and universities as white students. Today, any minority wanting to go to college will likely have many choices. Since the Civil Rights Movement, university and college boards have attempted to make up for past discrimination by enacting policies that increase enrollment of minorities. Special minority scholarships (of which many are listed in the resource section of this book), recruitment programs, and preferences given minority applications have helped minorities gain access to higher education. These efforts are not only in the name of fair practice; colleges also recognize the educational value of a racially diverse environment and social interaction between students of differing backgrounds and cultures. In the book *The Shape of the River: Long-Term Consequences of Considering Race in College and University Admissions* (Princeton University Press, 1998), William Bowen and Derek Bok provide evidence that racial preferences greatly benefit minorities, and therefore society, and argue that eliminating preferences would have very little positive effect on the majority.

Despite these findings, universities in Georgia, Texas, Massachusetts, California, and Washington have eliminated certain minority application procedures, and other schools are following suit. As a result, the University of Michigan in 1999, faced by lawsuits by white students accusing the institution of reverse discrimination in its application policies, put together a defense that shows, through extensive research by social scientists, that such racial preferences are of great value to the success of the university and its students. Meanwhile, a group of minority students and organizations filed suit against the University of California at Berkeley, charging that the school's emphasis on standardized test scores violates anti-bias laws.

Standardized test scores, such as the SAT, have long been criticized as inadequate measures of student success. In 1997, an advisory group of professors and community activists in Texas stated that classroom performance in high school is a more effective gauge of a graduate's potential. The "percent" plans initiated in Texas and California, which effectively increase minority enrollment without using racial consideration, bypass SAT scores in the application process. Though standardized testing will likely continue to be used in evaluating college applicants, more universities may adopt new policies for evaluation in order to increase minority enrollment while avoiding reverse-discrimination lawsuits.

While it's uncertain what role affirmative action will play in the nation's future, the issue at hand—establishing equality among the races—will likely continue to inspire great controversy. As affirmative action is eliminated in some states, there remains hope for something more effective and less divisive to take its place.

Legal Rights and Recourse

How Am I Protected From Discrimination?

Affirmative action as we now know it may be in trouble (see "Leveling the Playing Field"), but programs to end workplace discrimination have been particularly effective in the last 40 years. These programs have succeeded in part because minorities have legal recourse and access to mediation when they feel they've been mistreated. Any kind of discrimination based on race, color, or national origin is prohibited by law. Minorities are protected from being excluded in job advertisements and training and recruitment programs, from being passed over for promotions and raises, and from being denied retirement plans. Not only intentional discrimination is illegal, but so are special workplace practices that result in discrimination, such as employers prohibiting the speaking of any language other than English in the office.

Thanks to the efforts of the Equal Employment Opportunity Commission (EEOC), employers and their employees often can reach agreement without the case going to court. The EEOC was formed as a result of the Civil Rights Act passed in 1964. This act prohibits employment discrimination on the basis of race, color, or national origin, as well as on the basis of religion, age, sex, and disability. Private employers, state and local governments, and educational institutions that employ 15 or more individuals are held accountable when discrimination occurs.

Some who oppose affirmative action make the claim that discrimination no longer exists. However, the EEOC continues to investigate thousands of cases every year. In 1998, there were over 35,000 individual filings with the EEOC charging discrimination on the basis of race and national origin. And many of these individual filings claim multiple types of discrimination. These numbers reveal that a great deal of disharmony among the races remains in the workplace, despite nearly 40 years of affirmative action. But the EEOC is resolving cases faster than they are being filed. And these resolutions, through settlement and conciliation, have helped those who have been discriminated against (including minorities, women, the disabled, those over 40 years of age, and other victims of discrimination) receive $169.2 million in monetary benefits. In litigation, the EEOC has helped win nearly $90 million in 1998 ($40 million more than the monetary benefits won in 1996). Though monetary awards don't make up for acts of discrimination, they do help to compensate individuals for unfair promotion practices, unfair raise and benefits distribution, and other discrepancies. And they require individual businesses to address issues of discrimination, and help to end unfair practices in the workplace.

What Can I Do If I've Been a Victim of Discrimination?

Though we often read in the newspaper of court cases involving workplace discrimination and large monetary settlements, litigation is usually a last resort for those who feel they have been the victim of discrimination. Court cases can be expensive, time-consuming, and incredibly disruptive to the lives of all involved. (And after you've sued your employer, you will most likely have to look for work elsewhere.) Many companies have established their own affirmative action policies and programs in efforts to eliminate discrimination and to avoid lawsuits. Human resources departments may employ professionals to deal with disputes in-house, and a company may employ diversity counselors to whom employees can voice complaints. Some companies also provide areas within their intranet systems (electronic networks used only within the company) for the posting of complaints. Mentors and special minority peer groups can also help guide individuals through a process of complaint.

According to a 1998 survey conducted by Korn/Ferry International, an executive placement firm, 40 percent of the minority executives surveyed believed they had been passed over for deserved promotions as a result of race discrimination. These executives believed that positive approaches were the most effective in dealing with unfairness in the workplace. Such positive approaches included direct feedback and careful analysis, which allowed them to handle the situations and to learn from them without damaging their careers.

In case you're unable to persuade the company to deal fairly with your complaint of discrimination, you may need additional assistance. In some states, outside mediation, or alternative dispute resolution (ADR), is required by the courts. Mediators are trained professionals, unbiased in the case, who listen to both sides of an argument and help employer and employee reach a satisfactory settlement. Both parties must agree before settlement can be reached. ADR seeks a quick resolution of the dispute, and helps to reduce backlogs in the courts. Your employer may even have it written into your contract that you must first seek mediation through a third party before filing a lawsuit. ADR has been encouraged by the Supreme Court, the Civil Rights Act of 1991, and the Americans with Disabilities Act. The Academy of Family Mediators states that mediated agreements are adhered to more often than judgments of the court.

If you choose to speak to your employer about your charges of discrimination, you may decide together to pursue mediation. The Mediation Information and Resource Center (MIRC) maintains a database of trained mediators, and can provide you with more information about mediation. You can also learn more about mediation from the National Association for Community Mediation, the American Arbitration Association, and the Academy of Family Mediators. (For the Web sites, phone numbers, and addresses of these organizations, see the "For More Information" section at the end of this essay.)

If you'd rather not pursue a discrimination case by yourself, you can seek help from the EEOC. If your workplace employs more than 15 individuals, your options in the event of discrimination must be posted somewhere in the workplace for all employees to read. A phone number may be all you need to contact the EEOC. The EEOC has 50 field offices across the country with employees who can help you file a charge. If there are state laws prohibiting the kind of discrimination you've experienced, you may file with your state's own equal opportunity office. These state offices are often called Fair Employment Practices Agencies (FEPAs). When a case of discrimination violates both state and federal laws, a FEPA will work together with the EEOC to resolve a problem. More than 48,000 discrimination charges are processed annually by the EEOC contracting with approximately 90 FEPAs across the country.

You only have 180 days from the date that an incident occurs to file a charge with the EEOC. If you feel that filing a charge may greatly jeopardize your professional standing in the workplace, you may ask someone else to file a charge for you. Any individual or organization can file on your behalf. You should keep in mind that, even if filing through someone else in order to remain anonymous, there is a level of risk involved. Should the case be investigated closely, your identity will likely become apparent to your employers. But, to rectify a case of discrimination, risks might be necessary.

If you are unable to find a posting about discrimination at your workplace, look in the federal government section of your telephone book for your local EEOC office. (If you're a federal employee, you'll have to contact the EEO counselor within your department.) You also can learn more information about EEOC by calling 1-800-669-4000 (voice) or 1-800-669-6820 (TTY). When filing a charge, you'll be asked to provide your name, address, and phone number, as well as that of whomever you're charging with discrimination. You'll also need to describe the act of discrimination, and the date it occurred. You also should know the approximate number of people employed by the company or organization charged.

After interviewing you about the situation, and asking you questions about how you believe you were discriminated against, the EEOC will then decide whether to proceed. The EEOC may dismiss your charge, determining that there is no case of discrimination. In this case, you'll be issued a notice, and you'll have 90 days to file your own lawsuit against the charged party if you choose. If your charge has merit, the EEOC will investigate by gathering information and documents and interviewing the various parties involved.

How Are Cases of Discrimination Settled?

As mentioned above, mediation has become a popular and effective form of settling employment disputes, even with charges handled by the EEOC. Since 1996, when the EEOC mediation program started, 2,400 charges have been settled through mediation, yielding $27.8 million for the victims of discrimination.

The EEOC's mediation program is offered as an alternative to investigation. When both employer and employee agree to use EEOC mediation, a third party will meet with them, listen to the complaint, and help them settle the issue within one to five hours of discussion. Once an agreement is reached, the charging party is not allowed to take the case to court (unless the agreement ultimately goes unrecognized by the employer). A settlement may allow you promotion, back pay, or other remedies of discrimination. If no settlement is reached, an investigation will continue without the involvement of the mediator. The mediation is entirely confidential, and no written record or tape recordings are made, so nothing discussed in the mediation session is used in the investigation. If no settlement can be reached, the EEOC may choose to sue, or to close the case, allowing the charging party to pursue litigation.

As the EEOC statistics demonstrate, the nation's workplaces have a long way to go before they will be free of discrimination. In the meantime, minority workers can rely on mentors, diversity departments, mediators, and the EEOC in getting the promotions, raises, and respect entitled to them.

For More Information

To contact the EEOC headquarters, or to find out the phone number for your area's field office:

Equal Employment Opportunity Commission
1801 L Street, NW
Washington, DC 20507
Tel: 800-669-4000
Web: http://www.eeoc.gov

Essays on Minority Topics

For information about free publications available from the EEOC:

EEOC
Publications Distribution Center
P.O. Box 12549
Cincinnati, OH 45212-0549
Tel: 800-669-3362
Web: http://www.eeoc.gov

Mediation Information and Resource Center
P.O. Box 51090
Eugene, OR 97405
Tel: 541-302-6254
Web: http://www.mediate.com

National Association for Community Mediation
1527 New Hampshire Avenue, NW
Washington, DC 20036-1206
Tel: 202-667-9700
Web: http://www.nafcm.org

American Arbitration Association
335 Madison Avenue, 10th Floor
New York, NY 10017-4605
Tel: 212-716-5800
Web: http://www.adr.org

Minorities in the Arts: Opportunities for Performers, Visual Artists, and Writers

Did you play in a band in high school? Write poetry or create original illustrations for your own magazine? Maybe you've grown up studying the skills and artistry of a parent or grandparent gifted in a particular art form. Or maybe you have little artistic background, but possess an original perspective on your life and the world around you. In any case, the art world, whatever the discipline, offers opportunities to help minorities develop as artists and to introduce their work to the public. Pursuing a career in the arts can be difficult—receiving recognition for your work can take years of dedication and involve much rejection, disappointment, and serious competition from the thousands of other talented people seeking the same awards and opportunities for exposure. Because of these challenges, organizations have evolved to help minority artists with scholarships, reaching an audience, and mentoring with established artists.

A number of organizations, such as the Association of Hispanic Arts, the Asian American Arts Alliance, and the International Agency for Minority Artists and Affairs, assist individual artists and groups, as well as promote the significance of the work of minority artists. Not only have these organizations created opportunities for artists, but also for those interested in careers supporting artists—including careers as arts administrators, gallery and museum curators, teachers, and agents. Colleges and universities across the country offer minority scholarships for their Masters of Fine Arts programs (studio-based graduate programs for writers, dancers, painters, actors, filmmakers, and other artists). There are many state art councils and leagues that offer special opportunities for artists, such as the Asian American Renaissance of Minnesota; the Multi-cultural Arts Development Program of the California Arts Council; and the Mentoring Program for Artists of Color and Traditional Artists sponsored by the Nebraska Arts Council. Minority artists should contact their own city and state arts organizations about such programs. (To find out the phone number and address of your arts organizations, contact the offices of your mayor and governor.)

With the exception of some art disciplines and opportunities, the arts do not typically offer a great deal of financial reward. Many artists must supplement their arts careers with jobs that may be outside their fields of interest, or do freelance work to afford them the freedom and time to commit to their art. According to the 1998-99 *Occupational Outlook Handbook* (OOH) of the Bureau of Labor Statistics, nearly 60 percent of visual artists are self-employed—about seven times the proportion in all professional occupations. The OOH also reports that photographers and musicians pursue self-employment in much higher numbers than average. Nearly three out of five musicians employed in 1996 worked part time. Many of the organizations and groups mentioned in this essay must struggle to survive and to secure funds for the artists they support. But, for artists with drive and ambition, the rewards of having work recognized and appreciated far outweighs financial reward.

The Performing Arts—Theater, Dance, Music, Film

In 1999, articles in *The New York Times, Newsweek, Rolling Stone,* and many other major publications heralded the cross-cultural appeal of Latin music. The spotlight on Ricky Martin, Jennifer Lopez, and Marc Anthony also cast some glow on many other Latin American musicians perhaps not as famous, but certainly benefiting from the growing success of Latin music in America. Clubs such as Sounds of Brazil in Manhattan are cropping up in major cities, giving more Hispanic musicians opportunities to perform and build an audience, and powerful people in the industry are paying close attention. David Byrne, former leader of the 1980s band Talking Heads, promotes world music with his record company Luaka Bop, and the Internet company Descarga.com has found great success selling only Latin music.

Though ballet does not typically have the same impact on American culture as pop music, the Ballet Hispanico is allowing many talented dancers the opportunity to perform in front of thousands of people across the nation. And with its school of dance, the Ballet Hispanico trains children in classical ballet and traditional Spanish dance (Jennifer Lopez is an alumnus of the school); with its arts education program, the Ballet Hispanico visits schools across the nation to work with kids of all ages.

For performers interested in theatrical opera, Opera Ebony provides opportunities for African American and other minority artists. The Opera stages such standards as Carmen and Madama Butterfly, while also showcasing the work of new minority composers. In addition to these performers and composers, Opera Ebony supports directors, choreographers, and technicians.

While many performing arts groups are based in New York City (including Ballet Hispanico and Opera Ebony), other major cities offer special opportunities for minority performers. The African-American Shakespeare Company tours throughout the Bay Area of California, and also performs a regular production season on its main stage in Oakland. Along with the tours and performances, the African-American Shakespeare Company invites high school students to take part in its Summer Youth Troupe. The program involves students in production, direction, and management of a touring show.

The East West Players (EWP) of Los Angeles is the nation's foremost Asian American theater, with main stage productions of new and classic plays and musicals, as well as a great deal of actor training. Workshops involve training in acting, voice, auditions, choreography, and other skills needed for stage and film work. The EWP's Actors Network allows for actors to meet with industry professionals.

Arguably the most competitive art form, filmmaking has provided great, albeit limited, opportunities for minorities. Many new Asian American filmmakers have had their work showcased as part of the San Francisco International Asian American Film Festival. Some of the films shown at the festival are funded in part by the National Asian American Telecommunications Association (NAATA), which has set out to develop new Asian Pacific American programs for public television.

To introduce more African American filmmakers to the world, the Urbanworld Film Festival (UWFF) is going beyond showcasing the works of African American directors, producers, and actors to New York audiences; it also sponsors a college tour which is designed to encourage young African American college students around the country. Having reached approximately 200,000 students at historically black colleges and colleges with film programs, the UWFF has helped African American students learn about the film industry and see films being made by African American filmmakers.

The Sundance Institute, long committed to new filmmakers, has established the Native American Initiative, a program which offers professional support to Native American filmmakers. Its efforts include the July Native American Screenwriting Workshop, and the showcasing of Native American films at the annual Sundance Film Festival. It also sponsors Native American producers who attend its Independent Producers Conference.

The Visual and Fine Arts—Painting, Photography, Sculpture

Toward the end of the 20th century, multiculturalism in the nation's universities and museums began to allow for a more inclusive display of the artwork created by minorities. Some of the traditional artistry of minority groups—such as the prayer books, jewelry, and altarpieces much a part of Hispanic culture—has been appreciated in the past by the mainstream art world, but mostly as folk art or handicraft, something less than fine art. These attitudes are changing with the efforts of such organizations as the National Hispanic Cultural Center of New Mexico, and the galleries and museums across the country which exhibit the works of Hispanic artists who break traditional molds and experiment with the art forms of their culture. Also, the popularity of Latin American artists Frida Kahlo, Fernando Boteros, and others has heightened interest in the collection of Hispanic art. Galleries such as the Galeria de La Raza in San Francisco regularly feature the work of new Hispanic artists. The Florida Museum of Hispanic and Latin American Art is dedicated entirely to promoting the work of Hispanic artists; not only does the museum exhibit the work, it also organizes art courses and lectures.

Many contemporary Native American and Asian American artists also are working within the traditions of their cultures, and exhibiting their work in galleries and museums nationwide. The Institute of American Indian Arts (IAIA) of Santa Fe helps Native American artists to develop and exhibit their work, and is also home to The National Collection of Contemporary Indian Art. The Asia Society and the Asia/American Center of Queens College support the work of Asian American artists through national exhibits and publications. The Asia/American Center also hosts an artist intern.

Literature—Poetry, Fiction Writing, Playwriting

Terry McMillan, Amy Tan, and Sherman Alexie are just a few of the minority writers whose work has gained wide readership around the world; and Oprah's Book Club has helped the novels of several African American writers reach the bestseller lists. While most writers of contemporary fiction, poetry, and theater write for relatively small audiences, the desire to publish, or to see a play produced, remains strong. Many publishing houses, literary magazines, and Web pages are devoted to the publication of work by minority writers. In the index of the *International Directory of Little Magazines and Small Presses*, approximately 60 publications and presses are listed under "African American," 55 under "Asian American," over 100 under "Latin American" and "Latino," and over 180 under "Native American." There are also hundreds more that encourage the submission of work by minority writers, and publish special issues showcasing such writing.

For Asian American playwrights, EWP sponsors the David Henry Hwang Writers Institute. Those writers accepted into the program have the opportunity to study with professionals, and are expected to complete a number of one-act and full-length plays. The Hispanic Playwrights Project of the South Coast Repertory in California is a workshop in which writers can develop their skills; the project also promotes the production of plays by new Hispanic writers. Twenty-seven of the plays developed within the project in the last 12 years have been produced in regional theaters across the country. African American playwrights can benefit from the Lorraine Hansberry Playwriting Award sponsored by the Kennedy Center American College Theater Festival. The first-place winner receives a cash award of $2,500, as well as a fellowship to attend a writing retreat. The winning play is published and leased for production. You can read some of the winning plays in *The Lorraine Hansberry Playwriting Award: An Anthology of Prize-Winning Plays* (Clark Publishing, 1996).

African American writers also can benefit from International Black Writers (IBW), an organization that helps writers through an annual conference, publications, and other support of the literary community. IBW's publications feature new fiction and poetry, as well as announcements of writing competitions and opportunities. At Medgar Evers College in New York, African American writers can become involved with the Black Writers Institute (BWI). BWI sponsors workshops and seminars, scholarships, and opportunities for new writers to meet established writers and publishing professionals. BWI has expanded to the Internet, allowing writers and scholars across the country to discuss writing. The Internet site is also exploring the possibilities of online publication and other methods of promoting new works.

The Asian American Writer's Workshop (AAWW) is the only organization of its kind in the country—it provides Asian American writers with opportunities to develop and publish their work. Based in New York City, the AAWW promotes the work of new writers nationwide, and sponsors an Arts-in-Education program.

Native American writers have the opportunity to publish with the prestigious University of Nebraska Press—the North American Indian Prose Award was initiated by the press to promote works of literary merit and originality in dealing with North American Indian life. Though the contest does not invite submissions of novels, plays, or poetry, it does invite autobiography and collections of essays.

The Inroads Mentorship Program sponsored by The Loft Literary Center of Minneapolis has offered special programs for Native Americans, Asian/Pacific Islanders, African Americans, and Hispanics. These eight-week programs allow students to mentor with well-established authors, read their work publicly, and workshop their writing with others in the program. The Open Book Committee of the PEN American Center also provides opportunities for African American, Native American, Hispanic, Caribbean, and Asian American writers. It features an online network, online job bank, and other programs to help writers gain access to publishers.

For More Information

Opportunities for Hispanic artists:

A clearinghouse of information about Hispanic arts organizations; publishes a newsletter and a directory of organizations, and also maintains a database of information about fellowships and grants:

Association of Hispanic Arts, Inc.
173 East 116th Street, 2nd Floor
New York, NY 10029
Tel: 212-860-5445

Main stage performances; school of dance; and arts-in-education program:

Ballet Hispanico
167 West 89th Street
New York, NY 10024-1901
Tel: 212-362-6710
Web: http://www.ballethispanico.org

Exhibitions of Hispanic artists; lectures and seminars on a variety of arts-related subjects:

Florida Museum of Hispanic and Latin American Art
4006 Aurora Street
Coral Gables, FL 33146
Tel: 305-444-7060

Sponsor of the Hispanic Playwrights Project:

South Coast Repertory
Literary Department
PO Box 2197
Costa Mesa, CA 92628-2197
Web: http://www.scr.org

Opportunities for Asian American artists:

Provides assistance to Asian American artists and art groups through publications, networking opportunities, and advocacy:

Asian American Arts Alliance
74 Varick Street, Suite 302
New York, NY 10013-1914
Tel: 212-941-9208
Web: http://www.aaartsalliance.org

Actors workshops; main stage productions; home of the David Henry Hwang Writers Institute:

East West Players
244 South San Pedro Street, Suite 301
Los Angeles, CA 90012
Tel: 213-625-7000
Web: http://www.bnw.com/eastwestplayers

A writer's organization with four divisions: Programs, Publications, Arts-in-Education, and the Booksellers:

Asian American Writer's Workshop
37 St. Mark's Place
New York, NY 10003
Tel: 212-228-6718

Funds public television projects developed by Asian Americans:

National Asian American Telecommunications Association
346 9th Street, 2nd Floor
San Francisco, CA 94103
Tel: 415-863-0814
Web: http://www.naatanet.org

Sponsors exhibits of Asian American art, and supports Asian American arts through a variety of programs; Web site features many links to other arts organizations around the world:

Asia Society
725 Park Avenue
New York, NY 10021
Tel: 212-288-6400
Web: http://www.asiasociety.org

Opportunities for African American artists:

Annual film festival; sponsors a college tour, bringing films to students across the country:

Urbanworld Film Festival
375 Greenwich Street
New York, NY 10013
Tel: 212-501-9668
Web: http://www.uwff.com

Introduces performers, conductors, stage directors, choreographers and others to theatrical opera:

Opera Ebony
2109 Broadway, Suite 1418
New York, NY 10023
Tel: 212-874-7245
Web: http://www.operaebony.org

Main stage productions; tours; student programs:

African-American Shakespeare Company
3200 Boston Avenue
Oakland, CA 94602
Tel: 415-333-1918
Web: http://www.african-americanshakes.org

Dedicated to the development of African American writers and the promotion of their work; associated with Medger Evers College in Brooklyn; reaches writers nationally through Web site:

Black Writers Institute
1650 Bedford Avenue
Brooklyn, NY 11225
Web: http://www.blackwriters.net

Represents beginning and established writers; sponsors an annual conference, and publishes a magazine and newsletter:

International Black Writers
PO Box 1030
Chicago, IL 60690-1030
Tel: 708-331-6421

First place award of $2,500 and publication for new playwrights in annual competition:

The Lorraine Hansberry Playwright Award
American College Theater Festival
Kennedy Center
Washington, DC 20566
Tel: 202-416-8850
Web: http://www.kennedy-center.org/education/

Sponsors a variety of programs and services for artists, including training, newsletter, information about jobs:

International Agency for Minority Artist Affairs
163 West 125th Street, 9th Floor
New York, NY 10027
Tel: 212-749-5298
Web: http://idt.net/~iamaa/

Opportunities for Native American Artists:

School for Native American artists, offering instruction in a variety of disciplines; home of the National Collection of Contemporary Indian Art:

Institute of American Indian Arts
Admission Office
PO Box 2007
Santa Fe, NM 87504
WWW: http://www.iaiancad.org

Sponsors workshops for Native American screenwriters, and professional support for filmmakers:

Sundance Institute
Native American Initiative
225 Santa Monica Boulevard, 8th Floor
Santa Monica, CA 90401
Tel: 310-394-4662
Web: http://www.sundance.org

Competition inviting the work (autobiography, biography, history, literary criticism, and essays) of Native American writers; winners published by the press:

North American Indian Prose Award
University of Nebraska Press
312 North 14th Street
Lincoln, NE 68588-0484

Other arts programs for minorities:

A committee to assist minority writers with publication:

Open Book Committee
PEN American Center
568 Broadway
New York, NY 10012-3225
Tel: 212-334-1660
Web: http://www.pen.org

Inroads program allows selected minority writers to take workshops with established writers:

The Loft
Pratt Community Center
66 Malcolm Avenue, SE
Minneapolis, MN 55414
Tel: 612-379-8999
Web: http://www.loft.org

Starting Your Own Business

You are your own boss: you set your own hours, hire your own staff, work in an office in your home, and make a comfortable living. Does this describe your job? Or just your dream? For many, success in small business is a reality. More and more people are setting out to be entrepreneurs. According to the U.S. government's Small Business Administration (SBA), the 23 million small businesses in America employ more than 50 percent of the private workforce, and generate more than 50 percent of the nation's gross domestic product. And in the past 10 years, this boom has been helped along by minority-owned businesses. A report released by the Milken Institute in 1999 found that minority-owned businesses are growing at double the rate of all firms in the U.S. economy. But the Institute, which published its findings as "Mainstreaming Minority Business," also reported that minorities are still underrepresented in business ownership, compared to non-minority males. Just as obstacles exist for minorities seeking employment, so do obstacles exist in the pursuit of self-employment.

However, obstacles aren't necessarily stumbling blocks: the SBA's Office of Advocacy reported that the 3.2 million minority-owned businesses in the United States generated $495 billion in revenues in 1997. In 1999, Miami-based MasTec became the first Hispanic company to have revenues exceeding $1 billion. And many organizations and lending institutions are becoming more involved in helping minorities develop businesses. Since 1998, the SBA has been working to double the number of guaranteed loans to African Americans, and to increase loans to Hispanics by $2.5 billion. Banks such as Wells Fargo and Bank One have begun special lending programs which allow minorities to invest in business ventures. The Federal Reserve Board has been closely studying disparities in access to loans between minorities and non-minorities, and Chairman Alan Greenspan has cited these disparities as an impediment to national wealth. "It is important for lenders to understand," Greenspan said in a 1999 speech, "that failure to recognize the profitable opportunities represented by minority enterprises not only harms these firms, it harms the lending institutions and, ultimately, robs the broader economy of growth potential."

A perfect example of a "broader economy" benefiting from the establishment of minority-owned businesses is the small town of Chamblee, Georgia. Profiled recently in *Inc. Magazine*, Chamblee, population 8,000, was contacted by the U.S. Department of Justice following a heated city council meeting. The meeting suggested the potential of violence as a means of dealing with the influx of foreign-born residents. An intervention led to sweeping changes in the town, as the white elite of Chamblee met with representatives from the Hispanic and Asian communities. Today, the "International Village," a development featuring the businesses of ethnically diverse entrepreneurs, and the International Farmers Market, featuring goods and produce from around the world, are expected to bring in annual revenues of over $180 million to Chamblee. And immigrant entrepreneurs continue to establish new businesses in distressed areas of Chamblee, renovating many buildings and neighborhoods.

Funding and Information

Money and know-how: the two go hand in hand in establishing a business. To get your small business off the ground, and to keep it growing and developing, you'll need financial support and as much information as you can find. You may know everything there is to know about the goods and services you'll be offering, but you also must know about all the different aspects of small business: financing, marketing, long-term planning, labor requirements, and area competition.

Without proper funding, it can be difficult to start a business. Though some small businesses have few start-up costs, others require thousands of dollars—potential entrepreneurs typically look to loans, grants, personal savings, and investments from friends and relatives. But for some minorities, such options are limited: they may come from poor families and neighborhoods; they may have unverifiable credit and no collateral; they may live in the inner-city, where few banks are located; and they may face discrimination by lenders who, new to making small loans, believe that investment in minority-owned business is too big of a risk. Though commercial banks are the leading source of credit for small businesses, 40 percent of minority-owned businesses with gross sales of $1 million or more have never received bank loans, according to the U.S. Department of Commerce. A 1997 study by Wells Fargo found that 50 percent of the Hispanic business owners surveyed had been turned down for credit, compared to only 38 percent of non-Hispanics. Fifty-three percent of the Hispanic business owners had not even approached a bank for a loan.

In the last few years, some banks have begun to recognize the benefits of helping small business owners grow and succeed. Many minorities have been aided by the SBA. The organization's many efforts are led by administrator Aida Alvarez, the first Hispanic woman to serve as a member of the President's cabinet. The SBA Office of Minority Enterprise Development is seriously dedicated to helping minority businesses by providing specialized training, professional consulting, and other assistance. The SBA works with banks, guaranteeing the loans offered to selected minority businesses. It also actively recruits banks and other funding companies to invest in small, unproven businesses, and to allow these businesses time to become established. The SBA also has been involved in the development of ACE-Net, an Internet database that links investors with small businesses.

The Minority Business Development Agency (MBDA), which is part of the U.S. Department of Commerce, also has dedicated itself to the creation and expansion of minority-owned businesses. Through their development and resource centers across the nation, MBDA offers assistance in management, financial planning, marketing, and information about sources of funding.

The National Minority Supplier Development Council (NMSDC) oversees the Business Consortium Fund; this fund provides minority businesses with contract financing through a network of local banks. The regional councils of the NMSDC certify minority-owned businesses and match them with member corporations needing to purchase goods and services, helping the businesses to expand clientele.

Of course, these and other organizations, along with the banks that offer special programs for minority-owned businesses, are faced with many more applicants than they can fund. This is where preparation and wealth of information may pay off. With a detailed business plan that shows you've done your research and clearly understand such things as the marketplace, future trends, the demands of the business, and the competition, you can show investors that you're a good risk. You also must be prepared for complicated and detailed loan applications.

To help you prepare for all the ins and outs of starting and running a business, and to direct you to the information you'll need for success, community colleges and universities across the nation offer courses in small business administration and management. Some schools of business administration, such as at the University of Wisconsin-Milwaukee, have specific programs geared toward minority entrepreneurship. There are also a number of organizations that offer training. MBDA regional centers are located all across the country, and offer one-on-one assistance in writing business plans, as well as help with financial planning and management. The NMSDC offers educational seminars and training, business opportunity fairs, and publications to help you learn about small business. The National Center for American Indian Enterprise Development also provides assistance with business plans, along with advice on loan packaging, taxes, and Web page design. Asian American Economic Development Enterprises sponsors workshops, events, and seminars to train Asian Americans in entrepreneurship, as well as arranges for financial support for new businesses. Other organizations focused on the success of minority businesses include the National Minority Business Council, the National Association of Black Women Entrepreneurs, and the American Association of Minority Businesses. Also, most states have minority councils and development centers for small business owners. Your local chamber of commerce and the offices of the mayor and governor can also direct you to relevant information.

A number of publications focus on minority-owned business, including the magazines *Minority Business Entrepreneur, Hispanic Business, The Network Journal: Black Professional and Small Business News,* and *Black Enterprise,* which also publishes a series of books that includes *The Black Enterprise Guide to Starting Your Own Business* by Wendy Beech. *Entrepreneur Magazine* announces its Minority Entrepreneur of the Year in a special annual issue, and *Hispanic Magazine* publishes an annual list of the fastest growing Hispanic-owned businesses in the United States. Relevant books of the last few years include *The Americano Dream: How Latinos Can Achieve Success in Business and in Life* by Lionel Sosa; *Race for Success: The Ten Best Opportunities for Blacks in America* by George C. Fraser; and *About My Sister's Business: The Black Woman's Road Map to Successful Entrepreneurship* by Fran Harris.

Technology and Internet resources also are becoming increasingly important to minority entrepreneurs. A survey conducted by the software company Intuit found that minority business owners use technology for managing finances, finding information on the Internet, tracking customers, and forecasting budgets. Databases, articles, editorials, and information about training are available through the Web sites of many of the organizations and magazines listed in this directory. Web sites such as www.ideacafe.com direct minority entrepreneurs to information about funding, as does www.creativeinvest.com, the Web site for Creative Investment Research. The site also includes lists of minority-owned banks. And a small business can greatly benefit from its own Web site; business owners use their own sites to promote their businesses, answer questions, and provide customer service through email.

All of the efforts mentioned above are paying off for minority business owners, as entrepreneurs post high revenues and set records for success. The SBA indicates that an estimated 79 percent of new businesses fail within 10 years—a discouraging statistic until you consider that the SBA's Minority Enterprise Development program has a success rate of 45 percent—more than twice the rate obtained by all businesses.

For More Information

National Minority Business Council
235 East 42nd Street
New York, NY 10017
Tel: 212-573-2385
Web: http://www.nmbc.org

National Center for American Indian Enterprise Development
953 East Juanita Avenue
Mesa, AZ 85204
Tel: 800-4-NCAIED
Web: http://www.ncaied.org

Asian American Economic Development Enterprises
216 West Garvey Avenue, Unit E
Monterey Park, CA 91754
Tel: 626-572-7021
Web: http://www.aaede.org

Part II

Directory

Section A
Financial Aid

This section includes fellowships, grants, loans, awards, scholarships, and internships/career guidance opportunities. Though some of these terms are used interchangeably, a *fellowship* is typically a sum of money awarded to individuals who have demonstrated serious interest in the subject matter, and have possibly earned a degree in the area. A *grant* is often a cash sum, and is not necessarily awarded to individuals pursuing academic study. A *scholarship* enables a student to meet the fees and tuition of higher education. In the section on *internships/career guidance,* you'll find programs that involve individuals in hands-on experience with a profession, usually for a summer between college semesters.

Fellowships

Academy for Educational Development
1825 Connecticut Avenue, NW
Washington, DC 20009
202-884-8000
http://www.aed.org/ppia/

The **Program in Public Policy and International Affairs** offers fellowships to minorities for studies in public policy and international careers. Applicants in their junior, senior, or graduate years are eligible.

African-American Institute
Atlas Fellowships
833 United National Plaza
New York, NY 10017

The **Atlas Fellowships** and the **African Training for Leadership and Advanced Skills Program** provide scholarships for Africans studying economics, agriculture, business, engineering, and public health in the United States. The program is primarily for people from nations that have no native universities. Women receive a third of the awards. Applications are accepted all year.

Alabama A&M University
Graduate School
Normal, AL 35762
256-851-5266
http://aamu.edu

The Graduate School offers **Patricia Roberts Harris Fellowships** to help minority students with a 2.8 GPA finance college study. Applications are due April 30.

American Academy of Allergy and Immunology
611 East Wells Street, Fourth Floor
Milwaukee, WI 53202-3889
414-272-6071
http://www.aaaai.org

The **Underrepresented Minority Investigators Award in Asthma and Allergy** provides $30,000 per year for postdoctoral asthma or allergy research conducted by minority scientists. Two awards are given annually. A component of the award is also open to Ph.D.s; recipients are given $50,000 annually.

Financial Aid

American Academy of Child and Adolescent Psychiatry

AACAP Office of Research and Training
3615 Wisconsin Avenue, NW
Washington, DC 20016
202-966-7300
http://www.aacap.org

Five $2,500 **Jeanne Spurlock Minority Medical Student Clinical Fellowships** are awarded annually for work during the summer with a child and adolescent psychiatrist mentor. The Fellowships also provide for 5 days at the AACAP Annual Meeting.

Twelve **James Comer Minority Research Fellowships** of $2,500 each are awarded annually to minorities for work during the summer with a child and adolescent psychiatrist researcher-mentor. The fellowship also includes 5 days at the AACAP Annual Meeting.

American Association of Family and Consumer Sciences

1555 King Street
Alexandria, VA 22314
703-706-4600
http://www.aafcs.org

One **Virginia F. Cutler Fellowship** of $3,500 is awarded to a minority student in the United States or an international student pursuing a graduate degree in the area of consumer studies.

The association awards the $3,500 **Flemmie D. Kittrel Fellowship for Minorities** to students in family and consumer sciences or a related field.

The association awards the $3,500 **Freda A. DeKnight Fellowship** to an African American graduate student in family and consumer sciences.

American Association of Health Plans

1129 20th Street, NW, Suite 600
Washington, DC 20036
202-778-3284

The AAHP offers a 10-month **fellowship** experience to help increase the numbers of talented,

minority managers in the health plan community. Twenty-six fellowships are awarded for training in the Mid-Atlantic Region. To be eligible, you must be a member of an ethnic minority group, have a baccalaureate or master's degree in health care administration, business or other health-related field, and have worked in a health care environment for at least 1 year. Or, you may have an associate's degree or an RN license and have 3 years or more of supervisory experience working in a health care entity. Fellowship includes taxable stipend of $27,000 for the 10-month training program.

American Association of Law Libraries

Scholarships and Grants Committee
53 West Jackson Boulevard, Suite 940
Chicago, IL 60604
312-939-4764
http://www.aallnet.org

Two **Minority Stipends** of at least $3,500 are available to minority graduate students who have worked in a law library. Applicants must be studying at a library or law school. Apply by April 1.

American Association of University Women, Hawaii

Scholarship Coordinator
1802 Keeaumoku Street
Honolulu, HI 96822
808-537-4702

The **Pacific Fellowship Fund** provides support to women who have been residents of Hawaii for at least 3 years and who wish to pursue a master's degree or a doctorate in/on the Pacific area (excluding the west coast of the mainland United States). The deadline is March 1.

American Association of University Women

Educational Foundation
1111 16th Street, NW
Washington, DC 20036
202-728-7602
http://www.aauw.org

Selected **Professions Fellowships** with stipends ranging from $5,000 to $9,500 are awarded in designated fields where women's participation has been low.

Focus Professions Group Fellowships are awarded to minority women in business administration.

American Fellowships support women doctoral candidates writing their dissertations and post-doctoral scholars conducting research.

One-year **research leave** or **postdoctoral fellowships** of $20,000 to $25,000 are available in arts and humanities, social sciences, and natural sciences; one fellowship is designated for a woman from an underrepresented minority group.

Dissertation fellowships of $14,500 are awarded to women who will complete their dissertations and receive a doctoral degree by the end of the fellowship year.

Summer fellowships of $5,000 for postdoctoral research are awarded to women faculty at colleges and universities.

International Fellowships for full-time graduate or postgraduate study or research are awarded to women who are not U.S. citizens or permanent residents. Applicants must hold a U.S. bachelor's degree and be conducting studies important to women and girls in their country of origin.

The foundation awards approximately 70 **fellowships** annually, ranging in amount from $20,000 to $25,000, to women U.S. citizens who have completed all their doctoral requirements except writing the dissertation. Awards also are made to women for postdoctoral research and for the final year of study in medicine.

In addition, minority women undertaking their final year of study toward the M.D. or D.O. degree may apply for **scholarships** of up to $9,500.

American Bar Foundation

750 North Lake Shore Drive
Chicago, IL 60611-3038
312-988-6500

Minority college sophomores or juniors with a 3.0 GPA are eligible for **Summer Research Fellowships** to study some aspect of law or social science. Stipends of $3,600 are available for the summer program. Apply by March 1.

American Indian Graduate Center

4520 Montgomery Boulevard, NE
Albuquerque, NM 87109-1291
505-881-4584
http://www.aigc.com

The center offers **graduate fellowships** for Native Americans and Alaska Natives to support master's, doctoral, or professional study. Awards are offered in medicine, business, law, science, and other fields. Applicants must belong to a federally recognized tribe in the United States or have at least one-fourth degree Indian blood. Fellowships are meant to meet the applicants' financial needs after all other sources of financial aid have been used. New students receive a maximum of $4,000 and continuing students a maximum of $6,000.

American Institute of Certified Public Accountants

1121 Avenue of the Americas
New York, NY 10036
212-596-6270
http://www.aicpa.org

The primary objective of the **minority fellowships** program is to make it possible for more minorities to enter or move ahead in the accounting professorate. The program provides competitive awards of up to $12,000 per year for accounting scholars who show significant potential to become accounting educators. The fellowships are awarded each April and are renewable for up to an additional five years. Fellowships were awarded to 17 Ph.D. candidates for the 1998-99 academic year. To date, the program has assisted 24 candidates in completing their doctorates.

Financial Aid

American Nurses Association, Inc.

Fellowship Director
600 Maryland Avenue, SW, Suite 100W
Washington, DC 20024-2571
202-651-7245
http://www.ana.org

Ethnic/Racial Minority Clinical Training and Research Fellowships of up to $10,800 are awarded to minority nurses pursuing doctoral study in some phase of mental health in minority populations. Applicants must be registered nurses who are U.S. citizens or legal residents. Applications are due January 15.

American Physiological Society

Education Office
9650 Rockville Pike, Room #4301
Bethesda, MD 20814-3991
301-530-7132
http://www.faseb.org/aps

The **NIDDK Travel Fellowship Awards** for physiologists from underrepresented minority groups (African Americans, Hispanics, Native Americans, and Pacific Islanders) are open to advanced undergraduate, predoctoral, and postdoctoral students. Students in the APS Porter Physiology Development Program are also eligible. The intent of this award is to increase participation of pre- and postdoctoral minority students in physiological sciences. Minority faculty members at MBRS and MARC-eligible institutions may also submit applicants. The recipients receive funds for travel and per diem to attend either the Experimental Biology meeting or one of the APS Conferences. Recipients are matched with APS mentors at the meeting.

The **William T. Porter Fellowship Award** is designed to support the training of talented students entering a career in physiology and to provide predoctoral fellowships for minority students, and limited sabbatical leave aid for faculty members of predominantly black schools who wish to update their expertise in physiology. In addition, funds have been made available for lectureships and laboratory equipment to develop teaching consortia linking predominantly black colleges with medical schools in the same area. Summer research fellowships are also awarded for minority undergraduate opportunities in physiological research. The recipients recieve basic stipends, and an insitutional allowance is given to the training department or laboratory where the recipient will work.

American Planning Association

1776 Massachusetts Avenue, NW
Washington, DC 20036-1904
312-431-9100
http://www.planning.org

The association offers the **APA Fellowship Program** to minority students (African-American, Hispanic, or Native American) recently accepted to, or currently enrolled in, a n Urban or Transportation Planning graduate program approved by the Planning Accredited Board.

American Political Science Association

Minority Graduate Fellowships
1527 New Hampshire Avenue, NW
Washington, DC 20036
202-483-2512
http://www.apsanet.org

The APSA offers five **fellowships** of up to $6,000 for minority graduate students pursuing a doctoral degree in political science. Applications are due in March. Applicants must be African American, Hispanic, or Native American. The association publishes an annual "Guide to Graduate Study in Political Science," which lists programs available and possible financial aid.

American Press Institute

11690 Sunrise Valley Drive
Reston, VA 20191-1498
703-620-3611
http://www.newspaper.org

The institute offers a **Minority Journalism Educators Fellowship** which pays the cost of attending an API seminar or other meeting. Eligible are minority instructors of journalism courses; costs covered include room, board, and registration or tuition.

The **Rollan D. Melton Fellowship** is open to minority members who teach college-level journalism, and provides tuition and living expenses for attendance at a seminar. Apply by November 15.

American Psychiatric Association

Office of Minority/National Affairs
1400 K Street, NW
Washington, DC 20005
202-682-6096

The **APA/CMHS Minority Fellowship Program** provides educational enrichment to psychiatrists-in-training and stimulates their interest in providing quality and effective services to minorities and the underserved. The APA/CMHS is currently a nine-month program, which begins September 1 and ends May 31. Fellows are assigned to work with an APA component that is of particular interest to the trainee and congruent with his/her career goals. The fellowship is open to residents who are in at least their second year of psychiatry training and who are U.S. citizens or permanent residents.

American Psychological Association

750 First Street, NE
Washington, DC 20002
202-336-6127
http://www.apa.org

The APA operates three **minority student programs** designed to help students finance doctoral study in psychology. The first supports training leading to work as a research scientist; the second helps students prepare for a career as a clinical psychologist; and the third, for counseling psychology. Students may apply to only one program. Awards provide $8,500 for 12 months of study; in many cases, universities contribute tuition and other forms of assistance. The APA publishes a "Guide to Graduate Study in Psychology" and has operated a Congressional Summer Internship Program in the past.

The **MFP in Neuroscience Training Fellowship** is available to both predoctoral and postdoctoral students.

American Society for Microbiology

Office of Education and Training
1325 Massachusetts Avenue, NW
Washington, DC 20005
202-942-9283
http://www.asmusa.org/edusrc/edu2.htm

The **ASM Minority Undergraduate Research Fellowship** encourages minority students to pursue careers or advanced degrees in the biological and microbiological sciences. The program provides an opportunity for students to participate in research projects at selected institutions and gain experience presenting the results of their research at a national or regional meeting. Students eligible for the fellowship must be enrolled as a full-time undergraduate student majoring in the biological or microbiological sciences, and must be involved in a research project.

The **Robert D. Watkins Minority Graduate Fellowship** encourages minority graduate students to conduct research in the microbiological sciences. The goal of the program is to increase the number of underrepresented minorities completing doctoral degrees in the microbiological sciences. The Watkins Minority Graduate Fellow receives a $15,000 annual stipend.

American Society of Mechanical Engineers

3 Park Avenue
New York, NY 10016-5990
202-785-3756
http://www.asme.org

The **ASME Graduate Teaching Fellowship Program** was established to encourage outstanding graduate students, especially women and minorities, to pursue the doctorate in mechanical engineering and encourage engineering education as a profession. Fellowship awards will be made for a maximum of 2 years. The amount of the stipend ($5,000 initially) is reviewed and approved annually by the ASME Board on Engineering Education in cooperation with the ASME Foundation.

Financial Aid

American Sociological Association

1307 New York Avenue, NW
Washington, DC 20005
202-833-3410
http://www.asanet.org

Through its **Minority Fellowship Program**, the ASA offers a number of awards with stipends of over $14,000 for graduate study to help minority candidates prepare for careers in mental health, either as researchers or teachers. Because the program is funded by the National Institute of Mental Health, recipients must agree to work in behavioral research or training for a period as long as the original grant. Applicants must be U.S. citizens or have Alien Registration Cards, and they must be accepted and/or enrolled in a full-time sociology doctoral program. They must be members of a racial/ethnic group, including black, Hispanic, Native American, Asian, or Pacific Islander. The MFP also facilitates students' placement in graduate programs.

American Speech-Language-Hearing Association Foundation

10801 Rockville Pike
Rockville, MD 20852
800-498-2071
http://www.ashfoundation.org

The foundation offers a number of **fellowships** to finance college study, including one graduate award set aside for a minority candidate.

American Vocational Association

1410 King Street
Alexandria, VA 22314-2749
703-683-3111

Fellowships of $3,000 to $4,000 a year are open to AVA members planning to study home economics at the graduate level. One award is reserved specifically for a minority candidate, but minorities, of course, are eligible for all the awards.

Argonne National Laboratory

9700 South Cass Avenue
Argonne, IL 60439
630-252-4495
http://www.dep.anl.gov

Minority students are recruited for **research positions** at the lab to support studies at the master's or doctoral level in math, science, or engineering. Students receive a stipend of $350 per week. Applications are due February 1, May 15, or October 15.

Arizona State University

Student Financial Assistance Office
Box 870412
Tempe, AZ 85287-0412
480-965-6292

The **Navajo M.B.A. Fellowship Program** offers a stipend of $15,000 for each of two years plus a computer allowance and relocation fund for persons selected for its graduate program in business management.

Native American graduate students in library science may apply for **awards** averaging $8,000.

Arizona, University of, Tucson

Student Financial Aid Office
Administration Building, Room 203
Tucson, AZ 85721
520-621-2169

The College of Education offers $10,000 **fellowships** and $9,000 **assistantships** for minority Ph.D. candidates in administration, teaching, student personnel, and finance.

Arkansas Department of Higher Education

Financial Aid Division
114 East Capitol
Little Rock, AR 72201-3818
800-547-8839
http://www.adhe.arknet.edu

Faculty/Administrators Development Fellowships are open to minority American teachers or administrators at, or alumni of, sponsoring Arkansas colleges or universities. Applicants must be Arkansas residents enrolled in a doctoral program. Recipients must return to full-time employment at the sponsoring institution for three years. Otherwise, the fellowship must be repaid in proportion to the unpaid obligation. Apply by June 1.

The **Minority Masters Fellows Program** offers a forgivable loan to African Americans, Hispanics, and Asian Americans admitted to a master's program in mathematics, science, or foreign languages at an Arkansas university. It is also open to African Americans who received a Minority Teacher Scholarship and are now in the fifth year of a teacher education program. Applicants must be Arkansas residents. The award is $7,500 for full-time students and $2,500 for part-time summer students. To receive forgiveness of the loan after graduation, recipients must teach in a public school in Arkansas for two years. Apply by June 1.

Arts International
Institute of International Education
809 United Nations Plaza
New York, NY 10017
212-984-5370
http://iserver.iie.org/ai/index.html

Cintas Foundation Fellowships of $10,000 are offered to Cuban artists currently living outside the country. Awards are for graduate study in the United States or another country approved by the foundation. Apply by March 1.

Asian American Journalists Association
1182 Market Street, Suite 320
San Francisco, CA 94102
415-346-6343
http://www.aaja.org

AAJA has established quarterly **fellowships** for members to participate in management and advanced skills training workshops. In addition, the **AAJA/Poynter Fellowship** is awarded to four members to participate in select leadership programs offered by the Poynter Institute.

The **AAJA-New York Times Management Fellowship** is awarded to one qualified member to attend a management training program at Northwestern University each year. Full and associate members with at least three years

of professional experience are eligible for these fellowship programs.

Asian Cultural Council
437 Madison Avenue, 37th Floor
New York, NY 10022-7001
212-812-4300
http://www.asianculturalcouncil.org

The council awards seven to nine **fellowships** ranging from $500 to $20,000 for research and travel in Asia. Applicants must be Asian citizens. Funds may be used to cover the costs of research, travel, and living expenses. Awards are available for graduate and postdoctoral study. Specialists and scholars may also apply. Awards are offered in various aspects of Asian culture, including ethnic music, museum science, art, and archaeology.

Association on American Indian Affairs
P.O. Box 268
Sisseton, SD 57262
605-698-3998
http://web.tnics.com/aaia

The association oversees the **Sequoyah Fellowship Program,** which provides a one-year, $1,500 unrestricted stipend to American Indian and Alaska Native graduate students.

AT&T Labs
Room C103
180 Park Avenue
Florham Park, NJ 07932-0971
http://www.research.att.com/academic/alfp.html

Minority students pursuing Ph.D.s in computer and communications-related fields are eligible for 2 types of awards: **fellowships** and **grants** renewable for up to 6 years.

Atlanta History Center
Headquarters for the National Museum Fellows Program
130 West Paces Ferry Road
Atlanta, GA 30305-1366
404-814-4024

Financial Aid

The **National Museum Fellows Program** (1998-2001 program sites are the Atlanta History Center, Chicago Historical Society, and Minnesota Historical Society) trains minority undergraduates to qualify for entry-level museum profession positions, paid museum internships, and graduate programs in museum studies or arts management. African, Hispanic, Asian, and Native Americans who are sophomores or juniors at any 4-year college or university in Atlanta, Chicago, or St. Paul/Minneapolis are eligible to be nominated by their major professors for 12 months of training. Fellows receive $6,000 stipend, all texts, travel to U.S. museums and historic sites.

Auburn University

Office of Financial Aid
Auburn University, AL 36849
334-844-4080
http://www.auburn.edu/academic/provost/pgop

African American students enrolled in a Ph.D. or Ed.D. program with the goal of becoming college or university professors are eligible for **President's Educational Opportunity Fellowships** of $15,000 or more. Contact the Graduate School, 106 Hargis Hall, 334-844-4700.

Austin Peay State University

College of Graduate Studies, Box 4458
Clarksville, TN 37044-4458
931-221-7414
http://www.apsu.edu/~cogs

The **Tennessee African American Graduate Fellowship** is open to African American students from Tennessee admitted to APSU's Graduate School. Applications are due March 1.

Bank of America Center

Fellowship Officer, Department 3246
Box 37000
San Francisco, CA 94137
415-953-0932

The bank provides **fellowship funds** for outstanding California minority business students at Stanford University, the University of California at Berkeley, the University of California at Los Angeles, or the University of Southern California. Apply through your school.

Bannerman Program

1627 Lancaster Street
Baltimore, MD 21231
410-327-6220

The **Charles Bannerman Memorial Fellowship Program** provides a three-month sabbatical and $15,000 grant for community activists of color. Applicants must have been in the field for at least 10 years.

The new fellowship for **Young Organizers of Color** offers $5,000 for a self-designed project of two months or more. Applicants must be at least 30 years old and have been organizing for five years. Deadline to apply for either fellowship is December 1.

Black Writers Institute

1650 Bedford Avenue
Brooklyn, NY 11225
415-333-1918
http://www.blackwriters.net

The **John Oliver Killens Chair in Creative Writing** at Medger Evers College was established in1988 to support the short-term appointment of visiting writers who will lead writing seminars and workshops for the public.

Bristol-Myers Squibb Foundation

345 Park Avenue
New York, NY 10154-0037
http://www.bms.com/aboutbms/founda.html

The **Bristol-Myers Squibb Fellowship Program in Academic Medicine for Minority Students** annually awards 35 second- or third-year minority medical students. Recipients spend 12 weeks in academic research at their institutions under the guidance of a mentor.

Brown University
Pembroke Center for Training and Research on Women
P.O. Box 1958
Providence, RI 02912
401-863-1000

Postdoctoral Fellowships averaging $25,000 are available for scholars to spend a year in residence at the center for work on themes relating to gender, culture, and society.

Buffalo, University at
School of Management
206 Jacobs Management Center
Box 604000
Buffalo, NY 14260-4000
716-645-3204

The **Carborundum Minority Student Fellowship** is granted to an exceptional minority student who will pursue an M.B.A. in the full-time program. This fellowship is a one-time award of $1,500.

The **State University of New York Underrepresented Minority Fellowship** for minority graduate students provides a stipend plus tuition scholarships.

The two-year **Westwood-Squibb Pharmaceuticals Minority Fellowship**, awarded every other year, provides a tuition scholarship, a $6,800 annual stipend, and potential summer employment. All fellowships administered by the School of Management are awarded on the basis of academic merit and do not require the recipient to work in return for a stipend. Write for details.

California Institute of Technology
Mail Code 210-31
Pasadena, CA 91125
818-395-6811

The **James Irvine Foundation Minority Fellowship** was established to help increase the representation of minorities in science and engineering, or in another field of interest to Caltech faculty members. Eligible are those who have received their doctoral degree in engineering or the sciences and who are Native American, African American, Hispanic, Native Alaskan, or Native Pacific Islander. Applications should include a letter outlining the desired field of research and a curriculum vitae.

California Institute of Technology
Minority Undergraduate Research Fellowships
Mail Code 139-74
Pasadena, CA 91125
626-395-2885
http://www.its.caltech.edu/~sfp

Caltech's **Minority Undergraduate Research Fellowships** (MURF) program provides support for talented undergraduates to spend a summer working in a research laboratory on the Caltech campus. The MURF program is aimed at improving the representation of African Americans, Hispanics, Native Americans, Puerto Ricans, and Pacific Islanders in science and engineering.

California State University, Northridge
Graduate Studies
18111 Nordhoff Street
Northridge, CA 91330-8222
818-677-2138

Minority Equity Fellowships are open to students pursuing advanced degrees.

California Student Aid Commission
Customer Service Branch
P.O. Box 416027
Rancho Cordova, CA 95741-9027
916-526-7590
http://www.csac.ca.gov

Each year the commission awards about 500 **fellowships** for graduate and professional study in law, ranging from $700 to $6,500 for tuition and fees.

California, University of, Berkeley
Office of the Chancellor
200 California Hall
Berkeley, CA 94720-1500
510-642-1935
http://www.chance.berkeley.edu/fea

Financial Aid

The **Chancellor's Postdoctoral Fellowship Program for Academic Diversity** was established to increase the number of ethnic minority faculty members at the University of California at Berkeley. The program provides postdoctoral fellowships, research opportunities, mentoring and guidance in preparation for academic career advancement. The program currently solicits applications from individuals who are members of ethnic minority groups that are underrepresented in American universities, but all qualified applicants will be considered without regard to race, gender, color, or national origin. Special consideration will be given to applicants committed to careers in university research, and teaching, and whose life experience, research or employment background will contribute significantly to academic diversity and excellence at the Berkeley campus.

California, University of, Los Angeles

Institute for American Cultures
Special Fellowships Office
405 Hilgard Avenue
Los Angeles, CA 90024
310-825-3521

Postdoctoral fellowships of $25,000 to $30,000 are offered to students for Asian American, African American, Hispanic, or Native American studies.

California, University of, Los Angeles

Graduate Division
1252 Murphy Hall
P.O. Box 951419
Los Angeles, CA 90095-1419
310-825-3521
http://www.gdnet.ucla.edu

The **Eugene Cota-Robles Award** is a four-year fellowship with an annual stipend of up to $12,500 plus registration fees for a limited number of students who are entering Ph.D. programs and are interested in college teaching or research. Applicants must be nominated by their department or school.

The UCLA Graduate Division offers a variety of **fellowships** for which students from underrepresented minority groups are strongly encouraged to apply. These include a recruitment fellowship for students applying to terminal master's degree programs (i.e., **Graduate Opportunity Fellowship**), and a **Research Mentoring Fellowship** for continuing doctoral students.Most graduate degree granting departments and programs also have fellowship funding as well as teaching assistant and research assistant appointments available to help support their students.

Other **grants** and **fellowships,** including postdoctoral awards, are awarded through the 4 ethnic studies centers (i.e., Center for Afro-American Studies; American Indian Studies Center; Asian American Studies Center, Chicano Studies Research Center). More detailed information on these and other student support resources is available on the Graduate Division's Web site.

California, University of, San Diego

Office of Graduate Studies
La Jolla, CA 92093-0003
619-534-3871
http://www.ogsr.ucsd.edu

The **Eugene Cota-Robles Award** offers $12,500 per year plus tuition and fees for students from diverse backgrounds undertaking graduate study.

California, University of, Santa Cruz

Santa Cruz, CA 95064
408-459-0111

The **Graduate Fellowship Program for Minority and Disadvantaged Students** provides financial assistance to individuals who cannot finance their education by any other means.

Carleton College

Minority Predoctoral Teaching Fellowships in American Studies
One North College Street
Northfield, MN 55057
507-646-5769

One-year **minority teaching fellowships** involve teaching part-time and working part-time to finish the doctoral dissertation. Fellows are awarded a stipend of $25,000 plus funds for attending a professional meeting.

Center for the History of the American Indian

60 West Walton Street
Chicago, IL 60610
312-255-3564
http://www.newberry.org

The **Frances C. Allen Fellowship** is available to women of American Indian descent who are pursuing programs beyond the bachelor level in library science.

Center of American Indian and Minority Health

University of Minnesota
2221 University Avenue SE
Minneapolis, MN 55414
612-262-2075

The **Health Service Research and Policy Fellowship for Native American Physicians** is available for Native Americans who have completed the MD degree. The fellowship term is for 2 years. Compensation includes a $40,000 annual stipend.

Chicago, University of

Graduate School of Business
Chicago, IL 60637
773-702-3076

Two-year **Minority Student Fellowships** of $5,000 to $20,000 per year offer full tuition waivers to students pursuing an advanced degree; other awards are available for minority students enrolled part-time. Unlike many other business schools, Chicago does not object to part-time students who combine study with practical experience on the job. Applicants must be African American, Hispanic, or Native American. Students admitted to the Graduate School of Business are automatically considered for the fellowship.

City University of New York, New York

Office of Educational Opportunity & Diversity Programs
Graduate School
365 Fifth Avenue
New York, NY 10016
212-817-7540
http://web.gc.cuny.edu/oeodp

The City University of New York encourages African American and Hispanic students to pursue careers in college and university teaching. Four-year **fellowships** are offered to U.S. citizens or permanent residents entering any of the 31 doctoral programs at CUNY. Awards are $16,000 per year plus full tuition. The fellowships are offered under the Minority Access/Graduate Networking (MAGNET) Program. Apply by February 1.

Clark Atlanta University

School of Library and Information Studies
223 James Braley Drive
Atlanta, GA 30314
404-653-8697

Several **fellowships** are available for students pursuing a master's degree in the library school. A number of other financial aid options also are open to library science majors.

Columbia University

Admissions Office
600 West 168th Street
New York, NY 10032
212-305-3927

The **Dubose and Dorothy Heyward Memorial Fund** provides fellowships to minority students in the Theatre Division of the School of Art.

Columbia offers a number of minority **fellowships**, including those established by Bristol-Myers, Salomon Brothers, Dun & Bradstreet, and Citibank. Some provide an internship with the sponsoring organization.

67

Financial Aid

Columbia University

Joseph L. Mailman School of Public Health
60 Haven Avenue, B-3
New York, NY 10032
212-304-5260

The Division of Population and Family Health offers **fellowships** for 1 or 2 Hispanic women or men interested in obtaining a Master's in Public Health (MPH) degree. Applicants must have a bachelor's degree, prior public health work experience with Hispanic populations, and a commitment to serve Hispanic populations in the future. The division offers full tuition support and research assistantship opportunities for qualified applicants.

Congressional Black Caucus Foundation

1004 Pennsylvania Avenue, SE
Washington, DC 20003
202-675-6739
http://www.cbcfonline.org

The **Public Health Fellows Program** helps students in the pursuit of advanced degrees in community-based health professions. This fellowship focuses on African Americans who are first-year MPH or first-year doctoral students. Selected participants must already be accepted or enrolled in a public health education institution at the master's or doctoral level. Fellows will receive a $10,000 grant for the 18-month fellowship.

The **Congressional Fellowship Program** offers nine-month fellowships to help prepare minority students for senior-level careers in legislation. Applicants must be a full-time graduate student or faculty member. Apply by April 1.

Congressional Hispanic Caucus Institute

504 C Street, NE
Washington, DC 20002
202-543-1771
http://www.chci.org

Telecommunications Fellows (two recent college graduates or graduate students) are afforded the opportunity to conduct substantive research and written work on policy issues related to telecommunications or the telecommunications industry.

The **Edward R. Roybal Fellowship** allows a graduate student who is pursuing a degree in a health-related field the opportunity to apply his/her academic expertise in the public policy arena. Applicants must be pursuing a degree in a non-clinical, non-hospital, health related field which includes: health care policy, health research, health administration, and health education.

Consortium for Graduate Study in Management

200 South Hanley Road, Suite 1102
St. Louis, MO 63105-3415
888-658-6814
http://www.cgsm.wustl.edu:8010/

The Consortium for Graduate Study in Management is a 12-university alliance working to facilitate the entry of minorities into managerial positions in business. The universities recruit college-trained African American, Hispanic American, and Native American United States citizens and invite them to compete for merit-based **fellowships** for graduate study leading to a Master's Degree in Business. Founded in 1966, the consortium was organized to assist qualified minorities in the process of enrolling in accredited graduate business programs. The original mission of the consortium was to ensure that talented minorities develop the business skills necessary to compete for entry-level positions in American businesses. Since its inception, the consortium has increased the number of annual fellowships awarded from 20 to over 350. These fellowships are funded by various American businesses and the 12 universities affiliated with the consortium.

Council on Social Work Education

1600 Duke Street
Alexandria, VA 22314-3421
703-683-8080

The council offers doctoral **fellowships** for minority students with a master's degree in social work interested in careers in mental health research, with support from the National Institute of Mental Health. Awards are for $10,008 a year. Tuition of up to $2,000 may be available. Priority is given to candidates planning careers in mental health research and teaching. Applications are due February 28.

The council, together with the Substance Abuse and Mental Health Services Administration, offers doctoral fellowships to minority students with a master's degree in social work who are interested in assuming a leadership role in mental health services to minorities. Fellowship awards include a monthly stipend of $958; some tuition support of up to $1,800 a year may be available. Applicants must be American citizens or have permanent resident status. A payback provision accompanies the fellowship. Applications are available in September and due February 28.

Dartmouth College

Dean of Graduate Study
Wentworth Hall, Room 304
Hanover, NH 03755-3526
603-646-2736
http://www.dartmouth.edu/artsci/gradstdy/
Fellows.html

The **Thurgood Marshall Dissertation Fellowship** is awarded to an African American who needs to complete his or her doctoral dissertation. Fellows receive support for one year, including a $25,000 stipend, housing allowance, and $2,500 research assistance. Applications are due January 10.

Residential fellowships of $3,500 are available to doctoral candidates in most humanities and social science fields. Awards may be applied to research costs, living or travel expenses, or support for a spouse and/or children. Applications are due in March.

Earthwatch Institute

680 Mt. Auburn Street
Box 9104
Watertown, MA 02471-9104
800-776-0188
http://www.earthwatch.org

The **Earthwatch Education Awards Program** provides fellowships for minority and under-resourced high school students and K-12 teachers to participate in scientific field research expeditions.

East-West Center

Burns Hall 2066
1601 East-West Road
Honolulu, HI 96848
808-944-7192
http://www.ewc.hawaii.edu

Jefferson Fellowships are awarded to six working print or broadcast journalists from the United States and six from Asian and Pacific nations. Recipients spend nine weeks participating in intensive seminars on East-West issues. Five of the weeks are spent in Hawaii, and four are spent in Asia or the U.S. mainland. Editors, editorial writers, and producers receive preference.

The East-West Center awards **Graduate Fellowships** to citizens from the United States or Asian or Pacific nations. Applicants must be enrolled in a master's or doctoral program at the University of Hawaii and must plan to participate in EWC's educational and research projects.

Emory University

Director of Recruitment
Graduate School of Arts and Sciences
202 Administration Building
Atlanta, GA 30322
404-727-2815
http://www.emory.edu/gsoas/gsas.html

The **Andrew Mellon Postdoctoral Fellowship in African American Studies and Theatre Studies** offers a two-year appointment to teach and/or direct a studio presentation, as well as a stipend of $24,000 plus some allowances. Students must write a 500-page research proposal as part of the application.

The graduate school offers the **Emory Minority Fellowship** for first-time applicants entering doctoral study. Awards are given solely on the basis of merit. Apply by January 20. The graduate school has doctoral programs in the humanities, sciences, and social sciences.

Entomological Society of America

9301 Annapolis Road, Suite 300
Lanham, MD 20706-3115
301-731-4535
http://www.entsoc.org

The **Stan Beck Fellowship** assists needy students at the graduate or undergraduate level of their education. The need may be based on physical limitations or economic, minority, or environmental conditions. This award is made annually. The annual fellowship is approximately $4,000. All ESA members are eligible to nominate candidates for this fellowship.

Florida Education Fund

201 East Kennedy Boulevard, Suite 1525
Tampa, FL 33602
813-272-2772
http://www.fl-educ-fd.org

The **Minority Participation in Legal Education (MPLE) Program** awards an average of 66 scholarships annually to Florida residents attending both public and private law schools in Florida. Scholarships cover full tuition with a living stipend for students attending public law schools and provide up to $19,000 at private law schools annually for 3 academic years.

Fred Hutchinson Cancer Research Center

Weiss/Daling (MP381)
1124 Columbia Street
Seattle, WA 98104-2092
206-667-4642

The University of Washington, the University of Arizona's Native American Research and Training Program, and the Indian Health Service Cancer Prevention and Control Program offer 3-week training fellowships in cancer prevention and control research, in a program called the **Native Researchers' Cancer Control Training Program.**

Fredrikson and Byron Foundation Minority Scholarship

1100 International Centre
900 Second Avenue South
Minneapolis, MN 55402-3397
612-347-7000
http://www.fredlaw.com

The $5,000 **fellowship** is awarded to first-year minority law students based on academic performance and potential. Applications are due in March. Up to two $5,000 awards are given annually.

Fund for Theological Education

825 Houston Mill Road, Suite 250
Atlanta, GA 30329
404-727-1450
http://www.thefund.org

About 15 **Doctoral Fellowships** of $15,000 are offered to African Americans entering their first year of an accredited graduate program leading to a Ph.D. or Th.D. in religious or theological studies.

Dissertation Fellowships are available to African American Ph.D. or Th.D. students in their final year of dissertation work in religion or theological studies. Fellows receive a stipend of up to $15,000 for 1 year, and may apply for an additional $10,000 to pay student loans upon completion of the degree.

Harvard Medical School

164 Longwood Avenue
Boston, MA 02115
617-432-2313

The **Commonwealth Fund/Harvard University Fellowship in Minority Health Policy** prepares physicians for leadership positions in minority health and public policy. A BC/BE is required, and experience with minority health issues, interest in public policy, and U.S. citizenship. The fellowship includes a $40,000 stipend, master's degree tuition, health insurance, professional meeting and site visit travel provision.

Harvard University

John F. Kennedy School of Government
79 John F. Kennedy Street
Cambridge, MA 02138
617-495-5315
http://www.ksg.harvard.edu/hpaied/fellow.htm

The *Christian A. Johnson Endeavor Foundation Native American Fellowships* are awarded annually on a competitive basis of merit and financial need to American Indian students planning a career in American Indian Affairs. To be eligible, you must be enrolled in a John F. Kennedy School of Government degree program.

Harvard University

Graduate School of Arts and Sciences, Byerly Hall
8 Garden Street
Cambridge, MA 02138
617-495-5315
http://www.gsas.harvard.edu

Minority students enrolled in a Ph.D. program at Harvard are eligible for three-year fellowships which provide an annual stipend of $13,500 plus tuition remission. Contact Stephanie Parsons.

Hastie (William H.) Fellowship Program

Assistant Dean Martha Gaines
Room 5105, Law Building
Madison, WI 53706
608-262-8557
http://www.law.wisc.edu

The William Hastie Program offers **fellowships** to minority students who have graduated from law school and wish to teach law.

Hispanic Bar Association

Public Interest Fellowship
P.O. Box 1011
Washington, DC 20013-1011
202-624-2904
http://www.hbadc.org/found.htm

The foundation awards **fellowships** to those seeking funding for summer public interest legal work. The fellowships are intended to provide funding for first- and second-year law students desiring opportunities in public interest law. Two fellowships of $3,000 are awarded.

Hispanic Link Journalism Foundation

1420 N Street, NW
Washington, DC 20005
202-238-0705

Hispanic journalists are eligible for a 1-year training **fellowship**. With a stipend of $20,000 plus benefits, the fellowship allows an aspiring reporter to work with the Hispanic Link News Service.

Hispanic-Serving Health Professions Schools

1700 17th Street, NW, Suite 405
Washington, DC 20009
202-667-9788
http://www.hshps.com

The **HSHPS Research Fellowship Program** is designed to develop young Hispanic physicians' research and training abilities in biomedical and health services areas at member institutions in order to increase Hispanic faculty in medicine.

Howard Hughes Medical Institute

Office of Grants and Special Programs
4000 Jones Bridge Road
Chevy Chase, MD 20815-6789
301-215-8500
http://www.hhmi.org

Part of the institute's mission is to increase the interest in science education and research careers among women and minority groups underrepresented in the sciences. Of the awards offered annually, about 15 percent have gone to minorities and about 45 percent to women. The institute offers biological science fellowships to graduate students, medical students, and physicians; aids undergraduate institutions through science education; and aids science museums and biomedical research institutions through pre-college and public science education. Write to this address for information on these three fellowship programs: **Research Training Fellowships for Medical Students, Research Scholars at the National Institutes of Health,** and **Postdoctoral Research Fellowships for**

Financial Aid

Physicians. For information on Hughes Predoctoral Fellowships, see the listing for the National Research Council.

Howard University College of Medicine

Porter Physiology Development Program
520 W Street, NW
Washington, DC 20059
202-806-6346
http://www.faseb.org/aps/educatn/porter1.htm

The Porter Physiology Development Program offers **Minority Fellowships in Physiology**, awarded annually. These pre-doctoral and post-doctoral fellowships can be extended for additional years.

Hunter College

Center for Puerto Rican Studies
695 Park Avenue
New York, NY 10021
212-772-5687
http://www.centropr.org

Rockefeller Fellowships in the Humanities are offered to proven scholars for a year's residence and study of social equity and cultural rights. Awards are for $34,000. Minority graduate students in history may apply for **fellowships** offering a $34,000 stipend plus a moving allowance. Apply by January 15.

Indiana University, Bloomington

Minority Faculty Fellowship Program
Memorial Hall West, Room 111
Bloomington, IN 47405-6701
812-855-0543

The **Minority Faculty Fellowship Program** offers minorities with the doctorate—or near completion—summer school and academic year teaching appointments to introduce them to the IU campus. Summer fellows usually teach 1 course and academic-year fellows teach in both the fall and spring terms. Recipients receive a $3,000 fellowship in addition to an appropriate salary from the department in which they teach. Applications are accepted year-round.

Indiana University, Indianapolis

Center on Philanthropy
550 West North Street, Suite 301
Indianapolis, IN 46202
317-274-4200
http://www.philanthropy.iupui.edu

The $15,000 **Hearst Minority Fellowship** funds a 10-month program to study nonprofit management in philanthropic organizations. The center also provides partial tuition remission and a $1,000 travel grant. Applicants should be enrolled in a master's program at the center; apply by February 1. The university also administers the **William G. Mays Award** of $200 for African American juniors and seniors in business administration and management.

Indiana University

Committee on Institutional Cooperation
Predoctoral Fellowships Program
803 East Eighth Street
Bloomington, IN 47405
800-457-4420

CIC Predoctoral Fellowships providing full tuition and a stipend of $11,000 to cover two academic years of graduate work toward a Ph.D. are awarded annually for study in music theory, art history, and literature. Applicants must be African American, American Indian, Mexican American, or Puerto Rican as well as U.S. citizens, and must pursue doctoral study at one of the participating CIC institutions. Participating universities are: University of Chicago, University of Illinois at Chicago, University of Illinois, Indiana University, University of Iowa, University of Michigan, Michigan State, University of Minnesota, Northwestern, Ohio State, Pennsylvania State, Purdue, University of Wisconsin-Madison, and University of Wisconsin-Milwaukee.

Industrial Relations Council on Goals

P.O. Box 4363
East Lansing, MI 48826-4363
800-344-6257

The council encourages minority students to enroll in programs leading to careers in industrial relations and human resources, and offers fellowships of $7,800 for students enrolled on a full-time basis.

Institute for the Study of World Politics

Fellowship Competition
1755 Massachusetts Avenue, NW
Washington, DC 20036
202-797-0882

Designed to increase the number of minorities in international careers, **Dorothy Danforth Compton Fellowships for Minority Group Students of World Affairs** are open to graduate students in world politics. The support is intended to provide thesis or dissertation assistance. About 20 fellowships are awarded annually.

International Business Machines, Yorktown Heights

Thomas Watson Research Center
P.O. Box 218
Yorktown Heights, NY 10598-2141
914-945-3000

IBM has a **fellowship program** for students pursuing the Ph.D. degree in areas of broad interest to IBM, including chemistry, computer science, electrical engineering, material science, mathematics, mechanical engineering, physics, and related disciplines. Students should be enrolled full time in an accredited U.S. or Canadian college or university and should have completed at least one year of graduate study. Students must be nominated by a faculty member and endorsed by their department head.

IBM fellowships are intended to help enlarge the pool of talented Ph.D.s in areas of importance to IBM. IBM values diversity in the workplace and encourages nominations of women, minorities, and others who contribute to that diversity.

Two types of fellowships are available: **Research Fellowships** and **Cooperative Fellowships**. IBM will award approximately 25 fellowships in each of these categories. Both fellowships cover tuition and fees, and provide a student stipend

of $15,000. In addition, each category of fellowship will provide for a small number of **Distinguished Fellowships** with stipends of $20,000. All fellowships are awarded annually and eligible for continuation based on academic standing, continued progress and achievement, and the level of interaction with IBM's technical community. **Research Fellowships** are intended for students wishing to pursue a career in research and will be administered by the IBM Research Division. Selection for the Research Fellowships will be based on research excellence and an assessment of the student's overall potential for a research career. **Cooperative Fellowships** are intended for students who wish to pursue a challenging technical career in advanced technology and product development as well as related research areas.

Faculty wishing to nominate a student for either fellowship can do so during the annual fall nomination period specified at the fellowship nomination Web site:
http://domino.watson.ibm.com/hr/research/fellows.nsf/nomination

Investigative Reporters and Editors

Missouri School of Journalism
Columbia, MO 65211
573-882-2042
http://www.ire.org

Investigative Reporters and Editors (IRE) offers more than 25 **fellowships** each year which provide minorities with a waiver for their registration fees ($150 - $200 for a conference, or $500 - $1,000 for a boot camp) plus $450 to spend on travel and hotel rooms when they attend IRE conferences.

Iowa, University of

Graduate College
205 Gilmore Hall
Iowa City, IA 52242
319-335-1039
http://www.uiowa.edu

The University of Iowa offers an array of fellowship programs, including the **University of Iowa Fellowship Program** and the **Iowa Arts and Performing Arts Fellowship Programs**.

Financial Aid

The Graduate School offers **Opportunity Fellowships** for minority students. These awards provide a stipend of $9,600 plus full tuition for the first year of study. After that, the department is expected to provide support. Applications are due in January.

Entering freshmen are eligible for **Opportunity at Iowa Awards** of $1,000 to $8,000. Candidates must have ranked in the top third of their high school class and be African American, Hispanic, or Native American.

Japan Foundation, New York

152 West 57th Street, 39th Floor
New York, NY 10019
212-489-0299
http://www.jfny.org/jfny

The foundation awards **doctoral dissertation fellowships** and **research fellowships** for academics for various fields related to the study of Japan. Funds may be used for research costs, living expenses, travel costs, and support for spouse/dependents. Awards vary from four to 14 months in length and are non-renewable. Applications are due on November 1.

Kaiser Family Foundation

2400 Sand Hill Road
Menlo Park, CA 94025
650-854-9400
http://www.kff.org

The **Henry J. Kaiser Family Foundation Native American Health Policy Fellowships** are designed to give Native American health and welfare leaders an opportunity to learn more about national health and welfare policy issues that affect Native Americans and gain a better understanding of the national policymaking process. Fellows have the opportunity to work full-time in a Congressional or Executive Branch office to gain first-hand knowledge of policy issues and how government works.

Kellogg Graduate School of Management

2001 Sheridan Road
Evanston, IL 60201
847-491-3308
http://www.kellogg.nwu.edu

More than $500,000 in **scholarships** and **grants** is available to minority applicants in obtaining a graduate business degree.

Kentucky, University of

Office of the Assistant Vice President for Research and Graduate Studies
Lexington, KY 40506-0286
606-257-3317
http://www.rgs.uky.edu/astecc/lyman.htm

The **Lyman T. Johnson Minority Postdoctoral Fellowship** program is open to postdoctoral students in any academic area in which the university offers a degree. Fellows are expected to pursue an individualized program of advanced research training under the mentorship of one or more UK professors. Fellows receive a $30,000 stipend and $5,000 for research support or travel expenses.

Kentucky, University of

School of Library and Information Sciences
Lexington, KY 40506
606-257-3317
http://www.uky.edu/comminfostudies/slis

In-state and out-of-state **Minority Fellowships in Library Science** are awarded to minority students. Apply by July 1.

LaFetra Operating Foundation

LaFetra Fellows Program
1221 Preservation Park Way, #100
Oakland, CA 94612
510-763-9206
http://www.lafetra.org

The **LaFetra Fellowship** allows minorities to experience cross-cultural exchange firsthand. Fellows receive a stipend, a travel grant, and training to support their work with both local and international organizations. These organizations respond to community needs in areas such as economic development, environment education, and public health. The program runs for 9 months in 3 stages: beginning with an internship at a Bay Area community-based organization, followed by a 2-3 month volunteer project abroad, and ending with a return to the Bay Area internship where Fellows focus on ways to remain in solidarity with the communities overseas while sharing the experience at home.

Los Angeles Philharmonic Fellowship for Excellence in Diversity

Education Department
135 North Grand Avenue
Los Angeles, CA 90012
213-972-0703

A **fellowship** of $500 to $2,000 is available for orchestral minority students in Southern California between the ages of 16 and 30.

Loyola College, Baltimore

Department of Multicultural Affairs
MD Hall 2274
501 North Charles Street
Baltimore, MD 21210
410-617-2988
http://www.loyola.edu

Loyola Teaching Fellowships of $27,000 are open to African American Ph.D. candidates who have completed all work toward a doctorate except the dissertation. Fellows teach two or three courses at Loyola during the year of fellowship. Applications are accepted at any time.

Mathematica, Inc.

Director of Human Resources
PO Box 2393
Princeton, MA 08543
http://www.mathematica-mpr.com

Mathematica, Inc. offers 4 summer **fellowships** to students enrolled in a master's or Ph.D. program in public policy or a social science.

Fellows will pursue independent research on a social policy issue of relevance to economic and/or social problems of minority groups

under the guidance of a faculty member from their university or college. Two fellows will work in Princeton, NJ, and 2 fellows will be located in Washington, DC.

Missouri, University of, Columbia

Graduate School
210 Jesse Hall
Columbia, MO 65211
573-882-0089
http://web.missouri.edu/~gradschl/

The Chancellor's **Gus T. Ridgel Fellowship** is open to minorities pursuing doctoral degrees. Fellows receive a stipend of $10,000. Applicants must be an underrepresented ethnic minority U.S. citizen (African American, Alaskan Native, Mexican American, Native American, or Puerto Rican).

Missouri, University of, Columbia

College of Agriculture, Food and Natural Resources
2-64 Agriculture
Columbia, MO 65211
573-882-0089

George Washington Carver Graduate Fellowships are available for minority master's or doctoral candidates in the agriculture and natural resources sciences. Research conducted by the recipient will be part of the Agricultural Experiment Station's research program.

Mystic Seaport Museum

Munson Institute of American Maritime Studies
P.O. Box 6000
Mystic, CT 06355-0990
860-572-5359
http://www.mysticseaport.org

Paul Cuffe Memorial Fellowships are open to researchers interested in the role of African Americans and Native Americans in maritime history. Fellows receive a monthly stipend of $1,500; applications are due in June.

Financial Aid

NALEO Educational Fund
5800 South Eastern Avenue, Suite 365
Los Angeles, CA 90040
http://www.naleo.org

The **Ford Motor Company Fellows Program** allows Latino college students to participate in a 6-week program which includes a 4-week fellowship with a member of Congress. To be eligible, you must be currently enrolled in or a recent graduate of an accredited 4-year institution.

National Academy of Education
New York University
School of Education
726 Broadway, 5th Floor
New York, NY 10003-9580
212-998-9035
http://www.hae.nyu.edu

The **Spencer Postdoctoral Fellowships** offer $45,000 research awards for one academic year and $22,500 awards for each of two contiguous years, working half-time. Applicants must already hold a doctoral degree in education, humanities, or the social sciences to support research matters relevant to the improvement of education. Applications are not mailed after November 18 and must be returned by December 1.

National Academy of Sciences
Program Director
National Research Council
2101 Constitution Avenue, NW
Washington, DC 20418
202-334-2872
http://www.nas.edu

Ford Foundation Dissertation Fellowships for Minorities offers 20 awards with stipends of $18,000 over three years to minority doctoral students beginning work on dissertations in science, math, biology, engineering, or humanities. **Ford Foundation Predoctoral Fellowships for Minorities** provide 50 awards with $12,000 stipends for minority students beginning doctoral studies in science, math, biology, engineering, or humanities. Apply by November 3 for either award.

National Action Council for Minorities in Engineering
The Empire State Building
350 Fifth Avenue, Suite 2212
New York, NY 10118-2299
212-279-2626
http://www.nacme.org

NACME Sustaining Fellows Awards provide up to $20,000 scholarships payable over four years. Undergraduate engineering students from underrepresented minority population groups may apply during their freshman year after completing one semester. Applicants must have a minimum grade point average of 3.0/4.0. Applications are mailed to selected institutions in December.

NACME established the **W. Lincoln Hawkins Undergraduate Fellowship**, in collaboration with the Hawkins family, to honor an extraordinary scientist and engineer for his remarkable life and career. The fellowship offers an exceptional opportunity to outstanding African American, Latino and American Indian chemical engineering students, providing early research experience, one on one faculty mentoring, and exposure to leading-edge technologies. The research award provides up to $20,000 over two years; $10,000 to be applied to a research project and $10,000 to be applied toward education costs. Students may apply during their second semester in the sophomore year. Applicants must have a minimum grade point average of 3.5/4.0. Applications are mailed to selected institutions in December.

The **Elizabeth and Stephen D. Bechtel Jr. Foundation Fellows Award** encourages and recognizes undergraduate engineering students with exceptional academic records and outstanding leadership skills. The award provides up to $10,000 over 2 years to engineering students from underrepresented minority population groups. Students may apply during their second semester in the sophomore year. Applications are mailed to selected institutions.

National Asian Pacific American Bar Association

1717 Pennsylvania Avenue, NW, Suite 500
Washington, DC 20006
202-974-1030
http://www.napaba.org

The **NAPABA Law Foundation Community Service Fellowship Program** offers an award of $5,000 to law school graduates and outgoing judicial law clerks.

National Association for Equal Opportunity in Higher Education

8701 Georgia Avenue, Suite 200
Silver Spring, MD 20910
301-650-2440
http://www.nafeo.org

Each year, **Mobil Faculty Fellowships** are awarded to faculty and administrators who, through application, demonstrate that their participation will enable them to contribute to the internationalization of their campus through activities such as adding new courses or enhancing existing courses, or encouraging the inflow of international students.

National Association of Black Journalists

8701-A Adelphi Road
Adelphi, MD 20783
301-445-7100
http://www.nabj.org

NABJ annually awards at least two **Ethel Payne Fellowships** to journalists interested in obtaining international reporting experiences through assignments in Africa. The fellowships, designed for journalists who have a strong interest in Africa but limited opportunities to cover the continent for their news organizations, allow the recipients to spend up to three weeks in Africa and to produce news reports for NABJ. A panel of judges selects the winners based upon the strength of project proposals to cover news events or issues that have a major impact on one or more African countries. Applicants must be NABJ members with at least five years of experience as full-time journalists or freelance writers for a newspaper, magazine, or broadcast station. Candidates must submit an 800-word project proposal, write a 300-word essay describing the applicant's journalistic experiences, and submit three work samples and two letters of recommendation.

National Black MBA Association

180 North Michigan Avenue, Suite 1400
Chicago, IL 60601
312-236-2622
http://www.nbmbaa.org

The **Ph.D. Fellowship Program** annually awards one $10,000 fellowship and one $5,000 fellowship to qualified minority students enrolled full-time in a doctorate program accredited by the AACSB: The International Association for Management Education. Field of study must be in a business discipline. Applicants do not have to be enrolled in a doctoral program at the time their scholarship application is submitted, but must be enrolled at the time the scholarship award is disbursed.

National Broadcasting Corporation

Minority Fellowship Program
30 Rockefeller Plaza
New York, NY 10112
212-664-4444

The **NBC Minority Fellowship Program** provides a fellowship of $8,000 for graduate studies in journalism, communications, or business. Each year, several universities working closely with NBC owned and operated stations in Burbank, Chicago, Miami, New York City, Philadelphia, and Washington, D.C., are invited to nominate students for this program who have distinguished themselves through academics, extracurricular activities, and work experience. Please contact your financial aid office to find out if your university participates in this program.

National Consortium for Graduate Degrees for Minorities in Engineering, Inc.

University of Notre Dame
P.O. Box 537
Notre Dame, IN 46556
219-287-1097
http://www.nd.edu/~gem/

The Consortium seeks to increase the participation of African Americans, Hispanics, and Native Americans in master's and doctoral programs in engineering and science. A cooperative program developed by 70 colleges and universities and 84 research centers, the Consortium provides minority students with **fellowships**, traineeships, mentoring, professional development assistance, academic enhancement, and helpful publications.

National Council of La Raza

1111 19th Street NW, Suite 1000
Washington, DC 20036
http://www.nclr.org

NCLR awards an **educational policy fellowship** of $12,000 to students who have at least a master's in public affairs or policy studies. Fellows work at the John F. Kennedy School of Government at Harvard University for 10 months. The program's aim is to develop the administrative and management skills of Hispanic organizational leaders.

National Heart, Lung, and Blood Institute

Division of Blood Diseases and Resources
6701 Rockledge Drive, MSC 7952
Bethesda, MD 20892
301-435-0064

The **Minority Institution Research Scientist Development Award** provides research support to faculty members at minority institutions who have the interest and potential to conduct high quality research in the areas of cardiovascular, pulmonary, hematologic, or sleep disorders.

National Institute of Allergy and Infectious Disease

Division of Allergy, Immunology and Transplantation
Solar Bldg, Rm 4A-14
6003 Executive Boulevard
Bethesda, MD 20892
301-496-5598

The **Minority Fellowship in Transplantation** is open to racial/ethnic minority individuals, or permanent residents who hold a PhD, MD, DO, DDS, OD, DPM, ScD, EngD, or equivalent degree. Applicants must be proposing a program of research training on the rejection of transplanted organs or tissues. The amounts of the awards depend on the availability of funds.

National Institute of General Medical Sciences

Minority Opportunities in Research
Center Drive, Building 45
Bethesda, MD 20892
301-594-3900

The **National Minority Predoctoral Fellowship Program** is designed to increase the pool of underrepresented minorities studying biomedical sciences who wish to pursue the PhD, MD/PhD or other combined professional degree/PhD. The annual stipend is $11,500 per year.

National Medical Fellowships

Scholarship Department
110 West 32nd Street
New York, NY 10001
212-714-1007
http://www.nmf-online.org

The **Clinical Training Fellowship Program for Minority Medical Students in Substance Abuse Research and Treatment** consists of eight- to twelve-week fellowships. Three, $6,000 fellowships are offered.

The **W.K. Kellogg Community Medicine Training Fellowship Program for Minority Medical Students** encourages students to enter or establish organized, community-based primary care practices. Students receive firsthand experience in community medicine under the guidance of senior staff at a participating community-based facility. The fellows assist in health care delivery, community epidemiology, and health education as appropriate. Fellows must agree to complete two, eight- to twelve-week rotations.Competition is open to second- and third-year underrepresented minority students attending accredited U.S. medical schools. Fifteen, $10,000 fellowships are presented annually. Fellows can also apply for $1,000 travel stipends to attend approved professional meetings.

The **Fellowship Program in Academic Medicine for Minority Students** helps minority medical students pursue careers in biomedical research and academic medicine and fosters mentor relationships between these students and prominent biomedical scientists. Competition is open to second- and third-year students attending accredited U.S. medical schools who have demonstrated academic achievement and show promise for careers in research and academic medicine. Thirty-five, $6,000 fellowships are awarded.

National Medical Fellowships

110 West 32nd Street
New York, NY 10001
212-714-1007
http://www.nmf-online.org

The **Josiah Macy, Jr. Substance Abuse Fellowship Program for Minority Students** is for second- and third-year minority medical students who have demonstrated outstanding academic achievement and are interested in pursuing careers in biomedical and clinical sciences research, epidemiology, and health policy.

National Organization for the Professional Advancement of Black Chemists and Chemical Engineers

Dr. Joseph Cannon
P.O. Box 77040
Washington, DC 20013
202-806-6626
http://www.imall.com/stores/nobcche

NOBCChE awards **fellowships** of $10,000 to $13,500 to minority graduate students in a Ph.D. program for chemistry, chemical engineering, or life sciences.

National Organization of Black Law Enforcement Executives

4609 Pinecrest
Office Park Drive, Suite F
Alexandria, VA 22312-1442
703-658-1529
http://www.noblenatl.org

The **NOBLE Fellowship Program** is a training program that provides experience in research, training, and administrative activities. The average fellowship lasts between 6 and 12 months.

National Physical Sciences Consortium

MSC-3NPS
P.O. Box 30001
Las Cruces, NM 88003-8001
800-952-4118
http://www.npsc.org

The consortium offers **Graduate Fellowships in the Physical Sciences**. Awards are offered in astronomy, chemistry, computer science, geology, materials science, mathematics, physics, and subdisciplines. Each award includes tuition, fees, and stipends for up to six years, valued to $200,000. Eligible are all qualified students, with continued emphasis toward recruitment of African Americans, Hispanics, Native Americans, and women who are U.S. citizens and have a 3.0 undergraduate GPA in a 4.0 system. Awards are for study at a participating NPSC member university. Students should access the NPSC Web site for information and to access the online application. Deadline: November 5, annually.

National Puerto Rican Coalition

1700 K Street, NW, Suite 500
Washington, DC 20006
202-223-3915
http://www.incacorp.com/NPRC

The NPRC sponsors the **Philip Morris Public Policy Fellowship**, a year-long, paid position in

Financial Aid

Washington, D.C. It is open to recent Puerto Rican college graduates interested in pursuing a career in public policy.

The coalition offers a **fellowship** of $25,000 plus health, life, and disability insurance to a candidate sensitive to the Puerto Rican community who wishes to learn more about government and public policy. Apply by April 19.

National Urban Fellows

55 West 44th Street, Suite 600
New York, NY 10036
212-921-9400
http://www.nuf.org

Each year the NUF chooses 25 to 30 minorities for its **National Urban/Rural Fellows Program** from a national recruitment campaign that generates an average of 2,400 applicants. Selected fellows receive a stipend of $20,000 for the full 14 months which is distributed on a monthly basis. Fellows attend Bernard M. Baruch College, City University of New York, and are awarded a master's degree in Public Administration upon successful completion of the program. Fellows attend 2 intensive summer sessions at Baruch College and 9 months at a mentorship assignment as a special assistant to a senior executive officer in a leading public, non-profit, or city agency nationwide. NU/RF is looking for fellows who are committed to addressing urban and rural economic and community development issues, and who demonstrate the skills, commitment, and interest to assume a high level of responsibility and leadership in management and policy-making in the public and non-profit sectors.

Native American Center of Excellence

T-545 Health Sciences Center
PO Box 357430
Seattle, WA 98195
206-685-2489

NACOE is recruiting for American Indian/Alaska Native M.D.s who have an interest in receiving training research in Indian health care. The **Indian Health Fellowship** is a 1- to 3-year fellowship preparing candidates for faculty positions. To be eligible, you must be an enrolled member of a recognized tribe, must have an M.D. degree and have finished a residency program, and must be Board Certified or Board eligible.

New Mexico Educational Assistance Foundation

P.O. Box 27020
Albuquerque, NM 87125
505-345-3371

Graduate **fellowships** of up to $7,000 are offered to New Mexico minority and female residents to help them prepare for careers with academic institutions. Applicants must be willing to work 10 hours per week in an assistantship position with no additional compensation. Priority is given to students in business, computer science, mathematics, engineering, or agriculture. Apply through the financial aid officer at the attending institution.

Newberry Library

Committee on Awards
60 West Walton Street
Chicago, IL 60610-3380
312-255-3666
http://www.newberry.org

The **Frances C. Allen Fellowship** is open to women of American Indian heritage who are pursuing graduate or professional study. Funds are generally used for travel, living expenses, conducting library and field research, or for supporting periods of independent study and writing; fellows are expected to spend a significant amount of time in residence at the Newberry Library. Fellowships may last from one month to a year; stipends vary according to individual need. Deadline to apply is February 1.

Newspaper Association of America

1921 Gallows Road, Suite 600
Vienna, VA 22182
703-902-1600
http://www.naa.org

The **New Media Fellowship** is designed to provide minorities and women with a basic understanding of new media, including underlying principles and operations, as well as to expose them to the products and services created by the newspaper industry. The fellowship focuses on hands-on training, Web-site development and creation, and dialogue with industry leaders.

The **NAA Minority Fellowships** provide funds for minorities who work at newspapers or teach journalism to help minority students enter and continue in newspaper management and administration. African American, Hispanic, Native American, Eskimo, and Asian applicants are considered.

North Carolina, University of, Chapel Hill

Vice Provost for Research and Graduate Studies, CB #4000
312 South Building
Chapel Hill, NC 27599
919-962-1319

The **Caroline Minority Postdoctoral Scholars Program** awards postdoctoral research appointments to encourage persons awarded the Ph.D. in the last four years to consider college research and teaching careers. Candidates in the social sciences or humanities are particularly sought. Scholars receive a $34,000 stipend annually. Apply by February 1.

Oak Ridge Associated Universities

P.O. Box 117
Oak Ridge, TN 37831-3010
423-241-4300
http://www.orau.org

The **National Science Foundation Graduate Research Fellowship** provides a thousand awards of up to $14,400 for graduate or doctoral studies and research in math, sciences, engineering, and social sciences. Native American, Hispanic, African American, Native Alaskan, and Native Pacific Islanders may qualify. Apply by November 4.

ORAU provides **fellowships** for African American and Native American graduate students majoring in materials science, materials engineering, metallurgical engineering, and ceramic engineering. Applicants must be gradu-

ating seniors or graduate students who have not completed their first year. The award pays tuition, fees, $1,200 per month in stipends, and a $300 dislocation allowance during the off-campus research appointment. Apply by the last day of February.

Ohio University

Communications Assistantships
Office of Student Financial Aid and Scholarships
Athens, OH 45701
740-593-4141
http://www.sfa.chubb.ohiou.edu

Six graduate **assistantships** are offered to minorities wishing to enter the one-year graduate program in public telecommunications management. Applicants should have a bachelor's degree and at least three years of public broadcasting experience. Apply by May 1.

Old Dominion University

Office of Research and Graduate Studies
Koch Hall, Room 210
Norfolk, VA 23529-0013
757-683-3460

The **President's Graduate Fellowship Program** is open to students who are enrolled in or accepted into a graduate program leading to a terminal degree. Fellows receive tuition reimbursement and a stipend. Applications are due February 1.

Omega Psi Phi Fraternity

3951 Snapfinger Parkway, Suite 330
Decatur, GA 30035
404-284-5533
http://www.omegapsiphifraternity.org

Creative and Research Fellowships of up to $1,000 are awarded to assist in the completion of a work in progress or to help publish a manuscript. Fellowships are open to black male college juniors or seniors who are members of Omega Psi Phi.

Financial Aid

Paul and Daisy Soros Fellowships for New Americans

400 West 59th Street
New York, NY 10019
212-547-6926
http://www.pdsoros.org

The purpose of the **Paul and Daisy Soros Fellowships for New Americans** is to provide opportunities for continuing generations of able and accomplished New Americans to achieve leadership in their chosen fields. A New American is an individual who is a resident alien (i.e., holds a green card), has been naturalized as a U.S. citizen, or is the child of two parents who are both naturalized citizens. The fellowships are granted for up to 2 years of graduate study in the United States. Each year the Fellow receives a maintenance grant of $20,000 and a tuition grant of one-half the tuition cost of the graduate program attended by the Fellow.

Pennsylvania, University of

Center for Study of Black Literature and Culture
3808 Walnut Street
Philadelphia, PA 19104
215-898-6081

The center awards **fellowships** to scholars in humanities who are studying Afro-American literature, music, history, film, and culture. Candidates must have completed the Ph.D. at the time of application.

Pittsburgh, University of, Bradford

Dean of Academic Affairs
300 Campus Drive
Bradford, PA 16701

Minority doctoral candidates who have completed all course work are eligible to apply for a $28,000 **fellowship**. Fellows spend one year at Bradford teaching two courses per semester while completing work on a dissertation. Applications are generally due in January.

Purdue University

Graduate Opportunities Doctoral and Master's Fellowships
West Lafayette, IN 47907
765-494-6963

Graduate Opportunities Doctoral and Master's Fellowships are awarded through a rigorous faculty selection process to African American, Hispanic American, Native American, and Pacific Island American graduate students. These awards are offered to beginning doctoral students and a highly competitive group of beginning master's degree students, as well as a selected few returning graduate students. These fellowships provide full tuition and most university fees and attractive stipends for 2 years of graduate study.

Radio and Television News Directors Foundation

RTNDF Scholarships
1000 Connecticut Avenue, NW, Suite 615
Washington, DC 20036-5302
202-659-6510
http://www.rtndf.org

The foundation offers the **Michelle Clark Fellowship** award of $1,000 to a journalist with fewer than five years' experience in electronic journalism wishing to further her education; minorities are given preference.

Robert a Toigo Foundation

350 University Avenue, Suite 250
Sacramento, CA 94111
916-564-1878

Fellowships are open to students of color who are planning a career in financial services. Applicants must be interested in pursuing an M.B.A. at Columbia University, Cornell University, the University of California at Berkeley, the University of California at Los Angeles, Clark Atlanta, Stanford University, Dartmouth, the University of Pennsylvania, the University of Chicago, Northwestern University, or M.I.T. Fellowships provide tuition and living expenses; some pay up to $20,000. In addition, RTF offers a mentor program that pairs students with experts in the investment community as well as summer internships with leading pension and investment management firms.

Salt Lake Community College

Human Resources
P.O. Box 30808
Salt Lake City, UT 84130-0808
801-957-4210
http://www.slcc.edu/hr/hr.htm

Diversity Lectureships bring minority scholars to the campus for one-year appointments; a salary and benefits are offered. Applications are due in June.

Schomburg Center for Research in Black Culture

515 Malcolm X Boulevard
New York, NY 10037
212-491-2203

Scholars in the humanities studying African American and African history and culture are eligible for residence **fellowships** of up to $50,000 per year. Fellows have access to the center's collections and program activities. Applications are due January 15.

School of American Research

Indian Arts Research Center
P.O. Box 2188
Santa Fe, NM 87504-2188
505-954-7205
http://www.sarweb.org

The **Ron and Susan Dubin Native American Artists Fellowship** supports Native American artists at the Indian Arts Research Center at the School of American Research. The mission of the Dubin Fellowship is to encourage traditional Native American arts through support of artists of high merit. The program offers financial support to artists and assistance with their study of the school's collections. The program awards summer fellowships to individuals who excel primarily in the visual arts which relate to the school's collecting emphasis, but artists who work in the verbal and performing arts will also be considered.

The **Harvey W Branigar, Jr., Native American Fellowship** is offered annually by the Indian Arts Research Center at the School of American Research to a Native American individual interested in developing his or her skills in all areas related to the study of Native American arts, with particular emphasis on curatorial work and collections management. Applicants must have at least a bachelor's degree in art, art history, anthropology, history, or museum studies, or equivalent training and experience. Applicants must demonstrate a serious interest in a career in a museum, cultural center, or similar setting. In order to be eligible, applicants must have a Native American tribal affiliation. The fellowship will provide an apartment and office, a stipend, library assistance, travel funds, and other benefits during a nine-month tenure.

Sealy Center on Aging

University of Texas Medical Branch
301 University Boulevard
Galveston, TX 77555-0860

The **Postdoctoral Fellowship in Minority Aging** funds research focusing on the health of older minorities, with a particular interest on older Hispanics. Applicants must have completed a doctoral level degree (Ph.D., Dr. P.H., Sc.D.) or an M.D. who has completed a 3-year residency in Internal Medicine or Family Medicine plus a 1-year fellowship in geriatrics.

Simmons College

Graduate Studies Admissions
300 The Fenway
Boston, MA 02115
617-521-3840
http://www.simmons.edu

ALANA students are eligible for **Teaching Leadership Fellowships** to help finance a master of arts degree in education. Apply by April 1.

Smithsonian Institution

Office of Fellowships and Grants
955 L'Enfant Plaza, Suite 7000
Washington, DC 20560-0902
202-287-3271
http://www.si.edu/research+study

Financial Aid

The institution offers **Native American Community Scholar Awards,** appointments in residence at the Smithsonian. The program is available to Native Americans to undertake projects on a Native American subject and use the resources of the Smithsonian. Write for applications and deadline information.

Society for Advancement of Chicanos and Native Americans in Science

P.O. Box 8526
Santa Cruz, CA 95061-8526
831-459-0170
http://www.sacnas.org

The **Neuroscience Scholars Fellowship Program** allows pre- and postdoctoral scholars to learn the latest trends in neuroscience research and to advance toward a health and research career in neuroscience. The program involves up to 3 years of participation, attendance at conferences, and meetings with prominent neuroscientists to plan a career in basic and clinical research in the neurological sciences.

Southern Illinois University, Carbondale

Graduate School
Carbondale, IL 62901-4702
618-453-4330

The **Proactive Recruitment of Multicultural Professionals for Tomorrow (PROMPT) Program** is an initiative developed by the Graduate School of Southern Illinois University, Carbondale, to increase the numbers of minorities receiving advanced degrees. The PROMPT fellowship consists of: a 2-year financial assistance package; a monthly departmental stipend raging from $850 to $1,092 for master's and doctoral students; a tuition scholarship; and a commitment of 20 hours per week in teaching or research activities in academic departments. Contact the Graduate School for a complete PROMPT application.

The **Illinois Minority Graduate Incentive Program** (IMGIP) offers fellowships to African American, Hispanic American, and Native American students accepted for admission to doctoral programs in the fields of life sciences,

physical sciences, engineering, and mathematics. Each recipient is awarded an annual stipend of $13,500; an allowance of $1,500 for books, supplies, equipment, and travel; and an institutional scholarship that will cover tuition and fees. The award is renewable for up to a maximum of 3 years. Upon completion of the degree, and acceptance of appropriate employment, recipients are eligible to receive a $15,000 placement incentive.

State University of New York System Administration

Office of Diversity and Affirmative Action, T-6
State University Plaza
Albany, NY 12246
518-443-5676

SUNY offers the **Graduate Fellowship Program for Underrepresented Students** (African Americans, Hispanics, and Native Americans) in fields leading to a master's or doctoral degree. Awards range from $7,500 to $10,000, and may include a graduate tuition scholarship granted annually to new students. (Individual awards may vary.) Participating campuses are: The University Centers at Albany, Binghamton, Buffalo, and Stony Brook; Health Science Centers at Brooklyn and Syracuse; the University Colleges at Brockport, Buffalo, Cortland, Fredonia, Geneseo, New Paltz, Oneonta, Oswego, Plattsburgh, Potsdam, and Purchase; Empire State College, the College of Environmental Science and Forestry, Maritime College, College of Optometry, Institute of Technology at Utica/Rome, the four statutory colleges at Cornell University, and the College of Ceramics at Alfred University. Applications can be requested from the participating institutions.

Substance Abuse and Mental Health Services Administration

U.S. Department of Health and Human Services
5600 Fishers Lane, Room 15C-26
Rockville, MD 20857
301-443-5850

The Substance Abuse and Mental Health Services Administration (SAMHSA) is awarding **fellowships** to help: 1) facilitate the entry of ethnic minority students into mental health and/or substance abuse careers; and 2) increase the number of nurses, psychiatrists, and social workers trained to teach, administer, and provide direct mental health and substance abuse services to ethnic minority groups. The project period is anticipated to be three years, and the first year will be funded for up to $400,000 for each.

Sundance Institute
Native American Initiative
225 Santa Monica Boulevard, 8th Floor
Santa Monica, CA 90401
310-394-4662
http://www.sundance.org

The Sundance Institute, in its commitment to promoting diversity and cultural integration has developed a program to assist in bringing the resources of the independent filmmaking community to the Native American filmmaking community. Through a multi-staged effort, the mandate of the **Native American Program** is to serve as a bridge to bring resources, professional support, and visibility to the creative enterprises of Native American filmmakers. The Native Program includes the exhibition of Native-made films at the Sundance Film Festival; the support of Native American writers and filmmakers as Fellows at the January Screenwriters Lab, the June Filmmakers Lab, and the July Native Screenwriting Workshop; and the sponsorship of three Native American producers to attend the Independent Producers Conference, also held at Sundance in July. An Advisory Committee has been constituted to include representatives from the Native American arts and filmmaking communities, as well as individuals from the world of independent filmmaking and the Hollywood film industry. The committee members will give support, direction, and guidance to the activities of the initiative.

Tennessee Student Assistance Corporation
404 James Robertson Parkway
Parkway Towers, Suite 1950
Nashville, TN 37243
800-342-1663
http://www.state.tn.us/tsac

The **Minority Teaching Fellows Program** provides $5,000 per year, for up to four years, to minority residents of Tennessee preparing for teaching careers. Loans or partial loans may be forgiven for service in the state. Candidates must rank in the top one-fourth of their high school class and be undergraduates enrolled in college. Hispanic, Eskimo, Indian, African American, and Asian American applicants are eligible. Apply by April 15.

Trinity College, Hartford
Professor Jan Cohn
Hartford, CT 06106
203-297-2000

The **Ann Plato Fellowship** supports a minority doctoral student who is completing a dissertation. The award consists of a $25,000 stipend and a campus apartment. Fellows are expected to teach one course and deliver a public lecture.

U.S. Department of Education
Indian Fellowship Program
Federal Student Aid Information Center
P.O. Box 84
Washington, DC 20044
800-433-3243
http://www.ed.gov

The **Indian Fellowship Program** offers awards averaging $12,590 to Indian undergraduate or graduate students in business administration, education, engineering, law, medicine, natural resources, and psychology. Apply by January 25.

U.S. National Endowment for the Humanities
Fellowships and Seminars Program
1100 Pennsylvania Avenue, NW, Room 316
Washington, DC 20004-2501
202-606-8400

Faculty members at historically black colleges are eligible for a **fellowship** to help them complete work toward the doctoral degree. Teachers of art are not eligible; applicants must be nominated by their college.

Financial Aid

U.S. National Research Council

Fellowship Office GR 420A
2101 Constitution Avenue
Washington, DC 20418
202-334-2872
http://www.nas.edu/fo/index.html

The **Ford Foundation Postdoctoral Fellowships** are awarded to Native American, Native Alaskan, African American, Mexican American/Chicano, Native Pacific Islander, and Puerto Rican teachers and scholars engaged in postdoctoral research and scholarship. About 20 one-year awards are given annually; they include a $25,000 stipend, a $3,000 travel and relocation allowance, and a $2,000 cost-of-research allowance to the fellowship institution. Applicants must have earned the Ph.D. or Sc.D. by March of the year of application and no more than seven years previously.

Utah, University of

Graduate School
201 South President's Circle
Salt Lake City, UT 84112-9016
801-585-3650

The **President's Graduate Fellowship Program** offers $10,000 stipends plus free tuition for up to four years to minority students from the state who are interested in pursuing careers in college teaching.

Virginia Polytechnic Institute

Graduate School
213 Sandy Hall
Blacksburg, VA 24061
540-231-6000

The **Minority Doctoral Students ABD Fellows Program** offers minority graduate students a stipend of up to $6,000 to teach one course and conduct research at Virginia Tech. Applications are due January 1.

Washington and Lee University

Vice President for Academic Affairs
24 Washington Hall
Lexington, VA 24450
540-463-8746
http://www.wlu.edu

Washington and Lee University offers a **Minority Teaching Fellowship** with a $20,000 stipend plus travel expenses to eligible candidates. Fellows are expected to teach one or two courses while completing their dissertation.

Washington University, St. Louis

Graduate School of Arts and Sciences
Campus Box 1187
One Brookings Drive
St. Louis, MO 63130-4899
314-935-6000
http://www.wustl.edu

The **Chancellor's Graduate Fellowship Program for African Americans** offers an exceptional opportunity to students who are embarking upon graduate study at Washington University for the purpose of acquiring training appropriate to careers in college or university teaching. For students in the Graduate School, Chancellor's Fellowship packages guarantee, in the presence of satisfactory academic progress, full tuition scholarships, 12 month annual stipends of at least $15,000, and annual educational allowances of $1,500, for up to 5 years of graduate study. In addition, a limited number of Special University Fellowships are offered annually to minority graduate students. Virtually all of the minority students admitted to the Graduate School for 1997-98 received some type of financial assistance.

Willamette University

College of Liberal Arts
Salem, OR 97301
503-370-6285
http://www.willamette.edu

The College of Liberal Arts sponsors a **Minority Fellowship Program** to support doctoral candidates as they complete degree requirements, encourage minority scholars to consider teaching careers in the liberal arts, and enrich the university's curriculum. Fellows are responsible for teaching one course each semester. Candidates must have completed all requirements for the Ph.D. except the dissertation.

Wisconsin, University of, Eau Claire
Office of the Provost
206 Schofield Hall
Eau Claire, WI 54702-4004
715-836-2320

The **UWEC Visiting Minority Scholars Program** offers short-term assignments to established scholars and artists from the United States as well as a junior program for candidates enrolled in terminal degree programs at Wisconsin, Minnesota, and Iowa universities. Terms for senior scholars usually range from 1 to 3 weeks. However, longer visits are possible. Junior scholars visit for 4 days. Both programs offer persons with good academic skills the chance to pursue scholarly activities and share their expertise on the Eau Claire campus.

Wisconsin, University of, Madison
School of Library and Information Studies
600 North Park Street, Room 4217
Madison, WI 53706-1474
608-263-2900
http://polyglot.lss.wisc.edu/slis

The library school offers **Advanced Opportunity Fellowships** to help minority students working toward a master's or doctoral degree. Contact the Admissions and Placement Advisor for more information or assistance.

Zeta Phi Beta Sorority
Scholarship Chairperson
1827 17th Avenue
Baton Rouge, LA 70807
202-387-3103

The **Zeta Phi Beta African Fellowship** is available to African American undergraduates.

Grants

Administration for Native Americans
Mail Stop HHH 348F
370 L'Enfant Promenade
Washington, DC 20447-0002

ANA provides **grants** to support projects in 4 competitive areas: Governance, Social and Economic Development, Social Development for Alaska Native Entities, Environmental Regulatory Enhancement, and Native American Language Preservation and Enhancement.

Alaska Native Health Career Program
3890 University Lake Drive
Anchorage, AK 99508

Minority students preparing for health careers are eligible for **financial aid**. Priority is given to those planning to work in rural areas of the state with centers serving Native Alaskans.

Alaska State Council on the Arts
411 West Fourth Avenue, Suite 1E
Anchorage, AK 99501-2343
907-269-6610

Traditional Native Arts Apprenticeships offer $2,000 grants to support the maintenance and development of the traditional arts of Alaska's native people. Application deadlines are March 1 and October 1.

American Association of State Colleges and Universities
1307 New York Avenue NW, 5th Floor
Washington, DC 20005-4701
202-293-7070
http://www.aascu.org

AASCU and the National Association of State Universities and Land-Grant Colleges jointly administer the **National Minority Graduate Feeder Program**. The NMGFP is a recruitment program which electronically links 32 minority institutions of higher education with 38 Ph.D.-granting institutions. The numbers of institutions will expand with time. Member Ph.D.-granting institutions pay for the graduate study of minority students they select for enrollment into their institutions.

American Digestive Health Foundation

ADHF/AGA Research Scholar Awards
7910 Woodmont Avenue, 7th Floor
Bethesda, MD 20814
301-654-2635
http://www.adhf.org

The **Research Scholar Awards** offers support for young investigators working toward an independent research career in any area of gastroenterology, hepatology, or related areas. One of the awards is reserved specifically for an underrepresented minority investigator.

American Nurses Association, Inc.

600 Maryland Avenue, SW, Suite 100W
Washington, DC 20024-2571
202-651-7245
http://www.ana.org

The **Nursing Research Grants Program** offers 25 awards of up to $2,700 each for projects being conducted by beginning nurse researchers or by more advanced nurse researchers exploring a new area of study. The **Minority Clinical and Research Training Fellowship** offers awards of $9,000 for doctoral studies in behavioral science or psychiatric nursing. Apply by January 15.

American Society of Mechanical Engineers

Washington Center
1828 L Street, NW #906
Washington, DC 20036-5104
202-785-3756
http://www.asme.org/bmw

The **Diversity Action Grants** (DAG) is a program sponsored by the Board on Minorities and Women (BMW) in cooperation with the Student Section Commmittee (SSC) whereby grants are awarded to ASME Student Sections for projects with the objective of increasing the participation of women and underrepresented minority students in student section activities.

Appalachian State University

Harry Williams, Associate Director of Admissions
Boone, NC 28608
828-262-2120

Minority Presence Grants are open to African American entering freshmen who are residents of North Carolina and demonstrate exceptional financial need.

Arkansas Department of Higher Education

Financial Aid Division
114 East Capitol
Little Rock, AR 72201-3818
800-547-8839
http://www.adhe.arknet.edu

The **Freshman/Sophomore Minority Grant Program—Arkansas** offers up to $1,000 to African American, Hispanic, and Asian American college freshmen and sophomores majoring in education at an Arkansas school. Applications are accepted all year; ask at the education office of your school.

Asian American Arts Foundation

http://www.aaafoundation.com

The **Asian American Arts Foundation Grants Program** awards grants to Bay Area Asian Pacific artists and arts organizations.

Asian Cultural Council

437 Madison Avenue, 37th Floor
New York, NY 10022-7001
212-812-4300
http://www.asianculturalcouncil.org

Fellowship Grants for Asian Citizens provide financial aid for graduate study, research, specialized training, or creative endeavors in the United States. Apply by February 1.

Bethel College

Office of Financial Aid
North Newton, KS 67117
316-283-2500

The **McKnight Grant** was established to recruit minority students. In addition, the **Minority Scholarship Grant Program** is open to Minnesota students of color. The Lane Multicultural Scholarship is offered to a minority student with strong leadership capabilities and character.

Blackfeet Nation
Blackfeet Adult Vocational Training Grants
P.O. Box 850
Browning, MT 59417-0850
406-338-7521
http://www.blackfeetnation.com

The **Blackfeet Adult Vocational Training Grants Program** provides financial assistance of $2,800 to $3,500 to enrolled members of a federally recognized tribe. Applicants must be Montana residents between the ages of 18 and 35, in need of employment training, and willing to accept full-time employment promptly after training. Grants are awarded in this order: 1) Blackfeet tribal members who reside on or near the Blackfeet Reservation, 2) Blackfeet tribal members who reside off the Blackfeet Reservation, 3) members of other tribes, 4) second training grant applicants. Apply by February, or by March for the summer term.

Business and Professional Women's Foundation
Scholarships/Loans
2012 Massachusetts Avenue, NW
Washington, DC 20036
202-293-1200

The BPWF operates a number of programs, including the **Sally Butler Memorial Fund for Latin Research**, which is open to a Hispanic woman pursuing a doctoral degree or who already has one. The grant allows for the attendance of an academic conference.

California Community Foundation
445 South Figuero Street, Suite 3400
Los Angeles, CA 90017-1638
213-413-4130
http://www.calfund.org

Grants averaging $2,500 each help emerging artists residing in Los Angeles County find time for creative endeavors. Artistic disciplines supported by these funds vary from year to year. Undergraduate students may not apply.

California Librarians Black Caucus, Greater Los Angeles Chapter
P.O. Box 2906
Los Angeles, CA 90078-2906
310-835-3350
http://www.clbc.org

African American college graduates who are interested in becoming librarians are eligible for a **stipend** of $500 or more based on financial need. Applicants must be library science students in California. Interviews are mandatory. Applications are due in October.

California State University, Dominguez Hills
Aide to Teacher Program (ATT)
Carson, CA 90747
310-243-3832
http://www.csudh.edu

The **ATT program** is designed to recruit more minority teachers into the Los Angeles area; it recruits instructional aides in 8 local school districts and partially supports them through their undergraduate classes.

California Student Aid Commission
Customer Service Branch
P.O. Box 416027
Rancho Cordova, CA 95741-9027
916-526-7590
http://www.csac.ca.gov

Each year the commission issues up to 200 conditional **warrants** to assist in repaying student loans for persons planning to teach in California at the college or university level.

Financial Aid

California Student Aid Commission

Customer Service Branch
P.O. Box 416027
Rancho Cordova, CA 95741-9027
916-526-7590
http://www.csac.ca.gov

The commission is dedicated to providing equal access to higher education. It offers a balanced program of grants, student loans, and other special programs for low- and middle-income students. **Cal Grant A Awards** are open to low-income residents of the state and help cover tuition and fees at public or independent colleges and universities. The grants may be renewed for three additional years if students continue to need financial assistance and meet the academic standards required for re-enrollment. Grants range from $600 to $4,500.

Cal Grant B Awards provide a living allowance for low-income college students, most of whom attend a community college. The award may be increased for students who transfer to a four-year institution to help cover tuition. Awards range from $600 to $1,200.

Cal Grant C Awards are given to vocationally oriented students who wish to acquire marketable job skills. These awards are for up to $2,000 plus $450 for books and supplies, and may be used at accredited proprietary schools and hospital schools.

Graduate Fellowships of $600 to $5,500 are awarded to California students for full-time graduate or professional study at an accredited California college or university. About 500 awards are made each year. Applicants should be planning college teaching careers.

Center for AIDS Prevention Studies

74 New Montgomery Street, Suite 600
San Francisco, CA 94105
415-597-9366

The **Collaborative HIV Prevention Research in Minority Communities** is a program funded by the National Institute of Mental Health designed to assist investigators already conducting HIV prevention research with ethnic minority communities to improve their programs of research.

Conference of Minority Public Administrators

P.O. Box 3010
Fort Worth, TX 76113
817-871-8325
http://www.compa.org

Students studying public administration and public affairs may receive $400 **travel grants** for attending the COMPA national conference. The checks will not be issued in advance of the conference. Special consideration will be given to those students who can leverage other sources of support to insure attendance.

Council for International Educational Exchange

Bailey Scholarship Program
205 East 42nd Street
New York, NY 10017
800-40-STUDY
http://www.ciee.org/study

The **Robert B. Bailey III Minority Scholarships for Education Abroad** provide $500 for council study programs. Applicants who are self-identified as members of underrepresented groups are eligible. Applicants must be U.S. citizens. Apply by October 26 and April 1. The organization also offers the **Bowman Travel Grants for Educational Programs in Developing Countries**, which provide airfare for students involved in educational programs in Africa, Asia, Eastern Europe, and Latin America. Applicants need not be members of a minority group.

Creek Nation of Oklahoma

Higher Education
PO Box 580
Okmulgee, OK 74447
918-756-8700

The **Undergraduate Grant Program** assists Indian students attending accredited institutions of higher learning.

East Carolina University
East Fifth Street
Greenville, NC 27858
252-328-6495
http://www.ecu.edu

The **Minority Presence Grant Program** is open to African American residents of North Carolina with financial need. The award provides an average of $4,000 for graduate or doctoral study at East Carolina.

Eastern College
Office of Financial Aid
1300 Eagle Road
Saint Davids, PA 19087
610-341-5842
http://www.eastern.edu

Eight **grants** ranging from $1,000 to $6,000 are offered to undergraduate students depending on the student's GPA and regardless of financial need.

Geological Society of America
P.O. Box 9140
Boulder, CO 80301-9140
303-447-2020
http://www.geosociety.org

The **Research Grants Program** provides partial support for graduate students in geology who are attending universities in the United States, Canada, Mexico, or Central America. In a recent year, 218 grants averaging $1,600 each were awarded. Deadline to apply is February 15.

Health Resources and Services Administration
5600 Fishers Lane
Rockville, MD 20857
301-443-1700

The administration assists organizations, allowing them to provide financial support for full-time financially needy disadvantaged health professions students who are enrolled in participating accredited schools. Eligible to submit **grant requests** are accredited schools of medicine, nursing, osteopathic medicine, dentistry, pharmacy, podiatric medicine, optometry, veterinary medicine, public health, chiropractic or allied health (baccalaureate and graduate degree programs of dental hygiene, medical laboratory technology, occupational therapy, physical therapy, radiologic technology, speech pathology, audiology, and registered dieticians), and graduate programs in behavioral and mental health practice, which includes clinical psychology, clinical social work, professional counseling, or marriage and family therapy; or programs providing training of physician assistants. They must be carrying out a program for recruiting and retaining students from disadvantaged backgrounds, including racial and ethnic minorities.

The **African American HIV Service Planning Grants** provide funding to community-based or public organizations to assist with the development of primary health care services for people with HIV.

Hispanic Theological Initiative
12 Library Place
Princeton, NJ 08540
609-252-1721
http://www.aeth.org

HTI awards 7 Hispanic doctoral students a $12,000 **grant**. This award is aimed at supporting the student for a maximum of 2 years of full-time course work.

Through the Association for Hispanic Theological Education's (AHTE) Hispanic Theological Initiatives, 2 **Research and Writing Grants** are offered each year. One award is a semester grant of $15,000, the second is a summer grant of $8,000. Contact AHTE, or visit the Web site, for complete application guidelines.

Hopi Tribe Grants and Scholarship Program
P.O. Box 123
Kykotsmovi, AZ 86039
800-762-9630
http://www.nau.edu/~hcpo-p/index.html

The **BIA Higher Education/Hopi Supplemental Grant** provides for Hopi students pursuing an associate, baccalaureate, graduate, or post-graduate degree. Awards are based on financial need as recommended by the college/university's financial aid officer. Entering freshmen must have a 2.0 Cumulative Grade Point Average (CGPA) for high school coursework or a minimum score of 45% on the GED Exam. The BIA Higher Education Grant provides a maximum of $2,500 per semester; the Hopi Supplemental Grant provides a maximum of $1,500 per semester.

Funds are available through the **Educational Enrichment Grant** to assist Hopi students who have been accepted to participate in special activities and events that offer unique opportunities to develop leadership, personal skills, or to acquire educational/pre-college experiences. Examples of such activities and events include: math camps, pre-college orientation, conferences, etc. This grant is open to Hopi students from fourth grade through college. Applications are accepted year round and must be submitted at least two weeks before the date of the activity.

Inter American Press Association

Scholarship Fund
2911 Northwest 39th Street
Miami, FL 33142
305-634-2465

Grants averaging $13,000 are available for working newspaper staff members or journalism students to study in Latin America or the Caribbean, or for Latin American and Caribbean students to come to the United States or Canada. Applicants must hold a journalism degree, speak the language of the country they will visit, and be 21 to 35 years old. Apply by December 31.

Iowa, University of

College of Dentistry
Iowa City, IA 52242
319-335-1039

A Dental Opportunity Program offers a **Student Support Grant** of up to $4,000 to aid minority students, as well as a special summer premedical orientation program.

Iowa, University of

Henry B. Tippie School of Management
Iowa City, IA 52242
319-335-1039
http://www.biz.uiowa.edu/mba

The Minority MBA Assistance Program provides tuition scholarships, **grants**, and assistantships to minority students pursuing full-time M.B.A. study. The average award in a recent year was $7,517. Applications are due April 15.

Jicarilla Apache Tribe

P.O. Box 507
Dulce, NM 87520
505-759-3616

The tribe offers **grant** assistance to help its members pursue undergraduate or graduate study.

Kiowa Tribe of Oklahoma

Higher Education Grant Program
P.O. Box 369
Carnegie, OK 73015-0369
405-654-2300

The Kiowa Tribe has programs that offer **grant awards** to eligible enrolled tribal members for attending accredited colleges and universities. Awards are also available for adult students seeking vocational training in a technical field.

Margaret McNamara Memorial Fund

World Bank Group, Room G-1000
1818 H Street, NW
Washington, DC 20433
202-473-8751

Grants of $6,000 are available to women from developing countries during their studies in the United States. Applicants must demonstrate a commitment to the needs of women or children, must be at least age 25 by January 1, and must be planning to return to their native countries within two years of receiving the grant. Apply by February 1.

Medical College of Pennsylvania

Career for Women and Minorities in Biomedical Research
3200 Henry Avenue
Philadelphia, PA 19129
215-842-4166

Minority Ph.D. students are offered a **grant** of $12,500 to research AIDS and other immunological diseases, aging, Alzheimer's disease, cancer, cardiovascular disease, and other health topics.

Menominee Indian Tribe of Wisconsin

Education Department
P.O. Box 910
Keshana, WI 54135
715-799-5118

Tribal members may apply for need-based **grants** of up to $2,200 to help finance postsecondary education. Applications are due in February for the fall semester. Applications are due in October for the spring semester.

Minnesota Higher Education Services Office

400 Capitol Square Building
550 Cedar Street
St. Paul, MN 55101
612-296-3974
http://www.mheso.state.mn.us/cfdocs/webdirectory/index.cfm

The **Minnesota Nursing Grants for Persons of Color** offer $2,000 to $4,000 for minorities with financial need who are studying nursing at a Minnesota school. Applicants must be residents of the state. Applications are accepted all year.

National Asian American Telecommunications Association

346 9th Street, 2nd Floor
San Francisco, CA 94103
415-863-0814
http://www.naatanet.org

Through funding from the Corporation for Public Broadcasting, NAATA produces, programs, and promotes Asian American stories on non-commercial, public television. For the past 18 years, NAATA has taken acclaimed shows into millions of American households to enliven the dialogue about race and ethnic identity, educate people about unknown histories and remind us of the value of a culturally pluralistic society. Since 1990, NAATA has provided over $2 million to more than 150 **projects**. NAATA is especially interested in: contemporary issues, e.g., where Asian Americans stand in an increasingly multicultural society; the ongoing debates around affirmative action and bilingual education; personal stories that look outward at the larger community; and works that look at historically underrepresented Asian American populations, especially South and Southeast Asians, or address youth, labor or refugee issues. Funded projects should provoke thoughtful dialogue and impact how the general public understands and interprets the Asian American experience. While proposals can take creative risks, ultimately, selected projects must appeal to a wide variety of television audiences.

National Black Programming Consortium

761 Oak Street
Columbus, OH 43205-0101
888-464-NBPC
http://www.blackstarcom.org

The **Program Development Fund** provides $1,000 to $50,000 to African American media artists with film and video projects.

National Cancer Institute

Comprehensive Minority Biomedical Branch
Executive Plaza North, Room 620
Bethesda, MD 20892
301-496-7344

Minority investigators engaged in cancer research are eligible for funding through the **Minority Health Professional Training Initiative.**

National Heart, Lung, and Blood Institute

Division of Epidemiology and Clinical Applications
6701 Rockledge Drive, MSC 7934
Bethesda, MD 20892
301-435-0709

Financial Aid

The **Mentored Minority Faculty Development Award** provides support to underrepresented minority faculty members with varying levels of research experience to prepare them for research careers as independent investigators.

National Hispanic Corporate Achievers

445 Douglas Avenue
Altamonte Springs, FL 32714
407-682-2883
http://www.hispanicachievers.com

National Hispanic Corporate Achievers provides a minimum of 5 students annually with financial aid in the form of **grants**.

National Institute of Arthritis and Musculoskeletal and Skin Diseases

Natcher Building Room 5AN44A
45 Center Drive
Bethesda, MD 20892-4500
301-594-5014

Grants are available to assist with research on the etiology, treatment, and prevention of arthritis, musculoskeletal, and skin diseases in minority populations. Members of minority groups are particularly encouraged to apply as principal investigators.

National Institute of Mental Health

Division of Epidemiology and Services Research
Parklawn Building, Room 10C-06
5600 Fishers Lane
Rockville, MD 20857
301-443-3364

Minority Dissertation Research Grants in Mental Health provide financial support to minority doctoral candidates planning to pursue research careers in any area relevant to mental health and/or mental disorders.

National Institute on Aging

Geriatrics Program
Building 31, Suite 5C05
31 Center Drive
Bethesda, MD 20892
301-496-5278

The **Aging, Race, and Ethnicity in Prostate Cancer Grants** support research that expands the understanding of biological and clinical factors leading to the development, progression, and treatment of prostate cancer in aging men. Racial/ethnic minority individuals are encouraged to apply as principal investigators.

National Institute on Aging

Office of Extramural Affairs
Gateway Building, Room 2C-218
7201 Wisconsin Avenue
Bethesda, MD 20892
301-496-9322

The **Minority Dissertation Research Grants in Aging** are small grants to support doctoral dissertation research on biological, neuroscientific, geriatric, or behavioral and social research on aging. Applicants must be underrepresented minority doctoral candidates.

National Institute on Deafness and Other Communication Disorders

6120 Executive Boulevard, Room 400-C
Bethesda, MD 20892-7180
301-496-5061

Minority Dissertation Research Grants in Human Communication assist with doctoral research in hearing, balance, smell, taste, voice, speech, and language.

National Institutes of General Medical Sciences

45 Center Drive, MSC 6200
Bethesda, MD 20892-6200
301-594-3833
http://www.nih.gov/nigms/

Principal investigators holding **NIGMS research grants** may request supplemental funds to support minority scientists and students. The aim of these supplements is to attract and encourage minority individuals to pursue biomedical research careers. The types of supplements available are: **Research Supplements for Minority High School Students**, which support minority high school students who have expressed an interest in the biomedical or behavioral sciences; **Research Supplements for Minority Undergraduate Students**, which support minority undergraduate students who have demonstrated an interest in the biomedical or behavioral sciences and wish to continue on to graduate-level training in these areas; **Research Supplements for Minority Individuals in Postdoctoral Training**, which provide an opportunity for minority postdoctoral scientists to participate in ongoing research projects to further their development into independent biomedical or behavioral researchers; and **Research Supplements for Minority Investigators**, which provide short- and long-term opportunities for minority investigators to participate in ongoing research projects while futher developing their own independent research potential.

National Institutes of Health

National Institute of General Medical Sciences
Natcher Building, Room 2AS.37
Bethesda, MD 20892
800-528-7689
http://www.nih.gov/nigms

The Honors Undergraduate Research Training (HURT) grant has been replaced with the **Undergraduate Student Training for Academic Research (USTAR) institutional grant**. This grant is awarded to 4-year colleges and universities with substantial enrollment of underrepresented minorities. Because this grant is awarded directly to the institution, students cannot apply. The institutional program director chooses students to participate in this program. The students who participate in this program are junior/senior honors students majoring in the biomedical or behavioral sciences, including mathematics. Application deadlines are January 10 and May 10.

National Latino Communication Center

3171 Los Feliz Boulevard, Suite 201
Los Angeles, CA 90039
213-663-8294

Research and development **grants** are available to filmmakers.

National Science Foundation

Division of Human Resource Development
4201 Wilson Boulevard
Arlington, VA 22230
703-306-1632

Organizations and academic institutions with significant underrepresented minority enrollment are eligible to apply for **grants** intending to increase the quantity and quality of minority students receiving baccalaureate degrees in science, engineering, and mathematics.

North Carolina State University

Graduate School
P.O. Box 7012
Raleigh, NC 27695
919-515-2011
http://www.fis.ncsu.edu/Grad/grants.htm

The Minority Presence Grant Program is open to African American residents of North Carolina with financial need. The award provides an average of $4,000 for graduate or doctoral study at North Carolina State University or the School of Veterinary Medicine at North Carolina State University.

Office of Indian Education

Bureau of Indian Affairs
1849 C Street, NW
Washington, DC 20240
202-219-1127

Grants are available to assist colleges sponsored by Federally Recognized Indian Tribes or tribal organizations. These grants are to help with the operation and improvement of tribally controlled community colleges to insure continued educational opportunities for Indian students.

The **Indian Education Higher Education Grant Program** provides financial aid to eligible Indian students to enable them to attend accredited institutions of higher education. Awards range from $300 to $5,000.

Financial Aid

Oncology Nursing Foundation

501 Holiday Drive
Pittsburgh, PA 15220-2749
412-921-7373

Ethnic Minority Researcher and Mentorship Grants assist minorities conducting oncology nursing research.

Pacific Islanders in Communications

1221 Kapiolani Boulevard #6A-4
Honolulu, HI 96814
808-591-0059
http://www.piccom.org

PIC awards **grants** to independent producers and public television stations to research and develop programs that originate from the Pacific Islander experience and are intended for national public broadcast audiences.

Paul Robeson Fund for Independent Media

Funding Exchange
666 Broadway, Room 500
New York, NY 10012
212-529-5300
http://www.fex.org/robeson

Film, video, and radio artists who create works that are tools for organizing change on critical social issues are eligible for **grants** from the Paul Robeson Fund to support projects.

Playwright's Center

2301 Franklin Avenue
Minneapolis, MN 55406
612-332-7481
http://www.pwcenter.org

The center awards 2 to 4 **Multicultural Collaboration Grants** of between $200 and $2,000 each to culturally diverse teams of 2 or more artists for collaboration on the creation and development of new theater pieces. The grants are intended to support early project collaborations, artistic research and development, and/or first productions.

Presbyterian Church USA

Financial Aid for Studies
100 Witherspoon Street
Louisville, KY 40202
502-569-5760
http://pcusa.org

Native American Education Grants of $200 to $2,500 are open to Indians, Aleuts, and Eskimos pursuing full-time postsecondary study. Applicants must have completed at least one semester at an accredited college or university, members of the Presbyterian Church, and members of Native American Tribes or Native Corporations. Deadline to apply is June 1.

Racial/Ethnic Leadership Supplemental Grants of $500 to $1,000 are available to Asian American, African American, Hispanic, and Native American members of the Presbyterian Church who plan a career in the seminary, theology, or religion.

Grants for Graduate Education are offered to minorities and women preparing for teaching careers at a Presbyterian college or theological seminary. Applicants must be Presbyterian.

Professional Women of Color

P.O. Box 5196
New York, NY 10185
212-714-7190
http://www.pwconline.org

The **PWC Dream Grant** is a cash award given annually to a member to assist in a business venture. Applicants are evaluated in 3 areas: executive summary/proposal, 2- to 5-minute presentation, and question-and-answer segment.

Pueblo of Acoma

Acoma Higher Education Grant Program
P.O. Box 307
Acoma, NM 87034
505-552-6604

Acoma Tribal members pursuing 2-year or 4-year degrees are eligible for **funding**.

Robert Wood Johnson Foundation

Route 1 and College Road East
P.O. Box 2316
Princeton, NJ 08543-2316
609-452-8701
http://www.rwjf.org

Minority Medical Faculty Development Awards
offer $35,000 per year to individuals who already
hold the M.D. and wish to teach college-level
courses in medicine. In addition, the foundation
has a special interest in the health problems of
minorities and in preparing minority students
for health care careers. It funds financial aid
programs offered by individual medical schools
and helps national groups recruit minorities for
the field.

Sachs Foundation

90 South Cascade Avenue, Suite 1410
Colorado Springs, CO 80903-1691
719-633-2353
http://www.frii.com/~sachs

The foundation helps African American residents of Colorado to fund their undergraduate
education. It provides **grants** to about 250 students each year, and selects approximately 50
new applicants each year. Each grant is about
$4,000 a year (depending on fund availabilty)
and may be renewed upon evidence of satisfactory progress. Applicants must have lived in
Colorado for at least five years and be high
school seniors with a GPA of 3.5 or higher.

Smithsonian Institution

Center for Museum Studies
Washington, DC 20560-0427
202-357-3101

Minority professionals working in museums are
eligible for a **travel allowance** to attend the
annual Diversity, Leadership and Museums
Seminar. The American Indian Museum Studies
Program offers travel grants to Native American
museum professionals to attend workshops
offered by the program.

Southern Illinois University, Carbondale

Graduate School
Carbondale, IL 62901-4702
618-453-4330

The Illinois Consortium for Educational
Opportunity Program (ICEOP) offers an annual
stipend of $10,000 and an institutional scholar-
ship to cover tuition and fees. Doctoral recipients may receive awards for up to 4 years; those
in master's or professional degree programs
may receive awards for up to 2 years. To be considered for an ICEOP Award, an applicant must
be: 1) an Illinois resident; 2) a member of an
underrepresented group in higher education
such as African American, Asian American,
Hispanic American, or Native American; 3) the
recipient of an earned baccalaureate degree; 4)
of above-average academic ability as evidenced
by admission to a graduate or professional
degree program; and 5) unable to pursue a
graduate or professional degree in the absence
of an ICEOP award.

Spring Arbor College

Office of Financial Aid
106 East Main Street
Spring Arbor, MI 49283
517-750-1200
http://www.arbor.edu

The college awards **grants** to African American
students.

Studio Museum in Harlem

144 North 125th Street
New York, NY 10027
212-864-4500
http://www.studiomuseuminharlem.org

African American artists are eligible for one-year
grants of $13,000 to support a period of independ-
ent work; the program also provides studio space.

U.S. Bureau of Indian Affairs

Office of Education
1849 C Street, NW
Washington, DC 20240-0001
202-208-3478
http://shaman.unm.edu/oiep/home.htm

Financial Aid

The bureau's Office of Indian Education Programs operates a number of financial aid, job training, and other programs to support Native American students. **Higher Education Grants** typically range from $500 to $4,000 per year. All fields of study are considered. Applicants must be members of a federally recognized Indian tribe or one-quarter Indian to qualify. Contact your tribal agency or tribe, or the above address for details.

U.S. Department of Agriculture
Proposal Services Unit
Grants Management, Extramural Programs
Cooperative State Research
Washington, DC 20250
202-720-2791
http://www.usda.gov

The **Higher Education Multicultural Scholars Program** offers about 100 grants to about 20 colleges and universities to be used to help minority agriculture majors. The scholarships are given to the colleges who, in turn, provide financial aid and other assistance to their students. Apply through your college, not directly through the Agriculture Department. The awards are available to blacks, Hispanics, Asians, Pacific Islanders, American Indians, and Alaska Natives.

U.S. General Accounting Office
441 G Street, NW
Washington, DC 20548
http://www.gao.gov

Doctoral candidates in economics, political science, federal government, and international affairs may be eligible for the **Doctoral Research Program**. Grants range from $26,000 to $28,000 and may be used for research costs, living expenses, tuition, and travel costs. Recipients are selected on the basis of the quality of proposed research.

U.S. National Park Service
Heritage Preservation Services (2255)
P.O. Box 37127
Washington, DC 20013-7127
http://www.nps.gov

Available are **grants** for documenting Native American cultural activities, oral history, and traditions; the funds may be applied toward video, audio, and/or still photography. Applications are due January 15.

Western Illinois University
One University Circle
Macomb, IL 61455-1390
309-298-2001
http://www.wiu.edu/foundation/scholarship.htm

The **Western Opportunity Grant** provides awards of up to $1,000 for freshmen students from underrepresented groups. Rank in upper 15 percent mandatory. Apply early.

The **President's Minority Graduate Access Program** provides grants for minority students pursuing an advanced degree. Acceptance into a WIU graduate program is mandatory. Deadline to apply is April 1.

Whatcom Museum of History and Art
Jacobs Research Fund
121 Prospect Street
Bellingham, WA 98225
360-676-6981

The Jacobs Research Fund offers renewable grants of up to $1,200 to support research on social and cultural anthropology among Native Americans. Priority is given to projects dealing with the Pacific Northwest. Field studies that address cultural expressive systems, such as music, language, dance, mythology, world view, plastic and graphic arts, intellectual life, and religion, including those which propose comparative psychological analysis, are appropriate. Projects in archaeology, physical and applied anthropology, applied linguistics, and archival research are not eligible. Formal academic credentials are not required, but applicants who are inexperienced in research should arrange for the collaboration or supervision of a research scholar. Apply before February 15.

Youth Opportunities Foundation

8820 South Sepulveda Boulevard, Suite 208
P.O. Box 45762
Los Angeles, CA 90045-4840
213-670-7664

The foundation provides one-time **grants** of $100 to $500 to Hispanic/Latino students from California high schools. Candidates must have ranked in the top 10 percent of their high school class, have strong academic records and SAT scores, and demonstrate leadership ability.

Zeta Phi Beta Sorority

1734 New Hampshire Avenue, NW
Washington, DC 20009-2595
202-387-3103
http://www.zpb1920.org

Black women are eligible for **grants** ranging from $500 to $1,000 to help finance medical or other health studies. Applicants may be either undergraduate or graduate students.

Awards and Loans

American College Theater Festival

John F. Kennedy Center for the Performing Arts
Washington, DC 20566
202-416-8850
http://www.kennedy-center.org/education/

Lorraine Hansberry Playwriting Awards honor student authors of plays reflecting the black experience in America; the play must be produced for the annual festival by a college or university. First prize is $2,500; second prize, $1,000.

Avon Latina Model of the Year

1251 Sixth Avenue
New York, NY 10020
800-FOR-AVON
http://www.avon.com

The Avon Latina Model of the Year contest is open to women of Hispanic descent, ages 17-25, who have never been professional models. The initial field of more than 1,000 entrants is narrowed to 100 semi-finalists, then reduced to 50 and, ultimately, to five on the basis of responses to a detailed questionnaire on personal goals and cultural pride. Winners typically receive $15,000 in educational awards and modeling fees, along with other prizes. First runner-up receives an educational award in the amount of $5,000.

Black American Cinema Society

Contest Coordinator
Western States Black Research Center
3617 Montclair Street
Los Angeles, CA 90018
323-737-3292
http://www.wsbrec.org

The **Filmmakers Competition** offers six scholarships of up to $1,500 for black high school graduates studying filmmaking at college. Applications are due February 15.

Black American students and film makers who are U.S. citizens between the ages of 21 and 34 are eligible for the **BACS Awards** of $250 to $3,000. Apply by March 6. There is a $25 application fee.

Black American film and video makers who are U.S. citizens are eligible for the **BACS Student and Independent Film Makers Awards** of $1,000 to $3,000. Apply by February 27. There is a $25 application fee.

California Chicano News Media Association

USC School of Journalism
3502 Watt Way, ASC G10
Los Angeles, CA 90089-0281
213-740-5263
http://www.ccnma.org

The Ruben Salazar Journalism Awards are given annually by the CCNMA to those Hispanic journalists who have achieved excellence in 1 of 4 categories: Print, Television, Radio, and

Photography. Cash prizes are awarded at a ceremony held in the fall in San Francisco.

Calvin Theological Seminary

3233 Burton Street, SE
Grand Rapids, MI 49546-4387
616-957-6036
http://www.calvin.edu/seminary

The **SCORR Multicultural Leadership Award** is given to a SCORR Multicultural Scholarship recipient who shows outstanding leadership performance on the campus, in the community, or in the local church. Nominations are made by the seminary through the registrar's office.

Chicano/Latino Literary Prize

University of California, Irvine
Department of Spanish and Portuguese
322 Humanities Hall
Irvine, CA 92697-5275
949-824-5443

The Chicano/Latino Literary Prize offers annual awards, rotating through the genres of novel, short story, poetry, and drama. Contact the Prize Coordinator to find out which genre is being judged. First prize is $1,000 and publication. Second prize is $500, and third is $250.

Columbia College

Theater/Music Center
72 East 11th Street
Chicago, IL 60605
312-663-1600

The **Theodore Ward Prize** awards $500 to $2,000 for the best full-length play related to the African American experience, written by an African American. Applicants need not be U.S. citizens. Scripts are accepted from May 1 to August 1 and should be typed, bound, and copyrighted. A resume, synopsis, and background information on the script should accompany the submission.

Committee on Institutional Cooperation

302 East John Street, Suite 1705
Champaign, IL 61820-5698
217-333-8475
http://www.cic.net/cic/cic.html

The CIC waives the application fee for up to 3 CIC Graduate Schools. African American, Mexican American, Native American, and Puerto Rican students applying for admission to Ph.D. programs or Master of Fine Arts programs at CIC universities are eligible to apply for **fee waivers**. CIC universities include: University of Chicago; University of Illinois; Indiana University; University of Iowa; University of Michigan; Michigan State University; University of Minnesota; Northwestern University; Ohio State University; Pennsylvania State University; Purdue University; and University of Wisconsin.

East West Players

244 South San Pedro Street, Suite 301
Los Angeles, CA 90012
213-625-7000
http://www.bnw.com/eastwestplayers

The **New Voices Project** is a multi-featured program sponsored by AT&T and was established to develop emerging playwriting talent and to strengthen EWP's literary department. In an effort to encourage Asian American writers from all over the country, the New Voices Project has implemented programs such as a National Playwriting Contest.

Health Resources and Services Adminstration

Bureau of Health Professions
Division of Student Assistance
5600 Fishers Lane, Room 8-34
Rockville, MD 20857

The **Loans for Disadvantaged Students (LDS) Program** provides funding to eligible health professions schools for the purpose of providing long-term, low-interest loans to assist full-time financially needy disadvantaged students to pursue a career in medicine, osteopathic medicine, dentistry, optometry, podiatric medicine, pharmacy or veterinary medicine. Funds are made available to participating schools for the establishment of revolving student loan funds.

Hispanic Association of AT&T Employees, New Jersey

HISPA-NJ "HIJOS"
290 Davidson Avenue, Room E4C102
Somerset, NJ 08873
http://home.att.net/~hispanj/

The **HIJOS essay contest** is open to high school seniors accepted to college. Visit the Web site for application information and essay topic.

Inner City Cultural Center

1308 South New Hampshire
Los Angeles, CA 90028
212-962-2102

Located in a predominantly minority area, the center organizes three competitions to display new talent to producers and publishers as well as to encourage creative newcomers to succeed. Available are the **Ira Aldridge Competition for Acting**, the **First Bar Songwriter's Competition**, and **Act II**, which involves the production of short original plays.

National Action Council for Minorities in Engineering

The Empire State Building
350 Fifth Avenue, Suite 2212
New York, NY 10118-2299
212-279-2626
http://www.nacme.org

High school seniors with records of outstanding academic achievement, community involvement, and participation in precollege math and science programs are eligible for the **TechForce Pre-Engineering Prize**. Ten prizes are awarded annually. Students must be nominated by directors of university-based programs. Each TechForce Scholar receives a $1,000 award, a plaque, and a paid trip to attend the annual NACME Forum to receive the award and to make a presentation to an audience of 300 corporate and academic leaders. Winners are also eligible for the **3M Engineering Award**—2

$10,000 awards of $2,500 annually are made to the 2 top TechForce Prize winners.

The **Philip D. Reed Undergraduate Award in Environmental Engineering** is designed to increase access to careers in this burgeoning area among African American, Latino and American Indian students. Made possible through an endowment from the Philip D. Reed Foundation, the award provides $10,000 payable over two years. Undergraduate students may apply during the second semester sophomore year. Applicants must have a minimum of 3.0/4.0 grade point average and a demonstrated interest in environmental engineering. Students may apply during their second semester in the sophomore year. Applications are mailed to selected institutions in December.

National Association of Black Journalists

870-A Adelphi Road
Adelphi, MD 20783
301-445-7100
http://www.nabj.org

The **National Media Awards Contest** recognizes excellence in the coverage of issues of importance to the African American community. NABJ members and other top journalists compete in 40 print and broadcast categories. First place winners receive a plaque and $100. Second and third place winners receive a certificate. Winners are honored at the annual convention.

National Association of Black Women Attorneys

3711 Macomb Street, NW
Washington, DC 20016

The association identifies and provides financial support to outstanding black women law students. The winners of an annual **trial memorandum** are awarded about $1,000. NABWA also sponsors an annual essay competition open to minority women law students, with awards ranging from $500 to $3,000. It is expected that any funds won will be used for educational purposes.

Financial Aid

National Association of Health Services Executives

8630 Fenton Street, Suite 126
Silver Spring, MD 20910
202-628-3953
http://www.nahse.org

The **Everett V. Fox Student Case Competition** gives first and second year graduate students the opportunity to apply their creativity and knowledge to the diverse issues facing a health care organization. Students make presentations to a panel of judges in competition for scholarship awards.

National Black Law Students Association

1225 11th Street, NW
Washington, DC 20001
http://www.nblsa.org

The **Frederick Douglass Moot Court Competition** is an annual competition allowing teams of African American law students to address issues facing the African American community.

National Black Programming Consortium

761 Oak Street
Columbus, OH 43205-0101
888-464-NBPC
http://www.blackstarcom.org

The **NBPC Prized Pieces Award** recognizes achievement in film and video programs affirming the universality of the African American experience. Winning filmmakers receive a cash award of $1,500.

National Medical Fellowships

Scholarship Department
110 West 32nd Street
New York, NY 10001
212-714-0933
http://www.nmf-online.org

The **C. R. Bard Foundation** offers a prize to a graduating, underrepresented medical student who intends to practice in the field of cardiology or urology. Eligible candidates must be in the senior year of medical school, pursuing careers in cardiology or urology. One award is presented annually; this honor includes a certificate of merit and a $5,000 stipend.

The **Ralph W. Ellison Prize** is presented to a graduating underrepresented medical student. Candidates must demonstrate outstanding academic achievement, leadership and potential to make significant contributions to medicine. One prize is presented each year; the honor includes a certificate of merit and a $500 stipend.

The National Medical Association annually recognizes and rewards African-American medical students for extraordinary accomplishments, academic excellence, leadership and potential for outstanding contributions to medicine. Programs include **The Slack Awards for Medical Journalism**, which recognize demonstrated skill in journalism and academic achievement, and **The NMA Merit Scholarships**, given for outstanding academic achievement and leadership. The NMA Merit Scholarships also have a need component. The number of awards for each program varies from year to year.

The **Wyeth-Ayerst Laboratories Prize in Women's Health** awards fourth-year female minority medical students, recognizing the outstanding talents and potential of a graduating female student who will practice or conduct research in the field of women's health. One prize is awarded annually; this honor includes a certificate of merit and a $5,000 stipend.

National Women's Studies Association

7100 Baltimore Avenue, Suite 500
College Park, MD 20740
301-403-0525

The **Pat Parker Poetry Award** of $250 is open to African American, lesbian, feminist poets. Poems up to 50 lines in length are accepted between May 1 and July 31. Send a stamped, self-addressed return envelope for contest rules.

Two $400 awards are given annually to emerging African American women scholars. Open to graduates and undergraduates, the **Abafazi-Africana Women's Studies Essay Awards** recognize scholarly essays on subjects relevant to African American women's issues and/or experiences. For more information, contact the NWSA, or write to The Editors, ABAFAZI, Simmons College, 300 The Fenway, Boston, MA 02115-5898.

Nebraska Press, University of
Northern American Indian Prose Award
312 North 14th Street
Lincoln, NE 68588-0484
402-472-3581
http://www.nebraskapress.unl.edu

The annual **North American Indian Prose Contest** accepts non-fiction entries from Native Americans. The winner will receive a $1,000 advance, and the award-winning manuscript will be published by the University of Nebraska Press. Deadline for submissions is July 1.

New York Association of Black Journalists
Rockefeller Center
P.O. Box 2446
New York, NY 10185
212-522-6969
http://www.nyabj.org

The **Stephen H. Gayle Memorial Essay Contest** is open to junior high school, high school, and university students. Grades 6-8 can win $250; high school students can win $750; and university students, $3,000. Essay subjects are related to the concerns of journalists.

Organization of American Historians
112 North Bryan Street
Bloomington, IN 47408-4199
812-855-7311
http://www.oah.org

Named for Benjamin Quarles and the late Nathan Huggins, two outstanding historians of the African American past, the **Huggins-Quarles Awards** are given annually to minority graduate students at the dissertation stage of their Ph.D.

programs. To apply, the student should submit a brief, two-page abstract of the dissertation project along with a one-page budget explaining the travel and research plans for the funds requested. The amount requested should not exceed $1,000. Each application must be accompanied by a letter from the dissertation adviser attesting to the student's status and the ways in which the Huggins-Quarles Award will facilitate the completion of the dissertation project. Contact the OAH for current deadlines.

Organization of Black Screenwriters
P.O. Box 70160
Los Angeles, CA 90070-0160
323-882-4166
http://www.obswriter.com

OBS sponsors a **National Writing Contest** open to full-length features, sitcoms, and one-hour episodics. The works of the winners are circulated to top agents for the purpose of representation and to industry personnel. The winners usually obtain meetings with studio, network, and production company personnel to aid them in furthering their careers. Submissions accepted in the fall. Write OBS or visit the Web site for submission guidelines.

Yolk Magazine-Asian American Media Development Screenwriting Competition
2005 Orange Street, Suite A
Alhambra, CA 91803
626-576-2173
http://www.yolk.com

Yolk, the electronic magazine for young Asian Americans, sponsors this competition for original, unproduced screenplays. Winners receive a monetary award, an invitation to attend a free workshop, and the opportunity to meet entertainment industry professionals. Visit the Web site for complete application guidelines.

Financial Aid

Disciples of Christ (Christian Church)

Scholarship Administrator
Department of Ministry
P.O. Box 1986
Indianapolis, IN 46206-1986
317-635-3100

The African American Loan Fund provides **assistance** to African American members of the church who are studying for careers in the ministry. Loans can be repaid with money or service. Apply by April 15.

Missouri Department of Health

Bureau of Health Systems Research & Development
P.O. Box 570
Jefferson City, MO 65102-0570
800-891-7415

Minority students and students from rural and underserved areas receive priority for the **Primary Care Resource Initiative for Missouri Program**, which offers loans of up to $20,000 for students in allopathic or osteopathic medicine, and $10,000 or $15,000 for primary care resident physicians in their second and third year of residency training, respectively. The loans must be repaid but may be forgiven in exchange for service in areas of the state with a health care shortage.

National Minority Supplier Development Council

1040 Avenue of the Americas, 2nd Floor
New York, NY 10018
212-944-2430
http://www.nmsdcus.org

The council assists minority business owners in gaining access to loans.

Sac and Fox Tribe of Oklahoma

Higher Education Department
Route 2, Box 246
Stroud, OK 74079-9802

The department operates a financial aid program to help tribal members finance higher education.

United South and Eastern Tribes

711 Stewarts Ferry Pike, Suite 100
Nashville, TN 37214
615-872-7900
http://www.oneida-nation.net/uset

A **scholarship program** helps Native Americans who are members of one of the 23 United South and Eastern Tribes. Awards are based on scholastic aptitude and financial need.

Scholarships

A. E. Church of St. Thomas

Townsend Scholarship in Music
Scholarship Committee
6361 Lancaster Avenue
Philadelphia, PA 19151

The $1,000 **James Townsend Scholarship** is open to an African American freshman, sophomore, junior, or senior under age 25, who is enrolled in an accredited college or university, or who is studying with a master teacher affiliated with an accredited school of music. A senior student must plan to continue studying as a graduate student. The $1,000 **Sidney Deknight Piano Scholarship Award** is open to an African American freshman, sophomore, or junior under age 25, pursuing a career in music in an accredited college or university. Senior students are also eligible if they are planning to enter graduate school the following semester.

Alaska Native Health Career Program

3890 University Lake Drive
Anchorage, AK 99508

The **Minority Nursing Scholarship** is available to nursing students.

Albertson College of Idaho
Office of Student Financial Services, #39
Caldwell, ID 83605-4432
208-459-5308

Diversity Scholarships are available for minority students; minorities with need also may apply to have the application fee waived.

All Indian Pueblo Council
Scholarship Coordinator
PO Box 3256
Albuquerque, NM 87190
505-884-3820

The council's **Scholarship-Grant Program** benefits high school graduates who are certified members of one of the following Pueblo Indian tribes: Zia, Tesuque, Taos, Santa Clara, Santa Ana, San Juan, San Ildefenso, San Felipe, Sandia, Pojoaque, Picuris, Nambe, Jemez, Isleta, and Cochiti.

Alpha Kappa Alpha Sorority
Educational Advancement Foundation
5656 South Stony Island Avenue
Chicago, IL 60637-1997
800-653-6528
http://www.akaeaf.org

AKA offers $500 to $1,500 **scholarships** to African American women. In addition, most of the 700 local chapters award scholarships to students who have completed their first year of college.

American Alliance for Health, Physical Education and Recreation
1201 16th Street, NW
Washington, DC 20036

The Alliance offers **scholarships** to Native American or Alaska Native students pursuing teaching careers in physical education.

American Association of Advertising Agencies
405 Lexington Avenue
New York, NY 10174-1801
212-682-2500
http://www.aaaa.org

The AAAA Foundation, Inc., a charitable institution founded and operated in cooperation with the AAAA, grants **scholarships** to multicultural university students of the advertising creative arts. With this key function, the foundation seeks to improve the level of cultural diversity among all advertising agencies. Under the scholarship program, the foundation works with selected post-graduate finishing schools to identify aspiring art directors and copywriters of diverse ethnic backgrounds who meet the qualifications for eligibility. Scholarship winners receive varying amounts of financial assistance, usually over a two-year period. Applicants must already have received an undergraduate degree, demonstrate financial need, be African-American, Asian-American, Hispanic-American, or Native-American, and a citizen or permanent resident of the U.S., and submit 10 samples of creative work in their respective field of expertise.

American Association of Hispanic Certified Public Accountants, Northern California Chapter
Scholarship Committee
P.O. Box 26109
San Francisco, CA 94126-6109
415-957-3100
http://www.hispanic-cpa.org

The association provides **scholarship** opportunities for its student members, including $1,000 scholarships presented each November.

American Association of Hispanic Certified Public Accountants
Scholarship Committee
100 North Main Street, PMB 406
San Antonio, TX 78205
203-255-7003
http://www.aahcpa.org

Financial Aid

The AAHCPA grants **scholarships** to undergraduate and graduate students in accounting. Scholarship awards are based primarily on academic achievement, financial need and community involvement. Eligible applicants must be of Hispanic descent, and be enrolled in a graduate program with an accounting emphasis or in the last year of a five-year accounting program.

American Chemical Society

1155 16th Street, NW
Washington, DC 20036
800-227-5558
http://www.acs.org

ACS operates **Project SEED**, in which economically disadvantaged high school students who have taken at least one year of chemistry work for 10 weeks in a business or government laboratory for the summer. The society's **Scholars Program** offers up to $2,500 scholarships for African American, Hispanic, Native American, or Eskimo undergraduate students pursuing degrees in chemistry, biochemistry, chemical engineering, or chemical technology. The award is based on need. Apply by February 15.

American College of Healthcare Executives

One North Franklin Street
Chicago, IL 60606-3491
312-424-2800
http://www.ache.org

The $3,000 **Albert W. Dent Scholarship** and the $3,000 **Foster G. McGaw Student Scholarship** are offered to minority graduate student associates of the American College of Healthcare Executives. Applicants must be majoring in health care management. Applications are accepted between January 1 and March 31.

American College of Sports Medicine

PO Box 1440
Indianapolis, IN 46206-1440
http://www.acsm.org

The American College of Sports Medicine annually awards graduate **scholarships**, for minorities and women, of up to $1,500 to be used to cover college or university tuition and/or fees. The purpose of the scholarships is to provide partial support toward the education of graduate and/or medical students with outstanding promise and strong interest in research and scholarly activities as they pursue a career in sports medicine or exercise science.

American Dental Association

Minority Dental Student Scholarship
211 East Chicago Avenue
Chicago, IL 60611-2678
312-440-2500
http://www.ada.org

Scholarships of $2,000 are available for minority students who are entering their second year of a dental program and have a minimum 2.5 grade point average. Candidates must demonstrate financial need. Application forms are available at the dental schools.

American Dental Hygienists' Association

Institute for Oral Health
444 North Michigan Avenue, Suite 3400
Chicago, IL 60611
312-440-8900
http://www.adha.org

The ADHA offers the **Colgate Minority Scholarships** to minority college students.

The ADHA **Institute Minority Scholarship** offers two, one-year awards of $1,000 to minority students in dental hygiene programs which lead to licensure as a dental hygienist. Eligible are Native Americans, African Americans, Hispanics, Asian Americans, and males (who do not have to be members of a minority group). Apply by June 1.

American G.I. Forum

Hispanic Education Fund
3301 Mountain Road NW
Albuquerque, NM 87104
505-243-7551
http://www.incacorp.com/agihef

Entering Hispanic freshmen may apply. The foundation awards its scholarships through the chapters of the American G.I. Forum of the United States. Apply to the nearest chapter. Contact the foundation for chapter information.

American Geological Institute

AGI Minority Geoscience Scholarships
4220 King Street
Alexandria, VA 22302-1502
703-379-2480
http://www.agiweb.org

AGI Minority Geoscience Scholarships are open to full-time undergraduate or graduate students majoring in the geosciences (geology, geophysics, geochemistry, hydrology, meteorology, physical oceanography, planetary geology, or earth-science) at an accredited institution. The program does not support students in other natural sciences, mathematics, or engineering. Applicants must be U.S. citizens and must be African American, Hispanic, or Native American.

American Health and Beauty Aids Institute

401 North Michigan Avenue
Chicago, IL 60611
312-644-6610
http://www.ahbai.org

AHBAI awards **scholarships** of $250 and $500 to college-bound students planning to major in chemistry, business, or engineering. A minimum 3.0 grade point average (4.0 scale) and two letters of recommendation are also required. Contact AHBAI for application guidelines.

Beauty school students can earn a **cosmetology scholarship** of between $250 and $500 from the AHBAI Fred Luster, Sr. Education Foundation. To be eligible for a scholarship, students must have an 85 percent or higher average in school and must have completed a minimum of 300 hours. Contact AHBAI for application guidelines.

American Hotel Foundation

1201 New York Avenue, NW
Washington, DC 20005-3931
202-289-3180
http://www.ei-ahma.org

The purpose of the **Hyatt Hotels Fund For Minority Lodging Management Students** is to provide financial aid to minority students pursuing a degree in hotel management. The **Hyatt Scholarship** is a national competition among the four-year universities that are members of the Council on Hotel, Restaurant and Institutional Education (see Web site for a list of universities). Each university nominates the one student most qualified according to the criteria to compete in the competition. The deadline for receipt of applications is April 1. Scholarship winners receive a $2,000 award. In 1999, a total of 14 scholarships were awarded. Students should inquire in their dean's office for consideration of the nomination.

American Indian Committee

3738 South Mission Drive
Lake Havasu City, AZ 86406-4250

Native Americans with financial need are eligible for $500 **American Indian Scholarships**.

American Indian Heritage Foundation

6051 Arlington Boulevard
Falls Church, VA 22044
703-237-7500
http://www.indians.org

The foundation operates several programs of interest to American Indian students, including **scholarships** of up to $500 for students with financial need. In addition, a comprehensive college scholarship of up to $27,000 is awarded to the winner of its **Miss Indian USA pageant**. Apply by February 3.

American Indian Science and Engineering Society

P.O. Box 9828
Albuquerque, NM 87119-9828
505-765-1052
http://www.aises.org

Financial Aid

A. T. Anderson Scholarships are open to Native American students who are AISES members for study in business, math, engineering, medicine, science, or natural resources. Award amount is $1,000 for undergraduates, $2,000 for graduates. Apply by June 15.

The **U.S. Environmental Protection Agency (EPA) Tribal Lands Environmental Science Scholarship** is provided to college juniors, seniors, and graduate students majoring in environmental science disciplines. Summer employment at an EPA facility and/or on an Indian reservation is also offered contingent upon the availability of resources. Award amount is $4,000 per academic year.

The **Burlington Northern Santa Fe Foundation Scholarship** provides $2,500 for Native American high school students who are residents of Arizona, Colorado, Kansas, Minnesota, Montana, New Mexico, North Dakota, Oklahoma, Oregon, South Dakota, Washington, or San Bernardino, California. Students majoring in health administration, education, science, or business are eligible.

American Institute for Foreign Study

River Plaza
9 West Broad Street
Stamford, CT 06902-3788
800-727-2437
http://www.aifs.org

One full scholarship plus five $1,000 grants are awarded each semester as part of the **AIFS Minority Scholarship Program**. The purpose of the Minority Scholarship is to help increase the participation of ethnic minority college students in study abroad programs. Recipients are expected to be ambassadors of international understanding within their communities upon return. Contact AIFS for more details.

American Institute of Architects/American Architectural Foundation

Minority/Disadvantaged Scholarship Program
1735 New York Avenue, NW
Washington, DC 20006-5292
202-626-7511
http://www.aiaonline.com

Twenty-five **scholarships** of varying amounts are offered each year to high school seniors, technical school/junior college students transferring to a school approved by the National Architecture Accrediting Board, and college freshmen enrolled or planning to enroll in an NAAB-accredited degree program. Students who have completed one or more years of a standard college curriculum are not eligible. Candidates must be nominated by December 6; eligible students then receive an application, due January 15. Awards are for one year but may be renewed for up to two additional years.

American Institute of Certified Public Accountants

1121 Avenue of the Americas
New York, NY 10036
212-596-6270
http://www.aicpa.org

Minority students are eligible for **awards** of up to $5,000 a year to study accounting at the undergraduate or graduate levels. Applicants must be enrolled as a full-time student. More than 500 awards are made each year based on academic achievement and financial need. Applicants must be Indian, black, or Hispanic. Apply by July 1.

American Institute of Chemical Engineers

Member Activity Groups—Awards
3 Park Avenue
New York, NY 10016-5991
212-591-7478
http://www.aiche.org

Minority Scholarship Awards for Incoming College Freshmen are available from AIChE. To receive 1 of the 6 scholarships presented annually, you must be nominated by an AIChE local section leader. You must be a high school graduate planning to enroll in a four-year university offering a major in chemical engineering. The scholarship is a one time award of $1,000 per student.

American Library Association
Office for Human Resource Development and Recruitment
50 East Huron Street
Chicago, IL 60611
800-545-2433

The **Spectrum Initiative Scholarship** provides $5,000 to help finance study toward a master's degree in library science. Applications are due April 1.The **Minority Scholarship in Library and Information Technology** awards $2,500 to students interested in applying automation to libraries. Apply by April 1.

American Meteorological Society
Fellowship/Scholarship Coordinator
45 Beacon Street
Boston, MA 02108-3693
617-227-2425
http://www.ametsoc.org

High school seniors who will be entering their freshman year of college in the fall may apply for the **AMS Minority Scholarships**. Applicants must be from minority groups traditionally underrepresented in the sciences, and they must plan to major in atmospheric or related oceanic and hydrologic sciences. The two-year scholarships are for $3,000 per year, with second-year funding dependent on successful completion of the first academic year.The AMS also administers a wide array of graduate fellowships and undergraduate scholarships for any qualified students, with awards ranging from $700 to $15,000. The society encourages applications from women, minorities, and disabled students. For a brochure and application forms, send a self-addressed, stamped envelope.

American Nuclear Society
555 North Kensington Avenue
La Grange Park, IL 60526
708-352-6611
http://www.ans.org

The **John and Muriel Landis Scholarship** provides financial support for students majoring in nuclear science, nuclear engineering, or a related field. The applicant must be a U.S. citizen or possess a permanent resident visa. Support is directed toward those from disadvantaged backgrounds.

American Philological Association
291 Logan Hall
University of Pennsylvania
Philadelphia, PA 19104-6304
215-898-4975
http://www.apaclassics.org

One **APA Minority Scholarship** of $3,000 is awarded annually to an African American, Hispanic American, Asian American, or Native American undergraduate wishing summer study to prepare for graduate work in classics in Italy, Greece, or Egypt. Selection is based on academic qualifications (especially in classics, including skill in at least one classical language) and financial need. Apply by February.

American Physical Society
Minority Scholarship Program
One Physics Ellipse, Fourth Floor
College Park, MD 20740-3844
301-209-3232
http://www.aps.org

The **Minority Undergraduate Scholarships for Physics** are $2,000 awards available to African American, Hispanic, or Native American high school seniors and to college freshmen and sophomores. Applicants must be U.S. citizens who plan to major in physics. Apply by February 2.

American Physical Therapy Association
1111 North Fairfax Street
Alexandria, VA 22314-1488
703-706-8505
http://www.apta.org

The **Minority Scholarship Fund** rewards senior physical therapy student and faculty members of the American Physical Therapy Association from racial/ethnic minority groups for their contributions to minority affairs and services while in pursuit of professional, para-professional, and post professional education in physical therapy. The awards are based upon academic achievement, potential to contribute to the profession of physical therapy, and contributions to minority services and communities.

American Planning Association

122 South Michigan Avenue, Suite 1600
Chicago, IL 60603-6107
312-431-9100
http://www.planning.org

The **APA/Planning and the Black Community Division Scholarship** is reserved for minorities (African-American, Hispanic, or Native American) entering their sophomore, junior, or senior year of college and majoring in planning or a planning-related field (such as public administration or environmental science) at a Planning Accredited Board-approved college or university.

American Respiratory Care Foundation

11030 Ables Lane
Dallas, TX 75229-4593
972-243-2272
http://www.aarc.org

The **Jimmy A. Young Memorial Scholarship** offers $1,000 to undergraduate minority students majoring in respiratory care. Applicants must have a GPA of at least 3.0. Apply by June 30.

American Society for Clinical Laboratory Science

Forum for Concern of Minorities Scholarship
7910 Woodmont Avenue, Suite 530
Bethesda, MD 20814
301-657-2768
http://www.ascls.org

The purpose of the **Forum for Concern of Minorities Scholarship** is to provide assistance to students in clinical laboratory scientist or clinical laboratory technician programs, who demonstrate evidence of financial need. Two scholarships are awarded annually.

American Speech-Language-Hearing Foundation

10801 Rockville Pike
Rockville, MD 20852
800-498-2071
http://www.ashfoundation.org

The **Young Scholars Award for Minority Students** offers $2,000 to help finance graduate study in speech-language-hearing. Decisions are based on a special paper written for a competition. Applications are due June 15.

Minority students majoring in communication science are eligible for the $2,000 **Kala Singh Memorial Scholarship**.

American Symphony Orchestra League

Music Assistance Fund Scholarship Program
33 West 60th Street, 5th Floor
New York, NY 10023-7905
212-262-5161
http://www.symphony.org/asol.htm

Music Assistance Fund Scholarships provide up to $2,500 to students pursuing careers with American symphony orchestras. Eligible are U.S. citizens of African descent who are seeking degrees at conservatories or university music schools. Selection is based on an audition, financial need, and written recommendations.

American University

Financial Aid Office
4400 Massachusetts Avenue, NW
Washington, DC 20016
202-885-1000

The **Hechinger Foundation Scholarship** is awarded to a black undergraduate business major from the District of Columbia. Award amount varies.

American Water Works Association

Scholarship Coordinator
6666 West Quincy Avenue
Denver, CO 80235
303-794-7711
http://www.awwa.org

The **Holly A. Cornell Scholarship** provides a one-time grant of $5,000 to a female and/or minority student pursuing a master's degree in the field of water supply and treatment. Apply by January 15.

Amigos Scholarship Foundation

901 Superior Avenue
Sheboygan, WI 53081
414-459-2780

Hispanic residents of Sheboygan County, Wisconsin, are eligible for **scholarships** of $1,500 to assist with college.

Amoco Foundation, Inc.

200 East Randolph Drive
Chicago, IL 60601
312-856-6306

Hispanic juniors and seniors majoring in engineering are eligible for the **Amoco Foundation Undergraduate Scholarship Program**. The scholarship is awarded by participating schools; check with your school's scholarship department.

Arizona, University of, Phoenix

Webber Scholarship Fund
Cooperative Extension Service
4341 East Broadway
Phoenix, AZ 85040
602-255-4456

Mexican American women from mining towns in Arizona are eligible for **scholarships** averaging $1,000 to help finance study in home economics and nutrition.

Arkansas Department of Higher Education

Financial Aid Division
114 East Capitol
Little Rock, AR 72201-3818
800-547-8839
http://www.adhe.arknet.edu

The $5,000 **Minority Teachers Scholarship** is available for African American, Hispanic, and Asian college students enrolled full-time in a teacher-certification program in Arkansas. Applicants must be Arkansas residents, have a cumulative GPA of at least 2.50, and have passed the PPST exam. After graduation, recipients must teach for five years in a public school in Arkansas; some reductions of this term are available. For instance, the requirement is three years for African American males teaching at the elementary level. Apply by June 1.

Arkansas, University of, Little Rock

Graduate School/TEAMS
2801 South University Avenue, ADN 306
Little Rock, AR 72204
501-569-8781
http://www.ualr.edu

Teacher Enhancements Affecting Minority Students provides **Tuition Assistance for Eligible Minority Students**, up to $600 per semester. Scholarships are competitive. Apply by August 1 for fall or by December 1 for spring.

Arrow, Inc.

1000 Connecticut Avenue, NW, Suite 1204
Washington, DC 20036
800-230-6261

A number of **scholarships** are available for Native American graduate students.

Asbury College

1 Macklem Drive
Wilmore, KY 40390
606-858-3511
http://www.asbury.edu

The **Harry Hosier Scholarship for African Americans** is open to first-year college students; deadline to apply is March 15.

Financial Aid

Asbury Park Press
3601 Highway 66, Box 1550
Neptune, NJ 07754-1550
908-922-6000
http://www.app.com

The Press' $2,000 **scholarships** for minority students are offered to one graduating high school student from Monmouth County, N.J., and one from Ocean County, N.J., who will enter college seeking a career in the communications field. Awards are renewable for one year with continued satisfactory work.

Asian American Journalists Association
1182 Market Street, Suite 320
San Francisco, CA 94102
415-346-6343
http://www.aaja.org

Scholarships for up to $2,000 will be awarded to students pursuing careers in broadcasting, print, or photojournalism. Applicants must be high school seniors or college or graduate students enrolling in an accredited institution for the upcoming academic year. Awards are based on involvement or interest in the Asian American community, scholastic achievement, demonstrated journalistic ability, financial need, and a desire to pursue a news career. Applications are available in January; deadline to apply is April 15.

Asian and Pacific Americans in Higher Education
Scholarship Program
c/o Chabot College
25555 Hesperian Boulevard
Hayward, CA 94545-5001
510-786-6916

Scholarships of $500 are available for California residents attending a California college or university.

Asian Pacific Women's Network
Scholarship Committee
P.O. Box 86995
Los Angeles, CA 90086
213-891-6040

Scholarships of $1,000 are available to women of Asian or Pacific Island ancestry and residents of Southern California.

Aspen Institute
Nonprofit Sector Research Fund
One Dupont Circle, NW
Washington, DC 20036
202-736-5831
http://www.aspeninst.org

The **William Randolph Hearst Endowed Scholarship for Minority Students** is available to African Americans, Asian Americans, Hispanics, Native Americans, or Eskimos studying volunteerism, philanthropy, and nonprofit organizations. Applicants must be U.S. citizens.

Association for the Advancement of Mexican-American Students
Vail High School
1230 South Vail Avenue
Montebello, CA 90640
323-887-7900

Hispanic/Latino high school seniors who are graduating from Bell Gardens, Montebello, Schurr, or Vail High School with a 2.5 GPA may apply for **scholarships** of $200 to $500 for college study.

Association for the Student of Afro-American Life and History
1407 14th Street, NW
Washington, DC 20005-3704
202-667-2822

The association awards a $500 **scholarship** to an undergraduate or graduate student in the first 2 years of African American studies.

Association on American Indian Affairs
P.O. Box 268
Sisseton, SD 57262
605-698-3998
http://web.tnics.com/aaia

AAIA offers one-term **scholarship** grants of $50 to $300 to help qualified persons of Native

American and Alaska Native ancestry excel in health care professions so they can minister to the needs of Native American communities. Applications are accepted year round.

The **Adolph Van Pelt Scholarship** offers $500 to $800 to Native Americans working toward a degree in any field. The award is renewable; each year, $100 is added to the award. Apply by June 1.

AAIA offers renewable **Displaced Homemaker Scholarships** to financially needy Native American women and men. The award can be used for transportation, child care, and certain other expenses. Apply by September 1.

AT&T Bell Laboratories, Holmdel

University Relations
101 Crawfords Corner Road, Room 1E-213
P.O. Box 3030
Holmdel, NJ 07733-3030
908-949-2943

The **Dual Degree Scholarship Program** and **Undergraduate Scholarship Program** offer three awards of full tuition, fees and other expenses, and summer employment for freshmen minority students majoring in engineering, computer science, math, or science at certain schools.

Bacone College

Office of Financial Aid
2299 Bacone Road
Muskogee, OK 74403
888-682-5514

Several Native American **scholarships**, ranging in value up to $2,800, are available for new freshmen attending Bacone. Contact the number listed for details and application materials.

Bainbridge-Smith Award

Fordham Law School, Office of Financial Aid
140 West 62nd Street, Room 5B
New York, NY 10023

Scholarships averaging $1,000 are open to minority students from the New York City area who attend a local law school. Contact the school of interest for details.

Ball State University

Financial Aid Office
2000 University Avenue
Muncie, IN 47306
317-285-5600
http://www.bsu.edu/finaid

Academic Recognition Scholarships are available for minority students from outside Indiana. Applicants must have a 3.0 high school GPA. The value of the award is a waiver of the nonresident portion of the tuition charge. The current value for 1998-2000 is $6,160.

Ball State's journalism department offers two $1,000 minority **scholarships**.

Baptist Health System

MHA Minority Scholarship Program
PO Box 830605
Birmingham, AL 35283-0605
http://www.bhsala.com

The **Master's in Healthcare Administration Minority Scholarship Program** is for students who have been accepted to an accredited program of study leading to the master's degree in health care administration. Baptist Health System will pay up to $10,000 per year toward tuition, fees, and expenses.

Bay Area Urban League

Scholarship Committee
2201 Broadway
Oakland, CA 94612-3017
510-271-1846

The league offers the $1,000 **Percy Steele Scholarship** to help African Americans from the San Francisco Bay Area who are preparing for careers in social work or community development. Applicants must have a 3.0 GPA and submit an essay on their goals. Applications are due in April.

Financial Aid

Bechtel Foundation Scholarships of $1,000 are offered to minority engineering students who live in the Bay Area and have a 3.0 GPA.

BECA Foundation
1070 South Commerce Street, Suite B
San Marcos, CA 92069
619-471-5465

Latino students from San Diego County, California, are eligible for renewable **Alice Newell Joslyn Scholarships**, ranging from $500 to $2,000 per year, to help finance study in various health fields. BECA also assigns a mentor to each scholarship recipient.

High school seniors of Latino descent who are graduating from schools in San Diego County are eligible for **Daniel Gutierrez Memorial General Scholarships** and **General Scholarships**, which range from $250 to $1,000 per year. Recipients may pursue any course of study at any school in the United States. BECA also assigns a mentor to each scholarship recipient.

BEEM Foundation for the Advancement of Music
3864 Grayburn Avenue
Los Angeles, CA 90008-1941
323-291-7252

Awards of $500 to $1,000 are offered to individuals and groups for excellence in the study, promotion, and/or performance of African American music or musicians. Monies may be applied toward college study or private instruction. Deadline to apply is March 15. Scholarships are available only to residents of Los Angeles, Los Angeles County, and southern California.

Beloit College
700 College Street
Beloit, WI 53511-5509
608-363-2500
http://www.beloit.edu

The $2,000-$10,000 **Charles Winterwood Scholarship** is awarded to an entering minority student based on financial need and academic record; the scholarship is renewable. An interview and essay are required. Beloit also provides **Upward Bound**, the **Educational Development Program**, and the **McNair Scholarship Program** to qualified students.

Bentley College
Graduate School of Business
175 Forest Street
Waltham, MA 02452-4705
781-891-2108
http://www.Bentley.edu

Diversity Scholarships are available to qualified applicants to the Graduate School of Business.

Bethune-Cookman College
Office of Admissions
640 Dr. Mary McLeod Bethune Boulevard
Daytona Beach, FL 32114-3099
904-255-1401
http://www.bethune.cookman.edu

More than 100 **Academic Merit Scholarships** of $2,000 to $2,400 are awarded to college freshmen, sophomores, juniors, and seniors. Freshmen must have at least a 3.0 GPA. Upperclassmen must have a GPA of at least 3.25.

Whitehead Foundation Scholarships are open to women from the Southeast attending this predominantly black college.

Bishop State Community College
351 North Broad Street
Mobile, AL 36603-5898
334-690-6801
http://www.bscc.cc.al.us

This historically black college administers various state and federal **scholarships**, fellowships, and grants.

Black Caucus of the American Library Association, Chicago Chapter
7305 South Eberhart Avenue
Chicago, IL 60619-1714

The $500 **Charlemae Hill Rollins Scholarship** is open to an African American student enrolled in the master's program in library science. Only legal residents of the Chicago metropolitan area are eligible, but the student may attend any ALA accredited program.

Black Caucus of the American Library Association

E.J. Josey Scholarship Committee
Clark Atlanta University
School of Library Sciences
Atlanta, GA 30314

Three **E. J. Josey Scholarship Awards** of $2,000 are given to African American graduate students in an ALA accredited Library and Information Science program in the United States or Canada.

Black Culinarian Alliance

P.O. Box 2044
North Babylon, NY 11703
http://www.blackculinarians.com

The **Jefferson Evans Scholarship Foundation** helps minority students attend the Culinary Institute of America.

Black Women in Sisterhood for Action

PO Box 1592
Washington, DC 20013
301-460-1565

The **BISA Scholarship Program** provides financial support to perspective college students who have been accepted for admission to a college or university and need financial assistance. Eligible are African American females graduating from high school in the year they are applying for scholarship assistance.

Black Writers Institute

1650 Bedford Avenue
Brooklyn, NY 11225
415-333-1918
http://www.blackwriters.net

The **DorisJean Austin Scholarship** offered by BWI (part of the creative writing program of Medger Evers College of Brooklyn) provides monetary prizes for creative writers in college.

Blackfeet Higher Education Program

P.O. Box 850
Browning, MT 59417
406-338-7521
http://www.blackfeetnation.com

Scholarships are available to financially needy members of the Blackfeet Tribe. Apply by March 1.

Blues Heaven Foundation

249 North Brand Boulevard #590
Glendale, CA 91203
818-507-8944
http://www.island.net/~blues/heaven.html

The **Muddy Waters Scholarship** is offered for undergraduate study in music, Afro-American studies, or a related field. A major in music or performing arts is not required but greatly increases one's eligibility.

Bradley University

Graduate School
118 Bradley Hall
Peoria, IL 61625
309-677-2375
http://www.bradley.edu

Academic Excellence and other minority **scholarships** are available for students in the graduate program; candidates should have financial need and a 3.0 GPA. Apply by March 1.

Briar Cliff College

Financial Aid Office
Sioux City, IA 51104
712-279-5440
http://www.briar-cliff.edu

Five minority **scholarships** are available. Write for details.

Calgary, University of

2500 University Drive, NW
Calgary, AB CN T2N
403-220-7872
http://www.ucalgary.ca

The **Alberta Law Foundation Scholarship** provides $3,500 to $5,000 for juniors and seniors who are Aboriginal Canadians majoring in law. Apply by May 1.

California Chicano News Media Association

USC School of Journalism
3502 Watt Way, ASC G10
Los Angeles, CA 90089-0281
213-740-5263
http://www.ccnma.org

The **Joel Garcia Memorial Scholarships**, ranging from $500 to $2,000 per student, are awarded annually to Hispanic students planning to pursue journalism careers. Financial need is considered along with academic achievement.

California Chicano/Latino Medical Student Association

CMSA MCAT Scholarship Fund
3737 Nobel Drive, #2105
San Diego, CA 92122

The **Latino Student MCAT Scholarship Fund** assists Hispanic students with MCAT application or preparation fees.

California College of Podiatric Medicine

1210 Scott Street
San Francisco, CA 94115-4000
415-292-0407
http://www.ccpm.edu

A minority recruitment program counsels, assists with admissions, and provides financial assistance to minority students interested in podiatric medicine.

California Japanese American Alumni Association, San Francisco

P.O. Box 15235
San Francisco, CA 94115-9991

California Japanese American Undergraduate Scholarships of $2,000 are open to undergraduates who are U.S. citizens of Japanese ancestry and who have good GPAs and a record of community service.

California Librarians Black Caucus, Northern Chapter

2326 Hood Street
Oakland, CA 94605
http://www.clbc.org

The **Eunice J. H. Parker Scholarship Award** assists African American students in the pursuit of graduate or post-graduate degrees in library and/or information studies. The amount of each award as well as the actual number granted depend upon available funds.

California Library Association

Scholarships
717 K Street, Suite 300
Sacramento, CA 95814
916-447-8541
http://www.cla-net.org

Two $2,000 **Edna Yelland Scholarships** are awarded to minority master's students enrolled in an accredited library science degree program in a California school. Applicants must be California residents with financial need. Apply by May 31.

California School Library Association

1499 Old Bayshore Highway, Suite 14Z
Burlingame, CA 94010
650-692-2350
http://www.schoolibrary.org

A $1,000 **Leadership for Diversity Scholarship** is offered to a traditionally underrepresented student preparing for school library work. Recipients must commit to work as a library media teacher in California for at least three years. Apply by June 1.

California School of Professional Psychology

2728 Hyde Street
San Francisco, CA 94109-1222
415-346-4500
http://www.cspp.edu

Minority **scholarships** for doctoral study are available to help finance the cost of attending the school, which has campuses in Alameda, Fresno, Los Angeles, and San Diego. Available programs include clinical psychology, organizational psychology and management, health psychology, forensic psychology, psychophysiology and biofeedback, behavioral health care management, and culture and human behavior.

California Teachers Association

1705 Murchison Drive
P.O. Box 921
Burlingame, CA 94011-0921
650-697-1400

The **Martin Luther King, Jr. Memorial Scholarship Fund** provides financial assistance to ethnic minority members of the California Teachers Association, their dependent children, or ethnic minority members of the Student California Teachers Association pursuing degrees or teaching credentials in public education. Apply by March 15.

California, University of, Los Angeles, Extension

Scholarship to Encourage Extensive Diversity
10995 LeConte Avenue
Office of the Dean
Los Angeles, CA 90024-2400
310-825-8261
http://www.unex.ucla.edu

SEED Scholarships are available through selected community organizations addressing the needs of underserved populations throughout Los Angeles County. SEED recipients are allowed to take up to eight UCLA Extension courses under the SEED Program.

California, University of, Santa Barbara

Center for Black Studies Advisory Committee
4603 South Hall
Santa Barbara, CA 93016-3140
805-893-3914

The $1,000 **Young Black Scholars Award** is open to African American students with a record of academic achievement; contact the financial aid office. In addition, the Center for Black Studies offers **Black Studies Dissertation Fellowships** for students who have completed all requirements for the Ph.D. except the dissertation.

Fellows receive a stipend of $16,000 plus $800 for research support.

Calvin College

3201 Burton Street, SE
Grand Rapids, MI 49546
800-688-0122
http://www.calvin.edu

Multicultural Scholarships of $1,500 are open to entering minority students with a 3.0 high school GPA; awards may be renewed with a 2.6 college GPA. Ten **Mosaic Scholarships** of $5,500 are awarded each year to first-year students who will enhance the cultural diversity of the student body. Mosaic scholarships typically are awarded to students with a high school GPA of 3.2 or higher; they may be renewed with a 3.2 college GPA.

Calvin Theological Seminary

3233 Burton Street SE
Grand Rapids, MI 49546-4387
616-957-6036
http://www.calvin.edu/seminary

The **Barney and Martha Bruinsma Scholarship** provides 1 or 2 scholarships of $500 per year. Its purpose is to promote the ministry of the gospel through North American ethnic-minority persons to their own groups. Degree candidates who are preparing to minister primarily to their own ethnic peoples are eligible. Criteria for selection include academic ability and achievement, Christian character and commitment, potential for ministry, and financial need. Further information and application forms may be obtained from the academic office.

The **John H. Kromming Scholarship** is open to minority students with financial need, prior academic achievement, and potential for leadership. Scholarship amounts are based on students' needs and may be used for study in any of the seminary's degree programs. Selection is made on the basis of Christian character, financial need, academic ability, and potential for Christian service. Applicants must be committed to serve in ministry in the Christian Reformed Church.

Financial Aid

Capital University Law School
303 East Broad Street
Columbus, OH 43215
614-236-6500
http://www.law.capital.edu

Several programs are available to help minority law students finance their education.

Career Opportunities for Youth
Collegiate Scholarship Program
P.O. Box 996
Manhattan Beach, CA 90266

Scholarships of $250 to $1,000 are available to full-time minority undergraduates at 4-year institutions majoring in engineering, science, mathematics, computer science, or business administration.

Carleton College
Office of Financial Aid
100 South College Street
Northfield, MN 55057
507-646-5769
http://www.carleton.edu

Carleton offers a number of awards for minority students who attend Carleton, including **Cowling Scholarships, McKnight Scholarships, Carolyn Foundation Scholarships**, and the **Alice Bean Frasier Scholarship**. All are based on need; award amounts vary. Eligible students may be considered for National Achievement or National Hispanic Scholarships.

Carnegie Mellon University
Office of Financial Aid
5000 Forbes Avenue
Pittsburgh, PA 15213
412-268-2082
http://www.cmu.edu

Hispanic students may apply for **National Hispanic Scholarship Awards** based on merit.

Central Florida, University of
Office of Undergraduate Admissions
Orlando, FL 32816
407-823-3000
http://www.ucf.edu

The **Hispanic Scholarship Program** provides 18 awards averagingg $3,000 for freshman finalists in the National Hispanic Scholarship Program. Apply by March 15.

The **Minority Academically Talented Scholarship** provides 150 awards averaging $3,000 for minority freshmen. Apply by March 15.

Central Michigan University
Minority Student Services
University Center 121
Mount Pleasant, MI 48859
517-774-3945

Central Michigan University's Minority Student Services is a comprehensive office which provides academic, personal, social, and cultural support to students. To empower and retain students, the MSS staff provides and enhances a campus environment where diversity is understood and celebrated. **Scholarships** are available beginning in October of each year.

Central Oklahoma, University of
Scholarship Coordinator
100 North University
Edmond, OK 73034
405-974-2727
http://www.ucok.edu

The **Minority Achievement Scholarship** provides 15 awards averaging $1,500 for minority freshmen from Oklahoma. Apply by March 1.

Cherokee Nation of Oklahoma
P.O. Box 948
Tahlequah, OK 74465
918-456-0671
http://www.cherokee.org

Students who belong to the Cherokee Nation of Oklahoma are eligible to apply for 400 **scholarships** of $750 to attend a U.S. college or university.

Chevrolet Excellence in Education Award

P.O. Box 80487
Rochester, MI 48308-9988

Hispanic high school graduates are eligible for 1 of 6 $1,000 **scholarships** to attend an accredited 4-year college.

Cheyenne-Arapaho Tribal Offices

Education Assistance Program
P.O. Box 38
Concho, OK 73022
405-262-0345

This **scholarship** provides financial assistance to Cheyenne-Arapaho tribal members pursuing a postsecondary education; selection is based on financial need.

Chicago Urban League

Scholarship Program
4510 South Michigan Avenue
Chicago, IL 60653-3898
312-285-5800
http://www.cul-chicago.org

African Americans may apply for the **Evangelical Hospital Nursing Scholarship** to help finance nursing training at the associate- or bachelor's-degree level. The process requires several interviews.

The **Benz Scholarship** is open to an African American student wishing to study engineering and work in the automotive field.

The **Duracell/National Urban League Scholarship Program** offers scholarships to minority college sophomores with career goals in engineering, sales, marketing, business administration, finance, and manufacturing operations. Selection is based on an academic portfolio and an overall assessment of the applicants.

The Urban League offers several scholarships to African American students. Renewable **Anheuser-Busch Scholarships** of $250 to $350 are available to male or female heads of households. Applicants must be enrolled in a two-year college, have financial need, and submit two letters of recommendation.

The **Edwin C. Berry Emergency Fund** provides financial assistance for students who enrolled in a four-year college and who have a GPA of at least 2.5. Applicants must demonstrate financial need and submit two letters of recommendation along with their college transcript.

Renewable **Whitney M. Young Memorial Scholarships** provide $250 to $400 to students enrolled in a postsecondary institution. Candidates must have a 2.5 GPA and financial need.

The **Coors Scholarship of Excellence** provides $2,000 to $3,000 for students attending a four-year college. Applicants must have financial need and a GPA of at least 3.0.

Mercedes-Benz of North America Scholarships provide $2,000 for graduating high school students who have completed two years of high school mechanic courses in which they earned a GPA of at least 2.5.

Chicana Latina Foundation

P.O. Box 1914
El Cerrito, CA 94530-4941
510-526-5861

Hispanic women attending college in Alameda, Contra Costa, Marin, Santa Clara, San Francisco, or San Mateo counties are eligible for $1,000 **scholarships**. Candidates may be undergraduate or graduate students. They should demonstrate leadership, community involvement, and academic achievement. Applications are due in March.

Financial Aid

Chinese American Citizens Alliance Foundation

1055 Wilshire Boulevard, Suite 1210
Los Angeles, CA 90017-2494
213-250-5515

Scholarships of $1,000 are available to students of Chinese ancestry.

Chinese American Educational Foundation

Scholarship Committee, CAEF
P.O. Box 728
San Mateo, CA 94401-0728

A **scholarship** is available to full-time undergraduate or graduate students of Chinese descent, studying in the United States. Apply by April 8.

Chinese American Engineers and Scientists Association of Southern California

Department of Electrical and Computer Engineering
Irvine, CA 92717
714-824-2164

A **scholarship** of $400 is available to full-time Chinese American students who have a sophomore or higher standing and a minimum 3.5 GPA.

Chinese American Medical Society

281 Edgewood Avenue
Teaneck, NJ 07666-3023
201-833-1506
http://www.camsociety.org

The society offers limited **scholarship** aid for Chinese American medical students.

Chinese Historical Society of Southern California

P.O. Box 862647
Los Angeles, CA 90086-2647
323-222-0856
http://www.chssc.org

Sophomores and juniors at southern California colleges and universities may apply for a $1,000 **scholarship** to help finance Chinese American studies; the award is intended for a social science or humanities major. Applications are due in March.

Chinese Professional Club of Houston

Scholarship Committee
14442 Moorfield Drive
Houston, TX 77083

The Chinese Professional Club (CPC) of Houston awards **scholarships** ranging from $500 to $1,500. Applicants are evaluated by their scholastic achievements, leadership qualities, writing proficiencies, and a personal interview for semi-finalists. Two awards are designated for applicants with demonstrated financial needs. One award is designated for applicants who are interested in a career in education/teaching. To qualify, an applicant must: be a student of Chinese descent (minimum 1/4) who is a resident of (or whose parent or guardian resides in) the greater Houston Metropolitan Area, and enrolled in an accredited high school or secondary school. Contact CPC for a full list of requirements, and for application materials.

Chinese-American Librarians Association

1100 Lawrence Street
Denver, CO 80204

The **Shelia Suen Lai Scholarship** of $500 is available for Asian Americans pursuing the library sciences.

Choctaw Nation of Oklahoma

Higher Education Program
Drawer 1210
Durant, OK 74702-1210
580-924-8280

Scholarships of up to $800 per semester are offered for study at an accredited college or university. Students must hold a tribal membership card and a Certificate of Degree of Indian Blood showing Choctaw descent. Applications are accepted from January 1 to March 15.

Cincinnati, University of

Cincinnati, OH 45221-0379

The **Graduate Yates Minority Fellows and Scholars Program** recruits minority students and provides scholarships and support services to foster pursuit of their professional goals in communication sciences disorder.

Cleveland Foundation Scholarship Program

1422 Euclid Avenue, Suite 1400
Cleveland, OH 44115
216-861-3810
http://www.clevelandfoundation.org

Cleveland students attending UNCF colleges and universities are eligible for **scholarships** administered through the UNCF. Contact your financial aid office.

Colby College

Mayflower Hill
Waterville, ME 04901
207-872-3168
http://www.colby.edu

Ralph Bunche Scholarships ranging from $200 to $4,650 are available for African American, Hispanic American, Asian American, and Native American students based on academic record, demonstrated leadership ability, and financial need. Applications must be received by the Office of Admissions and Financial Aid prior to the applicant's admission to the college.

College of New Jersey

PO Box 7718
Ewing, NJ 08628-0718
609-771-2131

Scholarships are awarded to minority students based on academic merit. The college also offers a minority mentoring program for students of color.

Colorado Commission on Higher Education

1300 Broadway, Second Floor
Denver, CO 80203
303-866-2723

Governor's Opportunity Scholarships are open to low-income students who are residents of Colorado and are enrolled as full-time students. Awards are based on merit and financial need. Contact the admissions director of your chosen 2- or 4-year college.

Colorado River Tribes

Career Development
Route 1, Box 23-B
Parker, AZ 84344
602-669-9211

Scholarships are available to members of a Colorado Indian Tribe; selection is based on financial need.

Colorado, University of, Boulder

Office of Financial Aid
Campus Box 106
Boulder, CO 80309-0106
303-492-5091
http://www.colorado.edu/finaid

American Indian students are eligible for the **White Antelope Scholarship Fund**, which provides more than 20 awards ranging from $1,500 to $5,000.

The **Lillian Gutierrez Scholarship** is open to minority students pursuing teacher licensure at the University of Colorado. Awards are for up to three semesters, and amounts vary. Preference is given to those who demonstrate financial need and have been active in their ethnic community.

The **Judy Carol Crites Herron Minority Scholarship** is offered to Colorado residents earning teacher licensure in secondary education, preferably in social studies or English.

Many local law firms provide money for scholarships, which are available to help incoming law students finance their studies. The **Holland and Hart Minority Scholarship** offers $5,000; apply promptly after January 1.

Columbia International University

Financial Aid Office
P.O. Box 3122
Columbia, SC 29230-3122
800-777-2227
http://www.ciu.edu

The **CIU Minority Scholarship** provides up to 20 scholarships of approximately $1,300 for African American, Hispanic, Native American, and Asian American students to attend Columbia Bible College or Columbia Biblical Seminary and School of Missions.

Columbus Foundation

1234 East Broad Street
Columbus, OH 43205
614-251-4000
http://www.columbusfoundation.org

The **Charlotte R. Haller Fund** supports UNCF students from Central Ohio. Contact your financial aid director for more information.

Colville Tribes

P.O. Box 140
Nespelem, NE 99155

Students of one-fourth or more Colville heritage may apply for **scholarship** assistance.

Comanche Tribe

Higher Education Program
P.O. Box 908
Lawton, OK 73502

The tribe operates a **financial aid** program for members seeking college or vocational training.

Community Foundation for Palm Beach and Martin Counties

324 Datura Street, Suite 340
West Palm Beach, FL 33401-5431
561-659-6800
http://www.cfpbmc.org

Inez Pepper Lovett Scholarship is open to an African American high school graduate from Palm Beach County who plans to major in elementary education.

Community Foundation for Palm Beach and Martin Counties

324 Datura Street
West Palm Beach, FL 33401-5431
561-659-6800
http://www.cfpbmc.org

The **Matthew "Bump" Mitchell/ Sun-Sentinel Scholarship** is given to a minority high school senior in south Palm Beach County who demonstrates scholastic excellence, community service, and financial need.

Community Foundation for Palm Beach and Martin Counties

324 Datura Street, Suite 340
West Palm Beach, FL 33401-5431
561-659-6800
http://www.cfpbmc.org

The **Stephen Madry Peck Scholarship** is open to an African American high school graduate from Palm Beach County who plans to major in French or Spanish.

Community Foundation for Palm Beach and Martin Counties

324 Datura Street
West Palm Beach, FL 33401-5431
561-659-6800
http://www.cfpbmc.org

The **NationsBank Minority Student Scholarship** helps minority students pursue higher education. Priority is given to economically disadvantaged minority students who plan to major in business.

Confederated Tribes of the Umatilla Indian Reservation

P.O. Box 638
Pendleton, OR 97801
541-276-3165

This Native American tribe offers **financial aid** to help its members meet the costs of postsecondary education.

Conference of Minority Public Administrators

P.O. Box 3010
Fort Worth, TX 76113
817-871-8325
http://www.compa.org

COMPA annually awards a $1,500 and $1,000 **scholarship**. Graduate and undergraduate students who are about to begin full-time or are enrolled in full time studies in public administration/public affairs are eligible to apply. The academic year scholarships will be awarded in increments of $750 and $500 per semester upon verification of enrollment and continued eligibility.

Conference of Minority Transportation Officials

National Scholarship Awards Program
c/o WMATA
600 5th Street, NW, Room 3A
Washington, DC 20001
http://www.comto.com

Student members of the Conference of Minority Transportation Officials who are currently enrolled in or accepted to a college program are eligible for $1,500 **scholarships**.

Congressional Black Caucus Foundation

1004 Pennsylvania Avenue, SE
Washington, DC 20003
202-675-6739
http://www.cbcfonline.org

The **Congressional Black Caucus Spouses (CBC Spouses) Education Scholarship** Fund provides tuition assistance to college students. Scholarships are awarded in the congressional district of each African American member of Congress.

Congressional Hispanic Caucus Institute

504 C Street, NE
Washington, DC 20002
202-543-1771
http://www.chci.org

The **CHCI Scholarship Connection** (CSC) is a program designed to help Hispanic students access scholarships and other sources of financial assistance free of charge. CHCI does not offer scholarships but provides Hispanic students with substantial financial aid information through the use of the Scholarship Resource Network (SRN), free of charge. SRN is a database equipped with more than 150,000 resources containing a wide variety of financial assistance opportunities. By using SRN, the CHCI Scholarship Connection conducts a personal scholarship search based on the specific characteristics of each individual student.

Connecticut, University of, West Hartford

School of Social Work
1798 Asylum Avenue
West Hartford, CT 06117
860-570-9135
http://www.socialwork.uconn.edu

Opportunity Scholarships covering full tuition and fees are offered to African American students and other minorities majoring in social work. Applicants must demonstrate financial need; applications are due in April.

Continental Society Daughters of Indian Wars

Route 2, PO Box 184
Locust Grove, OK 74352-9652

The Continental Society Daughters of Indian Wars, an organization of descendants of Native Americans and immigrants who participated in the early conflicts, 1607-1900, is offering a **scholarship** of $1,000. This scholarship is awarded each year and is based on academic achievement and commitment to the field of education or social service. Applicants must be a certified tribal member; plan to work on a reservation with Native Americans in the field of education or social service; be accepted in, or already attend, an accredited college or university; enrolled in an undergraduate degree program and preferably entering the junior year; and maintain a 3.0 average and carry at least 10 quarter or 8 semester hours.

Council for Exceptional Children

1920 Association Drive
Reston, VA 20191-1589
703-620-3660
http://www.cec.sped.org

The $500 **CEC Ethnic Diversity Scholarship** and **Student CEC/Black Caucus Scholarship** are awarded to minority students preparing for careers in special education. Candidates must be student members of the council. Deadline to apply is early December. Call CEC for more information, or contact Dr. Kayte Fearn, Special Assistant for Diversity Affairs, 888-232-7733. The Council for Exceptional Children (CEC) is the largest international professional organization dedicated to improving educational outcomes for individuals with exceptionalities—students with disabilities and/or gifts. CEC advocates for appropriate government policies; sets professional standards; provides continual professional development; advocates for newly and historically underserved individuals with exceptionalities; and helps professionals obtain conditions and resources necessary for effective professional practice.

Council of Energy Resource Tribes

1999 Broadway, Suite 2600
Denver, CO 80202-5726
303-297-2378

American Indian undergraduate or graduate students in engineering, science, or another energy- or environmental-related field are eligible for one-year **CERT Scholarships**. Candidates must have completed a CERT pre-college summer program or a CERT 10-week summer internship.

Scholarships of $1,000 per year are offered to Native American high school graduates pursuing undergraduate or graduate study; candidates must have completed CERT's eight-week college preparatory program and have a 3.0 GPA. Applications are due August 1 for undergraduates, June 1 for graduates.

Council on International Educational Exchange

Scholarship Committee
205 East 42nd Street
New York, NY 10017
800-4-STUDY
http://www.ciee.org

The **Bailey Scholarship** is intended to promote increased participation in the council's International Study Programs by members of groups that have traditionally been underrepresented in study abroad, especially ethnic minority students. Awards are usually made in the amount of $500. The award will be applied toward the applicant's program fee. Contact the council, or visit the Web site, for more information about the program.

Cox Enterprises, Inc.

Minority Journalism Scholarship
P.O. Box 4689
Atlanta, GA 30302
800-846-6672

Cox Enterprises Inc., a multi-media company headquartered in Atlanta, offers a full paid, 4-year **scholarship** to high school seniors who will graduate from the metro school system served by one of the following newspapers: *West Palm*

Beach Post (Florida), *Austin-American Statesman* (Texas), and *Atlanta Journal-Constitution* (Georgia). Only one scholarship is offered each calendar year and only one newspaper is selected to administer the program. This decision is made in January. The scholarship is intended to provide financial support for highly motivated minority students (African-American, Hispanic, Asian-American, and Native Americans) who are citizens and who wish to pursue a career in the newspaper industry. All education expenses will be paid for 4 years of college, including tuition, room, board, and books. It is renewable for up to 4 years as long as the student maintains a "B" average and fulfills his or her internship requirements. The student is expected to intern at the newspaper during the summer and holiday breaks throughout the 4 years of college. This scholarship is valued at $40,000 total.

Crow Tribe
Crow Indian Agency
Crow Agency, MT 59022
406-638-2601

The tribe operates a **financial aid** program for members seeking postsecondary or vocational training.

Cuban American Scholarship Fund
P.O. Box 6422
Santa Ana, CA 92706
714-543-9656

Undergraduate students of Cuban descent attending a two- or four-year college or university in California are eligible for **scholarships** ranging from $500 to $1,000; candidates must have a 3.0 GPA or higher. Applicants must be U.S. citizens or legal residents of California. Applications are available after January 15 and due April 15.

Cuban American Teachers' Association
12037 Peoria Street
Sun Valley, CA 91352-2320
818-768-2669

CATA awards **scholarships** of $300 to $1,000 to students of Cuban descent who reside in Los Angeles County. Applicants must hold a 3.0 grade-point average, speak Spanish, and be interested in their cultural heritage. Apply by April 1.

D-Q University
P.O. Box 409
Davis, CA 95617
530-758-0470
http://www.dqu.cc.ca.us

The university offers a number of support programs for enrolled American Indian students and others, including **financial aid**, counseling, tutoring, child care, and campus housing. They offer AA and AS degrees; certificate programs; and Adult Education (Academic Basic Skills) program.

Daughters of the American Revolution
1776 D Street, NW
Washington, DC 20006-5303
202-628-1776
http://www.dar.org

Up to 50 **American Indian Scholarships** of $500 are awarded to Native American students pursuing college or vocational training. Candidates must have financial need, academic achievement, and a 2.75 GPA.

Delaware, University of
College of Business and Economics
Newark, DE 19716
302-831-4369

The **Mid-America Scholarship** for minority students in business or economics is available; apply for admissions and scholarship at the same time. In addition, MBNA America, one of the nation's largest credit card companies, provides scholarship assistance for minorities to attend the college.

Financial Aid

Des Moines Register

715 Locust Street
Des Moines, IA 50311
515-284-8559
http://www.dmregister.com

The newspaper offers the **Des Moines Register and Tribune Minority Journalism Scholarship** to students from Iowa. Drake University assists in the selection process.

Detroit Free Press

321 West Lafayette Boulevard
Detroit, MI 48226
313-222-6490

Minority residents of the Greater Detroit area are eligible to compete via an essay for several **scholarships** ranging from $750 to $1,000. Applicants must be planning to major in journalism. Write for deadline information.

The **Knight Ridder, Inc., Minority Scholarship** provides three awards of $1,000 to minority high school seniors interested in journalism or communications. Apply by December 15.

Development Fund for Black Students in Science and Technology

2705 Bladensburg Road, NE
Washington, DC 20018
202-635-3604

Scholarship awards of up to $2,000 per year, for a maximum of 4 years, are available to students enrolled in the engineering or science departments of predominantly black colleges and universities. Scholarships are based on merit and financial need. Applications are only available through the financial aid offices of pre-qualified schools.

Dialog Information Services

3460 Hillview Avenue
Palto Alto, CA 94304
415-858-6162

Minority students from the San Francisco Bay area are eligible for $500 **Dialog Scholarships** to support study in journalism and information science. Applicants compete on the basis of an essay and past experience on school and other papers. Awards may be renewed for up to four years.

Disciples of Christ (Christian Church)

Scholarship Administrator
Department of Ministry
P.O. Box 1986
Indianapolis, IN 46206-1986
317-635-3100

Forty **David Tamotsu Kagiwada Memorial Scholarships** offer $1,500 each to Asian American members of the Disciples of Christ who are planning a career in religion. Apply by March 15.

Forty **Star Supporter Scholarships** of $1,500 are offered to African American members of the Disciples of Christ who are preparing for careers in the ministry. Apply by March 15.

The **Hispanic Scholarship** is available to members of the church who are enrolled in seminary school and have financial need. Apply by March 15.

Dr. Rosa Minoka Hill Fund

5661 Airport Boulevard
Boulder, CO 80301-2339
303-939-0023

Dr. Rosa Minoka Hill, a Mohawk, was one of the first American Indian female physicians. The fund seeks to encourage young people to follow in her footsteps through various supportive programs: scholarships for students in medical school, a placement service for high school students into private schools and cultural awareness programs, and other activities.

Duke University

Office of Financial Aid
2106 Campus Drive
Durham, NC 27706
919-684-6225
http://www.registrar.duke.edu/finaid

The full-tuition **Reginald Howard Memorial Scholarship** is awarded annually to five African American entering freshmen.

At the graduate level, **Duke Endowment Fellowships** of $12,000 a year plus tuition are offered for African American, Hispanic, or Native American students nominated by their department.

East Carolina University
East Fifth Street
Greenville, NC 27858
252-328-6495
http://www.ecu.edu

The **Chancellor's Minority Student Leadership Scholarship** offers up to 15 awards of $1,000 for African American freshmen committed to leadership and community involvement.

Eastern College
Office of Financial Aid
1300 Eagle Road
St. Davids, PA 19087
610-341-5842
http://www.eastern.edu

The **McCarthy American Indian Scholarship Fund** provides financial support for Native American students.

Eddie G. Robinson Foundation
P.O. Box 50609
Atlanta, GA 30302
877-284-3473
http://www.eddierobinson.com

Eighth grade students and high school seniors are eligible for scholarships which recognize students who have distinguished themselves as leaders among their peers in their school and community. Awards are continuous scholarships of $20,000 each.

Evangelical Lutheran Church in America
Scholarship Fund
8765 West Higgins Road
Chicago, IL 60631-4194
312-380-2855

Minority students are eligible for an $800 scholarship; you must be nominated by an ELCA pastor.

Evansville, University of
1800 Lincoln Avenue
Evansville, IN 47722
812-479-2364
http://www.evansville.edu

Two special programs are available to aid minority students: the **Multicultural Scholars Award** and the **Martin Luther King, Jr. Scholarship Program**. Both require recommendation from a counselor or employer as well as academic promise in the field of choice.

Evergreen State College
Dean of Enrollment Services Office
Olympia, WA 98505
360-866-6000

Undergraduate students of color may apply for **scholarship** assistance; apply by February 31.

Falu Foundation
220 East 106th Street
New York, NY 10029
212-360-1210
http://www.ubms.edu

The Falu Foundation offers $1,000 **scholarships** to young Hispanic students interested and pursuing a career in technology.

Florida Department of Education
Office of Student Financial Assistance
124 Collins Building
325 West Gaines Street
Tallahassee, FL 32399-0400
888-827-2004
http://www.firn.edu

Financial Aid

The **Rosewood Family Scholarship Fund** pays tuition and fees up to 30 credit hours, not to exceed $4,000, to minority students with financial need. Descendants of affected African American Rosewood families receive priority consideration; it is expected that all available scholarships will be awarded to them.

The **Mary McLeod Bethune Scholarship Challenge Grant** provides up to $3,000 a year for residents of Florida attending one of the four historically black colleges in the state. Candidates must have a 3.0 high school GPA and demonstrate financial need.

The **Seminole and Miccosukee Indian Scholarship Program** is open to full-time and part-time undergraduate or graduate students with financial need who are members of the Florida Seminole or Miccosukee Indian Tribe. Awards are for study at a college or university in the state. The tribes determine the amount of the award and the application deadline.

The **Nicaraguan and Haitian Scholarship Program** provides $4,000 to $5,000 awards for Nicaraguan and Haitian students to pursue higher education in the Florida State University system. Applicants must be U.S. citizens or permanent residents, must reside in Florida, must have been born in or be citizens of Haiti or Nicaragua, and must have a GPA of at least 3.0.

The $2,000 **Jose Marti Scholarship Challenge Grant** is awarded to an Hispanic undergraduate or graduate student with a 3.0 GPA. Applicants must be residents of Florida, and attending a college or university in the state. They must also have been born in or have a natural parent who was born in Mexico, Spain, South America, Central America, or the Caribbean.

Scholarships of $13,020 are available to Latin American and Caribbean citizens attending institutions of higher education in Florida. The award is available for undergraduates studying the economic and social needs of their countries.

Florida Education Fund
201 East Kennedy Boulevard, Suite 1525
Tampa, FL 33602
813-272-2772
http://www.fl-educ-fd.org

The **Minority Participation in Legal Education (MPLE) Program** offers pre-law scholarships, valued at up to $7,000 annually, to juniors and seniors at Florida colleges and universities each year.

Fort Berthold Community College
Office of Financial Aid
P.O. Box 490
New Town, ND 58763
701-627-3665

This reservation-based community college offers **financial aid**; write for information.

Fort Lewis College
Office of Financial Aid
Durango, CO 81301
970-247-7010
http://www.fortlewis.edu

Full **tuition waiver** is available for all certified or registered members of recognized American Indian or Alaskan Native tribes.

Fort Peck Tribes
P.O. Box 1027
Poplar, MT 59255
406-768-5551

The tribe operates a **financial aid** program for members seeking college or vocational training.

Foundation for Exceptional Children
Scholarship Department
1920 Association Drive
Reston, VA 20191
703-264-3507
http://www.cec.sped.org/fd-menu.htm

The **Stanley E. Jackson Scholarship for Students with Disabilities** offers $1,000 to a freshman minority student who is disabled and intending to enroll in vocational, technical, or fine arts studies.

Fukunaga Scholarship Foundation
P.O. Box 2788
Honolulu, HI 96803
808-521-6511

The foundation awards **scholarships** to Hawaii high school students to encourage them to pursue higher education in business administration. Between 12 and 20 scholarships of $6,000 to $8,000 are awarded based on recommendations, academic record, and financial need. Applications are due March 15.

Future Farmers of America
National FFA Center
6060 FFA Drive
P.O. Box 68960
Indianapolis, IN 46268-0960
317-802-6060
http://www.ffa.org

FFA administers many scholarship programs, including the **Booker T. Washington Scholarships**, which offer financial assistance to minority students pursuing a 4-year college degree in any area of agriculture. One **scholarship** of $10,000 and 3 of $5,000 are available annually.

Garden City Community College Endowment Association
801 Campus Drive
Garden City, KS 67846-6333
316-276-9570
http://gccc.cc.ks.us

The association administers about 300 **scholarships**, including those listed here. The $200 **Angie Gonzales Posey Memorial Scholarship** is offered to minority students with a 2.5 high school GPA. Seven $300 **GI Forum Scholarships** are available to minority students with a 2.0 GPA; apply by April 1. The **American GI Forum Scholarship** is open to GI Forum members and their children with a 2.0 GPA; apply by April 1. Four $300 L.U.L.A.C. Scholarships are available to L.U.L.A.C. members and their children with a 2.0 GPA.

The $1,000 **Garden City Police Department Law Enforcement Scholarships**, are available to U.S. citizens and to international students who are at least 50 percent Hispanic. Applicants must have a GPA of at least 2.5.

General Board of Higher Education and Ministry
Office of Loans and Scholarships
P.O. Box 871
Nashville, TN 37202

The **Ethnic Minority Scholarship** is available for Methodist minority students attending college.

General Hospital #2 Nurses Alumnae
Scholarship Program
P.O. Box 413657
Kansas City, MO 64141

African American students enrolled in nurses training are eligible for this $500 **scholarship**.

George Bird Grinnell American Indian Children's Fund
11602 Montague Court
Potomac, MD 20854
301-424-2440

The **Al Qoyawayma Award** offers a $1,000 scholarship award (contingent on available funds) to a Native American undergraduate or graduate student majoring in science or engineering and who has demonstrated an outstanding interest and skill in any one of the arts. Recent high school graduates, adults who are returning to school, and single parents are all welcome to apply. Applicant must: be American Indian/Alaska Native (documented with Certified Degree of Indian Blood); be enrolled in a college or university; be able to demonstrate commitment to serving community or other tribal nations; document their financial need. Applications are available after January 1. Completed applications must be submitted by June 1.

The **Schuyler M. Meyer, Jr., Scholarship Award** (contingent upon available funds) offers up to $1,000 per school year to Native American students enrolled in either undergraduate or graduate programs in any field. Consideration is also given to students enrolled in a 2-year college leading to an academic degree. Students in all fields of study are eligible to apply. Recent high school graduates, adults who are returning to school, and single parents are all welcome to apply. This scholarship is renewable. Applicant must: be American Indian/Alaska Native (documented with Certified Degree of Indian Blood); be enrolled in a college or university; be able to demonstrate commitment to serving community or other tribal nations; document their financial need. Applications are available after January 1. Completed applications must be submitted by June 1.

Georgia, The University of

Grady College of Journalism and Mass
Communications
Athens, GA 30602-3018
706-542-7833
http://www.grady.uga.edu

Regents Opportunity Scholarships of $5,000 are available to financially disadvantaged graduate students.

Geronimo Corporation

Scholarship Committee
206 Zion Road
Salisbury, MD 21804
http://www.geronimo.org/scholarship.html

The Geronimo Corporation, Inc., offers the **William B. Klusty Memorial Scholarships** to Native American undergraduate and graduate students. The awards are $1,000 each. Scholarship awards are made for one academic year (fall quarter through spring quarter). Contact the corporation, or visit the Web site, for application requirements.

Golden State Minority Foundation

1055 Wilshire Boulevard, Suite 1115
Los Angeles, CA 90017-2431
800-666-4763
http://home.earthlink.net/~gsmf/

The foundation offers **scholarships** to African Americans, Latin Americans, Native Americans,

and other underrepresented ethnic minority students majoring in business, economics, life insurance, or related fields. Applicants must be residents of California or be attending school there. They must be full-time students with a 3.0/4.0 overall GPA or be students in good standing at an accredited four-year college or university with no GPA scale. They must have completed at least 60 units of college credit (junior, senior, or graduate status). If employed, they cannot be working more than 28 hours per week. U.S. citizenship or permanent legal U.S. residency is required. Contact the financial aid office at your school or send a self-addressed, stamped envelope to the foundation for information. Applications are accepted only February 1 to April 1.

Grambling State University

Department of Mass Communications
P.O. Box 45
Grambling, LA 71245
318-274-3811
http://www.gram.edu

This historically black university offers approximately 20 **scholarships** for mass communications majors.

Guilford College

5800 West Friendly Avenue
Greensboro, NC 27410-4108
336-316-2100
http://www.guilford.edu

Honors Scholarships are offered to incoming students based on standardized test scores, high school achievement, written recommendations, and extracurricular activities. Particular consideration is given to students who demonstrate outstanding performance relative to challenging circumstances. Special **Guilford Scholar Awards** include full tuition, room and board, books, and travel.

Hamilton College

Anderson-Connell Alumni Center
198 College Hill Road
Clinton, NY 13323
800-843-2655
http://www.hamilton.edu

Minorities receive preference for various awards administered by Hamilton College. Among them are the **George I. Alden Scholarship**, the **Class of 1981 Roy Alexander Ellis Memorial Scholarship**, the **George J. Finguerra-CIT Group Scholarship**, the **Hilde Surlemont Sanders Memorial Scholarship**, and the **Grant Keehn Prize Scholarship**.

The **Arturo Domenico Massolo Memorial Scholarship** is awarded with preference given first to a LINK student from Chicago. If there is no such LINK student at Hamilton, it is awarded to an African American student from Chicago. If there is no such student, it may be awarded to any other African American student at the college.

The **Clara B. Kennedy Scholarships** are awarded with preference given to entering minority students who show promise in terms of their ability to contribute to academic and campus life at Hamilton. The scholarships are renewable.

The **William and Ethel Marran Scholarship** is awarded to a woman minority student.

Hamline University
1536 Hewitt Avenue
St. Paul, MN 55104-1205
800-753-9753
http://www.hamline.edu/admin/admis/viewbook.html

Native American students are eligible for **Engquist Scholarships**. **Minority Student Grants** of up to $5,000 are made each year to help students with strong academic records. The school's main telephone number is 651-523-2800.

Hampshire College
Amherst, MA 01002
413-582-5471
http://www.hampshire.edu

Ten **Arturo Schomburg Scholarships** of $7,500 are awarded to minority students each year. The telephone number for Hampshire College admissions is 413-559-5471.

Hampton University
American Indian Educational Opportunities Program
Hampton, VA 23668
757-727-5251
http://www.hamptonu.edu

The **American Indian Educational Opportunities Program** provides scholarships and other services to eligible students accepted for admission at Hampton University at the undergraduate or graduate level.

Hartford Courant Foundation, Inc.
285 Broad Street
Hartford, CT 06115-2500
203-241-6472

A limited number of **scholarships** of $1,000 to $5,000 are available to Hispanic students who are Hartford residents attending Kingswood-Oxford, Watkinson, Northwest Catholic, or East Catholic high schools. Scholarships are awarded by the schools.

Haskell Indian Nations University
Financial Aid Office
155 Indian Avenue #5027
Lawrence, KS 66044
785-749-8468

American Indian students are eligible for **scholarship** assistance; write for details.

Haverford College
Financial Aid Office
Haverford, PA 19041-1392
610-896-1350
http://www.haverford.edu

The **J. Henry Scattergood Scholarship Fund** and the **Class of 1912 Scholarship Fund** are used to fund the need-based grants to African American or Asian American students who attend Haverford College. All the school's financial aid is based on need; none is merit-based.

Financial Aid

Hawaii Community Foundation

900 Fort Street Mall #1300
Honolulu, HI 96813-3713
808-537-6333
http://www.hcf-hawaii.org

The **Blossom Kalama Evans Memorial Scholarship** is available for Hawaiian studies or Hawaiian languages majors at a college or university in the state.

The foundation, which seeks to support study and research that will contribute to international and interracial understanding, offers the **Mildred Towle Scholarship** to help finance graduate study in the social sciences. Priority is given to black Americans attending a college or university in Hawaii. Applications are due in February.

Fo Farm Fund Scholarships are open to Chinese Americans who are residents of Hawaii and have a strong academic record and financial need.

The **Henry and Dorothy Castle Memorial Fund** offers scholarships to students from Hawaii who are majoring in early childhood education.

Helen Gough Scholarship Foundation

P.O. Box 69—Courthouse
Stanley, ND 58784-0069
701-628-2955

Native American graduates and undergraduates who are enrolled members of the Three Affiliated Tribes of North Dakota are eligible for a $500 **scholarship**.

Herbert Lehman Education Fund

99 Hudson Street, Suite 1600
New York, NY 10013
212-219-1900

This is the **Special Scholarship Project of the NAACP Legal Defense and Educational Fund, Inc.** It aims to facilitate a flow of black students to colleges and universities in the South formerly restricted to white students only. Between 50 and 60 awards of $1,400 are granted to freshmen each year.

Hispanic Alliance for Career Enhancement

Student Development Program
14 East Jackson Boulevard, Suite 1310
Chicago, IL 60604
312-435-0498
http://www.hace-usa.org

For nine years HACE has been providing **scholarship** support to outstanding Hispanic college students across the nation. To be eligible, you must be an undergraduate or graduate student enrolled full-time in an accredited four-year institution of higher education pursuing a bachelor's degree or above. Undergraduates must carry at least 12 hours of college course work for each term. Graduate students must carry at least 6 credit hours each term. Applicants must have completed a minimum of 12 credit hours of college course work from an accredited college or university prior to submitting the application. Applicants must have a grade point average of at least 2.50/4.0 or 3.50/5.0 scale. Students can request a scholarship application through HACE's Student Development Program by sending a self-addressed stamped envelope.

Hispanic Association of AT&T Employees, New Jersey

HISPA-NJ Scholarship Program
290 Davidson Avenue, Room E4C102
Somerset, NJ 08873
http://home.att.net/~hispanj/

Hispanic students attending a 4-year college or university are eligible for this **scholarship** program. Applicants must demonstrate financial need.

Hispanic College Fund Scholarships

One Thomas Circle, NW, Suite 375
Washington, DC 20005
800-644-4223
http://www.hispanicfund.org

To be eligible for an **Hispanic Fund Scholarship** for business majors, you must have been accepted or be enrolled as a full-time undergraduate student at an accredited institution of higher education. You must also demonstrate financial need.

Hispanic Dental Association

188 Randolph Street, Suite 1811
Chicago, IL 60601-3001
800-852-7921
http://www.hdassoc.org

Dr. Juan D. Villarreal and the HDA Foundation provides **scholarships** to Hispanic undergraduates currently enrolled in an accredited dental school in Texas. These scholarships are in the amounts of $1,000 and $500.

The **Procter and Gamble Oral Care and HDA Foundation** awards numerous scholarships in amounts of $1,000 and $500. Applicants, accepted into an accredited dental, dental hygiene, dental assisting, or dental technician program, are judged on demonstration of scholastic achievement, community service, leadership skill, and commitment to improving health in the Hispanic community.

Hispanic Designers, Inc.

1101 30th Street NW, Suite 500
Washington, DC 20007
703-620-9004
http://www.incacorp.com/hdi

This organization provides **scholarships** of $500 to more than $1,500 to Hispanic students enrolled in an accredited school of fashion design. Applicants must have a 2.5 GPA. Apply by September 30.

Nonprofessional Hispanic models ages 18 to 25 are eligible for the **National Hispanic Model Search**, in which winners participate in a televised fashion show in Washington, D.C.; appear in J.C. Penney advertisements and promotions; and receive a $1,000 scholarship for college study. Prizes are awarded to one male and one female each year.

Hispanic Link Journalism Foundation

1420 N Street, NW
Washington, DC 20005
202-238-0705

Hispanic Link offers 20 to 25 undergraduate and graduate **scholarships** of $1,000 for journalism students. High school and college students are considered. The Mark Zambrano Scholarship is awarded to college students in print or broadcast journalism.

Hispanic Outlook Scholarship Fund

P.O. Box 68
Paramus, NJ 07652
http://www.hispanicoutlook.com

The **Hispanic Outlook Scholarship** is open to high school seniors planning to attend one of the schools on the annual listing of the "Publisher's Picks" which is published in the November 19th issue of the Hispanic Outlook in *Higher Education Magazine.* For information and an application, send your request along with a business size self-addressed, stamped envelope. No phone or email requests for information are accepted.

Hispanic Scholarship Fund

One Sansome Street, Suite 1000
San Francisco, CA 94104
877-473-4636
http://www.hsf.net

The Community College Transfer Program assists Hispanic students in making the transition from community college to 4-year institutions. Many **scholarships** of $2,500 are available.

The fund provides scholarships of $500 to $1,000 to United States citizens or permanent residents of Hispanic heritage; applicants must be full-time undergraduate or graduate students at any United States (including Puerto Rico) college or university. They must have completed at least 15 credit hours of course work. Selection is based on academic achievement, personal qualifications, and financial need.

The high school program assists Hispanic students in making the transition from high school to college. Seniors are eligible for scholarships if they have a minimum GPA of 3.0 and have been accepted to attend college in the fall. In addition, there are a small number of other targeted regional programs.

Hispanic Women's Council Scholarship Program

5803 East Beverly Boulevard
Los Angeles, CA 90022
213-725-1657

Hispanic women who are at least 25 years old and residents of Los Angeles County are eligible for **scholarships**.

Hofstra University

School of Law
121 Hofstra University
Hempstead, NY 11550
516-463-4239
http://www.hofstra.edu

The **Dwight L. Green Memorial Scholarship** is awarded to an entering law student who is committed to the ideals of equality, justice, diversity, and excellence. The scholarship provides full tuition plus a stipend for living expenses.

Hopi Tribe Grants and Scholarship Program

P.O. Box 123
Kykotsmovi, AZ 86039
800-762-9630
http://www.nau.edu/~hcpo-p/index.html

The **Private High School Scholarship** assists Hopi students who want to attend an accredited private high school. Two awards are made annually by the Hopi Tribe. Entering freshman must have an eighth grade CGPA of 3.50. Continuing students must have a CGPA of 3.25.

The **Hopi Scholarship** is awarded to eligible Hopi students on the basis of academic merit. Entering freshmen must be in the top 10 percent of their graduating class or score a minimum of 21 on the ACT or 930 on the SAT; undergraduates must maintain a 3.0 CGPA; graduate, post-graduate/professional students must maintain a 3.2 CGPA for all coursework. The maximum award for the Hopi Scholarship is $1,000 per semester.

The **Tuition/Book Scholarship** provides financial assistance to Hopi students pursuing post-secondary education for reasons of personal

growth, career enhancement, career change, and/or continuing education for part-time students.

The **Tribal Priority Scholarship** is awarded to encourage Hopi college students to obtain degrees in areas of interest to the Hopi Tribe, and to encourage these graduates to apply their degrees to Hopi Tribal goals. This scholarship is only available to college juniors, seniors, and graduate students pursuing a degree in law, natural resources, education, medicine/health, engineering, or business.

The **Standardized Test Fee Scholarship** provides Hopi individuals financial assistance for standardized tests such as college entrance examinations or professional certification. This includes, but is not limited to, the ACT, SAT, GRE, GMAT, CPA examinations, bar examination, etc. Applications are accepted year-round and must be submitted thirty days prior to the test date.

Hualapai Nation Education Office

Office Manager, Hualapai Employment Assistance
P.O. Box 179
Peach Springs, AZ 86434
520-769-2200

Tuition is paid for tribal members, including high school students, in need of vocational training and job placement. Apply four weeks before school begins. Applicants must be U.S. citizens. **Hualapai Higher Education Scholarships** provide up to $5,000 for tribal members attending a two- or four-year college. Applicants must have financial need and a GPA of at least 2.0. Apply four weeks before school begins.

Huntington College

2303 College Avenue
Huntington, IN 46750-1237
800-642-6493
http://www.huntington.edu

American Black Scholar Awards are made each year to entering students with strong academic records. The amount is $4,500 per year, renewable. The school's main telephone number is 219-356-6000.

Illinois Board of Higher Education

500 West Monroe Street, Third Floor
Springfield, IL 62704
217-782-6767

Financial assistance is available for Illinois residents as well as students attending a college or university in the state. The Teachers in Special Education program offers **scholarships** for education majors preparing to teach the handicapped; minorities and women pursuing study toward a career in educational administration also are eligible for awards covering tuition and fees. Applicants must be state residents.

Illinois Student Assistance Commission

1755 Lake Cook Road
Deerfield, IL 60015-5209
800-899-4722
http://www.isac1.org

The **Illinois Minority Teachers Scholarship Program** provides grants of up to $5,000 to assist minorities with strong GPAs in preparing for teaching careers at the elementary or secondary level. Students must have finished their first year of college to be eligible, and must agree to later teach in Illinois for a specified number of years. Indian, Eskimo, Hispanic, black, and Asian residents of Illinois, enrolled at a college in the state, are eligible to apply. Apply by August 1.

The **David A. DeBolt Teacher Shortage Scholarship** provides $3,000 to undergraduate and graduate education majors who are residents of Ilinois. Minorities receive preference. Recipients must be enrolled in a teacher-shortage discipline. Apply by May 1.

Indiana State Student Assistance Commission

150 West Market Street, Fifth Floor
Indianapolis, IN 46204-2806
317-232-0550
http://www.ai.org/ssaci/

The commission offers $1,000 to $4,000 **Minority Teacher and Special Education Services Scholarships** to African Americans and Hispanics who are Indiana residents and attending an accredited college or university in the state. Recipients must teach in Indiana for 3 out of 5 years upon certification.

Indiana University of Pennsylvania

Clark Hall
Indiana, PA 15705
724-357-2218

Approximately 70 undergraduate **Board of Governors Scholarships** averaging $3,000 are awarded to African Americans or Hispanics who meet leadership and scholarship criteria. Applications are accepted all year.

Institute of Industrial Engineers

Scholarship Programs
25 Technology Park/Atlanta
Norcross, GA 30092
404-449-1460
http://iienet.org

The **United Parcel Service Scholarship for Minority Students** is available to undergraduate students enrolled in any school in the United States and its territories, Canada, and Mexico, provided the school's engineering program or equivalent is accredited by an agency recognized by IIE and the student is pursuing a course of study in industrial engineering. One scholarship of $4,000 was awarded for the 1999-2000 academic year.

Institute of Real Estate Management Foundation

IREM Foundation Coordinator
430 North Michigan Avenue
Chicago, IL 60611-4090
800-837-0706
http://www.irem.org

Three **George M. Brooker Collegiate Scholarships for Minorities** are available: one graduate level award of $2,500, and two undergraduate level awards of $1,000 each. Apply by March 15.

International Order of the King's Daughters and Sons

North American Indian Scholarship
4831 Kempsville Greens Parkway
Virginia Beach, VA 23462-6439
757-474-1488

Approximately 50 **grants** of $650 each are awarded each year to American Indian undergraduate students and high school seniors. For application materials, send a self-addressed, stamped envelope. Apply between September 1 and March 1. Completed applications must be postmarked by April 30.

Inter-Tribal Council of Nevada

680 Greenbrae Drive, Suite 280
Sparks, NV 89431
702-355-0600
http://itcn.org

The **Health Occupations Indian Scholarship Program** offers awards of $200 or more to Native American students from Nevada to finance training in a health field. Applications are due in August.

Intertribal Timber Council

Education Committee
4370 Northeast Halsey Street
Portland, OR 97213
503-282-4296
http://www.itcnet.org

Eight **scholarships** of $1,500 are available to Native American/Alaska Native students pursuing college study in natural resources. Apply by February 1.

Iowa, University of

Office of Admissions
Iowa City, IA 52242
319-335-1039
http://www.uiowa.edu

The **Opportunity at Iowa Scholarship** provides 50 awards of $5,000 each for African American, Hispanic, Native American, or Alaskan Native freshmen with academic merit. Qualified students are automatically considered upon admission.

Jackie Robinson Foundation

3 West 35th Street, 11th Floor
New York, NY 10001-2204
212-290-8600
http://www.jackierobinson.org

One hundred four-year **Jackie Robinson Scholarships** provide up to $5,000 per year for students interested in careers in postsecondary education. Applicants must be members of an ethnic minority group, U.S. citizens, high school seniors, and accepted into a four-year college or university. They must be able to demonstrate high academic achievement, financial need, and leadership potential. Apply by March 1.

Japanese American Citizens League

1765 Sutter Street
San Francisco, CA 94115
415-921-5225

The league offers the **Hayashi Law Scholarship** to help students finance legal training. Actual amount of the award varies. Also available to students currently enrolled or planning to enroll in an accredited law school is the **Sho Sato Memorial Law Scholarship**. Apply by April 1 for both awards.

The **Magoichi and Shizuko Kato Memorial Scholarships** provide financial assistance to students pursuing graduate education in the ministry or medicine. Also available are **Dr. Kiyoshi Sonoda Memorial Scholarships** for graduate students studying dentistry, and the **Chiyoko and Thomas T. Shimazaki Memorial Scholarship** to assist students in cancer research at the graduate level. All graduate scholarship applications are due April 1.

The JACL offers a number of other scholarships for Japanese Americans, including the **Alice Yurkio Endo Scholarship** for a student planning a career in public or social service; the **Minoru Yasui Memorial Scholarship** to JACL-member students pursuing careers involving human and civil rights, including education; **Sumitomo Bank of California Scholarships**, **Union Bank Scholarships**, and the **Yamashita Memorial Scholarship** for students studying business; the **Kyutaro and Yasuo Abiko Scholarship** for a student in journalism or agriculture; the **Sam**

Kuwahara Memorial Award provides a college scholarship for entering freshmen; the **Abe and Ester Hagiwara Student Aid Scholarship** is available to students with insufficient funds to continue their education; the **Henry and Chiyo Kuwahara Creative Arts Scholarship** for an art student whose work reflects the Japanese American experience and culture; and the **Aiko Susanna Tashior Hiratsuka Performing Arts Scholarship** is available for Japanese American students in the performing arts.

Jesse Arias Scholarship Fund

181 North E Street
San Bernardino, CA 92401
909-384-9957

The **scholarship** provides funds for Hispanic students pursuing careers in law or public policy.

Joint CAS/SOA Minority Scholarship Program

Minority Scholarship Coordinator
475 North Martingale Road, Suite 800
Schaumburg, IL 60173-2226
847-706-3500
http://www.soa.org

African American, Native North American, or Hispanic undergraduate students in actuarial science are eligible for **scholarship** assistance on the basis of academic merit and financial need. Awards range from $500 to $3,000. Submit a Financial Aid Form to the College Scholarship Service by March 31. Applications due May 1.

Kalispel Tribe

Kalispel-Spokane Higher Education Scholarship Committee
P.O. Box 38
Usk, WA 99180-0038

The Kalispel Tribe and Spokane Tribe jointly operate a **financial aid** program for members seeking college or vocational training. Contact the Kalispel-Spokane Higher Education Scholarship Committee for an application.

Kansas Board of Regents

700 SW Harrison, Suite 1410
Topeka, KS 66603-3760
785-296-3517
http://www.ukans.edu/~kbor

The **Kansas Minority Scholarship Program** offers a scholarship of $1,500 per year for study at a Kansas college or university. Applicants must show financial need and academic ability. The application deadline is April 1.

Kansas, University of, Lawrence

Office of Admissions and Scholarships
Lawrence, KS 66045
785-864-3881
http://www.admissions.ku.edu

The Boeing Company has funded two **scholarships** for minority students. The 2 acceptable majors are business administration and engineering.

National Achievement and National Hispanic scholars who specify KU as their first choice with the National Merit Corporation will receive a four-year scholarship of tuition and campus fees (15 credit hours per semester) and room and board in one of the university's scholarship halls.

Kaw Tribe of Oklahoma

Education Department
P.O. Drawer 50
Kaw City, OK 74641

Tribal members pursuing college or vocational training are eligible for **scholarship** assistance.

Kenyon College

Office of Admission
Ransom Hall
Gambier, OH 43022
740-427-5776
http://www.kenyon.edu

Kenyon offers African American and Latino **scholarships** to students who have distinguished accomplishments in academic and extracurricular activities in secondary school. The average scholarship is approximately $12,000.

Financial Aid

Knight-Ridder, Inc.
Minority Scholarship Program
50 West San Fernando Street, #1500
San Jose, CA 95113
http://www.kri.com

African American students attending Howard University, Spelman College, or Florida A and M University are eligible for several **scholarships** of $5,000 each to study business or journalism; the program also offers summer employment and a job prospect following graduation.

KNTV NewsChannel 11
645 Park Avenue
San Jose, CA 95110
408-286-1111
http://www.kntv.com

NewsChannel 11's **Minority Scholarship Program** provides scholarship assistance to students attending four-year colleges and universities in California. In addition to scholarship funding, recipients also receive a paid summer internship at the station. Email the station at melba@kntv.com for more information.

Korean American Scholarship Foundation
3435 Wilshire Boulevard, Suite 2450
Los Angeles, CA 90010
213-380-KASF
http://www.kasf.org

Scholarships of up to $1,000 are awarded to Korean American undergraduate college students. Apply by January 31.

Korean-American Scientists and Engineers Association
Scholarship Committee
1952 Gallows Road, Suite 300
Vienna, VA 22182
703-748-1222
http://www.ksea.org

About 7 **KSEA Scholarships**, 1 **Inyong Ham Scholarship**, and 2 **Hyundai Scholarships**, all offering $1,000 each, are available to outstanding Korean American students who have excelled in academics as well as public service, and who show promise for becoming future leaders. Eligible are Korean American juniors, seniors, or graduate students, who have graduated from a high school in the United States. Applicants must major in science, engineering, or related fields and be members of KSEA (may apply for KSEA membership at the time of scholarship).

KPMG Foundation
Minority Doctoral Scholarship Program
3 Chestnut Ridge Road
Montvale, NJ 07645
201-307-7628
http://www.kpmgfoundation.com

The program provides up to 20 **awards** yearly of $10,000 each to Africans Americans, Native Americans, or Hispanics who are pursuing a Ph.D. in either accounting or information systems. Apply by April 1.

Lambda Theta Phi
National Scholarship Program
703 73rd Street
North Bergen, NJ 07047
888-4-A-LAMBDA
http://www.lambda1975.org

The program grants **scholarships** to incoming Hispanic freshmen demonstrating financial need.

Landscape Architecture Foundation
636 Eye Street, NW
Washington, DC 20001-3736
202-216-9034
http://www.asla.org

The **Thomas P. Papandrew Scholarship** in the amount of $1,000 is intended for meritorious minority students interested in pursuing a career in landscape architecture. Students must study at Arizona State University.

The **Edward D. Stone, Jr. and Associates Minority Scholarship** was established to help African American, Hispanic, Native American, and minority students of other cultural and ethnic backgrounds entering their final two years of undergraduate study in landscape architecture continue their education. $1,000 scholarships are available.

Latin American Educational Foundation

930 West Seventh Avenue
Denver, CO 80204
303-446-0541
http://www.laef.org

Scholarship awards vary. You must be a Colorado resident, and of Hispanic heritage or actively involved in the Hispanic community. You must have a minimum 2.5 GPA, and must be enrolled in an accredited college, university, or vocational school. Yearly deadline: February 15. For an application, call, send a SASE, or visit the Web site.

Latin Business Foundation

Scholarship Program
P.O. Box 63337
Los Angeles, CA 90063-0337
213-269-0751

Hispanic high school seniors, undergraduates, and graduate students who are California residents are eligible for **scholarships**.

League of United Latin American Citizens

2000 L Street, NW, Suite 610
Washington, DC 20036
202-833-6130
http://www.lulac.org

The **Kraft/LULAC Scholars Program** provides 10 scholarships of $5,000 for full-time undergraduate students majoring in marketing, finance, or business administration. Applicants must have a minimum 3.25 GPA and apply during the spring before their junior year in college. Send a self-addressed, stamped envelope for a list of LULAC councils, and apply directly to your local chapter.

Hispanic, Native American, Eskimo, African American, and Asian undergraduate students majoring in engineering are eligible for **General Motors/LULAC Scholarships** of up to $2,000.

The **General Electric/LULAC Scholarship** offers $5,000 to Hispanic, African American, Native American, Eskimo, or Asian American sophomores, juniors, or seniors majoring in engineering or business.

LULAC administers a number of financial aid programs for Hispanic students. The **National Scholarship Fund** provides $1,000 awards which recognize student achievement in the Hispanic community. Candidates must attend a two- or four-year college or university, have a 3.5 GPA and an ACT score of 23. Apply by March 1. Contact your local LULAC council for details, or send a self-addressed, stamped envelope to the above address for a list of councils.

Lincoln University, Missouri

820 Chestnut Street
Jefferson City, MO 65102-0029
800-521-5052
http://www.lincolnu.edu

Lincoln offers a wide variety of institutional **scholarships** to eligible students.

Los Angeles Council of Black Professional Engineers

P.O. Box 881029
Los Angeles, CA 90009
310-635-7734
http://www.lablackengineers.org

The **Al-Ben Scholarship Fund** makes aid available to pre-college and undergraduate students enrolled in engineering, mathematical computer studies, and scientific studies. The Council offers: the **Scholastic Achievement Awards**; **Professional Merit Awards**; and **Academic Incentive Awards**. Each scholarship is between $500 and $1,000.

Louisiana State University

Scholarship Coordinator
School of Mass Communication
Baton Rouge, LA 70803
504-388-3226
http://www.jour.lsu.edu/manship

Financial Aid

During the annual, 10-day workshop for minority students, journalists lecture and critique students' work. Applications are due in April. In addition, the school offers the **New York Times Multicultural Scholarship** to minorities who wish to pursue a career in news-editorial journalism.

Lower Brule Sioux Tribe

Higher Education Department
P.O. Box 187
Lower Brule, SD 57548
605-473-5561

Tribal members pursuing college or vocational training are eligible for scholarship assistance.

Maryland, University of, College Park

Center for Minorities in Science
1134 Engineering Classroom
College Park, MD 20742-7225
301-405-3878
http://www.bsos.umd.edu/aasp/scholarship.html

The **John B. and Ida Slaughter Endowed Scholarship in Science, Technology and the Black Community** fosters increased minority participation in the fields of science and technology. The scholarship is intended to encourage students to apply scientific and technological knowledge in solving the complex problems facing the African-American community. The scholarship covers in-state tuition costs for one year, and is renewable for up to 2 additional years, based on satisfactory academic performance, as evidenced by a grade point average of 2.8 or better.

McDonald's

Public and Community Affairs
Kroc Drive
Oak Brook, IL 60523
http://www.mcdonalds.com/community/education/scholarships

The **Ronald McDonald House Charities' HACER Scholarship Program** is a high school to college initiative, awarding one-time scholarships of $1,000 and up to promising college-bound Hispanic students.

Media Action Network for Asian Americans

P.O. Box 11105
Burbank, CA 91510
213-486-4433
http://janet.org/~manaa

The Media Action Network offers **Annual Media Scholarships** of $1,000 each for high school and college students interested in pursuing careers in film and TV.

Medical Library Association

Program Services
65 East Wacker Place, Suite 1900
Chicago, IL 60602-4805
312-419-9094

MLA offers various grants and **scholarships** to qualified students in graduate library science programs. Awards range from $1,000 to $3,000.

Minority graduate students may apply for $2,000 scholarships in medical librarianship.

Meharry Medical College

School of Graduate Studies and Research
1005 D. B. Todd, Jr. Boulevard
Nashville, TN 37208
615-327-6223
http://www.mmc.edu

This professional school offers M.D., D.D.S., and Ph.D. degrees and provides significant **financial assistance** to underrepresented minority students pursuing doctoral degrees in biochemistry, microbiology, pharmacology, and physiology. In addition, opportunities for subsidized, laboratory-based summer science study and enrichment activities are extended to precollegians and collegians, as well as collegiate faculty and high school teachers.

Mescalero Apache Tribe

Tribal Scholarships
Education Department
P.O. Box 176
Mescalero, NM 88340
505-671-4494

The Mescalero Tribe offers **scholarships** to tribal members for undergraduate or graduate study in any discipline. Applicants must be U.S. citizens who have graduated from high school or earned a GED. Apply by July 1.

Mexican American Business and Professional Scholarship Association
P.O. Box 22292
Los Angeles, CA 90022

Mexican American undergraduates who are residents of Los Angeles county and demonstrate financial need are eligible for **scholarships** of $100 to $1,000.

Mexican American Grocers Association
405 San Fernando Road
Los Angeles, CA 90031
213-227-1565

The association offers limited **financial aid** to Hispanic students from the area who are studying for a degree in business. Candidates must have completed at least their freshman year, demonstrate financial need, and have a 2.5 GPA. Apply between May 1 and June 30.

Mexican American Legal Defense and Educational Fund
Law School and Communications Scholarship Programs
634 South Spring Street, 11th Floor
Los Angeles, CA 90014
213-629-2512
http://www.maldef.org

The Mexican American Legal Defense and Educational Fund (MALDEF) awards **scholarships** to Latino students entering law school and to students pursuing a graduate or professional degree in communications. Applicants must have a commitment to pursue a career in one of these fields. Applicants must demonstrate financial need, a commitment to serve the Latino community, and strong academic achievement. All applications must be received before June 30th. Faxed applications will not be accepted.

Mexican American Women's National Association
Scholarship Committee
1725 K Street, NW, Suite 501
Washington, DC 20006
202-833-0060

The **Raquel Marquez Frankel Scholarship** provides $200 to $1,000 for Hispanic women studying at vocational or postsecondary schools. Financial need, academic merit, and leadership promise are considered. Apply by April 1. There is a $10 processing fee.

The **Rita Dimartino Scholarship in Communications** provides funds for Hispanic women studying communications. Financial need, academic merit, and contribution to the Hispanic community are considered. Apply by April 1. There is a $10 processing fee.

The **MANA National Scholarship Program** assists Latina students enrolled full-time in an accredited college and/or university in the United States. This scholarship is open to graduate students.

Michigan State University
Graduation Education Opportunity Program
112 West Owen Hall
East Lansing, MI 48824
517-353-1803
http://www.msu.edu/unit/uap

Michigan State University is committed to increasing the enrollment of minorities and women at the graduate level and providing them with a quality education. Adequate **financial support** is crucial to the success of this commitment, because it is often a determining factor in the recruitment of underrrepresented minority students as well as in their retention and degree completion. The 3 main categories of graduate finanical support are: 1) departmental/school teaching and research assistantships, 2) fellowships and scholarships, and 3) funds administered by the Graduate Education Opportunity Program (GEOP). For specific information regarding GEOP, please contact Dr. Maxie C. Jackson, Jr., Assistant Dean, at the office listed above.

Microsoft National Minority Technical Scholarship

One Microsoft Way
Redmond, WA 98052-8303
http://www.microsoft.com/college/scholarship.htm

Microsoft offers 5 $1,000 **scholarships** to undergraduate minority students in their sophomore or junior year. Applicants must be enrolled full-time, pursuing degrees in computer science, computer engineering, or related technical disciplines. Applicants should have a passion for technology. Selected scholarship winners are considered for paid summer internships with Microsoft.

Milwaukee Foundation

1020 North Broadway
Milwaukee, WI 53202
414-272-5805
http://www.milwaukeefoundation.org

African American students from the Milwaukee area are eligible for **Wilbur and Ardie A. Halyard Scholarships** to study business or finance. Up to $39,000 in funds is distributed each year.

Milwaukee Institute of Art and Design

Financial Aid Officer
273 East Erie Street
Milwaukee, WI 53202
414-276-7889
http://www.miad.edu

The **Miller Brewing Company Scholarship** provides $3,500 to a Hispanic, Native American, African American, or Asian American student majoring in design or fine or applied arts. Apply by February 2. Awards are offered based on a portfolio competition.

Minnesota Higher Education Services Office

1819 Bemidji Avenue
Bemidji, MN 56601
218-755-2926
http://www.mheso.state.mn.us/cfdocs/
webdirectory/index.cfm

Minnesota Indian Scholarships provide funds to Minnesota residents who are members of a state-recognized Indian tribe. Awards are for study at a college or university in the state, and average $1,850 per year.

Minnesota, University of, Morris

600 East 4th Street
Morris, MN 56267
800-992-8863
http://www.mrs.umn.edu/

The university offers **Freshman Academic Scholarships** and the **President's Outstanding Minority Scholarship**, which can be worth up to $3,000, depending on financial need, and is renewable for up to 4 years.

An **American Indian Tuition Waiver** is available in recognition of the Morris campus' history as an Indian Boarding School in the 1800s. The Minnesota Legislature mandated that American Indians attending Morris not be required to pay tuition.

Missouri Department of Education

Teacher Education Scholarships
P.O. Box 480
Jefferson City, MO 65102
573-751-1668
http://www.dese.state.mo.us

Students with a strong academic record may apply for **minority teaching scholarships** of $3,000 per year, renewable for up to four years. High school graduates, college students, or individuals with a baccalaureate degree who are returning to an approved math or science teacher-education program are eligible. Applications must be postmarked by February 15.

Modesto Bee

Scholarship Program
P.O. Box 3928
Modesto, CA 95352
209-578-2351

This Central California newspaper offers two $500 **scholarships** for minority high school seniors planning to enroll in journalism degree programs in the fall. Candidates should be from an area served by the Bee.

Montana State University, Billings

Office of Financial Aid
1500 North 30th Street
Billings, MT 59101
406-657-2011
http://www.msubillings.edu

Montana residents of at least one-fourth American Indian blood who demonstrate financial need may apply for a **State Fee Waiver** of up to $2,181.60 per year. In addition, a Multicultural Student Services Program assists students in making cultural, academic, and social adjustments at MSU-Billings. A Native American Studies Program also is available.

Morongo Indian Reservation

Malki Museum Scholarship Program
11-795 Fields Road
P.O. Box 578
Banning, CA 92220
909-849-7289

Scholarships are available for members of a Southern California Indian tribe.

Morris Scholarship Fund

525 SW 5th Street, Suite A
Des Moines, IA 50309-4501
515-282-8192
http://www.assoc-mgmt.com/users/morris/
morris.html

The Morris Scholarship Fund was established to provide financial assistance, motivation and counseling for minority students desiring to pursue secondary and postsecondary education. All **Morris Scholarship** recipients must be students of minority ethnic status (as defined by the Equal Employment Opportunity Commission). Scholarships are awarded on the basis of academic achievement, community service, and financial need. Preference is given to Iowa residents who are attending an Iowa-based college or university.

National Action Council for Minorities in Engineering

The Empire State Building
350 Fifth Avenue, Suite 2212
New York, NY 10118-2299
212-279-2626
http://www.nacme.org

The **Bechtel Undergraduate Fellowship Award** is a financial support program that encourages and recognizes high academic achievement of students interested in pursuing a corporate career in construction-related engineering disciplines. The award is accompanied by internship and mentoring opportunities. The scholarship provides up to $10,000 over 2 years to engineering students from underrepresented minority population groups majoring in a construction-related engineering field. Students may apply during their second semester in their sophomore year. Applications are mailed to selected institutions.

NACME awards the **William Randolph Hearst Scholarships**. Two $10,000 awards of $2,500 annually are given to students who have demonstrated academic excellence, leadership skills, and a commitment to a career in engineering. A 3.0 GPA is required for renewal.

The **Engineering Vanguard Program** is a ground-breaking high school-to-university initiative that targets and recruits students from underserved communities, and provides intense preparation and full tuition and housing scholarships at selected universities. Using a non-traditional assessment process, the program identifies seniors who are likely to be overlooked by student recruitment practices at engineering schools, but who possess the skills, motivation, and interest to be successful in top tier engineering education environments.

The **NACME Corporate Scholars Program** offers high performing first-year students financial assistance, corporate mentoring, paid summer internships, and professional leadership development. Full-time students with a grade point average of 2.75 or better after the first semester, attending selected institutions, may apply. Corporate Scholars receive annual awards of up to $5,000 a year, based on academic performance, and attend special NACME leadership development conferences.

National Alliance of Black School Educators

2816 Georgia Avenue, NW
Washington, DC 20001
202-483-1549
http://www.nabse.org

The institute awards **financial aid** to eligible students pursuing careers in education. Additionally, research grants are available.

National Asian Pacific American Bar Association

1717 Pennsylvania Avenue, NW, Suite 500
Washington, DC 20006
202-974-1030
http://www.napaba.org

The **NAPABA Law Foundation Scholarship** is awarded each fall on a nationwide basis to law students committed to serving the Asian Pacific American community.

National Association for Black Geologists and Geophysicists

U.S. Geological Survey
2255 North Gemini Drive
Flagstaff, AZ 86001-1698
520-556-7220
http://iapetus2.bgsu.edu:1003/nabgg.html

At least ten target schools, with minority students in their graduate or undergraduate geoscience programs, are selected annually for the **scholarship** program. The department chairman of each school is asked to select three scholarship candidates. Minority students enrolled in geoscience programs at colleges or universities which are not in the target group may also apply.

National Association of Black Accountants, Inc.

7249-A Hanover Parkway
Greenbelt, MD 20770-3608
301-474-6222
http://www.nabainc.org

Scholarships are available for undergraduate and graduate accounting students with a 3.3 GPA in accounting and/or overall. Applicants who are not already association members must join when they submit their applications. NABA has awarded in excess of $2.6 million in scholarships on the local, regional, and national levels.

National Association of Black Journalists

8701-A Adelphi Road
Adelphi, MD 20783
301-445-7100
http://www.nabj.org

NABJ annually awards a minimum of ten $2,500 **scholarships** to African American college students, and two four-year sustaining scholarships to high school students who are planning to pursue a career in journalism. Any foreign or U.S. student currently attending an accredited four-year college or university, or any foreign or U.S. high school senior, is eligible to compete for a NABJ scholarship.

National Association of Black Management Consultants

888-410-5398
http://www.nabmc.org

Scholarships are available to NABMC members. Funds available are based on corporate donations.

National Association of Black Social Workers

8436 West McNichols
Detroit, MI 48221
313-862-6700
http://www.nynet-ac.com/~nabsw/

The **Cenie Jomo Williams Tuition Scholarship** and the **Selena Danette Brown Book**

Scholarship are available for students enrolled full time in an accredited U.S. social work program. Applicants must be members of NABSW.

National Association of Black Telecommunications Professionals

c/o Bell Atlantic
1710 H Street, NW, 10th Floor
Washington, DC 20006
800-946-6228
http://www.nabtp.org

NABTP offers the following scholarships: the **NABTP Scholar** for the college bound student planning to study telecommunications or a related field; the **NABTP Collegian** for the student who is presently studying telecommunications or a related field at an accredited college/university; and **WAVE Technologies scholarships** for data networking training.

National Association of Colored Women's Clubs

Scholarship Committee
5808 16th Street, NW
Washington, DC 20011
202-726-2044

All minority undergraduate students who are United States citizens are eligible for **Hallie Q. Brown Scholarships** of up to $1,000. Applicants must demonstrate financial need and be recommended by a member of the NACWC.

National Association of Health Services Executives

8630 Fenton Street, Suite 126
Silver Spring, MD 20910
202-628-3953
http://www.nahse.org

The NAHSE scholarship program helps financially disadvantaged African Americans to pursue careers in health care administration. **Scholarships** of $2,500 are awarded to those majoring in health care administration.

National Association of Hispanic Journalists

Scholarships
1193 National Press Building
Washington, DC 20045-2100
202-662-7145
http://www.nahj.org

The **Newhouse Foundation** sponsors a two-year scholarship program (awarding $5,000 annually for 2 years) for college juniors and seniors majoring in print journalism. Applicants must be current college sophomores. The recipient is required to intern at a Newhouse newspaper the summer following his/her junior year. The program provides a stipend to attend NAHJ's annual convention.

NAHJ scholarships of $1,000 to $2,000 are awarded based on the student's academic excellence, a demonstrated interest in pursuing a journalism career, and financial need. Applications and materials may be submitted in either Spanish or English. Scholarships are available for students in broadcast (radio or television), print, or photojournalism (broadcast or print). Applicants must be high school seniors or college undergraduate or graduate students majoring in print or broadcast journalism. (Students majoring in other fields must be able to demonstrate a strong interest in pursuing a career in journalism.)

National Association of Hispanic Nurses

1501 16th Street, NW
Washington, DC 20036
202-387-2477
http://www.incacorp.com/nahn

The **National Association of Hispanic Nurses National Scholarship Awards** provides financial assistance for Hispanic nursing students. Applicants must be members of NAHN, be in good academic standing, and demonstrate financial need.

Financial Aid

National Association of Negro Business and Professional Women's Clubs

1806 New Hampshire Avenue, NW
Washington, DC 20009
202-483-4206
http://www.afrika.com/nanbpwc/

The association awards **scholarships** from $300 to $1,000 based on merit and financial need.

National Association of Negro Musicians

1954 West 115th Street
Chicago, IL 60643-0484
773-779-1325
http://www.edtech.morehouse.edu/cgrimes/scholars.htm

Scholarships of $250 to $1,500 are awarded to non-professional musicians between the ages of 18 and 30 years. A contestant must be sponsored by a branch in good standing and need not be a member of a local branch or the national organization. The winners' financial awards will go toward payment of tuition at the college of their choice or private teachers. Contact the association for guidelines.

National Association of Urban Bankers

1300 L Street, NW, Suite 825
Washington, DC 20005
202-289-8335
http://www.naub.org

The **Graduate Degree Scholarship** is a one-time, once a year contribution of $2,500 to an NAUB member in good standing.

The **Undergraduate Degree Scholarships** offer a maximum of $8,000 per year to 4 students, at $2,000 each over a 4-year period.

National Association of Women in Construction

Founder's Scholarship Foundation
327 South Adams
Fort Worth, TX 76104
800-552-3506

Minority students enrolled in construction-related degree programs are eligible for **awards of $500 to $2,000.**

National Black Association for Speech, Language, and Hearing

Speech and Hearing Clinic
University of the District of Columbia
Washington, DC 20008
http://www.nbaslh.org

The association hosts an annual research competition for African American students enrolled in a graduate program for speech-language and hearing. The recipient receives a $1,000 **scholarship**.

National Black Law Student Association

Director of Educational Services
1225 11th Street, NW
Washington, DC 20001
202-583-1281
http://www.nblsa.org

The **Sandy Brown Memorial Scholarship** is awarded to a first- or second-year law student at the National BLSA Convention. The recipient is chosen by an essay competition whose topic reflects the theme of the National Convention.

The **Nelson Mandela Scholarship** is awarded to one incoming first-year African American law student from each of the six NBLSA regions. A $500 monetary award and a certificate are given to each student. The scholarship provides financial support for those whose financial condition is minimal. The scholarship can be used by the student in whatever capacity need be. Applicants must write a proposal geared toward an area of law (i.e., African Law, Property, Civil Rights, etc.) as specified by the NBLSA.

National Black MBA Association

180 North Michigan Avenue, Suite 1400
Chicago, IL 60601
312-236-2622
http://www.nbmbaa.org

Approximately 25 **scholarships** are awarded annually to qualified minority MBA students, each ranging from $2,500 to $4,000. Recipients must be minority students enrolled full-time in an MBA program.

Each year the NBMBAA national office provides a $1,000 scholarship to each of its chapters for awarding to a qualified minority undergraduate student. Although the national office develops the application and process, the program is actually implemented by the local chapters. Interested students must contact their nearest NBMBAA chapter to find out their calendar for instituting the program. For a list of chapters, visit the Web site, or contact NBMBAA directly.

National Black Nurses' Association

1511 K Street, NW, Suite 415
Washington, DC 20005
202-393-6870
http://www.nbna.org

Members are eligible for the $500 to $2,000 **Lauranne Sams Scholarship** and the **National Black Nurses' Association Scholarship.**

National Black Police Association

3251 Mt. Pleasant Street, NW, Second Floor
Washington, DC 20010-2103
202-986-2070
http://www.blackpolice.org

The **Alphonso Deal Scholarship Award** is open to qualified high school graduates pursuing college study in law enforcement or criminal justice. Recipients must have a 2.5 GPA.

National Center for American Indian Enterprise Development

953 East Juanita Avenue
Mesa, AZ 85204
800-4-NCAIED
http://www.ncaied.org

Each year, the National Center for American Indian Enterprise Development awards five **scholarships** to American Indian college or graduate students majoring in business. Scholarships are awarded at the Indian Progress

in Business (INPRO) awards banquet at the Biltmore Hotel in Los Angeles, California. In addition to the scholarship, recipients will be provided airfare and lodging to attend INPRO and must be available to attend. Eligible students must be enrolled full-time and be at the junior, senior, or graduate level. Contact NCAIED for application information.

National Center for Farmworker Health

PO Box 150009
Austin, TX 78715
512-312-2700

The **Migrant Health Scholarship Award** is for those who are committed to, and have a career interest in, migrant health. The following criteria are considered: applicability of educational goals to migrant health; length of service in the field of migrant health; former or current farmworker status; bilingual or multi-lingual ability; personal statement of experience and/or commitment to migrant health; letters of reference; financial need; and current employment position or student status. Scholarships range from $500-$1,000 per individual, depending on available funds and qualified applicants.

National Collegiate Athletic Association

700 West Washington Avenue
P.O. Box 6222
Indianapolis, IN 46206-6222
317-917-6222
http://www.ncaa.org

The **Ethnic Minority and Women's Enhancement Program** offers 12 **scholarships** to ethnic minorities who are college graduates entering the first semester of their postgraduate studies. The applicant must be accepted into a sports-administration or related program. Each award is valued at $6,000.

National Hispanic Foundation for the Arts

Hispanic College Fund
One Thomas Circle, NW, Suite 375
Washington, DC 20005
800-644-4223
http://www.hispanicfund.org

The **scholarship** is available to students pursuing disciplines leading to careers in the entertainment arts and industry. These disciplines include, but are not limited to: Acting; Theater; Radio and Television; Film; Music; Set Design; Costume Design; Lighting Design; Motion Picture Production; and Playwriting. To be eligible, you must have been accepted or be enrolled as a full-time graduate student at one of the following universities: New York University, Columbia University, Yale University, the University of California at Los Angeles, and the University of Southern California.

National Institutes of Health

Office of Loan Repayment and Scholarship
7550 Wisconsin Avenue, Room 604
Bethesda, MD 20892-9121
800-528-7689
http://ugsp.info.nih.gov/

The renewable **Undergraduate Scholarship Program for Individuals from Disadvantaged Backgrounds** provides up to $20,000 for undergraduate studies in biomedical and behavioral sciences. For each year awarded, recipients are required to work for NIH for a year. Applications are accepted all year.

National Medical Fellowships

Scholarship Department
110 West 32nd Street
New York, NY 10001-3205
212-714-0933
http://www.nmf-online.org

The **Hugh J. Andersen Scholarship** is available to minority Minnesota residents enrolled in any accredited U.S. medical school or students attending Minnesota medical schools. Two awards are presented annually; the honor includes a certificate of merit and $2,500 stipend.

Competition for the **Cadbury Scholarship** is open to senior, underrepresented minority students enrolled in accredited U.S. medical schools. Candidates must demonstrate outstanding academic achievement and leadership. One award is presented annually; the designated Cadbury Scholar is honored during the annual meeting of the Association of American Medical Colleges. The award includes a certificate of merit and $2,000 stipend (not renewable).

The **Metropolitan Life Foundation Awards Program for Academic Excellence in Medicine** awards 14 need-based scholarships annually to second- and third-year underrepresented medical students. Up to fourteen, $3,500 scholarships are awarded each year.

The **Irving Graef Memorial Scholarship** is presented annually to a third-year medical student. The scholarship is renewable in the fourth year if the award winner continues in good academic standing. One new scholarship is awarded annually; this honor includes a certificate of merit and annual stipend of $2,000.

Each year, the **Benn and Kathleen Gilmore Scholarship** is given to a third-year, African-American medical student in recognition of outstanding academic achievement and leadership. Candidates must be residents of Michigan; Illinois; Indiana; Ohio; or the District of Columbia; and must attend one of the following medical schools: University of Michigan Medical School; Wayne State University School of Medicine; or Michigan State University College of Human Medicine. One new scholarship is awarded annually; this honor includes a certificate of merit and a $3,000 stipend.

National Merit Scholarship Corporation

1560 Sherman Avenue, Suite 200
Evanston, IL 60201
312-866-5100
http://www.nationalmerit.org

The **National Achievement Scholarship Program** provides awards of $500 to $8,000 for African American high school students who have taken the PSAT/NMSQT and have met participation requirements. For details, ask your counselor for a PSAT/NMSQT Student Bulletin and about taking the PSAT/NMSQT in October of your junior year.

National Minority Junior Golf Scholarship Association

1140 East Washington Street, Suite 102
Phoenix, AZ 85034

Minority golfers in college are eligible for **scholarships** of $500 to $5,000.

National Newspaper Publishers Association

3200 13th Street, NW
Washington, DC 20010-2410
202-588-8764
http://www.nnpa.org

The association, representing the publishers of black-readership newspapers, coordinates the award of several $2,000 **scholarships** for journalism study.

National Organization for the Professional Advancement of Black Chemists and Chemical Engineers

Dr. Joseph Cannon
P.O. Box 77040
Washington, DC 20013
202-806-6626
http://www.imall.com/stores/nobcche

The **Rohn and Haas Awards** (3 in chemistry, 3 in chemical engineering) are awarded to college students. Winners in each category receive $1,000 and runners-up receive $250.

Two **Avlon Industries Awards** of $2,500 each are presented to outstanding students in chemistry and chemical engineering.

The **James E. Evans Award** of $5,000 is presented to a high school graduate planning on majoring in chemistry or chemical engineering.

National Organization of Black Law Enforcement Executives

4609 Pinecrest Office Park Drive, Suite F
Alexandria, VA 22312-1442
703-658-1529
http://www.noblenatl.org

Some of the 35 NOBLE chapters throughout the country offer **scholarship** awards. Contact the national office about the local chapter in your area.

The **Irlet Anderson Scholarship** is a $1,000 award for African American graduating seniors interested in a criminal justice career.

National Press Club

529 14th Street, NW, 13th Floor
Washington, DC 20045
202-662-7500
http://npc.press.org

The **Ellen Masin Persina Scholarship for Minorities in Journalism** is available for high school students planning to study journalism in college. Each year, the National Press Club offers a $20,000 college scholarship awarded over 4 years ($5,000 a year).

National Society of Black Engineers

1454 Duke Street
Alexandria, VA 22134
703-549-2207
http://www.nsbe.org

The **Seagate Scholarship** of $2,000 is awarded to students majoring in one of the following: chemical engineering, computer science, electrical engineering, information technology, material science, mechanical engineering, or physics. Applicant must demonstrate financial need, as well as demonstrate leadership abilities via campus activities.

The **Ernst & Young LLP Scholarship** of $2,500 is available to freshmen, sophomore, or junior NSBE members, engineering or technical majors, who demonstrate an interest in the consulting industry. Must attend a selected university. Visit the Web site for list of 14 eligible universities.

Financial Aid

The **IBM Student Research Scholarship** ($2,500 per year for two years) was established to encourage students to pursue graduate studies in science and engineering fields. The scholarship is available to college sophomore or junior NSBE members in good standing. Qualified fields of study may be any of the following: chemistry, physics, applied or engineering physics, materials science or engineering, math, computer science, computer engineering, chemical, electrical, mechanical, or optical engineering. The scholarship also includes a summer internship at IBM's Almaden Research Center in San Jose, California (salary commensurate with experience).

NSBE Fellows Scholarships are given to approximately 75 students who have held high scholastic standards, shown dedicated service to the society and other organizations, and who possess high professional promise. Of all applications received, one will be designated as the Mike Shinn Distinguished Fellow. Recipients of the Fellow Scholarship will receive: Mike Shinn Distinguished Fellow: $2,500 cash award; NSBE Fellows: $1,500 cash award (checks will be distributed at the National Convention.

The **Microsoft Corporation Computer Science Scholarship** of $2,500 was established to encourage students to pursue collegiate studies in computer science and technology fields. Available to college freshmen, sophomore, junior, and senior NSBE members in good standing. Qualified fields of study must be computer science or computer engineering.

The National Society of Black Engineers— Alumni Extension awards three (3) $2,000 **Technical Scholarships**. One will go to an NSBE graduating senior (who is planning to join the Alumni Extension and must have joined before entering graduate school to receive the award) and two will go to NSBE - AE members who are in graduate school, with at least one more academic year before graduation. All applicants must be paid members of the National Society of Black Engineers.

The **GE African American Forum Scholarship** is awarded to undergraduates majoring in one of the programs offered by a School of Business or Engineering. To qualify you must have a minimum cumulative grade point average of 3.2 on a 4.0 scale and have completed at least 12 hours of credit in your major or school of concentration by the spring semester of your sophomore year. All applicants except freshmen and graduate students will be considered for this scholarship. The GE African American Forum Scholarship recipients will receive a $1,500 cash award, along with travel, hotel accommodations, and registration to the National Convention.

The **Fulfilling the Legacy Scholarship** provides cash awards to be determined by the total amount contributed by members to the scholarship fund.

National Society of Black Physicists

NSBP Scholarship, L-716
Lawrence Livermore National Lab
Livermore, CA 94550
925-422-0894
http://www.nsbp.org

The National Society of Black Physicists (NSBP) and the University of California Lawrence Livermore National Laboratory(LLNL) sponsor an **undergraduate scholarship** to encourage African American students who plan to pursue degrees in physics. Graduating high school seniors, and undergraduate students already enrolled in college as physics majors may apply for the scholarship. The scholarship is in the amount of $5,000 and is renewable for up to four years - provided that the student maintains a B average and continues to be an undergraduate majoring in physics. The recipient of the scholarship is required to accept a summer internship at Lawrence Livermore National Laboratory for at least one summer during his or her undergraduate education.

National Society of Colonial Dames

Indian Nurse Scholarship
2305 Gillette Avenue
Wilmington, NC 28403

The **Indian Nurse Scholarship** offers $500 to $1,000 for American Indian students in prenursing programs. Applications are accepted all year.

National Society of Hispanic MBAs

Scholarship Program
8204 Elmbrook, Suite 235
Dallas, TX 75247
877-467-4622
http://www.nshmba.org

The **NSHMBA Scholarship Program** assists Hispanic students pursuing a master's degree in management/business. Scholarships range from $2,000 to $5,000 and one for $10,000. Applicants must have financial need. Visit the Web site, or contact the organization, for application forms and guidelines.

National Student Nurses' Association

555 West 57th Street
New York, NY 10019
212-581-2215
http://www.nsna.org

The **Breakthrough to Nursing Scholarships for Ethnic People of Color** are open to nursing or prenursing students who indicate on the application that they are members of one of the minority groups listed. There is an application fee of $10. Apply by February 1. Write for details.

National Technical Association

6919 North 19th Street
Philadelphia, PA 19126-1506
215-549-6509
http://www.ntaonline.org

With the **Charles E. Price Scholarship**, NTA provides financial assistance to a minority student pursuing a college degree in either electrical or mechanical engineering. The scholarship is renewable each year for up to four years. The scholarship grants will be made to those students who, in the judgment of the NTA/ABB Service Inc. selection panels, have demonstrated superior scholarship and show great promise as future electrical or mechanical engineers. The scholarship winner will receive a cash award of $6,000. Other scholarship aid is available by application from local chapters of the National Technical Association. That information can be made available upon request.

The **Science Scholarship Awards Program** is designed to identify potential science students and research scholars, and to inspire others to follow an academic science career. Each scholarship, ranging from $5,000 to $5000, is available for 1 year.

National Urban League, Inc.

Scholarship Coordinator
120 Wall Street
New York, NY 10005
212-558-5300
http://www.nul.org

The **Duracell/NUL Scholarship and Intern Program** is open to minority college juniors and seniors majoring in engineering, sales, marketing, and business administration. Awards are for $5,000 per year. Applications are due in mid-March.

National Youth Ministry Organization

Director of Financial Aid
P.O. Box 840
Nashville, TN 37202
615-340-7184

The **United Methodist/Richard S. Smith Scholarship** of $1,000 is available to a minority youth active in a local United Methodist Church. Applicants must be entering their freshman year of college.

Native American Journalists Association

3359 36th Avenue South
Minneapolis, MN 55406
612-729-9244
http://www.naja.com

Scholarships of up to $4,000 are available to Native American graduate and undergraduate students in journalism, communications, photography, radio, television, and new media. Apply by March 31.

Native American Scholarship Fund

8200 Mountain Road, NE, Suite 203
Albuquerque, NM 87110
505-262-2351
http://www.nasf.com

Financial Aid

Designed to provide financial assistance to Native Americans to help prepare them for work in fields which are critical for the economic, social, business, and political development of Indian tribes, the fund offers two programs for Native American college students: The **Math, Engineering, Science, Business, Education, and Computers (MESBEC) Program** provides scholarships for students majoring in these fields. The **Native American Leadership in Education (NALE) Program** offers awards of $500 to $5,000 to students in education. Deadlines to apply are April 15, September 15, and March 15.

The fund offers renewable **scholarships** of $500 to $5,000 a year for Native Americans with a GPA of at least 3.0 to study education, computer science, math, engineering, business, or science. Undergraduate and graduate students may apply. There is a one-time-only processing fee. Deadlines vary.

Navajo Generating Station
Salt River Project
P.O. Box W
Page, AZ 86040
602-645-8811

The **SRP/NGS Navajo Scholarship Program** provides for Navajo Tribe members enrolled in college.

Nebraska, University of, Omaha
Office of Financial Aid
Omaha, NE 68182-0187
402-554-2327
http://www.ses.unomaha.edu

The university offers several opportunities for minorities for scholarships. The **Rick Davis Scholarship** provides at least $2,000; apply by January 15. The Isaacson Incentive Scholarship provides $1,000; apply by January 15.

New Mexico State University
Director of Financial Aid
Box 30001, Department 5100
Las Cruces, NM 88003-0001
505-646-0111

Minority Presidential Scholarships provide $500 for entering minority students with a 2.5 high school GPA; awards are renewable. In addition, the **Chicano Faculty Staff Fund** offers full-tuition scholarships to Chicano students who have completed at least one year of study with a 2.0 GPA or higher.

The **Clara B. Williams Scholarship** provides $1,100 annually to one African American undergraduate with academic distinction. Apply by March 1.

The Department of Waste Management Education and Research supports minority undergraduates who have a 2.5 GPA or better. The Department of Computer Science offers the **El Paso Natural Gas Scholarship** of $1,000 to help finance the final year of computer science study. These awards are limited in number and very competitive.

New Mexico, University of, Albuquerque
Native American Studies
Mesa Vista 3080
Albuquerque, NM 87131
505-277-3917

The center offers a number of academic services for Native American students, faculty, and community members, including research and writing skills development, academic advising, and an Intervention Project which helps students locate **scholarship and financial aid information**. Also available for entering Native Americans is a handbook titled "Pathways off the Rez." The university also provides scholarship assistance for Native American students.

New York Association of Black Journalists
Rockefeller Center
P.O. Box 2446
New York, NY 10185
212-522-6969
http://www.nyabj.org

The **Sylvia L. Wilson Memorial Scholarship** is awarded to a minority student in Columbia's

Graduate School of Journalism, with preference given to aspiring editors.

New York State Education Department
HEOP/UTEA Scholarships
Room 1071 EBA
Albany, NY 12234
518-483-1319

Regents Professional Opportunity Scholarships are available to New York residents enrolled in undergraduate or graduate studies in various health fields, including nursing. Awards are for $1,000 to $5,000 a year for up to four years for study at a New York State institution. Preference is given to low-income students and minorities historically underrepresented in the field. Recipients must practice their professions within the state for one year for each year of financial assistance.

The **Regents Health Care Scholarships for Medicine and Dentistry** award $1,000 to $10,000 a year for up to four years to New York residents enrolled in approved medical or dental schools in the state. Recipients must agree to work for a specified number of years after graduation in an area of the state with a shortage of health workers. A hundred awards are given annually. Applicants must be minorities and/or financially needy. Apply by March 1.

New York State residents attending postsecondary institutions in the state may apply for **scholarships** of $1,550 per year. Applicants must be members of a New York state tribe, including the Iroquoian Tribes, the Shinnecock Tribe, and the Poospatuck Tribe. Apply by July 15 for the fall semester, December 31 for spring, and May 20 for summer. Applicants must reapply each semester.

Newcombe (Charlotte) Foundation
35 Park Place
Princeton, NJ 0854-6918
609-924-7022

The foundation provides grants to selected Presbyterian colleges to that they may offer **scholarships** to economically disadvantaged or minority students. Fourteen colleges related to the Presbyterian Church (USA) are currently in the program. Write or call the foundation for a list. Apply through your schooi; individuals may not apply directly to the foundation.

Nez Perce Tribe
P.O. Box 305
Lapwai, ID 83540

The tribe operates a **scholarship** program to help its members finance postsecondary education.

North Carolina Central University
School of Library and Information Science
P.O. Box 19586
Durham, NC 27707
919-560-6100

A number of **scholarships** and **assistantships** are available through the library school of this largely black university.

North Dakota State University
College of Pharmacy
123 Sudro Hall
Fargo, ND 58105-5055
701-231-8205
http://www.ndsu.nodak.edu/instruct/hanel/pharmacy/pharmacy.html

The **Native American Pharmacy Program** offers a variety of support services and $500 scholarships. Applications are due March 1.

North Dakota, University of
College of Nursing
P.O. Box 9025
Grand Forks, ND 58202-9025
701-777-3037
http://www.und.nodak.edu/dept/nursing

The **Recruitment of American Indians into Nursing (RAIN) Program** helps with admissions and financial aid.

North Dakota, University of

Enrollment Services
University Station
Grand Forks, ND 58201
701-777-3037
http://www.und.nodak.edu

The University of North Dakota awards several **tuition waivers** to broaden the cultural diversity on campus. Cultural diversity for this waiver is defined as individuals who come from historically underrepresented groups (African American, American Indian, Asian American, Hispanic American, and the economically disadvantaged).

Northeastern University

Office of the Provost
112 Hayden Hall
Boston, MA 02115
617-437-2170
http://www.neu.edu

The **Minority Faculty Recruitment and Retention Fund** and the **Minority Faculty Development Fund** provide resources to support the hiring of minority faculty and to support the research and scholarship of minority faculty.

Northern Arapaho Tribal Scholarships

Community Development Office
Wind River Indian Agency
Fort Washakie, WY 82514

These **scholarships** award up to $1,700 per academic year to members of the Northern Arapahoe Indian Tribe for full-time study at a college or university in Wyoming. Applications must be submitted at least six weeks before the beginning of the school year.

Northern Illinois University

Graduate School
DeKalb, IL 60115-2864
815-753-0142
http://www.niu.edu/grad

The following financial support is available for minority graduate students: **Rhoten A. Smith graduate assistantships** are teaching, research, and staff assistantships that provide a full waiver of tuition and a 1999-2000 stipend of $580 to $1,160 per month. **Jeffrey T. Lunsford Fellowships** for master's degree students carry a full tuition waiver and an annual stipend of at least $6,000. **Carter G. Woodson Scholars** are doctoral students who receive a full tuition waiver and an annual stipend of $14,300. Students are nominated for these awards, as well as for tuition-waiver scholarships, by the academic department in which they will pursue a graduate degree. The university also participates in state-wide minority fellowship programs: **The Illinois Consortium for Educational Opportunity Program** (ICEOP) awards a full tuition waiver and an annual stipend of $10,000, and the **Illinois Minority Graduate Incentive Program** (IMGIP) provides a full tuition waiver and an annual award of $15,000. Students are nominated for these two programs by the Graduate School.

Northwest Journalists of Color Scholarship Program

The Seattle Times
P.O. Box 70
Seattle, WA 98111
206-464-2092

This minority fellowship program for print, broadcast, and photojournalists allows high school seniors and undergraduates access to mentors. The fund includes a **grant** of up to $1,000.

Northwest Minority Media Association

c/o The Seattle Times
P.O. Box 70
Seattle, WA 98111
206-464-3343

Minority high school and undergraduate students from the Northwest may apply for **scholarships** of up to $1,000 to help finance study in journalism at an area college or university. Applications are due April 1.

Northwest Pharmacists Coalition Scholarships

Scholarship Coordinator
P.O. Box 22975
Seattle, WA 98122
206-746-9618

African American students are eligible for **financial aid** to help finance training in prepharmacy. Apply by May 1.

Nurses' Educational Funds, Inc.

555 West 57th Street, Suite 1327
New York, NY 10019-2925
212-399-1428

This organization grants **scholarships** to registered nurses pursuing further full-time study through degree programs. Two awards are specifically for black students: the **Osborne Scholarship** for a master's level candidate and the **Carnegie Scholarship** for a doctoral student. Men and women who are members of a nursing association and who qualify for these awards study in an accredited nursing program of their choice. Awards range from $2,500 to $10,000. Application forms are available between August 1 and February 1 and are due March 1. There is a $10 fee for the application packet. Also, GRE or MAT scores are required.

Oak Ridge Associated Universities

P.O. Box 117
Oak Ridge, TN 37831-3010
423-241-4300
http://www.orau.org

The organization provides **scholarships** from the U.S. Department of Energy for undergraduate students pursuing degrees in areas related to managing radioactive waste (science, math, engineering technology, or social science) at historically black colleges and universities. Juniors and seniors are eligible to receive tuition, fees, and a monthly stipend of $600. Applications are due in June. Students at historically black colleges and universities are also eligible for scholarships related to nuclear energy technology. Juniors, seniors, and graduate students are eligible for tuition, fees, and up to $14,400 per year in stipends. Apply by the third Tuesday in January.

Oglala Sioux Tribe

Box H
Pine Ridge, SD 57770
605-867-5821

Tribal members may apply for **scholarships**. Application deadlines are July 1, November 15, and May 1.

Ohio State University

Office of Minority Affairs
1000 Lincoln Tower
1800 Cannon Drive
Columbus, OH 43210-1230
614-292-0964
http://oma.ohio-state.edu

Martin Luther King, Jr., Scholarships are provided for African American students.

Ohio University

Office of Student Financial Aid and Scholarships
Athens, OH 45701
740-593-4141
http://www.sfa.chubb.ohiou.edu

Approximately 40 **Minority Scholar Awards** are offered annually to qualified applicants. Write for selection criteria and application deadlines.

The **John Newton Templeton Scholarship** pays in-state tuition for 10 minority freshmen each year. Apply by February 15.

Minority M.B.A. candidates are eligible for partial- and full-tuition **scholarships** as well as graduate assistantships.

Omega Psi Phi Fraternity

3951 Snapfinger Parkway, Suite 330
Decatur, GA 30035
404-284-5533
http://www.omegapsiphifraternity.org

Black men who belong to OPP are eligible for $500 **grants** to help finance undergraduate or graduate study. In addition, **Founders Memorial Scholarships** of $300 are offered to members with a 3.0 GPA and a record of campus involvement. Candidates must be in their sophomore year or higher.

Financial Aid

Oncology Nursing Foundation
501 Holiday Drive
Pittsburgh, PA 15220-2749
412-921-7373

The **Ethnic Minority Bachelor's Scholarship**
provides financial assistance to ethnic minorities for undergraduate studies in nursing.
Eligible candidates must be a registered nurse
with a demonstrated interest in and commitment to cancer nursing; be enrolled in an
undergraduate nursing degree program at an
NLN-accredited school of nursing (the program
must have application to oncology nursing);
must have a current license to practice as a registered nurse; not have previously received a
bachelor's scholarship from the Oncology
Nursing Foundation; and be a member of an
ethnic minority group.

Oneida Tribe of Wisconsin Higher Education
Financial Aid Director
Oneida Education Office
P.O. Box 365
Oneida, WI 54155
414-869-4333

Scholarships of up to $3,000 are open to
enrolled members of the Oneida Tribe of
Wisconsin for study at a postsecondary institution; awards are based on financial need.
Applications are due May 1 for the fall semester,
October 1 for the spring, and May 1 for the summer. The number of awards is based on the
availability of funds.

ONS Foundation
501 Holiday Drive, Building 4
Pittsburgh, PA 15220-2749
412-921-7373

Registered nurses who are studying or have an
interest in oncology nursing are eligible for
$2,000 to $3,000 scholarships. The **Ethnic
Minority Bachelor's Scholarship** offers $2,000.
There is a $5 application fee. Apply by February
1. Three awards are available. The **Ethnic
Minority Master's Scholarship** offers
$3,000. There is a $5 application fee. Apply
by February 1.

Organization of Black Screenwriters
P.O. Box 70160
Los Angeles, CA 90070-0160
323-882-4166
http://www.obswriter.com

In conjunction with the UCLA Extension
Program, OBS offers 2 **scholarships**, one
through the Writers' Department and one
through the SEED program.

Organization of Chinese Americans
Avon Scholarship
1001 Connecticut Avenue, NW, Suite 707
Washington, DC 20036

Asian-Pacific women in financial need are eligible for $1,000 **scholarships** to pursue college
study.

Osage Tribe
Muskogee Area Office
BIA Old Federal Building
Muskogee, OK 74401
918-687-2460

Financial assistance of up to $2,000 per year is
offered to tribal members for college or vocational training; applications are due in April,
June, or December.

Otoe Missouri Tribe of Oklahoma
Education Department
P.O. Box 68
Red Rock, OR 74651

Tribal members are eligible for **scholarships** to
help finance college study.

Pacific Gas and Electric Company
College Relations Department
P.O. Box 770000
San Francisco, CA 94177-0001
415-973-7000
http://www.pge.com

The **Asian Employees Association** (AEA) of
Pacific Gas and Electric Company awards six
$1,000 scholarships annually to outstanding
high school seniors planning to attend an

accredited college or university. Applicants are evaluated on their community involvement, academic achievement, leadership skills, financial needs, and their response to an essay topic. Contact the company for further information.

Papago Tribe

P.O. Box 837
Sells, AZ 85634

The tribe makes **financial aid** awards to help its members finance college training.

Pawnee Nation of Oklahoma

Education and Training Department
P.O. Box 470
Pawnee, OK 74058
918-762-2541

Tribal members pursuing education (including college, voc-tech, short-term courses, GED certificates) are eligible for **scholarship** assistance.

PCP Bar Association

P.O. Box 866
Orlando, FL 32808

The **Paul C. Perkins Bar Association Scholarship** of $1,000 is available to a senior at a university in Florida. Applicants must be accepted to an accredited law school.

Peninsula Community Foundation

1700 South El Camino Real, Suite 300
San Mateo, CA 94402-3049
650-358-9369
http://www.pcf.org

Up to 6 **scholarships** for gay/lesbian Asian students, of between $2,000 and $12,000 are awarded annually. This program is open to gay/lesbian high school seniors graduating from a San Mateo County public or private high school. Applicants must be United States citizens or legal residents of Asian descent. Asian countries are defined for the purpose of this grant as: Burma, Cambodia, China, Indonesia, Japan, Korea, Laos, Malaysia, Philippines, Singapore, Taiwan, Thailand, and Vietnam.

One **African-American Scholarship** of $5,000 is awarded annually. Applicants must be African-American, current graduating seniors of a high school in San Mateo or Northern Santa Clara Counties (Daly City to Mountain View), and must have a grade point average of at least 2.5. The award is contingent upon acceptance at a California Community College, State University or branch of the University of California (UC).

Pennsylvania, University of

Vice Provost for University Life
3611 Locust Walk
Philadelphia, PA 19104-6222
215-898-6081
http://www.upenn.edu

The **Andrew Mellon Minority Undergraduate Scholarship Program** is open to undergraduate students interested in pursuing college teaching careers in humanities or social sciences.

Pinellas County Education Foundation

775 Ulmerton Road, Suite 222
Largo, FL 34641

The **Samuel Robinson Scholarship** of $1,000 a year is open to a minority student from the St. Petersburg area who plans to study music in college.

Ponca Tribe of Oklahoma

Higher Education Program
P.O. Box 2, White Eagle
Ponca City, OK 74601
580-765-6871

Tribal members pursuing college study may apply for **financial aid**.

Presbyterian Church USA

Office of Financial Aid for Studies
100 Witherspoon Street
Louisville, KY 40202-1396
502-569-5760
http://pcusa.org

Financial Aid

Ira Page Wallace Bible Scholarships are awarded to African American students majoring in religion at related Historically Black Colleges.

Native American Seminary Scholarships help Native Americans, Aleuts, and Eskimos who have been accepted into a theological seminary.

Graduating high school seniors who are members of a racial minority may apply for up to 158 renewable **Student Opportunity Minority Scholarships** of $100 to $1,400. Applicants must be members of the Presbyterian Church (USA) and U.S. citizens. Hispanic, African American, Asian American, and Native American applicants are eligible. Apply by April 1.

Professional Hispanics in Energy

Scholarship Coordinator
P.O. Box 862616, Terminal Annex
Los Angeles, CA 90086-2616
909-396-3214

Hispanic students from the area who are preparing for careers in energy or the environment are eligible for **financial assistance**; candidates must have a 3.0 GPA.

Project Cambio Foundation

Program Director
P.O. Box 3004-227
Corvallis, OR 97339
503-929-6108

This organization offers $1,000 **scholarships** to Hispanic women planning to enter, re-enter, or advance in business careers. Apply by May 1.

Public Relations Society of America

33 Irving Place
New York, NY 10003-2376
212-995-2230
http://www.prsa.org

The PRSA Foundation offers two $1,500 **Multicultural Affairs Scholarships** annually to full-time minority communications students. Applicants must be in their junior or senior year at the time the scholarship is used. Membership in the Public Relations Student Society of America and a major or minor in public relations is preferred.

Pueblo of Acoma

Higher Education Programs Coordinator
P.O. Box 307
Pueblo of Acoma, NM 87034
506-552-6604

Scholarships are available for graduating seniors who belong to the Pueblo of Acoma Tribe and who are U.S. citizens. Applications are due May 1 and September 1.

Puerto Rican Legal Defense and Education Fund

99 Hudson Street, 14th Floor
New York, NY 10013
212-219-3360

This organization helps needy first- and second-year law students who have demonstrated a commitment to service with **awards** ranging from $500 to $1,000. Apply by September 15.

Puget Sound, University of

Office of Financial Aid and Scholarships
Tacoma, WA 98416
253-879-3214

Will and Susanna Thomas Scholarships of $7,000 are awarded annually, one each to an African American, Asian American, Hispanic American, and Native American freshman attending the University of Puget Sound. Selection is by academic merit and financial need. Apply by February 1. The award is renewable.

Bakke Scholars Program awards assist Christian students with financial need. Members of an ethnic minority are especially encouraged to apply. Three renewable scholarships are awarded annually to incoming freshmen attending the University of Puget Sound. Academic merit and financial need are considered.

Pyramid Lake Paiute Tribe

P.O. Box 256
Nixon, NV 87501

The tribe operates a **financial aid** program to help its members finance higher education.

Quinault Tribe

P.O. Box 189
Taholah, LA 98587
360-276-8211

The tribe provides **financial aid** to help its members finance vocational or college study.

Quinnipiac College

Mount Carmel Avenue
Hamden, CT 06518
203-281-8600
http://www.quinnipiac.edu

Diversity Scholarships are awarded to minority students and are renewable with satisfactory progress.

Radio and Television News Directors Foundation

1000 Connecticut Avenue, NW, Suite 615
Washington, DC 20036-5302
202-659-6510
http://www.rtndf.org

The $2,000 **Carole Simpson Scholarship** is available for a minority undergraduate student. Candidate must be a full-time college student whose career objective is electronic journalism. Applicant must have at least one full year of college remaining. To receive full award, winners must be officially enrolled in college and be in good standing. Scholarship is paid in semi-annual installments for one year of study.

The $2,500 **Ken Kashiwahara Scholarship** is awarded to a minority undergraduate student. Candidate must be a full-time college student whose career objective is electronic journalism. Applicant must have at least one full year of college remaining. To receive the full award, winners must be officially enrolled in college and be in good standing. Scholarship is paid in semi-annual installments for one year of study.

The **Ed Bradley Scholarship** offers one-year, $5,000 awards for college students in broadcast journalism. Preference is given to minorities. Applicants must have at least one full year of college remaining.

Real Estate and Land Use Institute

Scholarship Selection Committee
7700 College Town Drive, Suite 200
Sacramento, CA 95826-2304
916-278-6633

Scholarships averaging $502 to $1,101 each are available each year for low-income and educationally disadvantaged students enrolled, at least part-time, in one of the 23 California State University campuses. Applicants must be pursuing careers in the real estate industry, demonstrate financial need, and have a minimum GPA of 2.5 (3.0 for graduates). Applications are due April 30.

Red Cloud Indian Art Show

Heritage Center, Inc.
P.O. Box 100
Pine Ridge, SD 57770-0100
605-867-5491
http://www.basec.net/~rcheritage/artshow.html

Native American tribal members age 18 or older who submit artistic works to the art show are eligible for the $5,000 **Thunderbird Foundation Scholarship**. Applications are due in May. Applicants must enter artwork in the Red Cloud Indian Art Show to be eligible for the scholarship.

Reforma

University of Arizona Library
P.O. Box 210005
Tucson, AZ 85721

REFORMA, a professional association of Hispanic librarians, offers a $2,000 **scholarship** for study toward a master's degree in library science.

Financial Aid

Rider University
2083 Lawrenceville Road
Lawrenceville, NJ 08648
609-896-5042
http://rider.edu

Merit scholarships are awarded to minority students with strong academic records. Candidates must apply to the university no later than March 1 of their senior year and pay their admission deposit by May 1.

Rochester Institute of Technology
One Lomb Memorial Drive
Rochester, NY 14623-5603
716-475-6631
http://www.rit.edu

Among the programs offered are $3,000 **Urban League Scholarships**; $3,000 **Ibero-American Action League Scholarships** for Hispanic candidates; and **Minority Transfer Scholarships** of $3,000. All awards are based on both financial need and academic merit. Minority candidates who are semifinalists or finalists in the National Achievement Scholarship or National Hispanic Scholars programs are guaranteed academic (merit-based) scholarships worth $10,000 or more per year.

Rutgers University, New Brunswick
Office of Financial Aid
New Brunswick, NJ 08903
201-932-7755

James Carr Scholarships provide up to $5,000 a year to aid students of color. These are also offered on the Camden and Newark campuses. In addition, **Rutgers University Awards for Academic Achievement** of $1,000 are offered to undergraduate students, and **Minority Academic Fellowships** of up to $14,000 a year plus tuition are open to graduate students. Write for application criteria and deadline information.

Sacramento Bee
Community Relations Department
P.O. Box 15779
2100 Q Street
Sacramento, CA 95852
916-321-1790

Mass media **scholarships** for minority students are open to residents of the Sacramento Bee's metropolitan, three-county, statistical circulation area. Students may be attending an accredited college or university in any part of the country. Awards are up to $3,000 per year.

Sacramento Hispanic Chamber of Commerce
P.O. Box 161933
Sacramento, CA 95816
916-554-7420
http://www.sachcc.org

Scholarships of $500 are available to eligible Hispanic students graduating from high school who are from the Sacramento area and are planning to attend a 2-year or 4-year institution. Applicants should be pursuing degrees in business, engineering, computer science, or a related field. Applications are due in January.

Saint John's University School of Law
8000 Utopia Parkway
Jamaica, NY 11439
718-990-6600

A joint-degree program is operated by the School of Law at St. John's and the United Negro College Fund. Students who have completed three years of undergraduate work at a UNCF institution are eligible for full, three-year law school **scholarships** from St. John's. Awards include tuition and books with the option of additional support, if needed. At the end of the three years of law school training, students receive both a bachelor's degree from their UNCF college as well as a law degree from St. John's.

Santo Domingo Tribe Scholarship Program
P.O. Box 99
Santo Domingo, NM 87052
505-465-2214

Scholarships are available to members of the Santo Domingo Tribe who demonstrate financial need.

Sara Lee Foundation

Scholarship Coordinator
Three First National Plaza
Chicago, IL 60602-4260
312-558-8448

The **National Achievement Scholarships** are open to African Americans who are the children of Sara Lee Corporation employees.

School for International Training

P.O. Box 676
Brattleboro, VT 05302-0676
800-336-1616
http://www.sit.edu

The school has **Diversity Scholarships** for minority students enrolled in any of the degree or study-abroad programs. Deadlines to apply vary; please check Web site or call for details. The school's toll-free telephone number is 800-336-1616.

Seminole Tribe of Florida

6300 Stirling Road
Hollywood, FL 33024-2161
800-683-7800
http://www.seminoletribe.com

Higher Education Awards are granted to enrolled tribal members who are at least one-fourth Seminole Indian for study at an accredited college or university in the state. Awards are renewable.

Seneca Nation of Indians

Scholarship Coordinator
Higher Education Program
P.O. Box 231
Salamanca, NY 14779
716-945-1790

Members of the Seneca Nation of Indians who are enrolled in an accredited postsecondary institution approved by the foundation's board of trustees are eligible for **scholarships** of up to $5,000. Applicants must be U.S. citizens. Application deadlines are July 15, December 31, and May 20.

Shell Oil Company Foundation

P.O. Box 2099
One Shell Plaza
Houston, TX 77252
713-241-3616
http://www.shelloil.com

The **Shell Incentive Funds Program** offers awards to ethnic minorities for undergraduate study in business or a technical field. Preference is given to Inroads students. Candidates must be nominated by the academic department or area in which the Incentive Fund is offered at the school they attend; individuals should not apply directly to the foundation.

Shoshone Higher Education Programs

Scholarship Coordinator
P.O. Box 628
Fort Washakie, WY 82514
307-332-2920

Scholarships for higher education are available to members of the Wind River Shoshone Tribe.

Simmons College

Graduate School of Management
Office of Student Financial Aid
409 Commonwealth Avenue
Boston, MA 02215
617-521-3840
http://www.simmons.edu/gsm

The school offers a one-year, full-time M.B.A. and a two- or three-year, part-time M.B.A. The **Graduate School of Management Minority Scholarship** assists minority women with demonstrated financial need. Apply by March 1. (Extensions beyond this date are granted on an individual basis.)

Sisters' Alumni of South Pacific

c/o Alpine Village
833 West Torrance Boulevard, Suite 1
Torrance, CA 90502

The **California Scholarship Fund** of $1,000 is available for students of Pacific Island heritage.

Sitka Tribe of Alaska Higher Education Program

456 Katlian Street
Sitka, AK 99835
907-747-3207

Scholarships are available for members of the Alaskan Sitka Tribes.

Society of Hispanic Professional Engineers Foundation

Scholarship Coordinator
5400 East Olympic Boulevard, Suite 210
Los Angeles, CA 90022
323-725-3970
http://www.shpe.org

Each year, $200,000 is given to outstanding science and engineering students from colleges and universities all over the country. The **scholarship** program is dedicated to providing financial assistance to students from 12th grade to college so they can broaden their opportunities in math, science, and engineering. Many of the recipients are SHPE student chapter leaders who are developing leadership skills and providing academic support to fellow students.

Society of Mexican American Engineers and Scientists

3780 Kilroy Airport Way, Suite 200
Long Beach, CA 90806
562-988-6585
http://www.tamu.edu/maes

Student members (high school and college) of the Society of Mexican American Engineers and Scientists (MAES) are eligible for **scholarship** awards through MAES local professional chapters and its National Symposium.

Society of Women Engineers

120 Wall Street, 11th Floor
New York, NY 10005-3902
212-509-9577
http://www.swe.org

The society administers a number of **scholarships** for women studying computer science or engineering, including the **Chrysler Corporation Scholarship** of $1,750 for minority

women who are juniors or seniors. Candidates must have a 3.5 GPA. Several awards are offered to members of the SWE only. Please send a self-addressed, stamped envelope with your request for information.

The **Rockwell International Corporation Scholarships** are awarded to minority women engineering or computer science students entering their junior years. Two awards of $3,000 are available. The recipients must have demonstrated leadership ability.

South Carolina, University of

College of Journalism
Columbia, SC 29208
803-777-4105
http://www.jour.sc.edu

USC offers a $6,000 **scholarship** to a minority student of journalism or mass communication.

South Dakota Board of Regents

306 East Capitol Avenue, Suite 200
Pierre, SD 57501
605-773-3455
http://www.ris.sdbor.edu

Native Americans living in North or South Dakota are eligible for the $500 **Ardell Bjugstad Scholarship** to help finance college study in environmental fields, including agribusiness, agriculture, and natural resources management. Only graduating high school seniors are eligible. Apply by February 18.

Southern Baptist Convention

Black Church Extension Division Scholarship
4200 North Point Parkway
Chicago, IL 60637
770-410-6000

This **scholarship** is available to African Americans pursuing Christian vocations.

Southern Methodist University

Office of Financial Aid
P.O. Box 181
Dallas, TX 75275
214-768-2058

SMU recognizes outstanding academic performance, talents, and leadership abilities by awarding numerous merit **scholarships** to students from broad economic, cultural, and geographic backgrounds.

Southwest State University

1501 State Street
Marshall, MN 56258-3306
507-537-7021
http://www.southwest.msus.edu

Bremer Scholarships and **SSU Grants** are available for minority students. The **Sather Scholarship** is awarded to a Native American student. To qualify for either scholarship, students must be attending Southwest State University.

Southwest Texas State University

601 University Drive
San Marcos, TX 78666
512-245-2315
http://www.swt.edu

The **LBJ Achievement Scholarship** provides up to a $2,000 award to freshman, transfer, and continuing students who are enrolled full-time, ranked in the top quarter of their high school graduating class (if an entering freshman), and are current or past participants in one of the following programs: Talent Search; Educational Opportunity Center; Student Support Services; High School Equivalency Program; College Assistance Migrant Program; Youth Opportunities Unlimited; Summer Enrichment Program; Subsidized Secondary Lunch Program.

Southwestern University, School of Law

675 South Westmoreland Avenue
Los Angeles, CA 90005-3992
213-738-6717
http://www.swlaw.edu

Scholarships from the **Dino Hirsch Memorial Endowment Fund** are awarded to Hispanic law students with financial need who are planning to pusue public interest careers.

Established by Ms. Sarah Kim, a prominent member of the Korean business community, the **Sarah Kim Endowment Fund** provides scholarships for Korean-American students with financial need.

The law school awards between 20 and 25 **John J. Schumacher Minority Leadership Scholarships** annually to first-year law students who possess outstanding academic and leadership qualities. Providing up to full tuition, the scholarships are renewed based on academic performance.

The **Beverly Hills Bar Association Scholarship** Foundation Board of Directors provides a number of scholarships to minority law students in need of financial assistance. Preference is given to second- or third-year students.

The **Y. C. Hong Memorial Scholarship** is awarded by the Southern California Chinese Lawyers Association in December of each year to a student who has completed the first year of law school.

Awards from the **Bernard Burch Memorial Scholarship Endowment Fund** are granted to minority evening students who are also working parents with demonstrated financial need.

Special Libraries Association

1700 18th Street, NW
Washington, DC 20009
202-234-4700
http://www.sla.org

The **Affirmative Action Scholarship Program** offers awards of up to $6,000 to help minority students complete a graduate degree in library science.

163

Financial Aid

Spelman College

Office of Financial Aid
350 Spelman Lane, SW
Atlanta, GA 30314-4399
404-681-3643
http://www.spelman.edu

Minority women pursuing study in medicine are eligible for **scholarships** provided with funds from the Noyes Foundation. Because Spellman is a predominantly black institution, most of the financial aid awards go to minority students.

This historically black college for women offers $2,000 **Academic Scholarships** and **Honors Scholarships** of $3,000 to $5,000 a year. Both are based on merit and academic record.

Spokane Tribe

Higher Education Department
P.O. Box 389
Wellpoint, IN 82514

A **financial aid** program is offered to help tribal members finance their postsecondary education.

State Student Assistance Commission of Indiana

150 West Market Street, Suite 500
Indianapolis, IN 46204
317-232-2350
http://www.ai.org/ssaci/

The **Minority Teacher Scholarship** addresses the critical shortage of African American and Hispanic teachers in Indiana. The maximum annual scholarship is $1,000. However, if the applicant demonstrates financial need he/she may be eligible to receive up to $4,000 annually. To apply, contact a high school guidance office or a college/university financial aid office. To be eligible you must be: 1) a minority student (defined as African American or Hispanic) seeking a teaching certification; or a student seeking a Special Education teaching certification; or a student seeking an Occupational or Physical Therapy certification; 2) an Indiana resident; 3) admitted to an eligible institution as a full time student or already attending as a full time student; 4) pursuing or intend to pursue a course of study that would enable the student upon graduation to teach in an accredited elementary or secondary school in Indiana.

State University of New York, Brockport

Office of Admissions
Brockport, NY 14420
716-395-2751
http://www.brockport.edu

African American freshmen are eligible to apply for the **Urban League Black Scholars** Award and SUNY Empire State/Brockport College Foundation Minority Honors Scholarship program. This is made available to both freshmen and transfers.

State University of New York, Fredonia

Fredonia, NY 14063
716-673-3251
http://www.fredonia.edu

Fredonia offers four **Empire Minority Honors Scholarships**.

Stetson University, Gulfport

School of Law
Gulfport, FL 33707-3299
727-562-7809
http://www.law.stetson.edu

The School of Law offers $1,000 to $2,000 **Stetson Grants** for which minority students are particularly sought. Application deadlines are in March and September. **Merit Scholarships** are offered to incoming applicants who demonstrate exceptional academic promise. These scholarships vary in amount and are renewable for three years. Selection is made solely on the basis of merit at the time of application to Stetson. **Need Based Scholarships** are offered to incoming applicants who complete the FAFSA as well as a Supplemental Need Based Application. The purpose of this scholarship program is to assist students with financial need in pursuing a legal education and to promote diversity in our student body. These scholarships vary in amount and are renewable for three years.

Studio Art Centers International

809 United Nations Plaza
New York, NY 10017-3580
800-344-9186
http://www.saci-florence.org

Founded in 1975, Studio Art Centers International (SACI) is a U.S. university level, studio art school based in Florence, Italy. One full **scholarship** and a number of partial in-house scholarships are awarded in two competitions held annually. SACI's scholarships are based on a two-part criteria—outstanding ability and demonstrated financial need. One of SACI's scholarships is the **International Incentive Awards**. This offers $2,000 per term to underrepresented minority students of art or art history with a minimum G.P.A. of 3.0 to study at SACI. Completed applications and supporting materials must be submitted to SACI's New York office by March 31 for the academic year beginning the following fall or by October 15 for the spring and/or late spring/summer terms.

Synod of the Covenant

Cabinet on Ethnic Church Affairs
6172 Busch Boulevard, Suite 3000
Columbus, OH 43229
614-436-3310
http://www.synodofcovenant.org

A $600 **scholarship** is offered to Presbyterians within the synod bounds (Ohio and Michigan) who are disadvantaged because of systematic racism and poverty. Awards may be used for post-high school education in undergraduate colleges and vocational schools. Up to $2,000 in scholarship money is available for study at an accredited theological seminary.

TELACU Education Foundation

5400 East Olympic Boulevard, Suite 300
Los Angeles, CA 90022
213-721-1655

The **TELACU Education Foundation's Scholarship Program** helps Latino college students in the Los Angeles area to attend Southern California colleges and universities. Scholarships range from $500 to $1,500 per year, and special awards of up to $10,000 are available to students in engineering, education and post-graduate law or public administration. Requirements: Students must be from Los Angeles city, unincorporated East Los Angeles or the cities/communities of Montebello, Commerce, Bell Gardens, or Monterey Park. They must attend one of 17 participating colleges: The Cal State campuses of Fullerton, Long Beach, Los Angeles, Northridge, and Cal Poly, Pomona; Azusa Pacific University, East L.A. College, Loyola Marymount, Mount St. Mary's, Harvey Mudd, Occidental, Pepperdine, University of La Verne, UC Irvine, UCLA, USC, and Whittier College.

Tennessee Technological University

Office of Financial Aid
P.O. Box 5076
Cookeville, TN 38505
615-372-3101

Approximately 40 **scholarships** averaging $2,000 each are awarded to minority students.

Tennessee, University of, Knoxville

Office of Financial Aid
320 Student Services Building
Knoxville, TN 37996
423-974-2341

Students of color are eligible for special **scholarship** assistance in the colleges of business, engineering, architecture, and education.

The **Minority Undergraduate Scholarship** provides $1,000 to $2,000 for African American freshmen who are finalists, semifinalists, or commended students in the National Achievement competition. Apply by January 15.

More than 50 **scholarships** averaging $1,000 each are reserved specifically for minority undergraduate students. Apply by January 15.

Texas A&M University, College Station

Office of Financial Aid
College Station, TX 77843-4233
409-845-3236

Financial Aid

Minority students with financial need who are majoring in agriculture may apply for $500 **scholarships**.

Thornton (Ann C.) Memorial Fund Scholarship

90633 Highway 240
Coos Bay, OR 97420-9645
541-888-4584
http://www.scoregon.com

These $750 scholarships are open to American Indian or Alaska Native students who are residents of the state and active in their school and community. Apply by May 1.

Thunderbird: The American School of International Management

Office of Admissions
15249 North 59th Avenue
Glendale, AZ 85306
602-978-7210
http://www.t-bird.edu

Thunderbird, the oldest graduate school of international management in the world, aims to increase enrollment among underrepresented minority groups and, to that end, offers tuition **scholarships** to qualified applicants.

Tonkawa Tribe of Oklahoma

Higher Education Department
P.O. Box 70
Tonkawa, OK 74653

The tribe offers **financial aid** to help its members finance study at a postsecondary institution.

Tulalip Tribe

Higher Education Department
6700 Totem Beach Road
Marysville, MA 98270

Tribal members pursuing college or vocational study are eligible for **scholarship** assistance.

Tuskegee University

Office of Financial Aid
Tuskegee, AL 36088
800-622-6531
http://www.tusk.edu

The music department at this historically black college offers a number of $800 **awards** to its choir students.

Tuskegee offers five **scholarship** programs to help African Americans pursuing careers in education.

Scholarships are offered to engineering technology majors at this historically black university. Also available are graduate assistantships in engineering, chemistry, and the natural sciences.

U.S. Department of Agriculture

14th and Independence Avenue, SW
Washington, DC 20250
202-720-2791
http://www.usda.gov

The National Scholars Program offers **scholarships** including tuition, books, and summer employment for students majoring in agriculture or a related field at one of 17 historically black colleges or universities. Apply through a participating school. The American Indian Natural Resource Program recruits Native Americans for U.S. Forest Service positions; for details, call 303/498-1793. The department also offers grants to colleges and universities to be used to help minority agriculture majors. These monies are given to the colleges who, in turn, provide financial aid and other assistance to their students.

U.S. Department of Energy

Office of Minority Economic Impact
MI-22 Forrestal Building, Room 5B-110
Washington, DC 20585
202-586-1953
http://home.doe.gov

A **Minority Honors Training and Industrial Assistance Program** provides scholarships for students enrolled in computer science, electronics, engineering sciences, or technology, or a related field at a two-year college. Apply through cooperating schools.

U.S. Department of Health and Human Services, Rockville

Twinbrook Metro Plaza Building
12300 Twinbrook Parkway, Suite 100
Rockville, MD 20852
301-443-6197

The **Health Professions Preparatory Compensatory Preprofessional Scholarship** provides financial support for Indian students to enroll in courses that will prepare them for acceptance into health professional schools.

The Indian Health Service offers a **Health Professions Pregraduate Program** which gives preference to undergraduate Native Americans studying medicine, osteopathy, or dentistry. Recipients must work a year in the Indian Health Service industry for each year they receive the scholarship.

The **Health Professions Scholarship** provides financial support to Indian students enrolled in health professions and allied health professions programs. Recipients of the scholarship incur a year of service for each year of scholarship support received. The minimum period of service is 2 years. Applicants must: 1) be an American Indian or Alaska Native; 2) be a high school graduate or equivalent; 3) be enrolled or accepted for enrollment in a full- or part-time study program leading to a degree in a health related professions school within the United States for one of the health career "Priority Categories" published annually in the *Federal Register*.

U.S. Department of Housing and Urban Development

University Partnerships Clearinghouse
P.O. Box 6091
Rockville, MD 20849
800-245-2691
http://www.oup.org

HUD offers the **Community Development Work Study Program** to low-income and minority graduate students in community development, economics, or related disciplines.

U.S. Department of the Interior

Bureau of Indian Affairs
1849 C Street, NW
Washington, DC 20240-0001
202-208-3711
http://www.doi.gov/bureau-indian-affairs.html

The **Higher Education Grant Program** provides scholarships to Native Americans and Alaska Natives with financial need.

U.S. Hispanic Chamber of Commerce

1019 19th Street, NW, Suite 200
Washington, DC 20036
202-842-1212
http://www.ushcc.com

Ten **scholarships** of $1,000 each are awarded annually to Hispanic students enrolled in a college, university, or vocational program. Selection is based on academic achievement, community involvement, and financial need; applications are due July 15. The USHCC also publishes the "National Hispanic Business Directory," which lists firms with Hispanic owners. There is no charge for the listing.

U.S. National Aeronautics and Space Administration

204 Engineering Tower
300 E Street, SW
Washington, DC 20546
714-824-4189
http://www.nasa.gov

The **Undergraduate Student Researchers Program** offers $12,000 awards to underrepresented students and students with disabilities who are interested in a career in science, mathematics, computer science, or engineering. Applicants must be United States citizens in good academic standing with no more than 32 credit hours by the end of the school year. Apply by April 26.

Financial Aid

United Church of Christ, Southern California Nevada Conference

Scholarship Chair
2401 North Lake Avenue
Altadena, CA 91001
626-798-8082

African American female members of the UCC church in the Southern California area are eligible for $500 **scholarships**; applications are due May 1.

United Methodist Communications

Scholarship Committee
P.O. Box 320
Nashville, TN 37202-0320
615-742-5140
http://www.umcom.org/scholarships

The **Leonard M. Perryman Communications Scholarship for Ethnic Minority Students** awards $2,500 to a college junior or senior for study emphasizing religious communications. Applications are due March 15.

United South and Eastern Tribes

711 Stewarts Ferry Pike, Suite 100
Nashville, TN 37214
615-872-7900
http://www.oneida-nation.net/uset

Native American students in the USET service area are eligible for **scholarships** in the amount of $500.

Ute Tribe

Higher Education Department
Fort Duchesne, UT 84026

The tribe operates a **financial aid** program for members seeking college or vocational training.

Vanderbilt University

Office of Undergraduate Admission
2305 West End Avenue
Nashville, TN 37203
800-288-0432
http://www.vanderbilt.edu

Chancellor's Scholarships providing four years of tuition are open to minority students based on academic merit.

Vermont, University of

Financial Aid Office
Burlington, VT 05401
802-656-3156
http://www.uvm.edu

UVM has a variety of merit and financial need-based scholarships. Several **scholarships** are available for students with a demonstrated commitment to diversity. There is no separate application process. By completing the UVM Admissions application, a student will automatically be considered for UVM-based scholarships.

Vikki Carr Scholarship Foundation

P.O. Box 57756
Sherman Oaks, CA 91413

Renewable **scholarships** of $500 to $3,000 are available to California residents of Mexican American ancestry who are 17 to 22 years old. Write for application by February 1; apply by March 1.

Wake Forest University

Office of Admissions
Box 7305, Reynolda Station
Winston-Salem, NC 27109
336-758-5201
http://www.wfu.edu

The **Joseph G. Gordon Scholarships** award 7 full-tuition scholarships each year to underrepresented students who show exceptional achievement and promise of leadership. At least 3 other students will receive partial tuition scholarships of $2,000 or more. This program was established to demonstrate Wake Forest's strong commitment to provide educational and professional opportunities for and to benefit from the contributions of diverse students. Candidates may file either the Reynolds or Carswell application.

Washington College

Financial Aid Office
Chestertown, MD 21620
410-778-2800
http://www.washcoll.edu

Starr Scholarships are open to minorities.

Washington Society of Certified Public Accountants

902 140th Avenue, NE
Bellevue, WA 98005-3480
425-644-4800
http://www.wscpa.org

The CPA Foundation for Education, Inc., offers a non-renewable tuition **scholarship** annually to a minority accounting student at an accredited four-year institution in Washington state. Applicants must have completed their junior year of study by June 1. The amount of the scholarship is based on annual tuition costs for Washington state public colleges and universities.

Washington University, St. Louis

Office of Undergraduate Admissions
One Brookings Drive
Campus Box 1089
St. Louis, MO 63130
314-935-6000
http://www.wustl.edu

In addition to awarding more than $40 million in scholarships and grants each year, Washington University's **John B. Ervin Scholarship Program** recognizes the educational and leadership achievements of African-American students by awarding students full tuition for 4 years and an annual stipend of $2,500. The scholarship, worth more than $100,000 in total, is renewed for each of the remaining 3 years provided the student maintains a satisfactory academic record. In addition to the financial award, recipients participate in an ongoing series of programs.

Designed to recognize Hispanic students of outstanding merit, the **Annika Rodriguez Scholarship** provides for full tuition with a $2,500 annual stipend. It's awarded for 4 years

of undegraduate study, provided the student maintains satisfactory academic progress.

Washington, University of

Financial Aid Office
1410 Northeast Campus Parkway
Seattle, WA 98195
206-543-9686

Freshman Merit Awards of $1,000 to $2,000 are available for residents of Washington State who are in the Educational Opportunity Program.

Weber State University

Scholarship Office
1137 University Circle
Ogden, UT 84408-1137
801-626-6029
http://www.weber.edu/scholarships

Special academic **scholarships** are available for minority students.

West Virginia University

Scholars Office
PO Box 6410
Morgantown, WV 26506
800-344-9881
http://www.wvu.edu

Incoming African American freshmen are eligible for **scholarships**. The university also awards more than 20 **Storer Scholarships** to first-year African American students with a minimum high school GPA of 3.25 and a minimum SAT composite score of 1050 or an ACT score of 23. The minimum value of this scholarship is $1,250 per year for four years. The maximum value of the award is $3,000 for 4 undergraduate years. Applications must be submitted by February 1.

Western Illinois University

One University Circle
Macomb, IL 61455-1390
309-298-2001
http://www.wiu.edu/foundation/scholarship.htm

The **DuSable Scholarship** provides 4 awards of up to $1,000 for freshman or transfer students from underrepresented groups. Minimum ACT

Financial Aid

of 22 and upper 15 percent for freshmen, and 3.0 (on 4.0 scale) cumulative GPA for transfer. Apply early.

The **Western Opportunity Scholarship** provides awards of up to $2,200 for freshmen students from underrepresented groups. Some awards are renewable at $1,000 level based on major and GPA. Minimum ACT is 25. Apply early.

Western Kentucky University

Department of Journalism
Bowling Green, KY 42101-3576
502-745-4143
http://www.wku.edu/journalism

The $500 **Joseph Dear Scholarship** for minority students in advertising, broadcasting, journalism, or photojournalism is awarded based on academics and publication experience. The journalism department also holds a workshop for minorities each summer.

Western Washington University

Student Support Services—Multicultural Support and Retention
Old Main 110
Bellingham, WA 98225
360-650-3844
http://www.wwu.com

The **Martin Luther King, Jr. Scholarship** is awarded to African American students with leadership ability and academic achievement. Deadline to apply is April 15.

Women of Evangelical Lutheran Church in America

Amelia Kemp Memorial Fund
8765 West Higgins Road
Chicago, IL 60631-4189
800-638-3522

Women of color belonging to the ELCA are eligible for the **Kemp Scholarship** to aid with undergraduate, graduate, professional, or vocational study.

Women On Books

Scholarship Committee
879 Rainier Avenue North, Suite A105
Renton, WA 98055
206-626-2323

Women On Books is an African-American women's book club that has created a scholarship to support educational opportunities for African-American students. The $1,000 **scholarship** is available to students of African-American descent attending a 4-year college or university pursuing a degree in English, journalism, or related field. Applicants should demonstrate financial need, and must have a minimum 2.5 GPA; they should also intend to pursue a writing career (creative or journalism). Write for more information and application guidelines.

Xerox Technical Minority Scholarship Program

907 Culver Road
Rochester, NY 14609
716-482-3887
http://www.xerox.com

The program awards **scholarships** to minority students enrolled in one of the technical sciences or engineering disciplines. This scholarship is available to U.S. citizens and individuals with Permanent Resident visas. An applicant must be a full-time student enrolled in a 4-year institution; have a B average or better; at graduation will receive a BS, MS, or PhD in a technical science or an engineering discipline; must be African American, Asian American, Pacific Islander, Native American, Alaskan, or Hispanic; and have outstanding expenses (tuition related) not covered by other scholarships or grants (excluding loans).

Yakima Nation

Yakima Indian Agency
Box 151
Toppenish, WA 98948
509-865-5121

Tribal members are eligible for **financial aid** to help meet the costs of undergraduate and graduate education. Awards average $1,000. Apply by July 1.

Youth For Understanding International Exchange

3501 Newark Street, NW
Washington, DC 20016-3199
800-TEENAGE
http://www.youthforunderstanding.org

The **Dewitt Wallace/Youth Travel Enrichment Fund** is a nationwide competition for 40 minority high school students in grades 9-12 to spend the summer in select countries. Students must have at least a 2.0 GPA and annual family income must not exceed $55,000. The scholarship includes domestic and international travel, insurance, and $150 toward spending money. Recipients must pay a $650 program contribution.

The **Young Leaders Fellowship Awards** provide full scholarships for up to 2 African-American students to participate in the Youth For Understanding (YFU) International Exchange year program to Germany.

Zeta Phi Beta Sorority, Washington

1734 New Hampshire Avenue, NW
Washington, DC 20009-2595
202-387-3103
http://www.zpb1920.org

The **Isabel M. Herson Scholarship** is open to African American women enrolled in an undergraduate or graduate program leading to a degree in elementary or secondary education. Stipends range from $500 to $1,000. Recipients need not be members of Zeta Phi Beta Sorority.

Undergraduate Scholarships of up to $1,000 are available for college study for black women in the top 25 percent of their high school classes. Applicants must be recommended by a ZPB chapter. Apply by February 1. **Deborah Partridge Wolfe International Fellowships** provide about $1,000 to help African American women pursue undergraduate or graduate study abroad. Applicants need not be Zeta members. Awards are renewable. African Fellowships of up to $1,000 are open to active black sorority members for graduate study. Apply by February 1.

Zuni Scholarship Program

P.O. Box 339
Zuni, NM 87327-0339
505-782-4481

Students of one-fourth or more Zuni blood are eligible for **scholarship** assistance to help finance college study.

United Negro College Fund Scholarships

United Negro College Fund

8260 Willow Oaks Corporate Drive
Fairfax, VA 22031
800-331-2244
http://www.uncf.org

UNCF is the nation's oldest and most successful African American higher education assistance organization. It is a consortium of 39 private, accredited 4-year historically black colleges and universities. UNCF offers programs designed to enhance the quality of education for America's brightest young minds, and is committed to providing financial assistance to deserving students, raising operating funds for member colleges and universities, and supplying technical assistance to member institutions. UNCF oversees more than 400 scholarship programs; visit the Web site for a listing of opportunities and application information. A sampling of UNCF scholarships is listed below.

A&P Grocery Management Program

Scholarships and summer internships in retail management are available for students attending UNCF schools. Apply through your financial aid department.

Financial Aid

Amway/Ebony Business Leadership Scholarship Program

Students majoring in business administration at UNCF colleges can apply for this scholarship through their financial aid offices.

Avon Women in Search of Excellence Scholarship

Female UNCF students majoring in business or economics can apply through their financial aid departments for a scholarship. At least half of the awards go to students of nontraditional college age.

Becton Dickinson and Company Scholarship Program

Students maintaining a minimum GPA of 3.5 at UNCF schools are eligible for this scholarship.

Bryant Gumbel/Walt Disney World Tournament Scholarship Program

Eighty scholarships per year are awarded to juniors and seniors of UNCF schools. Students must major in liberal arts, maintain a 3.0 GPA, and apply through their financial aid offices.

CBS Career Horizons Internship/Scholarship Program

Sophomores and juniors enrolled at HBCUs are eligible for a summer internship, a $5,000 stipend, and an $8,000 scholarship. Students must be majoring in accounting, business, finance, marketing, mass communications, or journalism; must have a minimum GPA of 3.0; and must be nominated by their financial aid departments.

Charles Schwab and Co. Scholarship

Business and economic majors attending Florida A&M, Bethune-Cookman, Morehouse, Spelman, or Clark Atlanta University are eligible for scholarship support.

Chemical Bank/John F. McGillicuddy Scholarship

Seniors at New York City's John Jay and George Washington High Schools planning to attend UNCF member colleges are eligible for this scholarship.

Chicago Inter-Alumni Scholarship

The Chicago Inter-Alumni Council sponsors a pageant competition for Chicago high school students planning to attend a UNCF school. Top winners receive up to $25,000. Contact your school guidance counselor or career advisor for application materials.

Chicago Public Schools

Students attending Chicago Public Schools are eligible for a tuition and fees scholarship administered through the UNCF.

Chrysler Fund Scholarship

Students attending Clark Atlanta University, Morehouse College, Spelman College, or Tuskegee University are eligible for scholarships from this fund. Apply through your college's financial aid department.

Consolidated Edison Scholarship Program

As administered by the UNCF, this scholarship provides for students of New York City and Westchester County, New York.

CSX Corporation Scholars Program

Students attending HBCUs and UNCF schools are eligible for an educational and internship program focusing on the environment.

Doris and John Carpenter Scholarship

Students attending UNCF schools and demonstrating financial need are eligible for renewable scholarships.

Duquesne Light Scholarship

Students attending a UNCF school and who reside in Allegheny and Beaver counties of southwestern Pennsylvania should contact their financial aid directors for scholarship information.

Eddie Bauer Scholars Program

This scholarship for students majoring in business administration, computer science, marketing, and other subjects related to the retail industry includes a summer internship.

Emerson Electric Company Endowed Scholarship

College students in St. Louis, Missouri, are eligible for scholarships.

GAP Foundation Scholars Program

UNCF students from Bethune-Cookman College, Clark Atlanta University, Atlanta University, Voorhees College, and Fisk University are eligible for scholarships. Students must be pursuing degrees in fashion design, merchandise management, retail management, or business administration.

General Motors Engineering Excellence Awards

Engineering students at UNCF colleges and other HBCUs are eligible for scholarships. Apply through your financial aid office.

Grumman Scholarship for Peace and Justice

Students who have demonstrated a commitment to social change can compete for these scholarships. Students must attend a UNCF school, and apply through their financial aid office.

Harry C. Jaecker Scholarship

UNCF premedical students can apply through their financial aid office for scholarship consideration.

Hewlett Packard Scholarship Program

California residents attending a UNCF school are eligible for scholarships.

Higgins Scholarship

Juniors and Seniors at UNCF schools pursuing premedical courses are eligible for scholarship support, as are first- and second-year Morehouse Medical School students.

Imperial Chemical Industries/Zeneca Scholarship Program

Students from Delaware are eligible for full-tuition scholarships. Applicants must be nominated by their financial aid director.

James M. Johnston Foundation Scholarship

Students from Washington, D.C., attending UNCF schools are eligible for financial aid from the James E. Johnston Trust for Charitable and Educational Purposes.

Financial Aid

Jay Levine Endowed Scholarship Program

Students from Detroit, Mich., can apply through their financial aid department for this UNCF scholarship.

John Lennon Scholarship Fund

UNCF students in the performing arts or communications can apply through their financial aid offices for this scholarship.

Ladders of Hope Program

Disadvantaged minority students from South Central Los Angeles are eligible for grants to help them to attend UNCF colleges and universities.

Laffey-McHugh Foundation Scholarship

Students from Delaware are eligible for this scholarship. Applicants must be UNCF students, and must be nominated by their financial aid department.

Leo Burnett Scholarship Program

Scholarships and internships are available to UNCF students majoring in liberal arts with concentrations in marketing or creative design. Apply through your financial aid office.

Lynde and Harry Bradley Foundation Scholarship

UNCF students from Wisconsin can apply through their financial aid departments for this scholarship.

Malcolm Pirnie Scholars Program

Scholarships and summer internships are available for students of UNCF schools. Students must be majoring in civil, chemical, or environ-mental engineering, and must be nominated by their financial aid department.

Malcolm X Scholarship Program

Students demonstrating academic excellence and community leadership can compete for a renewable scholarship. Contact your financial aid department for application details.

Metropolitan Life Scholarship Program

UNCF juniors and seniors majoring in teacher education and health-related fields can apply through their financial aid offices for this scholarship.

Michael Jackson Endowed Scholarship Fund

Students majoring in the performing arts or communications at a UNCF school can apply through their financial aid department for this scholarship.

Minnesota/Iowa/Nebraska Student Aid Program

Scholarships of $2,500 a year are available to students in the 3 state area who demonstrate financial need and attend UNCF schools. Students must maintain a GPA of 2.5, and must apply through their financial aid departments.

Mitsubishi Motors Young Entrepreneurs Program

Students attending UNCF schools, or Hispanic Associated Colleges and Universities, are eligible for this business training program and $5,000 scholarship.

Morgan Stanley/Richard B. Fisher Scholars Program

Scholarships and summer internships are available to students pursuing careers in finance and banking, and who attend Spelman, Morehouse, or Fisk.

New York Health and Human Services Fund

New York City residents attending UNCF schools can apply through their financial aid departments for this scholarship.

NYNEX Scholarship

UNCF students who reside in the NYNEX service area are eligible for scholarships. Contact your finacial aid department.

Pacific Northwest Scholarship Program

Residents of Washington, Alaska, Oregon, Idaho, Montana, and Wyoming are eligible for scholarships as administered by the UNCF. Apply through your financial aid department.

PaineWebber Scholarships

Students attending a UNCF school who are interested in business-related fields can apply for this scholarship through their financial aid department.

Pennsylvania State Employees Scholarship Fund

UNCF students from Pennsylvania are eligible for scholarships from this fund created by Pennsylvania state employees. Applicants must be nominated by their financial aid directors.

Principal Financial Group

Students enrolled in UNCF colleges and universities can apply for this scholarship. Contact your financial aid department for details.

Quaker Oats Scholarship Program

Students at UNCF schools pursuing degrees in business administration, accounting, engineering, or liberal arts are eligible for scholarships. Contact your financial aid office.

Raymond W. Cannon Memorial Scholarship Program

Majors in pharmacy or pre-law at UNCF colleges can apply through their financial aid offices for this scholarship.

Reader's Digest Scholarship

Journalism majors at UNCF schools can apply for this scholarship through their financial aid offices.

Revlon Creme of Nature Scholarship

Scholarships are awarded by Revlon and UNCF to students on the basis of 150 word essays. Grand prize winner receives a scholarship of $25,000 and 5 runners-up receive $5,000 scholarships.

Rhythm Nation/Janet Jackson Scholarship

Students majoring in communications, music, performing arts, and the fine arts are eligible for these scholarships. Applicants must be nominated by their financial aid director.

Financial Aid

Richmond, Virginia Health and Human Services Fund

Virginia students attending UNCF colleges are eligible for scholarships that assist with living expenses. Apply through your financial aid department.

Ridgeway/Denny's Scholarship

Residents of California are eligible for this scholarship. Applicants must attend UNCF schools, and must be nominated by their financial aid directors.

SBC Foundation Scholarship

Students attending UNCF institutions in Texas and Arkansas are eligible for scholarships. Apply through your financial aid department.

Southwestern Bell 21st Century Scholarship

Students of UNCF colleges in Texas and Arkansas are eligible for scholarships. Apply through your financial aid department.

Stan Scott Scholarship

UNCF journalism students are eligible for 4 year scholarships. Contact your financial aid department about applying.

Sterling Winthrop Scholarship Program

Students from the New York area are eligible for Sterling Winthrop scholarships. Applicants must be nominated by their financial aid directors.

Tenneco Scholarship

Scholarships are available to UNCF students majoring in math, science, or business. Contact your school's financial aid department.

UNCF Bristol-Myers Squibb Scholarship Program

Students pursuing degrees in math or science at a UNCF school can apply for this scholarship.

UNCF Citibank Fellows Program

Fellowships include a $6,400 scholarship, a mentor, internship, and a conference. Apply through your financial aid office.

UNCF Hotel Management and Hospitality Program

Students majoring in hotel and hospitality management are eligible for scholarships. Apply through your financial aid office.

UNCF John Heins Environmental Fellows Program

Pennsylvania students interested in environmental careers, and who attend a UNCF college, are eligible for scholarship and internship support.

UNCF Manor Care Scholarship Program

Students pursuing degrees in business related fields, hotel and food service management, health care administration, and human resources are eligible for scholarships. Contact your school's financial aid department for application details.

UNCF Revlon Women's Health Scholars Program

Scholarships of up to $10,000 are available to female students in their junior year pursuing degrees in pre-medicine or other health care related fields. Students must be attending a UNCF school, and must apply through their school's department of financial aid.

UNCF Rite Aid Pharmacy

Students entering their sophomore year in an HBCU undergraduate pre-pharmacy program or enrolled in an HBCU school of pharmacy are eligible for $2,500 scholarships.

UNCF Toyota Scholarship Program

Each year, 20 students are awarded grants of $7,500 and 10 week internships. Apply through your college's financial aid office.

UNCF University of Minnesota Graduate Fellows Program

Graduates of UNCF colleges can apply to this program to pursue graduate work at the University of Minnesota. Fellows receive an assistantship, a scholarship, and a summer internship.

UNCF University of Minnesota Scholars Program

UNCF students from Minnesota can apply through their financial aid departments for scholarship support. Students also receive a summer research internship.

UNCF William Wrigley, Jr. Company Scholars Program

Scholarships and summer internships are available for seniors majoring in business, engineering, or chemistry at a UNCF school.

UNCF Wyeth/Ayerst Scholars Program

Scholarships and summer internships are available for students of UNCF schools pursuing science-based or health related careers.

US West Foundation Scholarship

Open to UNCF students from Washington, Oregon, Colorado, Iowa, Minnesota, Nebraska, Arizona, and Atlanta, Georgia, are eligible for scholarship support.

USENIX Association Scholarship

Undergraduate and graduate students majoring in computer science, computer engineering, or systems administration. Students must be attending a UNCF school, and must be nominated by their financial aid department.

Whirlpool Scholarship

Students participating in the Whirlpool Corporation's INROADS programs in Northwest Indiana, Benton Harbor, Mich., and Nashville, Tenn., are eligible for renewable scholarships.

Internships

Alvin Ailey American Dance Theater
Ailey School Summer Intensive Program
211 West 61st Street, 3rd Floor
New York, NY 10023
212-767-0590
http://www.alvinailey.org

The **Ailey School Summer Intensive Program** offers young teens (ages 12-15) and older, more advanced dance students (ages 16-25) the opportunity to study dance in a 7- or 8-week program at the Dance Theater in New York City.

American Association of Advertising Agencies

405 Lexington Avenue
New York, NY 10174-1801
212-682-2500
http://www.aaaa.org

The **MultiCultural Advertising Intern Program** (MAIP) program encourages African American, Asian American, Hispanic American, and Native American college students to strongly consider advertising as a career. In recent years, the program has been expanding with more students and more agencies becoming involved. Each year, approximately 75 to 100 qualified undergraduate and graduate students are selected from colleges and universities nationwide to spend 10 summer weeks interning at member agencies in various U.S. cities.

American College of Neuropsychopharmacology

320 Centre Building
2014 Broadway
Nashville, TN 37203
615-322-2075

Minority graduate students and residents interested in preparing for a career in psychopharmacology or the neurosciences are eligible to apply for the **Pharmacia & Upjohn, Inc. Minority Summer Fellow Program.**The grant provides enough to cover room and board, a stipend that ranges from $1,000 to $2,000, transporation to and from the laboratory site, and funds to allow the trainee to attend the American College of Neuropsychopharmacology's annual conference.

Black Law Institute

10625 Wilmington Avenue
Watts, CA 90002
323-563-0508
http://www.blacklawinstitute.com

The **Law Clerk Program** of the Black Law Institute is the only year-round clerk program dedicated to the development and training of African American law students nationally. The program introduces these students to BLI and its objectives, while also providing legal training and networking.

Case Western Reserve University, School of Medicine

Director of Minority Programs
10900 Euclid Avenue
Cleveland, OH 44106-4920
216-368-1914

The **Health Careers Enhancement Program for Minorities** (HCEM) offers basic science lectures, career, and school counseling for preparation for the MCAT and other requirements for applying to medical school, MCAT classes. It offers a stipend, housing, meals, and a travel allowance.

Cross Cultural Health Care Resources

1200 12th Avenue S
Seattle, WA 98144
206-326-4161
http://www.xculture.org

"Bridging the Gap" is a 40-hour basic/intermediate training course which covers basic interpreting skills, information on health care, culture in interpreting, communication skills for advocacy, and professional development.

Environmental Education Outreach Program

Northern Arizona University
PO Box 15004
Flagstaff, AZ 86011
520-523-1275
http://jan.ucc.nau.edu/~man5/eeop

The program offers summer programs and **internships** in environmental science for Native American students at a number of schools across the country.

Harvard School of Public Health

Division of Biological Sciences
655 Huntington Avenue, Building 2-111
Boston, MA 02115-6018
617-432-4470
http://www.hsph.harvard.edu/academics/dbs

The **Undergraduate Minority Summer Internship Program** is designed to expose minority college science students to the rewards of research directed toward solving important public health problems such as cancer, cardiovascular disease, infections, etc. To qualify for this program, you must be a U.S. citizen or permanent resident and a member of an ethnic group currently underrepresented in science: African American, Mexican American, Chicano, Native American (American Indian, Aleut, Eskimo), Pacific Islander (Polynesian or Micronesian), or Puerto Rican. The 10 week internship includes a stipend of $2,500, a travel allowance of up to $475 and free dormitory housing.

Hispanic Health Council

175 Main Street
Hartford, CT 06106
860-527-0856
http://www.hispanichealth.com

The **Hispanic Health Council Internship Program** provides graduate and undergraduate students with an opportunity to acquire direct experience working with the Puerto Rican and African American communities, and to familiarize themselves with the operation of a community-based organization. Specific activities vary depending on areas of interest and level of training and may include: development of educational materials; data collection; data entry; preparation of reports; and provision of training to families and community groups in areas such as nutrition, violence prevention, child abuse prevention, prenatal care, AIDS, and lead poisoning. Students in the social and behavioral sciences (e.g., anthropology, sociology, social work) as well as those in health-related areas are specially encouraged to participate in the program. Fluency in Spanish is preferred.

Indians Into Medicine

University of North Dakota
School of Medicine
PO Box 9037
Grand Forks, ND 58202-9037
701-777-3037

The **INMED Program** is designed to produce Indian health professionals in the areas of medicine, dentistry, nursing, medical technology, and other health professions. This program makes scholarship support available for up to 2 years of compensatory preprofessional education.

Kaiser Family Foundation

2400 Sand Hill Road
Menlo Park, CA 94025
415-854-9400

Kaiser Media Internship in Urban Health Reporting provides work experience to minority college or graduate students who want to specialize in urban health reporting. Minority college or graduate students studying journalism or a related field may apply for this program if their career goals are to be reporters on urban health matters. This program provides a stipend of $500 per week, all travel expenses, and a grant of $1,000 to participants who complete the program.

National Caucus and Center on Black Aged

1424 K Street, NW, Suite 500
Washington, DC 20005
202-637-8400

The **Minority Training and Development Program in Long-Term Care** provides on-the-job training, licensing preparation, and appropriate in-service training for minorities interested in administrative positions in nursing home facilities. Prospective trainees should be African Americans with a master's degree in a related field or a bachelor's degree with a minimum of 2 years of full-time work experience in a nursing home.

National Heart, Lung, and Blood Institute

Division of Lung Diseases
6701 Rockledge Drive, MSC 7952
Bethesda, MD 20892

The **Minority Institutional Research Training Program** is a National Research Service Award

Financial Aid

Program intended to support training of graduate and health professional students and individuals in postdoctoral training at minority schools. Training is intended to increase students' awareness of cardiovascular, pulmonary, hematologic, and sleep disorders.

National Medical Fellowships
110 West 32nd Street, 8th Floor
New York, NY 10001-3205
212-714-1007

The **Technology Training Program for Minority Medical Students and Medical Residents** is designed to introduce underrepresented minority medical students and residents to the role and applications of telecommunications technology in medicine and public health practices. The program offers two, day-long training sessions conducted by Lucent Technologies staff at 3 sites: Basking Ridge, N.J., Washington, D.C., and Los Angeles, Calif.

Utah Department of Health
288 North 1460 West
PO Box 141011
Salt Lake City, UT 84114-1011
801-538-6965

The Utah Department of Health offers a part-time paid internship to minority students through the **UDOH Ethnic Health Workforce Program**. The intern works within the Office of Ethnic Health on various projects aimed to ensure that Utah's ethnic populations are adequately served and represented in respect to health services. The student will have a background in sociology, ethnic studies, anthropology, family and consumer studies, or related subject with a demonstrated interest in ethnic minority issues.

Washington Center for Internships and Academic Seminars
1101 14th Street, NW, Suite 500
Washington, DC 20005
202-336-7600

Offered by the Washington Center for Internships and Academic Seminars, the **Minority Leaders Fellowship Program** gives minority students the opportunity to explore various issues of leadership in the Washington, D.C. metropolitan area. Program components include a week-long academic seminar to develop students' leadership skills; an internship experience affording them the chance to compare theory with daily experience within a given academic field; and an academic course that challenges fellows to connect their academic background with their respective field experiences.

Section B
Organizations

This section includes professional organizations, minority colleges, fraternities and sororities, and other groups that assist individuals with the pursuit of career, education, and community. In the section on professional organizations, you'll find nonprofit associations composed of individuals working together to further minorities and students within their particular professions; the section on minority colleges includes those two-year and four-year institutions that have historically demonstrated a commitment to furthering minority students; the section on fraternities and sororities provides a list of some of the national organizations, and their chapters, serving minority college students and alumni; and the section on other organizations includes foundations, Indian tribes, job banks, employment services, and other groups that assist minorities.

Professional Organizations

African American Chamber of Commerce
15 East Kirby Street, Suite 1218
Detroit, MI 48202
313-875-5094
http://www.aacofc.org

The African American Chamber of Commerce helps to develop African American businesses through education, information sharing, advocacy, and building alliances with a global network of companies and organizations. It offers training and workshops for small business owners in the use of the Internet.

African Scientific Institute
P.O. Box 12153
Oakland, CA 94609
510-653-7027

The institute helps enhance the awareness and participation of African Americans in science and technology. It also seeks to acquaint youth with opportunities in scientific fields and helps them prepare for careers in those fields. The institute offers consulting and research services. Through conferences and workshops, it allows for professionals to network while developing their skills. The institute also sponsors community and youth programs.

African-American Women Business Owners
3363 Alden Place, NE
Washington, DC 20019
202-399-3645

This association is open to any type of business. Benefits of membership include financial support and information, and networking opportunities.

Alliance of Black Entertainment Technicians
1869 Buckingham Road
Los Angeles, CA 90019
323-933-0746
http://www.abetnetwork.com

The alliance is a professional association for black technicians in the motion picture and entertainment industry. Benefits include a job referral resource directory, networking conferences, seminars and workshops, and youth programs.

Organizations

American Association of Blacks in Energy

927 15th Street, NW, Suite 200
Washington, DC 20005
202-371-9530
http://www.aabe.org

This national association of energy professionals is dedicated to serving as a resource for discussion of the economic, social, and political impact of environmental and energy policies on African Americans and other minorities. The association also encourages students to pursue careers in energy related fields by offering scholarships and other financial aid.

American Association of Hispanic Certified Public Accountants

Scholarship Committee
100 North Main Street, PMB 406
San Antonio, TX 78205
203-255-7003
http://www.aahcpa.org

The American Association of Hispanic Certified Public Accountants is a national organization dedicated to helping Hispanic students, accountants, and CPAs enhance their professional capabilities while expanding Hispanic representation in the nation's work force. As the only nationwide Hispanic CPA organization, the AAHCPA works to increase enrollment of Hispanic accounting students and to promote the hiring and retention of Hispanic accounting graduates throughout the Big Five accounting firms, other major international and national firms, and regional and local firms. It also assists these firms in the recruiting, developing, and promoting of Hispanic professionals, provides networking and career opportunities for its members, and expands business relationships between Hispanic CPA firms, the corporate sector, and major accounting firms.The AAHCPA is open to all Hispanic CPAs, CPA candidates, and accounting students. The AAHCPA each year holds an Annual National Convention and offers its participants quality continuing professional education, along with networking and career opportunities.

American Health and Beauty Aids Institute

401 North Michigan Avenue
Chicago, IL 60611
312-644-6610
http://www.ahbai.org

AHBAI represents the ethnic health and beauty aids (HBA) industry. AHBAI consists of 20 member companies with more than 100 associate members in a variety of fields. AHBAI assists those in the industry with job searches, scholarships, internships, and training. Among its services, AHBAI helps to strengthen the link between professionals and product manufacturers, sponsors a trade show, conducts workshops, and offers scholarship opportunities.

American Indian Library Association

University of Minnesota
229 19th Avenue South
Minneapolis, MN 55455

This affiliate of the American Library Association serves Native American library professionals through conferences, newsletters, and other services.

American Indian Science and Engineering Society

P.O. Box 9828
Albuquerque, NM 87119-9828
505-765-1052
http://www.aises.org

The AISES supports many programs and opportunities for students and professionals in the fields of science and engineering. AISES sponsers a national conference, a student science fair, college scholarships, and publishes a magazine. AISES is composed of both professional and college chapters.

Asian American Arts Foundation

http://www.aaafoundation.com

The Asian American Arts Foundation, a Northern California-based non-profit organization, promotes the support of the arts and provides financial support to Asian Pacific artists and arts organizations.

Asian American Journalists Association

1182 Market Street, Suite 320
San Francisco, CA 94102
415-346-6343
http://www.aaja.org

The Asian American Journalists Association (AAJA) was formed in 1981 and seeks to: increase employment of Asian American print and broadcast journalists; assist high school and college students pursuing journalism careers; encourage fair, sensitive, and accurate news coverage of Asian American issues; and provide support for Asian American journalists. The AAJA hosts a national convention, sponsors scholarships and fellowships, publishes a newsletter, an employment handbook, and other publications, provides job services, offers national awards, and maintains an informative Web site.

Asian American Law Enforcement Association

P.O. Box 56652
Chicago, IL 60656-0652
http://www.aalea.org

This not-for-profit organization represents Asian Americans in law enforcement agencies in Chicago and the Greater Chicagoland area. It encourages the recruitment, hiring, and promotion of Asians in all areas of law enforcement.

Asian American Manufacturers Association

770 Menlo Avenue, Suite 201
Menlo Park, CA 94025
650-321-2262
http://www.aamasv.com

The association is a non-profit organization of corporations and individuals promoting the growth and success of U.S. technology manufacturing and related enterprises throughout the Pacific Rim.

Asian American Psychological Association

3003 North Central Avenue, Suite 103-198
Phoenix, AZ 85012
602-230-4257
http://www.west.asu.edu/aapa/

Among its purposes, the AAPA seeks to advance the welfare of Asian Americans by encouraging, assisting, and advocating research on and service to Asian Americans. The AAPA also conducts meetings, issues publications and other educational materials, and informs others of socio-psychological issues facing Asian Americans.

Asian American Women's Alliance

1894 18th Street
San Francisco, CA 94122
415-681-9229

This non-profit organization develops community leaders and promotes leadership opportunities for its members. It provides networking, mentoring, scholarship, and other opportunities.

Asian Political Scientists Group in the USA

Department of Government
University of Maryland
College Park, MD 20742

This group was formed to promote common professional and ethnic interest of Asian American political scientists in the United States. It offers placement services.

Asian Professional Exchange

11464 Yolanda Avenue
Northridge, CA 91326
310-558-6683
http://www.apex.org

The Asian Professional Exchange (APEX) is a community-based organization with goals and purposes that are charitable, cultural, and educational in nature. APEX is generally comprised of Asian Americans in their 20s and 30s, who are professionals, entrepreneurs, and graduate students in the Southern California area. APEX serves as a medium to bring increased awareness about and to Asian Americans through community service, fellowship, charitable fund-raisers, cultural events, professional networking, and educational seminars.

Association for the Advancement of Creative Musicians

P.O. Box 5757
Chicago, IL 60680
312-752-2212
http://aacmchicago.org

The association is a collective of musicians and composers dedicated to nurturing, performing, and recording serious, original music. The AACM pays homage to the diverse styles of expression within the body of black music in the United States, Africa, and throughout the world. It sponsors public concerts and a free music training program for city youth.

Association of African American Sales Professionals

909A Broad Street, Suite 258
Newark, NJ 07102
732-246-5236
http://www.salesnetwork.org

The association is composed of sales professionals from all industries. Local chapters conduct seminars on selling and negotiating skills, job searching, time management, and organization skills. The association conducts a national annual conference and circulates a quarterly newsletter.

Association of African American Web Developers

88 Raymond Street
Malone, NY 12953
http://www.adkwebdesign.com/aaawd/

The association is a professional association for African Americans in all phases of Web development.

Association of African Women Scholars

French and Women's Studies
Cavanaugh Hall 001C
Indiana University
425 University Boulevard
Indianapolis, IN 46202
317-278-2038
http://www.iupui.edu/~aaws

This worldwide organization is dedicated to promoting and encouraging scholarship on African women in African studies, forming networks with scholars, activists, students, and policy makers inside and outside Africa.

Association of American Indian Physicians

1235 Sovereign Row, Suite C-9
Oklahoma City, OK 73108
405-946-7072

The association seeks to develop a national plan for Native American health personnel development.

Association of Black Cardiologists

6849 B-2 Peachtree Dunwoody Road NE
Atlanta, GA 30328
404-582-8777
http://www.abcardio.org

Representing African American cardiologists and medical professionals, the ABC sponsors a number of programs including training and legislative programs.

Association of Black Psychologists

P.O. Box 55999
Washington, DC 20040-5999
202-722-0808
http://www.abpsi.org

The association works to address the psychological needs of African Americans through research publications and assessment techniques. It is currently working to establish professional certification, training, and development programs.

Association of Hispanic Advertising Agencies

8201 Greensboro Drive, Suite 300
McLean, VA 22102
703-610-9014
http://www.ahaa.org

The mission of the AHAA is to promote the growth, strength, and professionalism of the Hispanic marketing and advertising industry to a diverse audience of business, government, and educational institutions.

Association of Mexican Professionals of Silicon Valley

P.O. Box 6484
Santa Clara, CA 95056-6484
http://www.mexpro.org

The association represents Mexican professionals in the technology industry. Composed also of students, it works to strengthen Mexico-United States relations.

Black Business Expo and Trade Show

Family Savings Bank Tower, Suite 502
3683 Crenshaw Boulevard
Los Angeles, CA 90016
323-290-4743
http://www.blackbusinessexpo.com

The Black Business Expo and Trade Show is an event in Los Angeles showcasing the products and services of black-owned businesses in such areas as health care, manufacturing, technology, and commerce.

Black Career Woman

P.O. Box 19332
Cincinnati, OH 45219
513-531-1932
http://www.bcw.org

This organization is devoted to the professional development of African American women. With nationwide contacts, BCW gives the working African American woman a forum for learning and for enriching her career. BCW hosts workshops and seminars.

Black Coaches Association

P.O. Box 443
Stone Mountain, GA 30086
877-789-1222
http://www.bca-org.com

BCA focuses on the concerns of minority coaches within the NCAA, the NAIA, and in the junior college, high school, and professional ranks. Projects include conventions and workshops.

Black College Communications Association

School of Communications
Howard University
Washington, DC 20059
202-806-7694
http://www.soc.howard.edu/bcca.htm

This nonprofit organization was created from a grant by the Freedom Forum, and consists of administrators at Historically Black Colleges and Universities (HBCUs) with communications programs. BCCA works to identify resources necessary for strengthening communications programs at HBCUs, to provide technical assistance to HBCUs seeking accreditation, and to establish hardware systems to be shared by member institutions.

Black Culinarian Alliance

P.O. Box 2044
North Babylon, NY 11703
http://www.blackculinarians.com

BCA addresses issues of multiculturalism within the hospitality industry. It hosts annual events, sponsors a scholarship program, and provides networking opportunities.

Black Data Processing Associates

8401 Corporate Drive, Suite 405
Landover, MD 20785
301-429-2702
http://www.bdpa.org

BDPA serves to strengthen the link between the information technology industry and African American communities. The organization consists of more than 40 local chapters across the country, and it offers many services including:

Organizations

career counseling, technological assistance, networking opportunities, workshops, and computer competitions. BDPA serves students and IT professionals seeking advancement. Through educational and executive programs, an annual conference, and online resources, BDPA assists its members with career development.

Black Women in Publishing

P.O. Box 6275
FDR Station
New York, NY 10150
212-772-5951
http://www.bwip.org

Black Women in Publishing, Inc. (BWIP) is an employee-based trade association. It works to increase the presence of African American women in the publishing industry.Through meetings and publications, BWIP creates networking forums, assists with career growth and entrepreneurial opportunities, and recognizes those successful in the industry. BWIP members work in many different areas of the publishing industry, including human resources, editorial and management, finance and production, art and design, marketing and sales, and wholesale and retail. They are writers, publishers, freelancers, agents, attorneys, CEOs, VPs, and business owners.

Blacks in Government

1820 11th Street, NW
Washington, DC 20001-5010
202-667-3280
http://www.bignet.org

Blacks in Government is an organization that provides employee support, advocacy, and resources for African American civil servants. It sponsors a national training conference and networking opportunities.

California Chicano News Media Association

USC School of Journalism
3502 Watt Way, ASC G10
Los Angeles, CA 90089-0281
213-740-5263
http://www.ccnma.org

The CCNMA serves media professionals and employers nationwide. It works to promote diversity in print and broadcast newsrooms and news coverage. CCNMA achieves this through internship and scholarship programs, networking opportunities for students and professionals, and job location services.

California Librarians Black Caucus

P.O. Box 2906
Los Angeles, CA 90078-2906
310-835-3350
http://www.clbc.org

The California Librarians Black Caucus is a statewide organization with branches in Northern and Southern California. It works to increase the numbers of African Americans in the library workplace and to assist them in their professional development. It also speaks on behalf of African American communities regarding the provision of library and information services, and promotes literature and information by and about African Americans.

Center for the Advancement of Hispanics in Science and Engineering Education

P.O. Box 34520
Bethesda, MD 20827
301-299-0033

The center seeks to overcome the underrepresentation of Hispanics in the engineering and scientific community by offering resources and opportunities to Hispanic youth for science and engineering education.

Chinese American Medical Society

281 Edgewood Avenue
Teaneck, NJ 07666-3023
201-833-1506
http://www.camsociety.org

This nonprofit organization works to promote medical professionals of Chinese descent through such activities as annual meetings, scientific research, and a scholarship program. CAMS also provides endowments to medical schools and hospitals. Members include physicians in primary care as well as various specialties in academic and research institutions, and medical students.

Conference of Minority Public Administrators

P.O. Box 3010
Fort Worth, TX 76113
817-871-8325
http://www.compa.org

The Conference of Minority Public Administrators (COMPA) is unique in that it is the only national entity devoted primarily to providing professional development opportunities for all America's racial minority public administrators. COMPA works to eliminate the institutional and social barriers to the professional development and employment of minority public administrators. Specific goals are to provide leadership in the elimination of discriminatory practices in the public sector; promote recruitment of minorities for leadership positions at all levels of government; provide a forum to promote, upgrade, and refine skills of minority administrators; and develop and maintain a roster of skilled minority professionals in public administration. COMPA sponsors an annual national symposium, publishes a journal and newsletter for its members, and awards scholarships to deserving students of public administration, public affairs, and public policy.

Conference of Minority Transportation Officials

1725 DeSales Street, NW, Suite 808
Washington, DC 20036
202-289-0567
http://www.comto.com

The conference represents those working in all areas of transportation. It maintains a job bank and offers opportunities in networking, training, education, and research. It also provides scholarships.

Congressional Hispanic Caucus Institute

504 C Street, NE
Washington, DC 20002
202-543-1771
http://www.chci.org

The Congressional Hispanic Caucus was established to monitor legislative and other government activity that affects Hispanics. It sponsors educational programs and other activities to increase the opportunities for Hispanics to participate in and contribute to the American political system. The board of directors includes influential Hispanic business persons from the private sector and community leaders from across the country who, in conjunction with the Hispanic Members of Congress, bring to the institute policy-related knowledge and experience at the local, state, and national levels. The institute offers programs designed to afford leadership development training for talented young Hispanics, as well as the opportunity to enter a wider range of professional areas.

E. J. Josey Scholarship Committee

Clark Atlanta University
School of Library Sciences
Winter Park, FL 32790-2228
http://www.bcala.org

This national organization of librarians promotes African Americans in the profession. It holds semi-annual meetings, conferences, and publishes a newsletter and awards scholarships.

Hispanic Bar Association

P.O. Box 1011
Washington, DC 20013-1011
202-624-2904
http://www.hbadc.org

The Hispanic Bar Association works to advance Hispanics in the legal profession. It encourages Hispanics to enter the legal profession, promotes the appointment of Hispanics to positions of leadership, and promotes the appointment of Hispanic judges. HBA hosts networking opportunities, seminars, and provides information on employment opportunities. It also publishes a newsletter, awards fellowships, and

Organizations

assists the Hispanic community in obtaining legal services.

Hispanic Dental Association

188 Randolph Street, Suite 1811
Chicago, IL 60601-3001
800-852-7921
http://www.hdassoc.org

The Hispanic Dental Association is a national organization with members all across the country. Members include Hispanic professionals and non-Hispanics; dentists and dental hygienists, dental assistants, dental technologists, academics and practicing professionals, students, and researchers.The HDA consists of 10 working committees, 20 regional affiliate chapters, and 31 institutional supporters. A Corporate Round Table composed of firms advise the association on its ongoing programs. A newsletter, "HDA News & Reports," is published quarterly. Due to the great demand for bi-lingual (English/ Spanish) dental professionals, the publication carries classified advertisements. It also includes relevant features, and updates on HDA scholarship programs and organizational business.

Hispanic Employment Program Managers

P.O. Box 44351
L'Enfant Plaza Station
Washington, DC 20026-4351
http://www.hepm.org

HEPM focuses on the needs of Hispanic Americans in all areas of federal employment. It provides information about job opportunities, Hispanic culture, and multicultural events.

Hispanic Public Relations Association of Greater New York

230 Park Avenue South
New York, NY 10003-1566
212-781-6728
http://www.hpragny.org

HPRA/GNY is a network of Hispanics working in public relations. It sponsors educational programs and provides assistance to students inter- ested in careers in public relations. It provides job and internship listings.

Hispanic-American Chamber of Commerce

67 Broad Street
Boston, MA 02109
617-261-HACC
http://www.hacc.com

The HACC is an organization of businesses, individuals, and institutions committed to the economic development of the Spanish and Portuguese speaking communities in the Northeast United States. It offers outreach information services to small businesses. Services include group health insurance, business referrals, and advocacy for business concerns.

Houston Hispanic Professional Coalition

http://www.houhispprof.org

The Houston Hispanic Professional Coalition aids the Houston Hispanic community with educational, scholarship, and professional development opportunities. It consists of a number of member organizations, including Houston chapters of Hispanic CPAs, Hispanic Nurses Association, and the Society of Hispanic Professional Engineers. Vist the Web site for a list of all the member professional associations, and for a list of special events. Contact the organization by email.

Institute for Tribal Environment Professionals

Northern Arizona University
P.O. Box 15004
Flagstaff, AZ 86011
http://www.cet.nau.edu/itep/

ITEP was created to act as a catalyst among tribal governments, research, and technical resources at Northern Arizona University, various federal, state, and local governments, and the private sector in support of environmental protection of Native American natural resources.

International Association of Black Professional Fire Fighters

8700 Central Avenue, Suite 306
Landover, MD 20785-4831
301-808-0804
http://www.vulcanet.mwinc.com

IABPFF serves fire fighters across the country through its many committees and local area chapters. It hosts an annual convention and announces job opportunities. It also sponsors a chapter for African American women in the fire service.

International Black Buyers and Manufacturers Expo and Conference

312 Florida Avenue, NW
Washington, DC 20001
202-797-9070
http://www.ibbmec.com

This conference allows business owners to meet with African American manufacturers, retailers, booksellers, importers/exporters, clothiers, fine artists/craftspeople, technology professionals, and service providers.

International Black Writers and Artists

P.O. Box 43576
Los Angeles, CA 90043
http://members.tripod.com/~IBWA/home.htm

IBWA/LA is devoted to fulfilling the need for information, resources, and services locally and abroad to those who value the unique contributions of writers and artists among the diaspora. Its vision is to expose and recognize writers and artists of color to ensure they are published, read, seen, and sought as a viable pool of talent —nationally and internationally. As a publishing group, IBWA solicits, critiques, selects, edits, and publishes manuscripts and visual arts in various forms. In addition, aid is offered to literary artists in their quests to prepare works for publication by themselves or others. IBWA provides visibility, information, education, and entertainment through a significant network of professionals and emerging faces. Benefits of membership include: "Black Expressions," the newsletter of the International Black Writers and Artists (which features job listings and intern-

ship opportunities); discounts on activities, services, and products of IBWA; priority consideration for UCLA Extension Scholarships; option of being listed in the IBWA Directory of Artists and Writers; connection with those who share similar goals; and being privvy to a network of professional guidance.

International Society of African Scientists

P.O. Box 9209
Wilmington, DE 19809
http://www.dca.net/isas

ISAS sponsors annual technical conferences, maintains a directory of technical professionals of African descent, and provides assistance to educational and research institutions in Africa and the Caribbean.

Korean-American Scientists and Engineers Association

1952 Gallows Road, Suite 300
Vienna, VA 22182
703-748-1222
http://www.ksea.org

The Korean-American Scientists and Engineers Association (KSEA) helps members develop their full career potential by providing professional opportunities in the areas of science, technology, and entrepreneurship. KSEA hosts an annual meeting and technical conference, provides a Web service, offers scholarships and summer internships, sponsors youth programs, gives job referrals, and provides many other services.

Latin Business Association

5400 East Olympic Boulevard, Suite 130
Los Angeles, CA 90022
323-721-4000
http://www.lbausa.com

The LBA serves Latin-owned businesses across the United States. It supports the LBA Institute which provides research, technical assistance, and access to capital for Latino entrepreneurs. Benefits of membership include subscriptions to the *Latin Business Association Journal,*

Organizations

monthly networking opportunities, and health care plans.

Latino Professional Network

P.O. Box 6019
Boston, MA 02209
617-247-1818
http://www.lpn.org

The Latino Professional Network is a membership organization for Hispanic professionals in the Boston area to network, learn about jobs, and to collaborate with other Hispanic professionals. It also offers scholarships for high school and college students.

Law Enforcement Association of Asian Pacifics

905 East 2nd Street, Suite 200
Los Angeles, CA 90012
http://members.tripod.com/~amerasia2/

This is a professional association of law enforcement officers in federal, municipal, state, county, and other agencies.

Los Angeles Council of Black Professional Engineers

P.O. Box 881029
Los Angeles, CA 90009
310-635-7734
http://www.lablackengineers.org

The Los Angeles Council of Black Professional Engineers works to enhance the educational, employment, and business opportunities of minority individuals. The council pursues personal contacts with students at all levels, curriculum advice in predominately minority educational institutions, consultations with colleges and universities, direct contact with potential employers, coordination with professional societies, and support and aid in business development. The council offers scholarship opportunities, job listings, and other benefits.

Minnesota American Indian Chamber of Commerce

212 3rd Avenue N, Suite 567
Minneapolis, MN 55401
612-333-0500
http://nnic.com/maicc/index.html

This organization supports American Indian entrepreneurs and the Native American community through programs and services. It provides education, training, and employment services to Native American youth and adults.

National Action Council for Minorities in Engineering

The Empire State Building
350 Fifth Avenue, Suite 2212
New York, NY 10118-2299
212-279-2626
http://www.nacme.org

NACME is a not-for-profit organization whose mission is to increase the representation of successful African Americans, Latinos, and American Indians in the engineering profession. NACME conducts research, analyzes and advances public policies, develops and operates precollege and university programs, as well as awareness and training programs, and disseminates information through publications, conferences, and electronic media. NACME is best known for its national scholarship program.

National Alliance of Black Interpreters

P.O. Box 70322
New Orleans, LA 70172-0322
504-943-6597
http://www.naobi.org

The alliance promotes African Americans in the profession of sign language interpreting. It consists of 5 local chapters across the country.

National Alliance of Black School Educators

2816 Georgia Avenue, NW
Washington, DC 20001
202-483-1549
http://www.nabse.org

NABSE is a nonprofit organization that serves as a network of African American educators. The organization develops instructional methods to improve the education of African American youth. NABSE focuses on professional development programs that strengthen the skills of teachers, principals, and other educators, and on advocacy for high standards in education. NABSE hosts conferences, awards scholarships and grants, sponsors research programs, and offers certification.

National Alliance of Market Developers

c/o Allen and Partners, Inc.
620 Sheridan Avenue
Plainfield, NJ 07060
908-561-4062
http://www.namdntl.org

Membership of this organization consists of African American professionals in marketing, management, advertising, sales, public relations, urban affairs, and related fields. In addition to offering professional support, the alliance offers education and guidance programs, and serves as a national African American consumer resource.

National Asian Pacific American Bar Association

1717 Pennsylvania Avenue, NW, Suite 500
Washington, DC 20006
202-974-1030
http://www.napaba.org

This is a national association of Asian Pacific American attorneys, judges, law professors, and law students. NAPABA advocates for the legal needs and interests of the Asian Pacific American community.

National Association for Black Geologists and Geophysicists

U.S. Geological Survey
2255 North Gemini Drive
Flagstaff, AZ 86001-1698
520-556-7220
http://iapetus2.bgsu.edu:1003/nabgg.html

The NABGG was organized to inform students of career opportunities that exist in the fields of geology and geophysics, and to encourage them to take advantage of scholarship programs, grants, and loans that are established for minority students. The association also aids minority students in the search for summer employment and aids corporate members interested in obtaining summer employees for positions that will enhance the students' background and marketability.

National Association of Black Accountants

7429-A Hanover Parkway
Greenbelt, MD 20770
301-474-6222
http://www.nabainc.org

The National Association of Black Accountants, Inc. (NABA) works to expand the influence of minority professionals in the fields of accounting and finance. In addition to helping members promote and develop their professional skills, NABA helps minority students enter the accounting profession. The association offers scholarships, hosts conferences, and maintains an online career center.

National Association of Black Hospitality Professionals

P.O. Box 195
Smiths, AL 36877
334-298-4121
http://www.blackhospitality.com

The association assists African Americans with finding work in the hospitality industry. It offers mentorships to students, assists students in seeking scholarships, and provides information on companies.

National Association of Black Journalists

870-A Adelphi Road
Adelphi, MD 20783
301-445-7100
http://www.nabj.org

Organizations

The National Association of Black Journalists, 3,000 members strong with 74 affiliated professional chapters and 51 student chapters, is the largest media organization for people of color in the world. Its mission is to strengthen ties among African-American journalists, promote diversity in newsrooms, honor excellence and outstanding achievement in the media industry, expand job opportunities and recruiting activities for established African American journalists and students interested in the journalism field, and expand and balance the media's coverage of the African-American community and experience. NABJ recently launched a $1 Million Endowment Campaign to provide a permanent source of funding for student scholarships and internships. Each year, NABJ awards nearly $100,000 in scholarships and internships to students throughout the country, as well as fellowships for seasoned professionals.

National Association of Black Management Consultants
888-410-5398
http://www.nabmc.org

The association serves minorities in the management consulting profession through consulting services and networking opportunities.

National Association of Black Procurement Professionals
P.O. Box 70738
Washington, DC 20024-0738
http://www.nabpp.org

The National Association of Black Procurement Professionals works to promote the selection of minorities for positions in the procurement profession. It sponsors the Procurement Training, Education, and Research Institute. It provides job listings, scholarships, mentoring, and certification prompting.

National Association of Black Social Workers
8436 West McNichols
Detroit, MI 48221
313-862-6700
http://www.nynet-ac.com/~nabsw/

The association promotes the welfare, survival, and liberation of communities of African ancestry. Through the development of national and international education conferences, the organization provides professional leadership to local, national, and global communities.

National Association of Black Telecommunications Professionals
c/o Bell Atlantic
1710 H Street, NW, 10th Floor
Washington, DC 20006
800-946-6228
http://www.nabtp.org

The National Association of Black Telecommunications Professionals has national and international membership of telecommunications professionals, small business owners, and students. NABTP targets talented young people for the development of interests and skills to enter the telecommunications field. NABTP sponsors national competitions which include seminars and workshops; publishes a newsletter; sponsors special community and education projects; and offers scholarships.

National Association of Blacks in Criminal Justice
North Carolina Central University
P.O. Box 19788
Durham, NC 27707
919-683-1801
http://www.nabcj.org

This is an association of criminal justice professionals and community leaders dedicated to improving the administration of justice.

National Association of Health Services Executives
8630 Fenton Street, Suite 126
Silver Spring, MD 20910
202-628-3953
http://www.nahse.org

The association works to promote the advancement and development of African American health care leaders. It is also dedicated to elevating the quality of health care services rendered to minority and underserved communities. It maintains a job bank and offers mentoring, scholarship, and internship opportunities.

National Association of Hispanic Journalists

1193 National Press Building
Washington, DC 20045-2100
202-662-7145
http://www.nahj.org

The National Association of Hispanic Journalists (NAHJ) is dedicated to the recognition and professional advancement of Hispanics in the news industry. NAHJ is governed by a 16-member board of directors that consists of executive officers and regional directors who represent geographic areas of the United States and the Caribbean. The national office is located in the National Press Building in Washington, D.C. NAHJ has approximately 1,500 members, including working journalists, journalism students, other media-related professionals and academic scholars. The goals of the association are: 1. To further employment and career development for Hispanics working in the news media. 2. To organize and provide mutual support for Hispanic journalists in English, Spanish, and bilingual media. 3. To encourage the study and practice of journalism and mass communication by Hispanics. 4. To promote fair treatment of Hispanics by the news media. 5. To foster greater understanding of the culture, interests, and concerns of Hispanic journalists. Programs of the NAHJ include: regional workshops and seminars; national convention and career expo; mid-career and professional development programs; online job bank; journalism awards; internship and fellowship listings; student journalism workshops; newsletter; and scholarships.

National Association of Hispanic Nurses

1501 16th Street, NW
Washington, DC 20036
202-387-2477
http://www.incacorp.com/nahn

As the only national organization representing Hispanic registered nurses in the United States,

the goal of the National Association of Hispanic Nurses (NAHN) is to increase the leadership development of Hispanic nurses and to improve the quality of health of Latino communities. NAHN analyzes the health care needs of the Hispanic community and works to deliver quality care. It helps Hispanic nurses receive education and training and assistance from local, state, and federal agencies. NAHN works to increase the number of bilingual and bicultural nurses. The association has chapters across the country, hosts an annual conference, and provides scholarship opportunities.

National Association of Hispanic Real Estate Professionals

1650 Hotel Circle North, Suite 215A
San Diego, CA 92108
800-964-5373
http://www.nahrep.org

The association serves Hispanic real estate professionals and works to increase home ownership among Hispanic Americans.

National Association of Mathematicians

Department of Mathematics
Atlanta University
Atlanta, GA 30314
404-681-0251

This membership organization serves teachers of mathematics in the Historically Black Colleges and Universities. The group works for ample resources for professors to pursue their studies and to encourage students to pursue mathematical careers.

National Association of Minorities in Communications

One Centerpointe Drive, Suite 410
La Palma, CA 90623
714-736-9600
http://www.namic.com

The National Association of Minorities in Communications promotes diversity in the telecommunications industry, focusing on the urban cable marketplace. Membership is comprised of 1,200 professionals in 16 chapters throughout the country. Members are cable operators, programmers, hardware suppliers, new media professionals, and entrepreneurs. The association publishes a membership directory and a newsletter, and hosts conferences. It also sponsors a national job bank and mentoring programs.

National Association of Minority Contractors

666 11th Street, NW, Suite 520
Washington, DC 20001
202-347-8259
http://namc.org

This non-profit association represents minority contractors across the country, helping contractors to find work opportunities. The NAMC also offers training programs.

National Association of Minority Media Executives

1921 Gallows Road, Suite 600
Vienna, VA 22182
703-893-2410
http://www.namme.org

NAMME was formed in 1990 to establish and maintain relationships among minority media executives and to promote the advancement of minorities into management of mainstream media. NAMME membership is open to senior managers and operational directors of newspapers, magazines, radio, and television stations.

National Association of Negro Musicians

1954 West 115th Street
Chicago, IL 60643-0484
773-779-1325
http://www.edtech.morehouse.edu/cgrimes/
scholars.htm

The National Association of Negro Musicians (NANM) is dedicated to the preservation, encouragement and advocacy of all genres of the music of African Americans in the world. It seeks to develop higher professional standards of all music through lectures, conferences, and conventions. Since its inception, it has provided encouragement, and support for thousands of African American musicians, many of whom have become widely respected figures in music and have contributed significantly to American music culture and history. In its almost 80-year history, NANM has awarded over 170 financial scholarships and awards to talented young musicians throughout the country. Foremost among the activities of NANM are its programs and activities which involve young people. These include NANM's national Junior and Youth Divisions, and Campus Branches comprised of collegiate young artists from colleges and universities all over the country. These young people participate in workshops and are presented in performances throughout each annual convention week.

National Association of Urban Bankers

1300 L Street, NW, Suite 825
Washington, DC 20005
202-289-8335
http://www.naub.org

The National Association of Urban Bankers is an organization of minority professionals in the banking and financial services industries. It supports programs that offer practical benefits for minority financial services professionals, banks, and financial institutions.

National Bankers Association

1513 P Street
Washington, DC 20005
202-588-5432

The NBA represents minority and women-owned banks and monitors legislative issues affecting minority institutions.

National Black Association for Speech-Language and Hearing

Speech and Hearing Clinic
University of the District of Columbia
Washington, DC 20008
http://www.nbaslh.org

The association is developed to meet the needs and aspirations of African American Speech-Language and Hearing Professionals, African American students, and the community. It sponsors educational seminars and conferences, as well as a bi-annual review course for the national exam.

National Black Caucus of State Legislators

444 Capitol Street, NW, Suite 622
Washington, DC 20001
202-624-5457
http://www.nbcsl.com

The National Black Caucus of State Legislators (NBCSL) represents minority legislators across the United States and offers associate membership to corporations and the public at large.

National Black Chamber of Commerce

1350 Connecticut Avenue, NW, Suite 825
Washington, DC 20036
202-466-6888
http://www.nationalbcc.org

The National Black Chamber of Commerce is the largest trade association in the United States that deals with issues of economics and entrepreneurship in the African American community.

National Black Law Student Association

Director of Educational Services
1225 11th Street, NW
Washington, DC 20001
202-583-1281
http://www.nblsa.org

This group helps black students enter legal studies programs by publicizing financial aid opportunities and publishing reports. It also sponsors a training program and hosts an academic retreat. Among its community service programs are voter registration drives, outreach programs for local schools, and a Computer in Schools Program.

National Black MBA Association

180 North Michigan Avenue, Suite 1400
Chicago, IL 60601
312-236-2622
http://www.nbmbaa.org

The NBMBAA serves business professionals around the world with an international affiliate in London and 38 chapters across the country. The organization offers scholarships, hosts a national conference, and maintains an employment network.

National Black Media Coalition

1738 Elton Road, Suite 314
Silver Spring, MD 20903
301-445-2600
http://www.nbmc.org

The National Black Media Coalition (NBMC) works to effect changes in the communications industry to benefit African Americans. NBMC's service program includes a summer internship program for students, research assistance for local affiliates, a speaker's bureau, publication of a broadcasting rights brochure, and the promotion of affirmative action among broadcasters and publishers.

National Black Nurses' Association

1511 K Street, NW, Suite 415
Washington, DC 20005
202-393-6870
http://www.nbna.org

This is a non-profit organization which seeks to advance and retain African Americans in the profession through improved working and economic conditions, improved patient care, and by recruiting students for the nursing profession. The association helps students obtain scholarships and other financial assistance for nursing education.

National Black Police Association

3251 Mt. Pleasant Street, NW, 2nd Floor
Washington, DC 20010-2103
202-986-2070
http://www.blackpolice.org

Organizations

The National Black Police Association is a nationwide organization of African American Police Associations dedicated to the promotion of justice, fairness, and effectiveness in law enforcement. The NBPA has several chartered organizations throughout the United States, and associate members in Canada, Bermuda, and the United Kingdom. The organization represents approximately 35,000 individual members. The principal concerns of the NBPA center upon law enforcement issues and the effect of those issues upon the total community. The NBPA serves as an advocate for minority police officers and establishes a national network for the training and education of all police officers and others interested in law enforcement. The NBPA hosts an Annual Education and Training Conference for its members and others interested in law enforcement. The conference is designed to provide workshops, discussion groups, and the dissemination of pertinent information to those who attend. The conference also provides an opportunity to network with fellow officers from across the country.

National Business League
Rep. Sherman N. Coplin Jr., President
107 Harber Circle
New Orleans, LA 70126
504-246-1166

The league works to create organizational unity, focusing on the public policy issues affecting African American business people.

National Coalition of 100 Black Women
38 West 32nd Street, Suite 1610
New York, NY 10001-3816
212-947-2196
http://orgs.womenconnect.com/ncbw/

The coalition is a volunteer organization dedicated to community service, leadership development, and the enhancement of career opportunities through programs and networking. It sponsors conferences, seminars, mentoring, and advocacy.

National Coalition of Black Meeting Planners
8630 Fenton Street, Suite 126
Silver Spring, MD 20910
202-628-3952
http://www.ncbmp.com

The National Coalition of Black Meeting Planners (NCBMP) is dedicated primarily to the training needs of African American meeting planners. The organization is committed to the improvement of the meetings, conferences, exhibitions, and convocations they manage. Members of NCBMP include meeting planners from numerous business, civil rights, church and fraternal organizations.

National Conference of Black Lawyers
2 West 125th Street, 2nd Floor
New York, NY 10027
212-864-4000

The organization consists of legal workers, including lawyers, legal scholars, judges, law students, and paralegals. It works for social, economic, and political justice for the African American community.

National Conference of Black Mayors
1422 West Peachtree Street, NW, Suite 800
Atlanta, GA 30309
404-892-0127
http://www.blackmayors.org

NCBM is a nonprofit service organization which provides management and technical assistance to black mayors and articulates the membership's concerns on national policy issues.

National Conference of Black Political Scientists
Department of History and Political Science
Albany State College
Albany, GA 31705

This organization of African American political scientists is dedicated to the exchange of scholarly works. The organization sponsors a graduate assistance program for African American students.

National Forum for Black Public Administrators

777 North Capitol Street, NE, Suite 807
Washington, DC 20002
202-408-9300

This organization of African American public administrators links professionals and organizations and offers mentoring programs for youth and programs in executive leadership development.

National Hispana Leadership Institute

1901 North Moore Street, Suite 206
Arlington, VA 22209
703-527-6007
http://www.nhli.org

The National Hispana Leadership Institute is an organization committed to the education and leadership development of Hispanic women. It offers a training program focusing on public policy and management.

National Hispanic Business Association

1712 East Riverside Drive, #208
Austin, TX 78741
512-495-9511
http://www.nhba.org

The National Hispanic Business Association comprises student organizations and alumni from around the nation and serves as a strong voice for the Hispanic business community across the United States. It addresses many educational and business issues related to Hispanics. It hosts an annual student leadership conference. Members have access to a newsletter, job listings, a resume database, and many networking opportunities.

National Hispanic Corporate Achievers

445 Douglas Avenue
Altamonte Springs, FL 32714
407-682-2883
http://www.hispanicachievers.com

The National Hispanic Corporate Achievers is a network of Hispanic professionals across the country. It works to stimulate job opportunties, introduce new business relationships, and create support for young Hispanics wishing to enter the business arena.

National Hispanic Medical Association

1700 17th Street, NW, Suite 405
Washington, DC 20009
202-265-4297
http://home.earthlink.net/~nhma

The association addresses the interests and concerns of licensed physicians and full-time Hispanic medical faculty dedicated to teaching medical and health services research.

National Institutes of Health Black Scientists Association

P.O. Box 38
Clarksburg, MD 20871
http://www.nih.gov/science/blacksci/index.html

This association of scientists, physicians, technologists, and science administrators at the NIH works as an advocate for health and scientific issues of importance to underrepresented minority communities. It is concerned with the recruitment and development of black scientists and clinicians.

National Network of Minority Women in Science

Office of Opportunities in Science
1333 H Street, NW
Washington, DC 20005

Minority women in the fields of science and engineering can network with other professionals through this organization.

National Newspaper Publishers Association

3200 13th Street, NW
Washington, DC 20010
202-588-8764
http://www.nnpa.org

Organizations

NNPA is a trade organization of publishers of African American owned newspapers. It provides news, features, and editorial content for the African American community. It also provides training sessions and conferences, as well as scholarship and internship opportunities for African American youth.

National Optometric Association

1489 Livingston Avenue
Columbus, OH 43205-2931
614-253-5593
http://www.natoptassoc.org

Optometrists throughout the country participate in the NOA's program, which recruits minority students interested in the field of optometry, counsels and assists them during training, and helps them establish a private practice or find professional employment.

National Organization for the Professional Advancement of Black Chemists and Chemical Engineers

Dr. Joseph Cannon
P.O. Box 77040
Washington, DC 20059
202-806-6626
http://www.imall.com/stores/nobcche

NOBCChE is committed to the professional and educational growth of underrepresented minorities in the sciences. It sponsors an annual meeting and a number of local programs through its network of local chapters. It also provides recognition awards and scholarships to students and professionals annually.

National Organization of Black Law Enforcement Executives

4609 Pinecrest Office Park Drive, Suite F
Alexandria, VA 22312-1442
703-658-1529
http://www.noblenatl.org

Membership of this professional organization consists of police chiefs, sheriffs, command-level officers and others. NOBLE conducts research, speaks out on the issues affecting the African American community, and performs a variety of outreach activities.

National Society of Black Engineers

1454 Duke Street
Alexandria, VA 22314
703-549-2207
http://www.nsbe.org

The objectives of the organization are to: stimulate and develop student interest in the various engineering disciplines; strive to increase the number of minority students studying engineering at both the undergraduate and graduate levels; encourage members to seek advanced degrees in engineering or related fields and to obtain professional engineering registrations; encourage and advise minority youth in their pursuit of an engineering career; promote public awareness of engineering and the opportunities for African Americans and other minorities in that profession; and function as a representative body on issues and developments that affect the careers of African American engineers. New and innovative project ideas are generated and implemented throughout the year on the chapter, regional, and national levels. Some of NSBE's present activities include tutorial programs, group study sessions, high school/junior high outreach programs, technical seminars and workshops, a national communications network (NSBENET), two national magazines (*NSBE Magazine* and the *NSBE Bridge*), an internal newsletter, a professional newsletter ("The Career Engineer"), resume books, career fairs, awards, banquets, and an annual national convention.

National Society of Black Physicists

NSBP Scholarship, L-716
Lawrence Livermore National Lab
Greensboro, NC 27441-1086
925-422-0894
http://www.nsbp.org

NSBP promotes the professions of African-American physicists within the scientific community and within society at large, through a number of activities and programs. NSBP hosts a national conference, names a Science Ambassador to give lectures to elementary, middle, high school, and university students, and awards undergraduate and graduate scholarships. It also honors oustanding African-American physicists with an Outstanding Career Achievement Award and the NSBP Society of Fellows.

National Society of Hispanic MBAs

Scholarship Program
8204 Elmbrook, Suite 235
Dallas, TX 75247
877-467-4622
http://www.nshmba.org

The National Society of Hispanic MBAs works to increase the enrollment of Hispanics in graduate management programs. It also assists corporations with the recruitment of Hispanic business professionals and provides many networking opportunities. Members have access to a national conference, newsletter, online resume database, and job listings. The society also offers scholarship opportunities.

National Society of Hispanic Physicists

Vanderbilt University
Department of Physics and Astronomy
P.O. Box 1807-B
Nashville, TN 37235
http://utopia.utb.edu/nshp/

The National Society of Hispanic Physicists works to improve the participation of minorities in science. NSHP sponsors workshops and meetings concerning educational and professional directives. The society publishes the newsletter "The Hispanic Physicist" and also directs undergraduates and graduates to fellowship and scholarship opportunities.

National Technical Association

6919 North 19th Street
Philadelphia, PA 19126-1506
215-549-6509
http://www.ntaonline.org

The National Technical Association is an organization for minority scientists and engineers. NTA is dedicated to: encouraging minority youth and women to choose careers in science and technology; creating access and opportunity to science/technology careers through academic preparation and awareness; building networks for practitioners and educators in fields of science and technology; and recognizing, honoring, and preserving the legacy of minority pioneers in technological fields. IT sponsors an annual conference and career fair. NTA consists of regional chapters, publishes *The Journal of the NTA*, and assists members with job searches.

Native American Journalists Association

3359 36th Avenue South
Minneapolis, MN 55406
612-729-9244
http://www.naja.com

NAJA, through many programs and activities, promotes journalism, native cultures, and a free press. NAJA monitors and analyzes tribal and national news, maintains educational services, and awards scholarships. It also supports various projects, such as the Rising Voices high school student journalism project.

Northwest Treeplanters and Farmworkers United

300 Young Street
Woodburn, OR 97071
http://www.pcun.org

This organization is Oregon's union of farmworkers, nursery, and reforestation workers, and is Oregon's largest Latino organization. It offers information to farmworkers about working conditions, union contracts, pesticides, and other issues of concern.

Oregon Association of Minority Entrepreneurs

4134 North Vancouver Avenue
Portland, OR 97217
503-249-7744

This organization focuses on the special concerns of minority business owners in the Pacific Northwest.

Organizations

Organization of Black Airline Pilots

2740 Greenbriar Parkway, Suite A3128
Atlanta, GA 30331
800-JET-OBAP
http://www.obap.org

The Organization of Black Airline Pilots (OBAP) is dedicated to the enhancement and promotion of educational opportunities in aviation, and the development of on-going mentoring of youth. OBAP also monitors the development of aviation projects.Working in cooperation with several airlines, government agencies, and other private organizations, OBAP maintains the Aviation Career Enhancement (ACE) Program, the Professional Pilot Development Program (PPDP), and the Type Rating Scholarship Program.

Organization of Black Designers

300 M Street SW, Suite N110
Washington, DC 20024-4019
202-659-3918
http://www.core77.com/OBD

The Organization of Black Designers is a national professional association for African American design professionals in the disciplines of graphics, interior, fashion, and industrial design.

Organization of Black Screenwriters

P.O. Box 70160
Los Angeles, CA 90070-0160
323-882-4166
http://www.obswriter.com

The Organization of Black Screenwriters (OBS), Inc. began in 1988 to address the lack of black writers represented within the entertainment industry. Its primary function is to assist screenwriters in the creation of works for film and television and to help them present their work. As a result of its efforts and the continued growth of the organization, OBS now networks with the Writers Guild of America, agents, producers, directors, and studios. OBS assists new writers in the creation of screenplays and helps present their work. OBS does not act as an agent or manager, only as a referral service for writers to the industry. However, upon joining OBS, the member agrees to donate a 3 percent finders fee to the organization for any works sold as a result of its efforts.

Professional Hispanics in Energy

20505 Yorba Linda Boulevard #324
Yorba Linda, CA 92886-7109
714-777-7729
http://www.phie.org

This is an association of Hispanic professionals working in the energy and environmental industries. It provides scholarships, training, and networking opportunities.

Professional Photographers Minority Network

Horace Holmes Studio, Inc.
352 Cotton Avenue
Macon, GA 31201
912-741-5151
http://www.ppa-world.org/minority_network.html

The purpose of PPMN is to enhance the professional development of minority professional image makers, photographers, videographers and artisans. Membership benefits include a mentor program, scholarship opportunities, technical support hotline, an annual convention, and educational programs.

Professional Women of Color

P.O. Box 5196
New York, NY 10185
212-714-7190
http://www.pwconline.org

Professional Women of Color is an organization providing workshops, seminars, group discussions, and networking sessions to assist women of color in the management of their personal and professional lives.

Puerto Rican Studies Association

CELAC/SS-247
University of Albany, SUNY
Albany, NY 12203
http://www.puertorican-studies.org

The PRSA is an organization of scholars in the field of Puerto Rican Studies.

Reforma

University of Arizona Library
P.O. Box 210005
Anaheim, CA 92815-0832
http://www.reforma.org

Reforma is an organization committed to the improvement of library and information services for Spanish-speaking and Hispanic communities. It's dedicated to developing Spanish-language library collections and recruiting bilingual library personnel. It sponsors programs and workshops, publishes a quarterly newsletter, and awards scholarships.

Sin Fronteras Organizing Project

201 East 9th Street
El Paso, TX 79901
915-532-0921
http://www.farmworkers.org

This project is organized to assist farmworkers in West Texas and Southern New Mexico.

Society for Advancement of Chicanos and Native Americans in Science

P.O. Box 8526
Santa Cruz, CA 95061-8526
http://www.sacnas.org

SACNAS encourages Chicano/Latino and Native American students to pursue graduate education and obtain the advanced degrees necessary for research careers and science teaching professions at all levels. SACNAS membership is composed of science professors, industry scientists, K-12 teachers, and students. Among SACNAS programs: conferences and workshops, fellowships and scholarships, and a quarterly journal.

Society of Hispanic Professional Engineers

5400 East Olympic Boulevard, Suite 210
Los Angeles, CA 90022
323-725-3970
http://www.shpe.org

SHPE promotes the development of Hispanics in engineering, science, and other technical professions to achieve educational excellence, economic opportunity, and social equity. The SHPE focuses on: increasing educational opportunities; promoting professional and personal growth; and carrying out social responsibility to be involved in education, business, and government issues. SHPE promotes educational opportunities for professionals, college, and K-12 students, and raises funds for scholarships. It develops internship agreements with government and corporate entities. It has developed a training program to enhance leadership skill development, and provides seminars on professional growth and career development. The organization promotes awareness of job opportunities and career guidance, and gathers and publicizes information on Hispanic entrepreneurship and business enterprises.

Society of Mexican American Engineers and Scientists

3780 Kilroy Airport Way, Suite 200
Long Beach, CA 90806
562-988-6585
http://www.tamu.edu/maes

The society works to increase the number of Mexican Americans and other Hispanics in the technical and scientific fields. It represents the Mexican American community in the technological arena on issues related to education, economics, environment, and research.

U.S. Hispanic Chamber of Commerce

1019 19th Street, NW, Suite 200
Washington, DC 20036
202-842-1212
http://www.ushcc.com

This network of nearly 250 Hispanic Chambers of Commerce and Hispanic business organizations communicates the needs and potential of hispanic enterprise to the U.S. government and Corporate America.

Walter Kaitz Foundation

436 14th Street, Suite 925
Oakland, CA 94612
510-451-9000
http://walterkaitz.org

The Walter Kaitz Foundation (WKF) is dedicated to assisting minority professionals in the cable/broadband industry. Training programs, networking, and mentoring opportunities offered by WKF allow professionals to develop skills and advance in the industry. The WKF also provides diversity information and resources to industry companies.

Other Organizations

A Better Chance
419 Boylston Street
Boston, MA 02116
617-421-0950
http://www.abetterchance.org

The mission of A Better Chance is to substantially increase the number of well-educated minority youth capable of assuming positions of responsibility and leadership in American society. Through a range of programs, A Better Chance works with students of color—from the sixth grade through college—to help them access expanded educational and career opportunities. Programs include the College Preparatory Schools Program in which academically talented students of color are placed in educational environments that affirm and nurture their academic talent. The Career Services Program provides an exclusive support network to assist students in career exploration and the preparation of individual career paths. The Pathways to College Program is a pilot program offering after-school support for promising students of color seeking ways to better prepare themselves for college.

Abya Yala Fund
P.O. Box 28386
Oakland, CA 94604
570-763-6553
http://ayf.nativeweb.org

The fund was created by and for indigenous peoples from Central and South America and Mexico. It funds projects that improve life for these people. Projects include a national rights training program for Mexican women and a community program for environmental entrepreneurs.

African American Shakespeare Company
3200 Boston Avenue
Oakland, CA 94602
415-333-1918
http://www.african-americanshakes.org

The African-American Shakespeare Company (AASC) is the only company of African-American actors that perform European classical works in the country. These time-honored works are told within the perspective and cultural dynamic of the African-American culture. The African-American Shakespeare Company's mission is to produce European classical works with an African-American cultural perspective and to provide opportunities and accessibility for minority artists and their community to view these works in a manner that is inclusive of their cultural heritage and identity. The AASC employs 15 actors and 8 designers a year. The company includes a full production season, an afterschool program, a school touring component, and a Summer Youth Troupe.

African American Speakers Bureau
P.O. Box 15490
San Francisco, CA 94115-5490
877-467-1735
http://www.aasb.net

The bureau provides speakers to address issues of interest to the African American community. Speaker categories include arts/literature, business, ethnic health, urban culture, and youth.

Alliance of African American Artists
4936-3 Columbia Road
Columbia, MD 21044-2176
410-740-0033
http://www.artists4a.com

The alliance works to support African American fine art by providing artists with information, consultation, and other support services.

Alpha Development Group

106 Truman Street, 3rd Floor
New London, CT 06320
860-443-8180
http://www.adgroup.org

This non-profit corporation focuses on the minority and disadvantaged community in promoting social, economic, and educational growth by providing activities and programs for increased awareness and success in the marketplace.

American Indian Chamber of Commerce of Oklahoma

2727 East 21st Street, Suite 102
Tulsa, OK 74114
918-743-1115

The Chamber of Commerce works to develop a stronger American Indian business community. It publishes a business directory, provides mentoring and networking opportunities, and advocates for American Indian interests.

American Indian College Fund

1111 Osage Street
Building D, Suite 205W
Denver, CO 80204
303-892-8312
http://www.collegefund.org

The American Indian College Fund raises money for the 30 tribal colleges in the United States. Money from the fund is distributed to these colleges, and the colleges then award scholarships to individual students.

American Indian Higher Education Consortium

121 Oronoco Street
Alexandria, VA 22314
703-838-9400
http://www.aihec.org

AIHEC is a support network for the newly established, tribally controlled colleges; 31 in the United States and one in Canada. The organization assists with areas such as faculty development, accreditation, and intergovernmental relations. AIHEC and the colleges publish a quarterly magazine, *Tribal College Journal.*

Arapaho Business Council

P.O. Box 217
Ft. Washakie, WY 82514
307-332-6120
http://tlc.wtp.net/arapaho.htm

Residents of the Wind River Reservation have access to a number of services and programs.

Asia Society

725 Park Avenue
New York, NY 10021
212-288-6400
http://www.asiasociety.org

The Asia Society is America's leading institution dedicated to fostering understanding of Asia and communication between Americans and the peoples of Asia and the Pacific. A national nonprofit, nonpartisan educational organization, the society provides a forum for building awareness of the more than thirty countries broadly defined as the Asia-Pacific region—the area from Japan to Iran, and from Central Asia to New Zealand, Australia, and the Pacific Islands. Through art exhibitions and performances, films, lectures, seminars, and conferences, publications and assistance to the media, and materials and programs for students and teachers, the Asia Society presents the uniqueness and diversity of Asia to the American people.

Asian American Arts Alliance

74 Varick Street, Suite 302
New York, NY 10013-1914
212-941-9208
http://www.aaartsalliance.org

Through its programs and services, the Asian American Arts Alliance provides managerial and artistic assistance to Asian American artists and art groups; informs and educates the public about Asian American arts; facilitates connections among Asian American artists; and advocates for increased visibility and opportunities for Asian American artists. Services include: Asian American Arts Calendar—a bimonthly calendar of performances, exhibits, and events

Organizations

happening nationwide that also features a Resources & Opportunities listing of jobs, open calls, grant opportunities, and workshops for artists and arts administrators; an information line which provides on-going assistance to callers and visitors seeking information and connections with other Asian American arts resources; an ongoing series of panel discussions, symposiums, and roundtables featuring artists and arts professionals speaking on issues relevant to Asian American arts and the Asian American community; a resource library consisting of a unique collection of books, periodicals, magazines, and interest binders related to Asian American arts; special projects such as the Asian American Arts Fund 1998 and Chase SMARTS Regrant Program, which provide technical assistance and cash regrants to New York City's community-based Asian American arts groups.

Asian American Arts Centre

26 Bowery, 3rd Floor
New York, NY 10013
212-233-2154

The centre exhibits works by Asian artists and photographers, and maintains an archive of art work.

Asian American Economic Development Enterprises

216 West Garvey Avenue, Unit E
Monterey Park, CA 91754
626-572-7021
http://www.aaede.org

The mission of AAEDE is to create business and personal growth for Asian Americans and others through education, employment, and enterprise. To do so, AAEDE provides group training in entrepreneurship, small business, and personal development; supplies management and technical assistance to new and fledgling businesses; and delivers financial support for growing ventures inside and outside the Asian American Community. For 20 years, AAEDE has provided training and employment services to thousands of Asian Americans throughout Southern California while collaborating with government, not-for-profit organizations, and

major corporations in providing programs. In 1998, AAEDE drew more than 1,000 attendees in workshops and seminars which covered topics from international trade and business growth to the commercial use of Internet and other career ideas. AAEDE now also offers language-specific workshops in addition to its usual workshops in English. AAEDE holds an annual job fair, Asian Career Transitions (ACT), specifically designed to meet the career transition needs of Asian Americans.

Asian American Network

9550 Flair Drive
El Monte, CA 91731
800-777-2582
http://www.aan.net

The Asian American Network provides Internet services such as Internet access and home page design for Asian American individuals, businesses, and organizations.

Asian American Service Agency

3610 DeKalb Technology Parkway, Suite 107
Atlanta, GA 30340
770-986-0055

This organization assists Asian Americans with their integration into American culture. Assistance includes computer-skill training, job-hunting skills development, and ESL classes.

Asian American Writer's Workshop

37 St. Mark's Place
New York, NY 10003
212-228-6718

Asian American Writer's Workshop is an organization dedicated to creative writers. It offers various programs, publications, and arts-in-education.

Asian Cultural Council

437 Madison Avenue, 37th Floor
New York, NY 10022-7001
212-812-4300
http://www.asianculturalcouncil.org

The Asian Cultural Council supports cultural exchange in the visual and performing arts between the United States and the countries of Asia. The central feature of the ACC is a program which grants fellowships to artists, scholars, and specialists from Asia for the purposes of research, study, and creative work in the United States. Some grants are also made to Americans pursuing similar activities in Asia and to educational and cultural institutions engaged in projects of special significance to Asian-American exchange.

Asian Media Access

3028 Oregon Avenue South
Minneapolis, MN 55426
612-376-7715
http://amamedia.org

Asian Media Access is a non-profit media art and education organization inspiring Asian American communities in the Midwest to use media as a means to promote positive social change.

Asian Pacific American Labor Alliance

1101 14th Street, NW, Suite 310
Washington, DC 20005
202-842-1263
http://www.apalanet.org

This national organization of Asian Pacific American union members seeks better pay, improved benefits, dignity on the job, and a voice in the workplace. It has a national office in Washington, D.C., and chapters across the country.

Aspira Association

1444 Eye Street, NW, Suite 800
Washington, DC 20005
202-835-3600
http://www.aspira.org

ASPIRA operates a number of programs across the country to help acquaint Hispanic students with opportunities in science and mathematics fields. It offers internship and scholarship opportunities, hosts education conferences, and sponsors a number of math and science initiatives.

Association for Hispanic Theological Education

P.O. Box 520
Columbia Theological Seminary
701 Columbia Drive
Decatur, GA 30031
404-687-4560
http://www.aeth.org

The AETH promotes and enhances theological education for Hispanic Americans in Bible institutes, Bible colleges, seminaries, and other programs in the United States, Canada, and Puerto Rico. Membership includes educators and students. AETH sponsors mentoring programs and a program for Hispanic women in the ministry, and provides technical assistance.

Association of Hispanic Arts, Inc.

173 East 116th Street, 2nd Floor
New York, NY 10029
212-860-5445

The association serves as a clearinghouse of information about Hispanic arts organizations. It publishes a newsletter and a directory of organizations, and also maintains a database of information about fellowships and grants.

Association on American Indian Affairs

P.O. Box 268
Sisseton, SD 57262
605-698-3998
http://web.tnics.com/aaia

The Association on American Indian Affairs (AAIA), is a citizen-sponsored, national, non-profit organization assisting American Indian and Alaska Native communities in their efforts to achieve full economic and social equality while preserving their unique culture. AAIA works on the national level to protect basic human rights for Native Americans at the request of tribal leaders. AAIA is governed by a board of prominent Indian people from such fields as law, education, health, and public

Organizations

service and is funded by over 40,000 members and contributors. Headquartered in Sisseton, South Dakota, AAIA also has a field office in California. The AAIA sponsors health programs, children and youth programs, and works to ensure tribes their sovereignty through federal acknowledgement. AAIA also sponsors 4 scholarship programs.

Atlanta Hispanic Chamber of Commerce Foundation

2964 Peachtree Road, NW, Suite 350
Atlanta, GA 30305
404-264-0879

This organization assists with the development of Hispanic businesses, and serves as an entrepreneurial resource center for small businesses.

Bad River Band of Lake Superior Chippewa

P.O. Box 39
Odanah, WI 54861
715-682-7111
http://www.glitc.org/badriv1.htm

The reservation offers a number of resources and community events.

Ballet Hispanico

167 West 89th Street
New York, NY 10024-1901
212-362-6710
http://www.ballethispanico.org

The Ballet Hispanico Company has been widely recognized as the foremost dance interpreter of Hispanic culture in the United States, with an innovative repertory which blends ballet, modern, and ethnic dance forms into a spirited image of the contemporary Hispanic world. Over 60 new works have been commissioned for Ballet Hispanico's repertory from choreographers of international stature. As part of the company's commitment to new work, Ballet Hispanico also conducts choreographer workshops, which have included a wide range of emerging artists.

Bay Area Urban League

Scholarship Committee
2201 Broadway Street
Oakland, CA 94612-3017
510-271-1846

The Bay Area Urban League is an interracial, non-profit community service organization which uses the tools and methods of social work, economics, law, business management and other disciplines to secure equal opportunities in all sectors of our society for African Americans and other minorities. It sponsors advocacy, and education and research programs. The On The Job Training program has proven a successful means for providing training and subsequent employment to San Francisco residents. Through North Cities Coalition (Alameda, Albany, Berkeley, Emeryville, and Piedmont), residents are enrolled in certified job training classes or directly into a guided job search program.

Black Academy of Arts and Letters

Dallas Convention Center Theater Complex
650 South Griffin Street
Dallas, TX 75202
214-743-2440
http://www.tbaal.org

The academy promotes the work of African Americans in the fine, literary, and performing arts. It supports arts education programs, exhibitions, special events, and music, theater, and dance performances.

Black and Puerto Rican Legislative Caucus

Legislative Office Building #442A
Albany, NY 12248
518-455-5347

To increase political involvement of minority populations, the annual caucus invites African Americans and Puerto Ricans to Albany for seminars and workshops.

Black Executive Exchange Program

120 Wall Street
New York, NY 10005
212-558-5320
http://www.beepusa.org

The Black Executives Exchange Program is dedicated to the need for quality education for African American students who are interested in high-level industry and government careers. It arranges for professionals to lecture at participating colleges.

Black Heritage Museum

P.O. Box 570327
Miami, FL 33257-0327
305-252-3535
http://gsni.com/bhm.htm

Black Literary Players

829 Langdon Court
Rochester Hills, MI 48307
810-556-7335

This literary agency represents African American writers.

Black Student Fund

3636 16th Street, NW
Washington, DC 20010-1146
202-387-1414
http://www.blackstudentfund.org

The Black Student Fund (BSF) offers financial assistance to African American students (grades K-12) and their families. It works to assure that African American students have equal access to quality educational opportunities. BSF programs include multiracial training to teachers and networking for African American educators.

Black Women in Sisterhood for Action

P.O. Box 1592
Washington, DC 20013
301-460-1565

This national non-profit corporation works to develop and promote alternative strategies for educational and career development of black women in the world of work; provide scholarship assistance to deserving youths; provide support and social assistance to senior black women in the community; share information and resources in meaningful ways with the community-at-large; and provide leadership, role models, and mentors for young people.

Black Writers Institute

1650 Bedford Avenue
Brooklyn, NY 11225
415-333-1918
http://www.blackwriters.net

The Black Writers Institute (BWI) is part of the creative writing program of Medger Evers College in Brooklyn, and serves as a resource for writers. The primary goal of the BWI is to make discussions about literature written by black writers accessible, relevant, and meaningful to the general public. BWI maintains Black Writers Institute Online where you can find resources, information and events related to the evolution of Black Literature. The Web site informs about the developments within the institute, particularly as they pertain to the world of black Literature. BWI wishes to act as an advocate for the many black writers whose writing, though meritorious, remains unpublished. BWI hopes to stem the trend that places more value on marketability of a work than on its aesthetic merits and its power to transform the world.

Blackfeet Nation

P.O. Box 850
Browning, MT 59417
406-338-7521
http://www.blackfeetnation.com

The Blackfeet Indian Reservation in Northern Montana is home to Blackfeet Community College, and provides information about jobs and economic development.

Blue Chip Foundation

4315 Donlyn Court
Columbus, OH 43232
614-861-0772
http://www.bbpa.org

The foundation is an organization that promotes the well-being of urban youth in central Ohio by helping them to develop leadership

Organizations

skills. Activities include mentoring, a training academy, and community service.

Blues Heaven Foundation

249 North Brand Boulevard #590
Glendale, CA 91203
818-507-8944
http://www.island.net/~blues/heaven.html

The Foundation is dedicated to perserving and promoting blues culture. It maintains a scholarship program, donates instruments to elementary and secondary school music education programs, sponsors an exhibit of photography of blues artists, and assists blues artists with copyright and royalty protection. The foundation is also restoring the building at 2120 S. Michigan Ave. in Chicago, former home of the Chess Records label, as a studio and gallery.

Brothers for Progress

30 3rd Avenue, Room 602
Brooklyn, NY 11217
718-222-1405
http://www.brooklynx.org/neighborhoods/
brothersforpro

This community service organization leads self-help and empowerment workshops for minority and disadvantaged people. Programs have included a Community Art Mentoring Program, Substance Abuse Prevention Project, and community outreach.

California Chicano/Latino Medical Student Association

http://latino.ucsf.edu/cmsa

The California Chicano/Latino Medical Student Association is an organization throughout the state of California, and in Tucson, Arizona, representing Hispanic students attending area medical schools. The organization works to promote the development of a communication network for Hispanic medical and premedical students. Contact one of these participating medical schools for more information: Stanford, UC Davis, UC San Francisco, UC Irvine, UC Los Angeles, UC San Diego, Charles R. Drew University of Medicine and Sciences, Western

University of Health Sciences, University of Southern California, and the University of Arizona.

California Indian Basketweavers Association

P.O. Box 2397
Nevada City, CA 95959
530-478-5660
http://www.ciba.org

The association works to preserve and promote California Indian basketweaving traditions.

Center for Pan-Asian Community Service

5302 Buford Highway, Suite B-3
Doraville, GA 30340
770-936-0969

This organization provides job training and other social services to the Pan-Asian community dealing with problems associated with immigration.

Center for the History of the American Indian

60 West Walton Street
Chicago, IL 60610
312-255-3564
http://www.newberry.org

The D'Arcy McNickle Center for American Indian History of the Newberry Library promotes research and teaching about the history of Native Americans. The center hosts pre- and post-doctoral scholars on long-term fellowships, generally of six to eleven months' duration. Short-term fellows spend between two weeks and two months. Over the years, these long- and short-term fellowships have resulted in nearly 40 books and dozens of scholarly articles. The McNickle Center has offered short-term fellowships for teachers of Native American history, published bibliographies, offered summer institutes for teachers of American Indian history and American Indian literature, and sponsored conferences, seminars, and workshops for scholars/teachers. The center also publishes "Meeting Ground," a national biannual newsletter.

Cheyenne River Sioux Tribe

P.O. Box 590
Eagle Butte, SD 57625
605-964-4155
http://www.sioux.org

The reservation colleges and the Game, Fish, and Parks Department are part of the tribe's resources.

Chickasaw Nation

P.O. Box 1548
530 East Arlington Boulevard
Ada, OK 74820
580-436-2603
http://www.chickasaw.com

Access to business enterprises, programs and services, and job information is available.

Chinese-American Planning Council

65-69 Lispenard Street, 2/F
New York, NY 10013
212-941-0920

The Chinese-American Planning Council is one of the largest social service programs serving the Chinese American population in the United States. It provides services through over 45 programs in 26 facilities located in the culture and arts, in the strengthening of the economy, and in the development of low-income housing. It also sponsors a Summer Youth Employment Program.

Chippewa Cree Tribal Council

R.R. 1, Box 544
Box Elder, MT 59521
406-395-4282
http://tlc.wtp.net/chippewa.htm

The tribe has formed a business committee and other developmental programs, and offers educational opportunities through the Stone Child College.

Choctaw Nation

Higher Education Program, Drawer 1210
Durant, OK 74702-1210
800-522-6170
http://www.choctawnation.com

The Choctaw Nation sponsors community events, programs, and a Web site which features the Choctaw Artists' Registry—a listing of Choctaw artists around the world.

Citizen Potawatomi Nation

1601 South Gordon Cooper Avenue
Shawnee, OK 74801-8699
405-275-3121
http://www.potawatomi.org

The nation sponsors programs and business enterprises to assist with economic development.

Columbia River Inter-Tribal Fish Commission

729 NE Oregon, Suite 200
Portland, OR 97232
503-238-0667
http://www.critfc.org

The commission represents the fisheries interests of the 4 Columbia River Treaty Tribes (Yakama, Umatilla, Warm Springs, Nez Perce).

Community Financial Investment Groups

P.O. Box 470077
Los Angeles, CA 90047
323-299-3297
http://www.investblack.com

This group is an African American financial and investment education membership association. Programs include the Black Business Enrichment Program and an entrepreneurship program.

Confederated Tribes of Siletz Indians

201 Southeast Swan Avenue
Siletz, OR 97380
800-922-1399
http://ctsi.nsn.us

Organizations

A number of tribal services are available, including career guidance.

Confederated Tribes of Warm Springs Oregon
http://www.warmsprings.com

The Web site provides community and historical information about the tribes, a directory of phone numbers, and other resources.

Congress of National Black Churches
1225 I Street, NW, Suite 750
Washington, DC 20005
202-371-1092
http://www.cnbc.org

The Congress of National Black Churches (CNBC) is an ecumenical coalition of 8 major historically African American denominations. These denominations represent 65,000 churches and a membership of more than 20 million people. CNBC's mission is to foster Christian unity, charity, and fellowship.

Congressional Black Caucus Foundation
Educational Programs
1004 Pennsylvania Avenue, SE
Washington, DC 20003
202-675-6739
http://www.cbcfonline.org

The Congressional Black Caucus Foundation, Inc. (CBCF), works to increase the influence of African Americans in the political, legislative, and public policy arenas. CBCF sponsors issue forums and leadership seminars, as well as national educational programs. These programs include the Congressional Black Caucus Spouses (CBC Spouses) Education Scholarship Fund, the Fellowship Program, and the Internship Program.

Cook Inlet Region, Inc.
P.O. Box 93330
Anchorage, AK 99509-3330
907-274-8638
http://www.ciri.com

An Alaska Native Regional corporation providing shareholder information, job listings, and community leadership.

Cow Creek Band of Umpqua Tribe of Indians
2371 Northeast Stephens, Suite 100
Roseburg, OR 97470
541-672-9405
http://www.cowcreek.com

The tribe sponsors economic development programs.

Dakota Indian Foundation
209 North Main
P.O. Box 340
Chamberlain, SD 57325
http://www.dakotaindianfoundation.org

The foundation grants funds to groups and organizations throughout the Sioux Nation to support a wide variety of activities directly related to the social enhancement, economic development, and cultural preservation of the Dakota Sioux Indian people.

Delaware Tribe of Indians
220 Northwest Virginia
Bartlesville, OK 74003
918-336-5272
http://www.delawaretribeofindians.nsn.us/

A number of services are available through the tribal council.

East West Players
244 South San Pedro Street, Suite 301
Los Angeles, CA 90012
213-625-7000
http://www.bnw.com/eastwestplayers

East West Players (EWP) is dedicated to the nurturing and promotion of Asian Pacific American and other culturally diverse talent through the arts. EWP encourages artists to express themselves by writing stories, creating and producing projects, expanding their performance repertoire, and sharing the work with the community. EWP's Mainstage season consists of productions from musicals, comedies, and dramas to Asian, European, and American classics and world premieres. EWP sponsors opportunities for new writers, hosts the EWP Actors Conservatory, and conducts seminars, workshops, and special benefits.

East-West Center

Burns Hall 20661
601 East-West Road
Honolulu, HI 96848
808-944-7111
http://www.ewc.hawaii.edu

The East-West Center is a national and regional source of information and analysis about the Asia-Pacific Region, including the United States. The center serves scholars, the government, business professionals, teachers, journalists, and others researching issues of contemporary significance. The center supports the East-West Center Research Program (EWCRP) which researches issues in order to promote understanding and mutually beneficial relations between the United States and the countries of Asia and the Pacific.

Eddie G. Robinson Foundation

P.O. Box 50609
Atlanta, GA 30302
877-284-3473
http://www.eddierobinson.com

The Eddie G. Robinson Foundation assists the youth of America with merit and need-based scholarships, grants, and charitable contributions.

Equal Rights Advocates

1663 Mission Street, Suite 550
San Francisco, CA 94103-2631
415-621-0672
http://www.equalrights.org

Law school students and graduates are sought by this organization to help with its ongoing program of research and legal action to help women attain equal rights. The group focuses on the needs of women from low-income or minority groups. This is a paid position; applications are due in May. Student law clerks are hired for the spring, fall, and summer to assist attorneys with legal research and writing and to staff ERA's Advice and Counseling Line. Students are encouraged to seek grants, work-study funding, and/or clinical credit for their work. The one-year Ruth Chance Fellowship is available for recent law school graduates; apply by November 1.

Falmouth Institute

3702 Pender Drive, Suite 300
Fairfax, VA 22030
800-992-4489
http://www.falmouthinst.com

The Falmouth Institute, Inc., offers training and consulting services to Native American communities. By researching the activities of Capitol Hill, the Department of Interior-Bureau of Indian Affairs, Department of Health and Human Services—Indian Health Service, Department of Education, Department of Housing and Urban Development, and other federal agencies, the institute can provide current training materials. With instructors, current textbooks, a wide range of course offerings and expert knowledge of Indian issues, the institute provides customized information, training, research, and technical assistance to the American Indian community. In addition, the Institute publishes the *American Indian Report* magazine, the *Native American Law Digest,* and the *Casino Crime Digest.*

First Nations Development Institute

11917 Main Street
Fredericksburg, VA 22408
540-371-5615
http://www.firstnations.org

This Native American non-profit organization promotes culturally appropriate economic development by and for native peoples. It provides education, advocacy, research, and funding. First Nations coordinates local grass roots projects with national programs and policy development to build capacity for its self-reliant reservation economics.

Organizations

Georgia Legislative Black Caucus

Legislative Office Building, Suite 602
Atlanta, GA 30334
404-651-5569

The caucus serves the African American community in Georgia, providing current information on government agencies.

Golden State Minority Foundation

1055 Wilshire Boulevard, Suite 1115
Los Angeles, CA 90017-2431
800-666-4763
http://home.earthlink.net/~gsmf/

GSMF strongly believes that the successful future of our nation requires the active participation of well-educated and qualified individuals from currently underrepresented minority groups. GSMF's mission is to financially and socially enable outstanding, economically disadvantaged minority students to achieve the comprehensive education necessary to realize their full potential as the essential voices of diversity in tomorrow's leadership. To reach its goals, GSMF awards grants to inner-city schools, scholarships to minority students, and offers mentoring opportunities.

Great Lakes Indian Fish and Wildlife Commission

P.O. Box 9
Odanah, WI 54861
715-682-6619
http://www.glifwc.org

Comprising 11 sovereign tribal governments located throughout Minnesota, Wisconsin, and Michigan, the commission's purpose is to protect and enhance treaty-guaranteed rights to hunt, fish, and gather on inland territories, and to provide cooperative management of these resources.

Great Plains Black Museum

2213 Lake Street
Omaha, NE 68110
402-345-6734

The museum serves as an educational resource for students and scholars, and is dedicated to preserving the African American experience of the Great Plains.

Heard Museum Library and Archives

2301 North Central Avenue
Phoenix, AZ 85004-1323
602-252-8840
http://www.heard.org

The library maintains an information file on 17,000 Native American artists. The file helps researchers, libraries, museums, and other artists learn of people working in all forms of Native American arts.

Hispanic Agenda for Action

U.S. Department of Health and Human Services
200 Independence Avenue, SW
Washington, DC 20201
http://www.haa.omhrc.gov

The HAA is a government initiative coordinated by the Office of Minority Health within the Department of Health and Human Services, focusing on such issues as health services and education for Hispanic Americans.

Hispanic Alliance for Career Enhancement

Student Development Program
14 East Jackson Boulevard, Suite 1310
Chicago, IL 60604
312-435-0498
http://www.hace-usa.org

Founded in 1982, the Hispanic Alliance for Career Enhancement (HACE) is a national pioneer in developing initiatives that provide opportunities for Hispanics to participate in professional and managerial positions, as well as in the educational advancement of college students. Its mission is to provide linkage and access for Hispanic professionals to private and public organizations, thereby strengthening the foundation for the professional and economic advancement of the Hispanic community. To achieve its goals, HACE offers such programs as the Employer Support Program (ESP)—a comprehensive candidate referral program designed to assist recruiters with their staffing and recruitment needs. HACE maintains a fully computerized database of over 3,500 professional profiles. HACE also sponsors the Annual Career Development Conference (which includes workshops and a 2-day career expo); professional development seminars; and a student development program.

Hispanic Association of Colleges and Universities

8415 Datapoint Drive, Suite 400
San Antonio, TX 78229
210-692-3805
http://www.hacu.net

As a national association representing Hispanic-Serving Institutions (HSIs), the Hispanic Association of Colleges and Universities works to promote non-profit, accredited college and universities where Hispanics constitute a minumum of 25 percent of the enrollment at either the graduate or undergraduate level. HACU works with its partners in business, government, and industry to accomplish this mission. The association also administers a national internship program for Hispanic students interested in careers with the federal government. Publications are produced periodically by the association, including a monthly newsletter, an annual report, and various research-related publications, and other multi-media products. It also maintains an informative Web site with a scholarship database.

Hispanic Association on Corporate Responsibility

1730 Rhode Island Avenue, NW, Suite 1008
Washington, DC 20036
http://www.hacr.org

HACR works to ensure that the Hispanic community has active participation in corporate America. HACR encourages corporations to adopt programs that support diversity. HACR conducts research on Hispanics in corporate America and publishes the results.

Hispanic Heritage Foundation

P.O. Box 2764
New Orleans, LA 70176-2764
504-582-4234

This group works on problems related to the Hispanic social and political presence in New Orleans.

Hispanic Radio Network

1030 15th Street, NW, Suite 400
Washington, DC 20005
202-637-8800
http://www.hrn.org

The Hispanic Radio Network is a series of Spanish language radio programs informing Hispanics about health, environment, education, social justice, information, and resources.

Hispanic-Serving Health Professions Schools

1700 17th Street, NW, Suite 405
Washington, DC 20009
202-667-9788
http://www.hshps.com

The mission of the HSHPS is to develop educational opportunities in health professions schools to increase the number of Hispanics in health professions careers.

Hispanics in Philanthropy

2606 Dwight Way
Berkeley, CA 94704
510-649-1692

Hispanics in Philanthropy (HIP) is an association of more than 350 grantmakers that advocates for increased philanthropic support of Hispanic communities and greater representation of Hispanics on boards and staff of foundations. HIP commissions and disseminates research findings, convenes conferences and briefings, provides information and referrals, and publishes regular newsletters and other reports.

Hispanics Organized for Political Equality

634 Spring Street, Suite 920
Los Angeles, CA 90014
213-622-0606
http://www.latinas.org

Organizations

HOPE is an advocacy organization dedicated to the political education and participation of Latinas and other women in the political process. It sponsors workshops and hosts annual symposiums.

Historically Black College and University Bandsmen of America

5640 Keele Street, Suite J-24
Jackson, MS 39206
601-899-5979
http://www.blackcollegebands.com

Historically Black College and University Bandsmen of America consists of students in HBCU bands across the country.

Hopi Tribe

http://www.hopi.nsn.us

The official site of the Hopi Tribe of northeastern Arizona provides information on tribal government and health and human services.

Native American Career Education in Natural Resources

Humboldt State University
Office of Financial Aid
Arcata, CA 95521
707-826-3011

Native American Career Education in Natural Resources offers Indians the opportunity to qualify for professional employment in natural resource management. Available at the bachelor's-degree level are majors in fisheries, forestry, oceanography, range management, wildlife management, and resources planning and interpretation; at the master's level, fisheries, forestry, wildlife, and interdisciplinary natural resources.

Indian Education Program

4600 De Barr Road
Anchorage, AK 99504
907-269-2311

The program seeks to increase the quality of education for Native Americans living in Alaska.

It is also concerned with providing more opportunities in academics for Native Americans.

Indian Family Services

1505 Park Avenue
Minneapolis, MN 55404
612-348-5788

This is a service organization concentrating on the needs of Indian elderly and disabled; it helps them become more independent by providing them with social and recreational activities.

Indiana Black Legislative Caucus

State House #405
Indianapolis, IN 46204
317-232-9646

The caucus works to keep the state's African American community informed about political issues.

Inter-Tribal Council of Nevada

680 Greenbrae Drive, Suite 280
Sparks, NV 89431
702-355-0600
http://itcn.org

The Inter-Tribal Council of Nevada, Inc. (ITCN), is a tribal organization serving the member reservations and colonies in Nevada. The governing body of ITCN consists of an executive board, composed of tribal chairmen from each of these tribes. The main intent of ITCN is to serve as a large political body for the small Nevada tribes. ITCN has played a major role in promoting health, educational, social, economic, and job opportunity programs. ITCN now manages federal and state funded programs aimed at improving the well-being of community members throughout the state of Nevada. Among the programs administered by ITCN are Headstart, the Job Training Partnership Act, and the Nevada Indian Environmental Coalition.

International Agency for Minority Artist Affairs

163 West 125th Street, 9th Floor
New York, NY 10027
212-749-5298
http://idt.net/~iamaa/

The International Agency for Minority Artist Affairs (IAMAA) is the Arts Council of Harlem. The IAMAA is committed to the long-range cultural development of Harlem. The council helps make a diversity of high-quality arts experiences available to the people of Harlem and assists resident art organizations and artists to reach their full potential.

Intertribal Timber Council

4370 Northeast Halsey Street
Portland, OR 97213
503-282-4296
http://www.itcnet.org

The ITC is a nationwide consortium of Indian Tribes, Alaska Native Corporations, and individuals dedicated to improving the management of natural resources of importance to Native American communities. The ITC works cooperatively with the Bureau of Indian Affairs (BIA), private industry, and academia to explore issues and identify practical strategies and initiatives to promote social, economic, and ecological values while protecting and utilizing forests, soil, water, and wildlife. Over 60 tribes and Alaskan Native Corporations currently belong to the ITC.

Jamestown S'Kallam Tribe

1033 Old Blyn Highway
Sequim, WA 98382
360-683-1109
http://www.olympus.net/personal/skallam/

Contact the tribal council for information about the tribe, tribal business enterprises, and special projects and programs.

Japan Foundation

152 West 57th Street, 39th Floor
New York, NY 10019-3310
212-489-0299
http://www.jfny.org

The Japan Foundation promotes international cultural exchange and mutual understanding between Japan and other countries. The foundation conducts a wide range of programs worldwide, including support for Japanese studies, Japanese language instruction, arts and cultural events, intellectual exchange, and the exchange of persons.

Japanese American Citizens League

1765 Sutter Street
San Francisco, CA 94115
415-921-5225
http://www.jacl.org

The Japanese American Citizens League works to fight discrimination against people of Japanese ancestry. It is the largest and one of the oldest Asian American organizations in the United States. The organization hosts conferences, publishes books, and supports scholarship, fellowship, and grant programs.

Japanese American Network

231 East 3rd Street, Suite G-104
Los Angeles, CA 90013
213-473-1653
http://www.janet.org

The Japanese American Network is a partnership of Japanese American organizations encouraging the use of the Internet to exchange information about the community.

Johns Hopkins University

Applied Physics Laboratory
11100 Johns Hopkins Road
Johns Hopkins University
Laurel, MD 20723-6099
http://www.jhuapl.edu/NAPD/contents.html

The association works to increase the pool of students pursuing engineering, mathematics, and technology-based college study. NAPD-program students are of ethnicities that are historically underrepresented in the science and engineering professions.

Organizations

Klamath Tribes

P.O. Box 436
Chiloquin, OR 97624
541-783-2219
http://www.klamathtribes.org

A number of tribal services and departments assist with economic, educational, and career development.

Latin American Educational Foundation

930 West Seventh Avenue
Denver, CO 80204
303-446-0541
http://www.laef.org

The Latin American Educational Foundation works to advance the economic and social status of the Hispanic community by improving access to higher education through scholarships, community collaboration, and support programs. Its programs include a high school network, mentoring, and relationships with institutions of higher education focusing on increasing Hispanic enrollment.

Latino International Film Festival

6777 Hollywood Boulevard, Suite 500
Hollywood, CA 90028
323-469-9066
http://www.latinofilm.org

This annual showcase of Latino films recognizes the makers of feature films, documentaries, and shorts.

Latino Issues Forum

785 Market Street, 3rd Floor
San Francisco, CA 94103
415-284-7200
http://www.lif.org

Latino Issues Forum is an advocacy institute focusing on public policy issues. It works for better access to higher education, health care, and telecommunications among Latinos. It provides community education and training, as well as policy analysis and development.

League of United Latin American Citizens

2000 L Street, NW, Suite 610
Washington, DC 20036
202-833-6130
http://www.lulac.org

The League of United Latin American Citizens (LULAC) operates community-based programs at more than 600 LULAC councils nationwide. LULAC focuses on education, civil rights, and employment for Hispanics. LULAC councils provide more than half a million dollars in scholarships to Hispanic students each year, conducts citizenship and voter registration drives, develops low income housing units, conducts youth leadership training programs, and seeks to empower the Hispanic community at the local, state, and national level. In addition, the LULAC National Educational Service Centers, LULAC's educational arm, provide counseling services to more than 18,000 Hispanic students per year at sixteen regional centers. SER Jobs for Progress, LULAC's employment arm, provides job skills and literacy training to the Hispanic community through more than forty-eight employment training centers located throughout the United States.

Lumbee Regional Development Association

P.O. Box 68
Pembroke, NC 28372
910-521-8602
http://www.lumbee.org

The association is dedicated to area development, and sponsors services and programs.

Magic Johnson Foundation

600 Corporate Pointe, Suite 1080
Culver City, CA 90230
888-624-4205
http://www.magicjohnson.org

The foundation supports community based organizations serving the health, educational, and social needs of children living in the inner-cities.

Marketing Opportunities in Black Entertainment

RAI Ltd.
6 North Michigan Avenue, Suite 909
Chicago, IL 60602
773-651-8008
http://www.mobe.com

MOBE sponsors a symposium series for marketers, entertainment executives, promoters, producers, and technologists.

Massachusetts, University of, Medical School

Summer Research Fellowship Program
Office of School Services
55 Lake Avenue, North
Worcester, MA 01610
508-856-2444

The Worcester Pipeline Collaborative encourages, educates, and challenges minority and/or disadvantaged students for success in health care and science professions where they are traditionally underrepresented. The WPC partnership includes professionals and K-20 educators from public schools, colleges, universities, biotechnology, health care, and science industries. WPC offers mentoring, internships, shadowing, after school programs, summer science camp, and professional development. In addition, students may delve into the exploratory nature of science in the Science Laboratory equipped with activities that enhance standards-based school curricula. A Technology Center with state of the art computers and Video Teleconferencing Equipment for distance learning will sustain WPC students into the 21st century.

Media Action Network for Asian Americans

P.O. Box 11105
Burbank, CA 91510
213-486-4433
http://janet.org/~manaa

The Media Action Network monitors all facets of the media for Asian American portrayals and subject matter. It recognizes the achievements of individuals in the entertainment and media industry for their efforts in presenting a balanced image of Asian Americans in the media. The organization also offers scholarship opportunities.

Mexican American Legal Defense and Educational Fund

634 South Spring Street, 11th Floor
Los Angeles, CA 90014
213-629-2512
http://www.maldef.org

The Mexican American Legal Defense and Educational Fund (MALDEF) works to promote the civil rights of Latinos living in the United States. MALDEF works through litigation, advocacy, community outreach, and education to secure the rights of Latinos, primarily in the areas of employment, education, immigration, political access, and public resource equity. Services include scholarship opportunities, legal programs, and programs in education and leadership development. MALDEF is headquartered in Los Angeles and has regional offices in Chicago, Los Angeles, San Antonio, San Francisco, and Washington, D.C.; a satellite office in Sacramento, California; and a program office in Phoenix, Arizona.

Mexican-American Women's National Association

1725 K Street, NW, Suite 501
Washington, DC 20006
202-833-0060
http://www.hermana.org

MANA is a membership organization dedicated to the empowerment of Latinas of all ages. It sponsors mentoring and community projects, awards scholarships, and hosts a leadership development conference.

Michigan Urban Indian Consortium

4990 Northwind Drive, Suite 100
East Lansing, MI 48823
517-333-6550

The consortium is a non-profit, statewide urban Indian organization. It consists of urban centers

217

Organizations

working together to address common problems in providing services for urban Indian people.

Minority Business Development Agency
14th Street and Constitution Avenue, NW, Room 5055
Washington, DC 20230
http://www.mbda.gov

The MBDA is an agency within the U.S. Department of Commerce, assisting minority-owned businesses. It oversees Minority Business Development Centers across the country, and the Native American Business Development Centers.

Mohegan Tribe
P.O. Box 488
Uncasville, CT 06382
860-204-6100
http://www.mohegan.nsn.us

The tribe sponsors education programs and other community development programs.

Multicultural Marketing Resources
286 Spring Street, Suite 201
New York, NY 10013
212-242-3351
http://www.inforesources.com

Multicultural Marketing Resources is a public relations and marketing company with resources for business executives and journalists. MMR publishes the bi-monthly "Multicultural Marketing News" newsletter and an annual directory, "The Source Book of Multicultural Experts."

NALEO Educational Fund
5800 South Eastern Avenue, Suite 365
Los Angeles, CA 90040
http://www.naleo.org

The National Association of Latino Elected and Appointed Officials Educational Fund promotes the participation of Latinos in the nation's civic life. It supports programs that promote the integration of Latino immigrants into American society. It also works to develop future leaders among Latino youth, and conducts research on issues of importance.

National African American Catholic Youth Ministry Network
320 Cathedral Street
Baltimore, MD 21201-4421
410-547-8496
http://www.nbccongress.org

The NBCC represents African American Roman Catholics. It offers training programs for clergy, and for religious and lay leaders, and hosts a high school consortium. Affiliated with the National Black Catholic Congress, the network provides a collective voice for youth and youth ministers.

National African American Student Leadership Conference
Rust College
150 Rust Avenue
Holly Springs, MS 38635
601-252-8000
http://www.naaslc.org

This annual conference concerns African American leadership. It consists of workshops and panel discussions on such topics as education, affirmative action, and international studies.

National Asian American Telecommunications Association
346 9th Street, 2nd Floor
San Francisco, CA 94103
415-863-0814
http://www.naatanet.org

NAATA seeks to advance the ideal of the U.S. as a pluralistic society where diverse cultures and people are empowered and respected. Through film, video, and new technologies, NAATA aims to promote better understanding of the Asian Pacific American experience to the broadest audience possible.

National Asian Women's Health Organization

250 Montgomery Street, Suite 1500
San Francisco, CA 94104
415-989-9747
http://www.nawho.org

The organization works to improve the health status of Asian American women and families through research, education, and public policy advocacy.

National Association for Bilingual Education

1220 L Street, NW, Suite 605
Washington, DC 20005-4018
202-898-1829
http://www.nabe.org

The National Association for Bilingual Education is a non-profit national membership organization founded to address the educational needs of language-minority students in the U.S. and to advance the language competencies and multicultural understanding of all Americans.

National Association for Equal Opportunity in Higher Education

8701 Georgia Avenue, Suite 200
Silver Spring, MD 20910
301-650-2440
http://www.nafeo.org

NAFEO is the national umbrella and public policy advocacy organization for 118 of the nation's historically and predominantly black colleges and universities (HBCU). NAFEO serves as an international voice for the nation's HBCUs; places and maintains the issue of equal opportunity in higher education on the national agenda; and increases the active participation of African Americans at every level in the forming of the policies and programs of higher education. Among NAFEO's programs and services: Mobil Faculty Fellowship Awards, National Conference on Blacks in Higher Education, the Coors African American Student Leadership Conference, and the NAFEO Internship Program.

National Association for Multicultural Education

733 15th Street, NW, Suite 430
Washington, DC 20005
202-628-6263
http://www.inform.umd.edu/NAME/

This organization promotes cultural and ethnic diversity in education, providing information to teachers, administrators, and other educators.

National Association of Black Scuba Divers

1605 Crittenden Street, NE
Washington, DC 20017
800-521-NABS
http://www.nabsdivers.org

The association promotes an appreciation of diving and an awareness of the aquatic environment. It sponsors an educational program and an annual convention, and provides scholarships for college students studying marine and environmental sciences.

National Association of Negro Business and Professional Women's Clubs

1806 New Hampshire Avenue, NW
Washington, DC 20009
202-483-4206
http://www.afrika.com/nanbpwc/

NANBPW is an organization composed of business and professional women devoted to community service projects. The organization also honors men, women, and youth who have demonstrated outstanding succcess in their professions and/or an exceptional commitment to the community.

National Baptist Convention of America

1327 Pierre Avenue
Shreveport, LA 71103
318-221-3701

The National Baptist Convention represents several thousand churches and millions of individuals. The convention promotes Christian education and missionary work.

National Baptist Convention USA

1700 Baptist World Center Drive
National Baptist World Center
Nashville, TN 37207
615-228-6292

Considered the largest African American organization in the world, this is the larger of the 2 Baptist conventions, serving more than 30,000 churches.

National Black Alcoholism and Addictions Council

285 Genesee Street
Utica, NY 13502
202-296-2696

The council is concerned with the effects of alcoholism among African Americans. It provides information to African American communities to inform them of the effects of addiction and conducts training on treatment.

National Black Family Summit

College of Social Work
University of South Carolina
Columbia, SC 29208

The National Black Family Summit is an annual event addressing vital issues impacting the African American family. The summit is a professional forum designed to examine issues from a scholarly perspective.

National Black United Fund

40 Clinton Street, 5th Floor
Newark, NJ 07102
http://www.nbuf.org

The fund promotes charitable giving among African Americans. It supports educational, cultural, socio-economic, and social justice programs.

National Bowling Association

377 Park Avenue South, 7th Floor
New York, NY 10016
http://www.inlink.com/~tnbainc/

Operated by African Americans, this association is 1 of the 3 major governing bodies for amateur bowling. Among its many programs is the Junior Bowling Program. It also sponsors national tournaments.

National Center for American Indian and Alaska Native Mental Health Research

4455 East 12th Street
Campus Box AO11-13
Denver, CO 80220
303-315-9232

The center pursues research to aid in the mental health care of Native Americans.

National Center for American Indian Enterprise Development

953 East Juanita Avenue
Mesa, AZ 85204
800-4-NCAIED
http://www.ncaied.org

The NCAIED offers economic development services to American Indians, Native Hawaiians, Alaskan Natives, and tribal governments. Currently the National Center provides services through three regional offices near the high-density Indian populations of Los Angeles, Phoenix, and Seattle. Its mission is to develop and expand an American Indian private sector which employs Indian labor, increases the number of tribal and individual Indian businesses, and positively impacts and involves reservation communitie, by establishing business relationships between Indian enterprises and private industry.

National Center for American Indian Enterprise Development

953 East Juanita Avenue
Mesa, AZ 85204
800-4-NCAIED
http://www.ncaied.org

The **Marketing and Procurement Services Program** (MPSP) is operated through a cooperative agreement and with partial funding from the U.S. Department of Defense's Defense Logistics Agency. The goal of this program is to provide contract identification and procurement assistance to reservation-based businesses throughout the western United States. MPSP makes available contract bid opportunities from federal, state, and local (including tribal) government agencies and large corporations doing business with the government throughout the country.

The **Native American Business Development Center** is a project operated by the National Center for American Indian Enterprise Development in cooperation with the U.S. Department of Commerce, Minority Business Development Agency. The NABDC provides management and technical assistance for Native Americans residing in the key states. This assistance extends to both tribes and individuals living both on and off the reservation. Assistance is available for all stages of business from start-up through expansion. Services provided include: financial and loan packaging; business plan preparation; procurement assistance; minority certification assistance; and 8(a) assistance.

The **Native American Business Consultant** is a project operated by the National Center for American Indian Enterprise Development in cooperation with the U.S. Department of Commerce, Minority Business Development Agency. The NABC provides management and technical assistance for Native Americans nationwide. This assistance extends to both tribes and individuals living both on and off the reservation. Assistance is available for all stages of business from start-up through expansion. Services provided include: internal computerized accounting; Web page design; tax advice; operating systems analysis; financial and loan packaging; business plan preparation; procurement assistance; and 8(a) assistance.

Management consulting services are available nationwide on a fee-for-service basis. Services are available to tribes, individuals, and corporations. Services provided include: business plan development; feasibility studies; entrepreneurial training; financial forecasting and budgeting; and commercial Web page development.

National Congress of American Indians

1301 Connecticut Avenue, NW, Suite 200
Washington, DC 20036
202-466-7767
http://www.ncai.org

The National Congress of American Indians works to inform the public and Congress on the governmental rights of American Indians and Alaska Natives. The congress consists of 250 member tribes from throughout the United States. Among the group's activities: promotion and support of Indian education, including adult education.

National Council of La Raza

1111 19th Street, NW, Suite 1000
Washington, DC 20036
http://www.nclr.org

The National Council of La Raza (NCLR) is a private, nonprofit, organization which works to reduce poverty and discrimination, and improve life opportunities for Hispanic Americans. The council helps to strengthen community-based organizations, offers advocacy, and supports research. In addition to resource development, the council publishes reports analyzing issues and policies of concern to the Hispanic community. It also publishes a quarterly newsletter, along with newsletters devoted to specific topics.

National Council of Negro Women

633 Pennsylvania Avenue, NW
Washington, DC 20004
202-737-0120
http://www.ncnw.com

This non-profit organization works at the national, state, local, and international levels to improve quality of life for women, children, and families. NCNW consists of 38 affiliated national organzations, 250 community-based sections chartered in 42 states, 20 college-based sections

Organizations

and 60,000 individual members. As the umbrella organization for this widely diverse group of organizations and individuals, ranging from college-based sororities and professional associations to civic and social clubs, NCNW has an outreach to over four million women.

National Image

930 West 7th Avenue
Denver, CO 80204-4417
303-534-6534
http://www.nationalimageinc.org

National Image, Inc., is a national Hispanic organization concerned with employment, education, and civil rights. It hosts a national training conference and convention.

National Indian Athletic Association

4084 Ibex NE
Salem, OR 97305

The association is dedicated to the promotion and coordination of sports education among the Indian people at local, regional, and national levels.

National Indian Council on Aging

10501 Montgomery Boulevard, NE, Suite 210
Albuquerque, NM 87111-3846
505-292-2001
http://www.nicoa.org

The council is a non-profit advocate for the nation's American Indian and Alaska Native elders. It aids indigenous seniors with employment training, dissemination of information, and data support.

National Indian Education Association

700 North Fairfax Street, Suite 210
Alexandria, VA 22314
703-838-2870
http://www.niea.org

NIEA was established to unite Indians in changing ineffective education laws and to ensure that the native voice is not excluded in policy decisions. NIEA provides a forum whereby Indian educators can discuss pertinent issues that require timely attention and those that depend on long range strategies. With many native languages and traditions near the brink of extinction, NIEA firmly believes that access to education can be used to help preserve rather than replace Indian traditions. For Indian people the link between education and culture is fundamental and cannot be stressed enough as they struggle to maintain their identity. Among NIEA's services are conventions and conferences, and the distribution of information about relevant legislation.

National Indian Health Board

1385 South Colorado Boulevard, Suite A-707
Denver, CO 80222
303-759-3075

The health board seeks to coordinate and improve Indian health programs and services, and to gather and disseminate information.

National Indian Justice Center

The McNear Building
#7 Fourth Street, Suite 46
Petaluma, CA 94952
http://nijc.indian.com/

The center is an Indian owned and operated non-profit corporation which works to design and deliver legal education, research, and technical assistance programs which seek to improve tribal court systems.

National Indian Telecommunications Institute

110 North Guadalupe, Suite 9
Santa Fe, NM 87501
505-986-3872
http://numa.niti.org

The National Indian Telecommunications Institute is a native-founded and run organization dedicated to using the power of electronic technologies to help American Indian, Native Hawaiian, and Alaskan Native communities in the areas of education, economic development, language and cultural preservation, tribal policy issues, and self-determination. Its activities include training sessions and lectures on issues of Native Americans and technology at national conferences and events. NITI also sponsors an internship program.

National Korean American Service and Education Consortium

900 South Crenshaw Boulevard, Suite 101
Flushing, NY 11355
718-460-5600
http://www.nakasec.org

The National Korean American Service and Education Consortium, Inc. (NAKASEC), is a national organization that seeks to educate and empower Korean American communities nationwide. Among its programs: NAKASEC produces bilingual educational materials on critical issues that affect the Korean American community. Resources include Legislative Updates, Fact Sheets, and Issue Papers. NAKASEC co-sponsors an annual Summer Youth Program with affiliates in Los Angeles, Chicago, and New York. Regular seminars, community forums, and conferences are organized on various issues of concern to the Korean American community. NAKASEC works with its affiliate cultural troupes to foster a new cultural awareness within the Korean American community. NAKASEC participates in multicultural and multidisciplinary workshops, concerts, and festivals. NAKASEC promotes the cultural development of Korean American artists as well as sponsors Korea-based artists in the United States.

National Minority AIDS Council

1931 13th Street, NW
Washington, DC 20009
202-483-6622
http://www.nmac.org

The council is dedicated to developing leadership within communities of color to address the challenge of HIV/AIDS. Works to promote sound health policies to diverse communities, and sponsors advocacy skills training and technical assistance sessions. It advocates for the development of AIDS treatment education programs.

National Minority Business Council

235 East 42nd Street
New York, NY 10017
212-573-2385
http://www.nmbc.org

The NMBC is an umbrella organization that encompasses thousands of small businesses located nationally and internationally. The primary purpose of the organization is to enhance the success and profitability of the small business community through the provision of high-quality services, programs, advocacy and networking support. The secondary purpose is to act as an information clearinghouse for the minority and women-owned business enterprise (MWBE) community. Given the various levels of managerial expertise among the membership, the NMBC strives to develop programs that are suited to the needs of the novice as well as the seasoned entrepreneur.

National Minority Supplier Development Council

1040 Avenue of the Americas, 2nd Floor
New York, NY 10018
212-944-2430
http://www.nmsdcus.org

The council works to provide a direct link between corporate America and minority-owned businesses. Membership benefits include certification of minority business enterprises, access to a computerized database of minority business suppliers, referrals, and capital loans.

National Native American AIDS Prevention Center

436 14th Street, Suite 1020
Oakland, CA 94612
510-444-2051
http://www.nnaapc.org

The center is the national headquarters for the campaign to educate Native Americans about AIDS.

Organizations

National Network for Immigrant and Refugee Rights

310 8th Street, Suite 307
Oakland, CA 94607
http://www.nnirr.org

The National Network works for immigrant rights across the country. It is composed of local coalitions and immigrant, refugee, community, religious, civil rights, and labor organizations.

National Organization of Black County Officials

440 First Street, NW, Suite 410
Washington, DC 20001
202-347-6953

This organization of African American county officials works with selected counties and assists them in resolving ongoing problems. The organization works on the national and local levels and provides project management in the areas of health, wellness, and environment.

National Organization of Concerned Black Men

1232 M Street, NW
Washington, DC 20005
888-395-7816
http://www.libertynet.org/cbmno

The organization serves as a positive and motivating environment for minority youth by helping them develop skills necessary for their success in the future. It sponsors a number of youth programs and activities, including essay contests, black college tours, sports programs, and mentoring. It also recognizes student academic achievement with scholarships and savings bonds.

National Political Congress of Black Women

8401 Colesville Road, Suite 400
Silver Spring, MD 20910
877-274-1198
http://www.npcbw.org

NPCBW works toward the political empowerment of African American women. Activities include mentorship, voter registration, and training in the political process. The organization is dedicated to assisting women in pursuing political office.

National Urban League

120 Wall Street
New York, NY 10005
212-558-5300
http://www.nul.org

Through advocacy and special programs, the National Urban League assists African Americans in a number of ways. Social and educational development programs help indivduals achieve economic self-sufficiency. This community-based organization has 115 affiliates across the country, and it offers scholarships, an online career center, assistance to small businesses, education and training programs, and many other resources.

Native American Public Telecommunications

1800 North 33rd Street
Lincoln, NE 68583
402-472-3522
http://www.nativetelecom.org

The mission of Native American Public Telecommunications (NAPT) is to inform, educate, and encourage the awareness of tribal histories, cultures, languages, opportunities and aspirations through the fullest participation of American Indians and Alaska Natives in creating and employing all forms of educational and public telecommunications programs and services.

Native American Rights Fund

1506 Broadway
Boulder, CO 80302-6217
303-447-8760
http://www.narf.org

Among its many activities, the fund offers summer internships for second-year law school students; undertakes litigation to help obtain Indian rights; and maintains the National Indian Law Library as a master file of information to help attorneys representing Indians. It also has compiled a bibliography of materials on Indian economic development to help tribes develop government tools essential for the protection and regulation of commercial activities on reservations.

Native American Scholarship Fund

8200 Mountain Road, NE, Suite 203
Albuquerque, NM 87110
505-262-2351
http://www.nasf.com

NASF works to raise funds to provide scholarship funding for American Indians in the fields critical to the economic, social, environmental, political, educational, and business development of Indian communities. It also sponsors programs to help Indian students prepare for college-level studies.

Native American Women's Urban Health Education Resource Center

P.O. Box 572
Lake Andes, SD 57356-0572
605-487-7072
http://www.nativeshop.org

The first resource center to be located on a reservation in the United States, the center is a project of the Native American Community Board of South Dakota. The center supports programs that benefit people locally, nationally, and internationally, including a domestic violence program, adult learning program, clearinghouse of educational materials, and scholarships for Native American women.

Native Americans in Philanthropy

PO Drawer 14291
102 1/2 East Second Street
Lumberton, NC 28358-1429
910-618-9749

Native Americans in Philanthropy (NAP) was created with a mission to advocate within the philanthropic community with promotion, development, effectiveness, and growth of Native American philanthropy. NAP also seeks to leverage and expand the sources of philanthropic dollars going toward American Indian issues and concerns, and to build the capacity for expanding and managing Native American philanthropic institutions.

Navajo Nation

http://www.navajo.org

At the Web site, read about the Nation, job openings, the Navajo Superfund Program, and Navajoland Tourism.

New Freedom Theatre

1346 North Broad Street
Philadelphia, PA 19121
215-765-2793

Freedom Theatre, founded in 1966, is Pennsylvania's oldest African American theater. Freedom Theatre presents more than 100 performances a year and includes a repertory theater company, a performing arts training program, a lecture series, and a readings series.

New Mexico State University

Chicano Programs Office
Las Cruces, NM 88003-8001
505-646-0111
http://www.nmsu.edu/~chicano

The office sponsors 8 student organizations: The Society of Hispanic Professional Engineers (SHPE), the Hispanic Business Student Association (HBSA), the Hispanic Educators Association (HEA), Movimiento Estudiantil Chicano de Aztlan (MECHA), Mexican American Engineers and Scientists (MAES), Kappa Delta Chi Sorority (KDChi), Omega Delta Phi Fraternity (ODPhi), and Latinos United Promoting Aspiring New Arts (LUPANA). These professionally oriented student groups offer such actitivies as guest speakers and minority career fairs. Chicano programs offers support and advocacy to NMSU students and Hispanic student organizations, as well as cultural events for NMSU and the community at large. The office also serves as a clearinghouse for several scholarships.

Organizations

New York African-American Research Institute

State University of New York
State University Plaza
Albany, NY 12246

The institute works to initiate historical research on African Americans of New York State. These studies are used in the development of public policy.

Northern California Indian Development Center

241 F Street
Eureka, CA 95501
707-445-8451
http://www.ncidc.org

The organization offers job and career counseling, a computer resource center, and a community mentoring project.

Office of Minority Health Resource Center

U.S. Department of Health and Human Services
200 Independence Avenue, SW
Washington, DC 20201
800-444-6472
http://www.omhrc.gov

The center is a nationwide service of the Office of Minority Health (OMH) within the U.S. Department of Health and Human Services. The mission of OMH is to improve the health of racial and ethnic populations through the development of effective health policies and programs that help to eliminate disparities in health. Through the center, minorities have access to an informative Web site and information specialists at the toll-free number.

ONABEN—A Native American Business Network

http://www.onaben.org

This non-profit corporation was created by Northwest Indian Tribes to increase the success of private businesses owned by Native Americans. ONABEN offers training and support focused on developing entrepreneurship,

and the Web site serves as a resource and directory.

Open Book Committee

PEN American Center
568 Broadway
New York, NY 10012-3225
212-334-1660
http://www.pen.org

The PEN Open Book Program encourages racial and ethnic diversity within the literary and publishing communities. Its committee works to increase the literature by, for, and about African, Asian, Caribbean, Latin, and Native Americans, and to establish access for these groups to the publishing industry. Its goal is to insure that those who are the custodians of language and literature are representative of the American people. The Open Book Peer Group serves as a forum for individuals interested in or already a part of the publishing industry. The group meets monthly at the PEN headquarters to discuss job concerns and strategies, develop special skills, and network among themselves. The program hopes to foster relationships between more senior publishing professionals and those in the early stages of their careers by pairing them in the Mentoring Program.

Opera Ebony

2109 Broadway, Suite 1418
New York, NY 10023
212-874-7245
http://www.operaebony.org

Opera Ebony, through mainstage productions, tours, and the performance of new and classical works, introduces performers, conductors, stage directors, choreographers, and other artists to theatrical opera. Opera Ebony's achievements range from stellar performances at home and abroad, to the development of commissioned works and a diverse repertoire of standard, new and neglected operas, to the creation of a unique professional platform in musical theatre for African-American talents, and female and minority composers.

Osage Tribe

Muskogee Area Office
BIA Old Federal Building
Pawhuska, OK 74056
918-287-1085
http://www.osagetribe.com

Tribal members are provided with access to employment opportunities and education programs.

Pacific Islanders in Communications

1221 Kapiolani Boulevard #6A-4
Honolulu, HI 96814
808-591-0059
http://www.piccom.org

Pacific Islanders in Communications (PIC) is a national nonprofit media organization working to increase national public broadcast programming by and about indigenous Pacific Islanders.

Pawnee Nation of Oklahoma

Education and Training Department
P.O. Box 470
Pawnee, OK 74058
918-762-2541
http://pawneenation.org

The Pawnee Nation sponsors councils, programs, and events in aid of the community.

Phelps-Stokes Fund

74 Trinity Place
New York, NY 10006
212-619-8100
http://www.psfdc.org

The fund focuses on the education of African Americans, Native Americans, Africans, and needy white youth. Over its 86-year history, the fund has sponsored educational surveys and research studies, administered scholarship and fellowship programs, and advocated on behalf of its constituents through public education programs.

Piney Woods Country Life School

Highway 49 South
Piney Woods, MS 39148
601-845-2214

One of the few remaining African American boarding schools in the the country, Piney Woods educates children in grades pre-K through 12.

Pinoleville Band of Pomo Indians

367 North State Street
Ukiah, CA 95482
707-463-1454
http://www.pinoleville.org

Port Madison Indian Reservation

15838 Sandy Hook Road
Suquamish, WA 98370
360-598-3311
http://www.suquamish.nsn.us

The reservation hosts a Tribal Center, and the Suquamish Community Learning Center, among other programs and resources.

Prairie Band Potawatomi

16281 Q Road
Mayetta, KS 66509-8970
785-966-2255
http://www.pbpindiantribe.com

The tribe sponsors a number of programs to assist with community development.

Pueblo of Santa Ana

2 Dove Road
Bernalillo, NM 87004
505-867-3301
http://www.santaana.org

The tribe has a development corporation, business enterprises, and sponsors community events.

Puerto Rican Traveling Theatre Company, Inc.

141 West 94th Street
New York, NY 10025-7016
212-354-1293

Organizations

In addition to its production and workshop program, the theater operates a training unit through which more than 250 students from low-income families receive instruction in acting, modern dance, music, and language.

Puerto Rico Council on Higher Education

P.O. Box 19900
San Juan, PR 00910-1900
787-724-7100

A state coordinating agency; licensing authority; state student assistance administrator; and data collection for higher education.

Quinault Indian Nation

P.O. Box 189
Taholah, WA 98587-0189
360-276-8211
http://www.techline.com/~ghrpc/quinpage.htm

Rainbow/PUSH Coalition

930 East 50th Street
Chicago, IL 60615-2702
773-373-3366
http://www.rainbowpush.org

The Rainbow/PUSH Coalition is a multiracial, multi-issue, international membership organization fighting for social change. Issues include job and economic empowerment, employee rights, and educational access.

Rankokus Indian Reservation

P.O. Box 225
Rancocas, NJ 08073
609-261-4747
http://www.powhatan.org

Social services and community events are sponsored by the tribe.

Rosebud Sioux Tribe

P.O. Box 430
Rosebud, SD 57570
605-747-2381
http://www.rosebudsiouxtribe.org

Economic development and other community programs are sponsored by the tribe.

Saginaw Chippewa Indian Tribe of Michigan

http://www.sagchip.com

At the tribe's Web site, learn about education and job opportunities, and services provided to tribal members.

Salish and Kootenai Tribes

P.O. Box 278
Pablo, MT 59855
406-675-2700
http://www.ronan.net/~csktadmn/

The Flathead Indian Reservation is home to the Salish Kootenai College, and offers residents a number of other educational and development resources.

Saludos Hispanos

73-121 Fred Waring Drive, Suite 100
Palm Desert, CA 92260
800-371-4456
http://www.saludos.com

This Hispanic employment service offers free resume postings to qualified bilingual professionals. It also publishes *Saludos Magazine* and visits job fairs across the country.

Sault Ste. Marie Tribe of Chippewa Indian

523 Ashmun
Sault Ste. Marie, MI 49783
906-635-6050
http://www.sootribe.org

Provides information on governmental services and economic development.

School of American Research

Indian Arts Research Center
P.O. Box 2188
Santa Fe, NM 87504-2188
505-954-7205
http://www.sarweb.org

The school's Indian Arts Research Center (IARC) houses one of the world's most significant collections of traditional Southwest Indian arts and artifacts, spanning the 450-year period from Spanish contact to the present. These collections and a range of associated programs have made the IARC an outstanding cultural and educational resource for the Native American community, researchers, scholars, and the public. Since 1987 more than 2,000 Native American artists and craftspersons have studied and been inspired by the IARC collections, with support from such SAR programs as the Native American Arts Education Program, the Native American Artist Mentor Program, and the Native American Artist Fellowships.

Secretariat for African American Catholics

3211 4th Street, NE
Washington, DC 20017-1194
202-541-3177

The organization provides education and social services to hundreds of Catholic parishes across the country.

Seminole Nation of Oklahoma

P.O. Box 1498
Wewoka, OK 74884
405-257-6343
http://www.cowboy.net/native/seminole/index.html

At the nation's Web site, read about projects, schools, and funds.

Seminole Tribe of Florida

6300 Stirling Road
Hollywood, FL 33024
800-683-7800
http://www.semtribe.com

The tribe sponsors a number of community development programs to assist with business and career development.

Seneca Nation of Indians

Scholarship Coordinator, Higher Education Program
P.O. Box 231
http://www.sni.org

The nation consists of 3 reservations in New York. Its Web site provides information about employment and economic development, education, and health services.

Sitka Tribe of Alaska

456 Katlian Street
Sitka, AK 99835
907-747-3207
http://www.sitkatribe.org

A number of tribal services are available to members seeking education and career guidance.

Soul in Motion Players

P.O. Box 5374
Rockville, MD 20848-5374
800-355-5374
http://www.us.net/simpinc/

This touring repertory theater company specializes in African drumming. The group performs for thousands of college students across the country.

Southern Ute Indian Tribe

http://www.southern-ute.nsn.us/index.html

This Web site serves the Southern Ute Tribe of Ignacio, Colo.. Provides information on Southern Ute government and enterprises.

SPANUSA

135 Beach Avenue
Mamaroneck, NY 10543
914-381-5555
http://www.spanusa.net

SPANUSA is an executive search firm specializing in the placement of bilingual Spanish-English speaking professionals and executives.

Organizations

Spirit Talk Culture Centre
http://www.blackfoot.org

This Internet site of the Blackfoot Confederacy Information Center provides information about seminars and discussions.

Studio Museum in Harlem
144 North 125th Street
New York, NY 10027
212-864-4500
http://www.studiomuseuminharlem.org

The museum offers an educational program, which includes seminars and workshops, that extends to national and even international communities through its collection and exhibition of African American, African-inspired, and Hispanic art.The museum's permanent collection consists of over 1,500 objects—a collection that exhibits traditional and contemporary African American art.

Talento Bilingue de Houston
333 South Jensen
Houston, TX 77003
713-222-1213
http://www.talento.org

Talento Bilingue de Houston (TBH), formerly the Teatro Bilingue, is Houston's largest Latino cultural arts organization. It is dedicated to presenting and preserving Latin America's rich cultural and artistic heritage, sponsoring varied performances, from ballet to hip-hop. Through mainstage performances, touring exhibitions, and a diverse schedule of cultural and education programs for children and adults, TBH works to instill a sense of cultural pride and affirmation for Latinos in Houston, and foster cross-cultural literacy and understanding for Houston's diverse communities.

Teach for America
315 West 36th, 6th Floor
New York, NY 10018
800-832-1230
http://www.teachforamerica.org

Teach for America is a national corps of diverse recent college graduates, of all academic majors, who commit 2 years to teach in under-resourced and rural public schools.

Thurgood Marshall Scholarship Fund
100 Park Avenue, 10th Floor
New York, NY 10017
917-663-2220
http://www.tmsf.org

The Thurgood Marshall Scholarship Fund is the only national organization founded for the sole purpose of providing scholarships to students attending the nation's Historically Black Public Colleges and Universities. In addition to scholarships, TMSF provides unrestricted and restricted support to its member universities. The fund partners with other organizations to support students in preparing for undergraduate and professional schools through its Test Prep Program.

Tlingit and Haida Indian Tribes of Alaska
320 West Willoughby Avenue, Suite 300
Juneau, AK 99801
800-344-1432
http://www.tlingit-haida.org

Vocational training and other services are available to tribal members.

Twenty-first Century Foundation
666 West End Avenue
New York, NY 10025
212-249-3612

The foundation assists the work of African American community and education based organizations, in the form of grants.

U.S. Indian Arts and Crafts Board
Department of the Interior, Room 4004
Washington, DC 20240
202-208-3773

The Indian Arts and Crafts Board is a clearinghouse of information on Indian arts and crafts. It assists federally recognized tribes and their members with economic development through the promotion and marketing of arts and crafts.

It also operates the Sioux Indian Museum in South Dakota, the Museum of the Plains Indian in Montana, and the Southern Plains Indian Museum in Oklahoma.

United Black Fund

1101 14th Street, NW, Suite 301
Washington, DC 20005
202-783-9300

The United Black Fund is a viable, non-profit grant-making institution giving general, programmatic, and emergency funding to community-based organizations. The United Black Fund presently supports 68 member agencies, and assists yearly over 100 non-member agencies on an emergency basis.

United Keetoowah Band of Cherokee Indians in Oklahoma

P.O. Box 746
Tahlequah, OK 74465-0746
918-456-5491
http://www.uark.edu/depts/comminfo/UKB/welcome.html

United National Indian Tribal Youth

P.O. Box 25042
Oklahoma City, OK 73125
405-236-2800
http://www.unityinc.org

UNITY promotes personal development, citizenship, and leadership among Native American youth. It sponsors workshops, a national training conference, and motivational speakers.

United Way of America

701 North Fairfax Street
Alexandria, VA 22314
703-836-7100
http://www.unitedway.org

This national service and training center assists minority communities in a variety of ways through local agencies.

Urbanworld Film Festival

375 Greenwich Street
New York, NY 10013
212-501-9668
http://www.uwff.com

The mission of the Urbanworld Film Festival (UWFF) is to expose independent minority films and entertainment to the widest audience possible. Held the first week of every August in New York City, UWFF features over 70 independent films from around the world. In continued efforts for audience exposure and education, UWFF launched the Urbanworld College Tour, a traveling version of the festival that visits more than 20 Historically Black Colleges as well as universities with film schools across the country. The tour hits an overall body of 200,000 students each year.

Ute Tribe Business Committee

P.O. Box 190
Fort Duchesne, UT 84026
801-722-5141
http://www.ubtanet.com/~northernute/

A resource for the Northern Ute Indian Tribe, providing access to information about tribal departments, enterprises, recreational activities, and events.

Vuntut Gwitchin First Nation

http://www.oldcrow.yk.net

The Web site provides information on education, tourism, government services, and social and youth programs. The site also lists employment opportunities.

Wampanoag Tribe of Gay Head

20 Black Brook Road
Aquinnah, MA 02535-1546
508-645-9265
http://www.wtgh.vineyard.net

The tribal council serves as a resource for information on education, health and human services, and economic development.

Organizations

Western States Black Research Center

3617 Montclair Street
Los Angeles, CA 90018
323-737-3292
http://www.wsbrec.org

Through its collection of films, books, fine art, memorabilia, and music, the Western States Black Research and Educational Center works to preserve the cultural heritage of African Americans. The center's assemblage of African American resource materials is unique in the Western United States because of its size and scholarly value. The center offers research services, workshops, and seminars, as well as grants to filmmakers.

Wichita and Affiliated Tribes

P.O. Box 729
Anadarko, OK 73005
405-247-2425
http://www.wichita.nsn.us

The official tribe Web site allows you to read about programs and organizations within the Wichita and Affiliated Tribes.

Yavapai-Apache Nation

http://yavapai-apache-nation.com

At the nation's Web site, access the online newsletter, and information about programs and events.

Minority Colleges

Historically Black Colleges and Universities (HBCU) accept applications from all students, but have historically served African American students. These institutions originated to serve the needs of African American communities in a time when black students could not gain entrance to most colleges. HBCUs continue to thrive, enrolling over 370,000 students and graduating about one-third of all African American students annually, according to the National Association for Equal Opportunity in Higher Education.

The government classifies a Hispanic-Serving Institution (HIS) as a college with at least 25 percent Hispanic undergraduate enrollment. Forty percent of the Hispanic students in post-secondary education are enrolled in Hispanic-Serving Institutions. You can learn more about HSIs with the HSI Information Kit which includes a video entitled "Hispanic Serving Institutions: Serving the Community, Serving the Nation." Order from:

> White House Initiative
> 400 Maryland Avenue, SW, Room 5E110
> Washington, DC 20202-3601
> 202-401-1411

Colleges controlled by tribal governments typically offer Native American students a unique education based on both traditional academics and native culture. According to the American Indian College Fund, fewer than 10 percent of Indian students graduate from public colleges, but more than 40 percent of tribal college graduates pursue further education, and another 50 percent find jobs.

Colleges in Puerto Rico are considered by the U.S. government as Hispanic-Serving Institutions.

Adams State College

208 Edgemont Boulevard
Alamosa, CO 81102
719-587-7011

Alabama A&M University Graduate School

Normal, AL 35762
256-851-5266
http://www.aamu.edu

Alabama Agricultural and Mechanical University is a traditional land-grant institution which combines professional, vocational, and liberal arts pursuits. The university provides baccalaureate and graduate studies.

Alabama State University

915 South Jackson Street
Montgomery, AL 36101
205-293-4100
http://www.alasu.edu

The Alabama State University campus is located only a short walk from the Alabama capitol, the state government complex, and downtown Montgomery. This location makes the downtown district, the Civic Center, museums, art galleries, theaters, medical centers, the state archives, and historical sites readily accessible to students. Across the street from the campus is the beautiful municipal Oak Park, which has one of the few space transit planetariums in the nation. Alabama State University is easily accessible from almost any point near Montgomery. The campus covers about 130 acres with 33 permanent buildings. The buildings are set in a landscape design that rivals the most beautiful urban campuses in the South. The replacement value of land, buildings, and equipment is estimated at $150 million.

Alan Hancock College

800 South College Drive
Santa Maria, CA 93454-6399
805-922-6966
http://www.hancock.cc.ca.us

Allan Hancock College is a community college serving a 3,000 square mile area on the Central Coast of California with a population of 235,671.

The college offers degrees and certificates in more than 100 areas of study in nine academic departments.

Albany State University

504 College Drive
Albany, GA 31705
912-430-4600
http://argus.asurams.edu/asu

Albany State University is a historically black institution in southwest Georgia. It offers bachelor's, master's and education specialist degrees and a variety of non-degree educational programs. The university emphasizes the liberal arts as the foundation for all learning by exposing students to the humanities, fine arts, social sciences, and the sciences. Global learning is fostered through a broad-based curriculum and diverse university activities.

Albuquerque Technical-Vocational Institute

525 Buena Vista, SE
Albuquerque, NM 87106
505-224-3000
http://www.tvi.cc.nm.us

Among the educational programs at this technical college are: arts and sciences, adult and developmental education, business occupations, health occupations, technologies, and distance learning.

Alcorn State University

1000 ASU Drive
Alcorn State, MS 39096
601-877-6100
http://www.alcorn.edu

Alcorn State was created in 1871 and has the distinction of being the first historically black land-grant institution and the first state-supported institution for the higher education of blacks in the United States. The more than 3,000 student body is predominantly black; however, it includes Caucasian, Asian, African, and West Indian students. The student population is composed of 60 percent female and 40 percent male. Situated on 1,700 acres, Alcorn has attracted students from all 82 counties in Mississippi, 42 other states, and from 18 foreign countries. Alcorn State University is accredited by the Commission on Colleges of the Southern Association of Colleges and Schools to award the associate, baccalaureate, master's and specialist degrees. It is also accredited by the National Council for the Accreditation of Teacher Education, the National League for Nursing, the National Association of Schools of Music, the National Association of Industrial Technology, and the Association of Family and Consumer Sciences, and approved by the American Dietetic Association. Currently more than 150 businesses, industries, governmental agencies, and school systems (including graduate and professional schools) recruit on the Alcorn campus.

Allen University

1530 Harden Street
Columbia, SC 29204-1057
803-254-9735
http://www.scicu.org/allen

Allen University, founded in 1870, is a small, coeducational, private institution located in Columbia, South Carolina. Its founding institution is the African Methodist Episcopal Church. Allen University is an academic community whose mission is to provide baccalaureate education with a strong, unalterable commitment to teaching and community service appropriate to the needs of its students. The university, with its enrollment of approximately 400 students from more than 12 states and 4 foreign countries, exists to serve students in an environment which fosters academic proficiency. The current open admissions policy is designed both for high school graduates, as well as those who complete and pass the equivalent General Education Development tests (GED). Allen University offers baccalaureate degrees in 8 majors of study.

American Indian College of the Assemblies of God

Office of Financial Aid
10020 North 15th Avenue
Phoenix, AZ 85021
602-944-3335

American University of Puerto Rico

P.O. Box 1082
Manati, PR 00674
787-854-2835

American University of Puerto Rico-Bayamon

P.O. Box 2037
Bayamon, PR 00960
787-798-2022

Arizona Institute of Business and Technical-Phoenix

6049 North 43 Avenue
Phoenix, AZ 85019
602-242-6265
http://www.aibt.edu

Arizona Institute of Business and Technology

925 South Gilbert Road #201
Mesa, AZ 85204
602-545-8755
http://www.aibt.edu

AIBT is a junior college accredited by the Accrediting Council for Independent Colleges and Schools to award certificates, diplomas, and Associate of Arts degrees.

Arizona Western College

9500 South Avenue 8E
Yuma, AZ 85365
520-317-6000
http://www.awc.cc.az.us

This two-year community college is located 5 miles east of the City of Yuma on a 640-acre site overlooking the Gila Valley. Thirty-three buildings, including three residence halls, student housing, and a college union serve more than 7,000 students from Yuma and La Paz counties. Course offerings include: agriculture, business, computer information systems, health, family and consumer sciences, fine arts, mathematics, nursing, physical education, recreation, science, and social studies. Day and evening classes are conducted on campus and throughout Yuma and La Paz Counties.

Arkansas Baptist College

1600 Martin Luther King Drive
Little Rock, AR 72202
501-374-7856

Arkansas, University of, Pine Bluff

1200 North University Drive
Pine Bluff, AR 71611
870-543-8000
http://www.uapb.edu

The University of Arkansas at Pine Bluff (UAPB) is a multi-cultural institution and one of 104 Historically Black Colleges and Universities (HBCU). There are 15 academic departments. Baccalaureate degrees are offered in several areas, as well as 3 master's degree programs: 2 in Education and 1 in aquaculture. These degrees are offered through the 4 academic schools: Arts and Sciences; Agriculture, Fisheries, and Human Sciences; Business and Management; and Education. There are also an Honors College, a University College, a Division of Continuing Education, a Military Science Program, and a Center for Multipurpose Research and Sponsored Programs. UAPB is accredited by the North Central Association (NCA).

Atlantic College

P.O. Box 1774
Guaynabo, PR 00970-1774
787-720-1022
http://www.atlanticcollege-pr.com

Bacone College

Office of Financial Aid
2299 Bacone Road
Muskogee, OK 74403-1568
888-682-5514
http://www.bacone.ed

Bacone College offers the associate of arts, associate of science, associate of applied science, certificate programs, and the accelerated associate degree program.

Bakersfield College

1801 Panaroma Drive
Bakersfield, CA 93305
661-395-4011
http://www.bc.cc.ca.us

Bakersfield College was founded in 1913 and is one of the nation's oldest continually operating community colleges. The college serves 13,000 students on the 153-acre main campus in northeast Bakersfield, at the Weill Institute in downtown Bakersfield, and at the Delano Center 35 miles north of Bakersfield. Classes are offered on a traditional 18-week semester calendar as well as in a variety of non-traditional scheduling options: evenings, weekends, short-term vocational programs, instructional television, and online. Bakersfield College offers students opportunities to earn an associate degree, transfer to a four-year institution, or to gain new job skills.

Barber-Scotia College

145 Cabarrus Avenue
Concord, NC 28025
704-786-5171
http://www.barber-scotia.edu

Barber-Scotia College offers a liberal arts education in a community concerned with the interaction of cultures, Christian heritage, scholarship, citizenship, and leadership. Barber-Scotia emphasizes a liberal arts education strengthened by advanced technology. The college has strong programs dedicated to teacher education, total student development, other service oriented majors, and community services. Students are expected to demonstrate a true sense of understanding and value of the local, national, and international communities.

Barry University

11300 NE 2nd Avenue
Miami Shores, FL 33161
305-899-3000
http://www.barry.edu

Barry is an independent, coeducational Catholic international university. Founded in 1940, the university is sponsored by the Adrian Dominican Order of Sisters from Adrian, Michigan. Barry offers over 60 undergraduate programs and 50 graduate degrees.

Organizations

Bay Mills Community College

12214 West Lakeshore Drive
Brimley, MI 49715
800-844-BMCC
http://www.bmcc.org

Bay Mills Community College is a tribally controlled community college located inside the boundaries of the Bay Mills Indian community on the Eastern Upper Pennisula of Michigan. Either the on-campus program at Bay Mills or the Bay Mills Nishnaabek Kinoomaadewin Virtual College program are based in Native American culture. Students attending the college at either the campus site or online receive an education integrated with American Indian wisdom, culture, and spirituality.

Bayamon Central University

Apartado 1725, Avenida Zaya Verde
Bayamon, PR 00960-1725
787-780-4040
http://www.ucb.edu.pr

Bee County College

3800 Charco Road
Beeville, TX 78102

Benedict College

Admissions Office
1600 Harden Street
Columbia, SC 29204
803-256-4220
http://www.benedict.edu

Benedict College, founded in 1870, is an independent, coeducational, private institution located in Columbia, South Carolina. The college, with its enrollment of approximately 2,100 students from more than 30 states and 9 foreign countries, offers bachelor degree programs in 22 major areas of study. The college's curriculum includes preparation of students for business, government, social and health service, public and private school instruction, military, civic, cultural, and scientific work. Students are provided opportunities to become involved in the arts and humanities, which will increase their aesthetic appreciation and enhance the quality of their lives, as well as promote their interests and talents.

Bennett College

900 East Washington Street
Greensboro, NC 27401
336-273-4431
http://www.bennett.edu

Located in Greensboro, North Carolina, Bennett College is a small, residential, four-year liberal arts college affiliated with the United Methodist Church. The average student enrollment at Bennett is 600 women, the majority of whom are of African American descent. These women bring with them the cultures of 29 states, including North Carolina, and 11 foreign countries, representing the continents of Africa, Asia, and Europe. More than 80 percent of the faculty hold doctorates from some of the most prestigious colleges and universities across the nation. The student/faculty ratio is 11:1. Bennett is accredited by the Southern Association of Colleges and Schools; Council on Social Work Education; American Dietetics Association; University Senate of the United Methodist Church; and National Council for the Accreditation of Teacher Education. Bennett offers 30 majors and awards the bachelor of arts, bachelor of science, bachelor of arts and sciences in interdisciplinary studies, and the bachelor of social work degrees. Bennett ranks fourth among all Historically Black Colleges and Universities in the percentage of alumnae earning doctoral degrees.

Bethune-Cookman College

Office of Admissions
640 Dr. Mary McLeod Bethune Boulevard
Daytona Beach, FL 32114-3099
904-255-1401
http://www.bethune.cookman.edu

Bethune-Cookman College, the 6th largest of the 41-member UCNF colleges, is located in the Atlantic coast city of Daytona Beach, Florida, which has a metropolitan area population of more than 160,000. Founded by Dr. Mary McLeod Bethune in 1904, the college is an historically black, United Methodist Church-related, liberal arts, career-oriented, coeducational, and residential institution offering the bachelor of science degrees in 39 major areas through 6 academic divisions: Business, Education, Humanities, Nursing, Science/Mathematics, and Social Sciences.

Bishop State Community College

315 North Broad Street
Mobile, AL 36603
334-690-6801
http://www.bscc.cc.al.us/

Bishop State Community College is a state-supported, open-admission, urban community college located in Mobile, Alabama. The college consists of four city campuses dedicated to serving the residents of Mobile and Washington counties in southwest Alabama. The college is part of the Alabama College System, the state-supported network of two-year community, junior, and technical colleges that serves the residents of Alabama. Bishop State offers university transfer programs for students wanting to continue their education at a four-year school, or for those who seek to start careers right away, the college's one- and two-year career programs can put students on the fast track to rewarding jobs.

Blackfeet Community College

P.O. Box 819
Browning, MT 59417
406-338-7755
http://www.montana.edu/wwwbcc/

The Blackfeet Community College is located in Browning, Montana. It is on the Blackfeet Indian Reservation, where the Rocky Mountains meet the plains of Northern Montana. The college is a fully accredited, two-year, higher education institution. It has degree granting powers sanctioned by the Northwest Association of Schools and Colleges.

Bluefield State College

219 Rock Street
Bluefield, WV 24701
304-327-4000
http://www.bluefield.wvnet.edu

Bluefield State College offers undergraduate liberal arts and professional programs in applied sciences, business, education, humanities, social sciences, engineering technologies, and allied health sciences leading to baccalaureate and Associate degrees, the nontraditional regents bachelor of arts degree, and continuing education opportunities. The college serves the citizens of southeast West Virginia by providing programs principally at sites in Mercer, Greenbrier, Monroe, McDowell, Raleigh, Pocahontas, and Summers Counties, and in some locations contiguous to its service area.

Boricua College

3755 Broadway
New York, NY 10032
212-694-1000

Boricua is a 4-year college focusing on the educational needs of Spanish-speaking students. associate and bachelor of arts degrees are offered, as well as post-graduate courses.

Bowie State University

14000 Jericho Park Road
Bowie, MD 20715
301-464-3000
http://www.bowiestate.edu

Bowie State University is an historically black university. Its academic programs consist of the School of Arts and Sciences, School of Education and Professional Studies, School of Continuing Education and Extended Studies, the Model Institute for Excellence (sponsored by NASA), the University College of Excellence, and the School of Graduate Studies and Research.

Bronx Community College

West 181st Street and University Avenue
Bronx, NY 10453
718-289-5100
http://www.bcc.cuny.edu

The Bronx Community College offers the associates in applied sciences degree (with career programs including: Accounting, Marketing, Nursing, Paralegal Studies), the associates in arts degree (Human Services, Liberal Arts, and Sciences), the associate in science degree (Business Administration, Computer Science), and certificate programs (Automotive Mechanics).

Organizations

California State University, Bakersfield

9001 Stockdale Highway
Bakersfield, CA 93311-1099
805-664-2011
http://www.csubak.edu

California State University, Dominguez Hills

1000 East Victoria Street
Carson, CA 90747
310-243-3300
http://www.csudh.edu

California State University, Fresno

5150 Maple Avenue
Fresno, CA 93740
209-278-4240
http://www.csufresno.edu

California State University, Los Angeles

5151 State University Drive
Los Angeles, CA 90032
323-343-3000
http://www.calstatela.edu

California State University, Los Angeles, is a comprehensive university that offers programs in more than 50 academic and professional fields. The university is organized into six schools that house nearly 50 academic departments and divisions. One quarter of the campus' 21,000 students are engaged in post-baccalaureate study in programs leading to master's and doctoral degrees; teaching, service, and specialist credentials; certificates; and other types of programs that prepare them for professional advancement.

California State University, Monterey Bay

100 Campus Center
Seaside, CA 93955-8001
408-582-3330
http://www.monterey.edu

California State University, Northridge

18111 Nordhoff Street
Northridge, CA 91330
818-677-1200
http://www.csun.edu

California State University, San Bernardino

5500 University Parkway
San Bernardino, CA 92407-2397
909-880-5000
http://www.csun.edu

Cañada College

4200 Farm Hill Boulevard
Redwood City, CA 94061-1099
650-306-3100
http://canadacollege.net

It is the mission of Cañada College to ensure that students from diverse backgrounds achieve their educational goals by providing quality instruction in transfer and general education courses, professional/technical programs, basic skills, and activities that foster students' personal development and academic success.

Cankdeska Cikana Community College

P.O. Box 269
Fort Totten, ND 58335-0269
701-766-4415
http://hoopster.little-hoop.cc.nd.us/

This college on the Fort Totten Reservation is operated by the Devils Lake Sioux Tribe and serves Indian students. Also known as Little Hoop Community College.

Caribbean Center for Advanced Studies

P.O. Box 3711
Old San Juan Station
San Juan, PR 00904-3711
787-725-6500

Caribbean Center for Advanced Studies—Miami
8180 N.W. 36th Street, 2nd Floor
Miami, FL 33166-6653
305-593-1223

Caribbean University—Bayamon
P.O. Box 493
Bayamon, PR 00960-0493
787-798-3400

Caribbean University—Carolina
Apartado 4760
Carolina, PR 009847
787-768-7850

Caribbean University—Ponce
P.O. Box 7733
Ponce, PR 00732-7733
787-840-2955

Caribbean University—Vega Baja
Apartado 4258
Vega Baja, PR 00763
787-858-3668

Center for Advanced Studies on Puerto Rico and the Caribbean
P.O. Box 902-3970
Old San Juan, PR 90239
787-723-4481

Central Arizona College
8470 North Overfield Road
Coolidge, AZ 85228
520-426-4444
http://www.cac.cc.az.us

Course offerings meet various student needs, including: transfer to a university; skills for direct employment; professional growth and development; GED (high school equivalency); and distance learning.

Central State University
1400 Brush Row Road
Wilberforce, OH 45384
513-376-6011
http://www.ces.csu.edu

With its origin as a state-financed department at the African Methodist Episcopal Church's Wilberforce University, Central State is unique as Ohio's only historically African American public institution of higher education. The enacting legislation, however, indicated that the Combined Normal and Industrial Department would be "open to all persons of good moral character." Central State has upheld that mandate while maintaining its historical concern for the African American youth of Ohio, the nation, and for students from throughout the world. Central State University currently grants the bachelor of arts, bachelor of science in education, bachelor of manufacturing engineering, bachelor of music degrees, and the master of education degree through the College of Arts and Sciences, College of Business and Industry, and College of Education.

Central Wyoming College
2660 Peck Avenue
Riverton, WY 82501-2215
307-855-2000
http://www.cwe.whecn.edu

This is a public, two-year college near the Wind River Reservation. About a fifth of the enrolled students are Native American.

Cerritos College
11110 Alonda Boulevard
Norwalk, CA 90650-6298
562-860-2451
http://www.cerritos.edu

Founded in 1955, Cerritos College is a public comprehensive community college serving an area of 52 square miles of southeastern Los Angeles County. The college offers degrees and certificates in 87 areas of study in nine divisions. Over 1,200 students successfully complete their course of studies each year. The Cerritos College student body is a majority of minorities: Hispanics, Asians, African Americans, Pacific Islanders, and Native Americans together account for more than 60 percent of the students.

Organizations

Chaffey College

5885 Haven Avenue
Rancho Cucamonga, CA 91737-3002
909-987-1737
http://www.chaffey.cc.ca.us

Charles Drew University of Medicine

1731 East 120th Street
Los Angeles, CA 90059
323-563-4800
http://www.cdrewu.edu

Born out of the ashes of the Watts Rebellion, Charles R. Drew Postgraduate School was founded in 1966 in response to the lack of adequate medical facilities in the area. The institution later became a university and changed its name in 1987 to reflect its expanded academic role and identity. Today, the university offers the M.D. degree, bachelor's of arts and sciences degrees, sssociate's of arts and sciences degrees, and certification.

Cheyenne River Community College

P.O. Box 220
Eagle Butte, SD 57625
605-964-6044

Cheyney University of Pennsylvania

Cheyney and Creek Roads
Cheyney, PA 19319-0200
610-399-2000
http://www.cheyney.edu

Founded in 1837 as the Institute for Colored Youth, Cheyney University of Pennsylvania is the oldest historically black institution of higher education in this nation. Cheyney is a comprehensive, coeducational, public institution, which admits all qualified students regardless of race, creed, or ethnicity. The university has a tradition of academic excellence while remaining faithful to its historical commitment to educate students whose academic development may have been limited by a lack of economic, social, or educational opportunity. Undergraduate degree programs are offered in the liberal arts and sciences and in teacher education, and master's degrees are offered in teacher education.

Chicago State University

9501 South Martin Luther King Drive
Chicago, IL 60628
312-995-2000
http://www.csu.edu

Chicago State University, a public, comprehensive, urban institution of higher learning located on the south side of Chicago, strives for excellence in teaching, research, creative expression, and community service. The university's academic programs include: arts and sciences, business, education, health sciences, graduate studies, continuing education, and library and learning resources.

Citrus College

1000 West Foothill Boulevard
Glendora, CA 91741-1899
http://www.citrus.cc.ca.us

Classes are offered on a traditional 18-week semester calendar, as well as in a variety of non-traditional scheduling options: evenings and weekends, late start and early end, summer session, and optional class formats, such as distance education online courses and distance education integrated classes.

City Colleges of Chicago, Harry S. Truman

1145 W. Wilson Avenue
Chicago, IL 60640
773-878-1700
http://www.ccc.edu

City Colleges of Chicago, Malcom X College

1900 W. Van Buren Street
Chicago, IL 60612
312-850-7031
http://www.ccc.edu

City Colleges of Chicago, Richard J. Daley

7500 S. Pulaski Road
Chicago, IL 60652
773-838-7500
http://www.ccc.edu

City Colleges of Chicago, Wilbur Wright College

4300 North Narragansett Avenue
Chicago, IL 60634
773-777-7900
http://www.ccc.edu

City University of New York, City College

Convent Avenue at 138th Street
New York, NY 10031
212-650-7000
http://www.ccny.cuny.edu

The City University includes the College of Liberal Arts and Science, along with Schools of Architecture, Education, Engineering, and the Sophie Davis School of Biomedical Education/CUNY Medical School. Long renowned as a great teaching institution, CCNY has also become internationally known for the research activities of its faculty in a host of fields such as molecular modeling, laser optics, and AIDS. During 1997-98, City's faculty received research grant support totaling over $27 million, the largest amount in The City University. CCNY has the largest undergraduate research program in the New York metropolitan area, giving students the chance to work side-by-side with world-renowned scientists.

City University of New York—Lehman College

250 Bedford Park Boulevard, West
Bronx, NY 10468-1589
718-960-8000
http://www.lehman.cuny.edu

Claflin College

700 College Avenue
Orangeburg, SC 29115
http://www.scicu.org/claflin/cchome.htm

Claflin College is a private, coeducational, historically black, United Methodist Church-related 4-year institution.Claflin offers a choice of 24 majors leading to the bachelor's degree. These majors help students pursue careers in fields such as teaching, the ministry, the service professions, government, business, scientific research, mass communications, and the arts.

The college also offers pre-professional programs in medicine, dentistry, law, Christian ministry, and engineering. The college has established a Center for Excellence in Science and Mathematics. The purpose of this center is to recruit, retain, and graduate students who plan to pursue careers in fields of science, engineering, mathematics, and technology.

Clark-Atlanta University

223 James P. Brawley DRSW
Atlanta, GA 30314
404-880-8000
http://www.cau.edu

Coahoma Community College

3240 Friars Point Road
Clarksdale, MS 38614
601-627-2571
http://www.clarksdale.com/ccc/ccc.html

Coahoma Community College is a 2-year coeducational community college offering degrees or certificates in more than 50 majors. Coahoma graduates are readily accepted by four-year colleges throughout the country. In particular, courses offered at Coahoma meet the requirements for transfer to the state's 8 four-year public universities. Nearly 20 clubs and organizations offer students the opportunity to develop leadership, teamwork, and management skills.

Coastal Bend College

3800 Charco Road
Beeville, TX 78102
361-358-2838
http://www.bcc.cc.tx.us

More than three-quarters of the graduates of Coastal Bend College are either working or earning university degrees, and CBC graduates have among the highest success rates in receiving university degrees — equal to those who began their studies at the large institutions. CBC also makes available scholarships, work-study programs, and grants to assist in funding. Apartments, dormitory, class buildings, and parking are arranged in consideration of students with disabilities. In the counseling center, you'll get assistance in preparing for a career.

Organizations

Colegio Biblico Pentecostal de Puerto Rico

P.O. Box 901
San Just, PR 00750-0901
787-761-0640

Colegio Tech del Municipio de San Juan

P.O. Box 701790
San Juan, PR 00936
787-250-7095

Colegio Universitario del Este-Carolina

P.O. Box 2010
Carolina, PR 00984-2010
787-257-7373

College of Aeronautics

La Guardia Airport
Flushing, NY 11371
800-PRO-AERO
http://www.aero.edu

The College of Aeronautics is one of the country's premier aviation institutions, and is located at LaGuardia Airport in Queens, New York. The college has more than 1,200 students, 60 faculty, and 67 staff members. It offers bachelor's and associate degrees in 5 primary areas: avionics (aviation electronics), flight, aviation maintenace, computerized design, and pre-engineering.

College of the Desert

43500 Monterey Avenue
Palm Desert, CA 92260
760-346-8041
http://www.desert.cc.ca.us

College of the Desert is organized around 9 academic divisions and offers degrees and certificates in over 70 disciplines.

College of the Menominee Nation

P.O. Box 1179
Keshena, WI 54135
715-799-4921
http://www.menominee.edu

The College of Menominee Nation is a tribal college offering many programs of study. It offers the associate of arts and sciences degree in liberal studies, business administration, elementary/early childhood education, gaming management hospitality and tourism, natural resources, nursing, human services/social work, and sustainable development. Also offered is the associate of applied science—technical studies for administrative assistant, microcomputer specialist, and timber harvesting. The certificate of mastery is offered in pre-apprenticeship electrical, pre-apprenticeship carpentry, building maintenance, and police science.

College of the Sequoias

915 South Mooney Boulevard
Visalia, CA 93277
559-730-3700
http://www.sequoias.cc.ca.us

Commonwealth International University

16000 East Canter Tech Parkway
Denver, CO 80221-3610
303-426-1000
http://www.commonwealth.edu

Community College of Denver

P.O. Box 173363
Denver, CO 80217
303-556-2600

Compton Community College

1111 East Artesia Boulevard
Compton, CA 90221
http://www.compton.cc.ca.us

Compton Community College is a single college district representing Carson, Compton, Lynwood, Paramount, and surrounding communities. Compton Community College is fully accredited, and offers a comprehensive program ranging from vocational programs to fine arts.

Confederated Salish and Kootenai Tribes

Kicking Horse Job Corps
Charlo, MT 59824
406-644-2217

The Job Corps helps young Native Americans learn vocational skills.

Confederated Salish and Kootenai Tribes Community College
Arlee, MT 59821
406-726-3224

Conservatory of Music of Puerto Rico
350 Rafael Lamar Street
San Juan, PR 00918
787-751-0160

Coppin State College
2500 West North Avenue
Baltimore, MD 21216
410-383-5400
http://www.coppin.umd.edu

Coppin provides an academic program which includes program offerings through the Division of Arts and Sciences, the Division of Education, the Division of Nursing, the Division of Graduate Studies, or the Division of Honors. In addition, Coppin students get valuable on-the-job training with national and local companies and agencies through the College's Cooperative Education and Internship Programs. Internships are offered in several majors and provide students with practical experience in the career they plan to enter. The Cooperative Education Program provides students with actual work experience for one or more semesters, interspersed with the regular college program of study.

Crownpoint Institute of Technology
P.O. Box 849
Crownpoint, NM 87313
505-786-4100
http://www.cit.cc.nm.us

Crownpoint Institute of Technology's two spacious campuses are situated on the eastern edge of the Navajo Nation in Crownpoint, New Mexico. Campus facilities are designed to blend with the Chaco Canyon's mesas and high plateau ranges. The institute was established in July 1979 as the Navajo Skill Center; since then, it has evolved into a technical-vocational education center well-known throughout the Southwest.

D-Q University
P.O. Box 409
Davis, CA 95617
530-758-0470
http://www.dqu.cc.ca.us

D-Q University is a two-year, private, accredited community college governed by a Native American Board of Trustees, recognized by the U.S. Department of Education as a tribally-controlled community college.

David N. Myers College
112 Prospect Avenue East
Cleveland, OH 44115-1013
877-DNMYERS
http://www.dnmyers.edu

This is a four-year college with a predominantly black enrollment. Myers College offers the master of business administration (MBA), bachelor of science (B.S.), associate in science (A.S.), and associate in arts (A.A.), in addition to a number of certificate programs.

Del Mar College
101 Baldwin Boulevard
Corpus Christi, TX 78404-3897
800-652-3357
http://www.delmar.edu

Del Mar College is a comprehensive community college located in Corpus Christi, Texas. The largest provider of post-secondary education south of San Antonio, Del Mar College enrolls about 25,000 students each year in academic, occupational, technical, and noncredit programs.

Delaware State University
1200 North Dupont Highway
Dover, DE 19901
302-739-4000
http://www.dsc.edu

Delaware State University is a public, comprehensive, 1890 land-grant institution. Degrees

243

offered consist of the bachelor's of art, science, social work, and technology, and the master's of art, science, business administration, and social work.

Dillard University

2601 Gentilly Boulevard
New Orleans, LA 70122
504-283-8822
http://dillard.edu

Dillard University is a private, undergraduate liberal arts university founded in 1869, and has been cited in *U.S. News and World Report* as a top southern liberal arts college. It is affiliated with The College Fund/UNCF, related to the United Church of Christ, and the United Methodist Church, and accredited by the Southern Association of Colleges and Schools, the National League for Nursing, and the Louisiana Department of Education. The university has 120 faculty members, and the average class size is 15 students. There are 36 undergraduate majors in six academic divisions.

Diné College

P.O. Box 97
Tsaile, AZ 86556
520-724-6633
http://www.ncc.cc.nm.us

Diné College was established to meet the educational needs of the Navajo people. As the only academic postsecondary institution chartered by the Navajo Nation Council, the college offers two-year programs according to the needs of the Navajo Nation. Diné College is a multi-campus institution. All campuses focus on the offering of educational programs which prepare the student for transfer to four-year colleges/universities and for entry into employment. Developmental studies are offered at all sites for students who need further preparation for college-level studies.

District of Columbia, University of

4200 Connecticut Avenue, NW
Washington, DC 20008
202-832-4888
http://www.udc.edu

The University of the District of Columbia is the only public institution of higher education in the District of Columbia. It was chartered in 1974 as an urban land-grant institution with an open admissions policy. As the public land-grant institution functioning as a graduate degree granting institution, baccalaureate degree granting institution, and as a community college, the university is responsive to the occupational needs of the residents of the District of Columbia metropolitan area and continues to design programs and produce competitive graduates in response to that need.

Dodge City Community College

2501 North 14th Avenue
Dodge City, KS 67801-2399
http://www.dccc.cc.ks.us

Don Bosco Technical Institute

1151 San Gabriel Boulevard
Rosemead, CA 91770-4299
626-940-2000
http://www.boscotech.tec.ca.us

Don Bosco Tech offers a unique college preparatory high school program and a two-year junior college program with an associate in science degree in one of several technology majors. The Salesian educational philosophy, emphasizing the personal, religious, and moral growth of the individual student, inspires campus life. The academic and technology programs offer students opportunities for career preparation as well as for higher education.

Dona Ana Branch Community College

MSC3DA, P.O. Box 30001
Las Cruces, NM 88003-8001
505-646-3211
http://dabcc-www.nmsu.edu

The academic programs of the Dona Ana Branch Community College consist of Business and Information Systems, Developmental Studies, Health and Public Services, Technical Studies, and General Education.

Dull Knife Memorial College

P.O. Box 98
Lame Deer, MT 59043
406-477-6215
http://www.montana.edu/~wwwai/DKMC.html

Dull Knife Memorial College is located on the Northern Cheyenne Indian Reservation in southeastern Montana, and serves the reservation and surrounding communities. The college offers associate in arts and associate in applied science degrees as well as Certificate programs. Students and faculty have the opportunity to interact with members of the community, mostly Cheyenne, thus being able to enjoy many of the traditional activities of the tribe.

East Los Angeles College

Upward Bound Program
1301 Avenida Cesar Chavez
Monterey Park, CA 91754-6099
323-265-8990
http://www.elac.cc.ca.us

East Los Angeles College has an international, multicultural student body that complements the 14 communities comprising its primary service area. The college offers both academic transfer courses which prepare students for admission to four-year colleges and universities and occupational programs which prepare students for careers in two years or less. Many of the students who transfer from East Los Angeles College to a four-year university move on to nearby California State University, Los Angeles, or to the University of California, Los Angeles (UCLA). The college is located in the suburban community of Monterey Park, California, ten miles east of downtown Los Angeles. Facilities include an instructional center; bookstore; cafeteria; Library; 20,000-seat sports stadium; 2,000 seat auditorium; and a 1,500-seat indoor swim stadium.

Eastern New Mexico University, Roswell

P.O. Box 6000
Roswell, NM 88201
505-624-7141
http://www.roswell.enmu.edu

Eastern New Mexico University—Roswell is a community college offering lower level course work applicable to baccalaureate degrees at ENMU and other institutions of higher education. It also offers vocational-technical education in selected occupations, continuing education opportunities, and developmental/basic programs to complement student development, including guidance, counseling, and advisement service.

Edward Waters College

1658 Kings Road
Jacksonville, FL 32209
904-355-3030
http://www.ewc.edu

Edward Waters College, the 133-year-old historically black college provides an environment where students achieve academic, social, economic, and spiritual success through appropriate development learning activities and community involvement in higher learning. The instructional program, applied research, and community services are strategically designed to assist students in discovering their innate abilities and talents that may upgrade and enrich the quality of their lives.

El Camino College

16007 Crenshaw Boulevard
Torrance, CA 90506
310-532-3670
http://www.elcamino.cc.ca.us

El Paso Community College

P.O. Box 20500
El Paso, TX 79998
915-831-2000
http://www.epcc.edu

The El Paso Community College offers associate degrees, certificates, and transfer courses. It also offers programs for career guidance and job placement.

Elizabeth City State University

1704 Weeksville Road
Elizabeth City, NC 27909
http://www.ecsu.edu

Organizations

Elizabeth City State University is a public baccalaureate university offering 25 degrees in the arts and sciences and in some professional and preprofessional areas; also offers a master's degree in elementary education.

Escuela de Artes Plasticas ICPR

P.O. Box 1112
San Juan, PR 00902-1112
787-725-8120

Estrella Mountain Community College

3000 North Dysart Road
Avondale, AZ 85323-1000
623-935-8000
http://www.emc.maricopa.edu

Estrella Mountain Community College is an institution of higher education serving the West Valley communities through general education, transfer education, developmental education, workforce development, community education, and student support services.

Faulkner University

5345 Atlanta Highway
Montgomery, AL 36109-3323
334-386-7324
http://www.faulkner.edu

Faulkner University has African American enrollment of about 25 percent. The university is dedicated to academic excellence and strong Christian commitment, endeavoring to help all students reach their full potential academically, socially, spiritually, and physically. The small class size and personal attention to each student allows the university to guide students to reach their full potential. Every subject is taught from a Christian perspective.

Fayetteville State University

1200 Murchison Road
Fayetteville, NC 28301-4298
800-222-2594
http://www.uncfsu.edu

Fayetteville State University is a constituent institution of the University of North Carolina. Its academic programs include the College of Arts and Sciences, School of Education, School of Business and Economics, and the Math/Science Education Center.

Fisk University

1000 17th Avenue, North
Nashville, TN 37208-3051
615-329-8500
http://www.fisk.edu

Fisk University was the first historically black college to gain accreditation by the Southern Association of Colleges and Schools; the first HBCU to be placed on the approved lists of the Association of American Universities; and the first HBCU to be granted a charter for the establishment of a chapter of Phi Beta Kappa. Some of the notable contemporary attributes of Fisk include: A recent National Science Foundation study revealed that more Fisk alumni earned doctorates in the natural sciences than African Americans from any other college or university; a significant percentage of the nation's black physicians, dentists, attorneys, and actuarial fellows have graduated from Fisk; and more than half of the university's graduates attend graduate and professional school. Fisk is home to a number of distinctive resources including The Fisk Jubilee Singers, the NASA Center for Photonic Materials and Devices, and the Fisk Race Relations Institute.

Florida Agricultural and Mechanical University

Tallahassee, FL 32307
850-599-3000
http://www.famu.edu

Florida Agricultural and Mechanical University was founded in 1887, thus making it one of the three oldest institutions of higher education in the state of Florida. It is a comprehensive, co-educational, residential, multi-level land-grant university offering a broad range of instruction, research, and service programs at the undergraduate, professional, and graduate levels. Baccalaureate and master's degrees are offered in a wide range of disciplines. Doctoral degrees are offered in pharmacy and engineering. As a land-grant institution, Florida Agricultural and Mechanical University maintains an abiding commitment to adult and continuing education outreach programs, and other ways of serving the needs of non-traditional learners. Agricultural research and the Cooperative Extension program serve Florida's citizens, with a special emphasis on the needs of the rural poor and the small farmer. The university is pre-eminent among the state universities for the cultural and racial diversity of its faculty. Florida Agricultural and Mechanical University will continue its focus on the educational needs of blacks and other ethnic minorities, while maintaining its leadership in racial desegregation, equal access, affirmative action, and cultural diversity.

Florida International University, University Park

Miami, FL 33199
305-348-2363
http://www.fiu.edu

A member of the State University System of Florida, FIU is a research university offering a diverse selection of undergraduate, graduate, and professional programs. Through its 16 colleges and schools, FIU offers baccalaureate, master's, and doctoral degree programs in more than 280 majors, conducts basic and applied research, and provides public service. Committed to both quality and access, FIU meets the educational needs of traditional students as well as the increasing number of part-time students and lifelong learners. Research and teaching which address economic and social concerns are conducted by interdisciplinary centers and institutes at the university.

Florida Memorial College

15800 Northwest 42nd Avenue
Miami, FL 33054
800-822-1362
http://www.fmc.edu

Florida Memorial College is a private, four-year, co-educational liberal arts college. FMC offers various academic programs in the liberal arts, business, sciences, computer science, dual degree engineering, education, and aviation.

Fond du Lac Community College

2101 14th Street
Cloquet, MN 55720
218-879-0800
http://www.fdl.cc.mn.us

Fond du Lac Tribal and Community College is unique in the United States because it is jointly a tribal college and a member of the Arrowhead Community College Region in Minnesota. Several two-year degree programs are offered, including a fully transferable associate in arts degree with specializations in accounting, business administration, liberal arts, Ojibwe specialist and law enforcement. An associate in applied science degree is available in the human services and human services/chemical dependency option. The latter is offered at the campus in Cloquet as well as in Duluth at Duluth Community College Center. Several study skills classes are in place to aid those who need additional assistance in their transition into college. These include study techniques, communication skills, and general life skills. A peer tutoring service is also available to help students through any class offered at Fort Belknap College.

Fort Belknap College

P.O. Box 159
Harlem, MT 59526
406-353-2607
http://www.montana.edu/~wwwse/fbc/fbc.html

The mission of Fort Belknap College is to provide quality post-secondary educational opportunities for Indian residents of the Fort Belknap communities. Fort Belknap College offers one degree, an associate of arts in general studies with an emphasis in business, human services, data processing, liberal arts, Native American studies, pre-professional, or natural resources. Offered also are certificates of completion in early childhood education and computer applications.

Fort Berthold Community College

Office of Financial Aid
P.O. Box 490
New Town, ND 58763
701-627-3665

Organizations

Fort Peck Community College

P.O. Box 398
Poplar, MT 59255
406-768-5551

Fort Valley State University

1005 State College Drive
Fort Valley, GA 31030
912-825-6211
http://www.fvsu.edu

Fort Valley State University is accredited by the
Commission on Colleges of the Southern
Association of Colleges and Schools to award
associate, baccalaureate, master's and special-
ist's degrees. The university consists of 4 aca-
demic colleges: Agriculture, Home Economics,
and Allied Programs; Arts and Sciences;
Education, Graduate, and Special Academic
Programs; and Weekend College. Additional
programs include: International Programs;
Learning Resources Center; Testing Center;
Office of Admissions and Enrollment
Management; and Continuing Education.
Extended educational outreach opportunities
are offered through Weekend College and university satellite centers in Macon and Dublin.

Fresno City College

1101 E. University Avenue
Fresno, CA 93741
209-442-4600
http://www.scccd.cc.ca.us

Fullerton College

321 East Chapman Avenue
Fullerton, CA 92832-2095
714-992-7568
http://www.fullcoll.edu

Gavilan College

5055 Santa Teresa Boulevard
Gilroy, CA 95020
408-847-1400
http://www.gavilan.cc.ca.us

Gavilan College is a public community college
committed to student success and offers a wide
range of services, including programs of continuing study in liberal arts, pre-professional, business, vocational, and technical fields, in day,

evening, and weekend classes designed to assist
students in meeting their educational needs and
life goals.

Grambling State University

P.O. Box 864
Grambling, LA 71245
318-274-3811
http://www.gram.edu

Founded in 1901 as a private industrial school
to educate African American citizens of north
central Louisiana, Grambling State University, a
constituent institution in the University of
Louisiana system, is now a comprehensive university offering undergraduate, graduate, professional, and continuing education programs.

Hampton University

School of Nursing
Hampton, VA 23668
757-727-5251

The Hampton University School of Nursing is
the oldest baccalaureate nursing program in
Virginia. The school offers traditional LPN-to-BS
and RN-to-BS programs. It has the oldest graduate nursing program in a Historically Black
College or University. Offers both the master's
and Ph.D. in nursing. Post-master's certification
as family, geriatric, or pediatric nurse practi-
tioner is available. The school operates a
Nursing Center with a Health Mobile that provides health care services for the community.

Hampton University

Hampton, VA 23668
757-727-5251
http://www.hamptonu.edu

Hampton University provides a liberal arts
foundation for its professional and scientific
disciplines. Some of the major areas of study
are: aviation science, architecture, entrepreneurship, environmental and marine science,
chemistry, electrical and chemical engineering,
music engineering technology, education,
English, business, computer sciences, mass
media, nursing, communicative sciences and
disorders, physical therapy, physics, paralegal
studies, fire administration, emergency medical

systems management, and systems management. Students may earn the bachelor's and/or master's degree in many areas. The Ph.D. is awarded in physics, physical therapy, and nursing; and the Pharm.D. is awarded in pharmacy.

Harris-Stowe State College

3026 Laclede Avenue
St. Louis, MO 63103
314-340-3366
http://www.hsscu.edu

The college's degree programs cover five main areas: Business Administration; Criminal Justice; Health Care Management; Teacher Education; and Urban Education. Harris-Stowe State College is also dedicated to professional development and achievement. The college regards its mission of service to the urban community with great importance. It is committed to providing the academic resources through which teachers and other professionals can keep abreast of new trends, upgrade skills associated with changing technology, and grapple with the complexity and intensity of educational /societal problems, all toward the objective of effecting viable options and solutions. The college provides this on-going education of professionals through a variety of courses, workshops, and seminars.

Hartnell College

156 Homestead Avenue
Salinas, CA 93901-1628
831-755-6700
http://www.hartnell.cc.ca.us

Hartnell College serves the Salinas Valley, a fertile agricultural region some 10 miles wide and 100 miles long. The college draws its students from Salinas and the surrounding communities of Bradley, Castroville, Chualar, Greenfield, Jolon, King City, Lockwood, Moss Landing, San Ardo, San Lucas, Soledad, and adjacent rural areas. Hartnell serves approximately 8,352 students with an ethnic profile that includes 48 percent Latino, 36 percent white, 5 percent Asian, 5 percent Filipino, 3 percent African American, 1 percent Native American, and 2 percent other minorities.The college offers the

first and second year of a college program and awards the associate of arts/sciences degrees and certificates of proficiency. The college also provides vocational training, work force and community development classes, Contract Education, and numerous cultural and recreational activities. The Computer Center is available to students for class and assignment use and provides access to the Internet and the World Wide Web.

Heald College School of Business and Technology—Hayward

777 Southland Drive, Suite 110
Hayward, CA 95134
408-370-2400
http://www.heald.edu

Heald College School of Business and Technology—Fresno

2665 North First Street
San Jose, CA 95134
408-370-2400
http://www.heald.edu

Heald College School of Business— Salinas

1450 North Main Street
Salina, CA 93906
408-757-1700
http://www.heald.edu

Heald College School of Business— Stockton

1605 East March Lane
Stockton, CA 95210
209-477-1114
http://www.heald.edu

Heritage College

3240 Fort Road
Toppenish, WA 98948
509-865-8500
http://www.heritage.edu

Heritage College is a non-profit, independent, non-denominational accredited institution of higher education offering undergraduate and graduate education. Its mission is to provide quality, accessible higher education to multicultural populations which have been educationally isolated. Within its liberal arts curriculum, Heritage College offers strong professional and career-oriented programs designed to enrich the quality of life for students and their communities.

Hinds Community College

505 East Main Street
Raymond, MS 39154-9799
601-352-3011
http://www.hinds.cc.ms.us

Dedicated to meeting the needs of the community, Hinds Community College is a comprehensive educational institution serving approximately 21,000 students each year. Hinds provides quality academic, technical, and vocational programs that are convenient and affordable.

Hostos Community College

City University of New York
500 Grand Concourse
Bronx, NY 10451
718-518-4444
http://www.hostos.cuny.edu

The college is accredited by the Middle States Association of Colleges and Schools and the Board of Regents of the University of the State of New York. The Allied Health programs are accredited by the appropriate agencies, including the American Dental Association, the American Medical Association, and the New York Department of Health. Of the faculty, 49 percent hold doctorates and 38 percent have master's degrees. The student population is diverse with nearly all cultures represented, the highest concentration coming from Puerto Rico, the Dominican Republic, and Central and South America. Financial assistance is provided to all eligible students and nearly 99 percent receive some form of federal or state aid.

Houston, University of (Downtown)

One Main Street, Suite 625-S
Houston, TX 77002
713-221-8000
http://www.dt.uh.edu

Howard University

2400 Sixth Street, NW
Washington, DC 20059-0001
202-806-6100
http://www.howard.edu

Chartered by the United States Congress in 1867, Howard University is one of only 88 Research I Universities in the United States, and the only predominantly African American university to be so designated. The private, comprehensive university comprises 12 schools and colleges in which more than 11,000 students are engaged in academic programs encompassing some 180 areas of study leading to undergraduate, graduate, and professional degrees. A national repository of research and scholarship, Howard University's faculty constitutes the largest assembly of African American scholars in the world. The university's Graduate School continues to produce more on-campus African American Ph.D.s than any other university.

Hudson County Community College

162 Sip Avenue
Jersey City, NJ 07306
201-714-2127
http://www.hudson.cc.nj.us

Hudson County Community College consists of four academic divisions, along with the North Hudson Center: Business and Allied Health Division; Culinary Arts Division; English, Humanities & Social Sciences Division; and the Mathematics, Science & Technology Division.

Humacao Community College

Apartado 9139
Humacao, PR 00792
787-852-1430

Huston-Tillotson College

900 Chicon Street
Austin, TX 78702
512-505-3000
http://www.htc.edu

Huston-Tillotson College is an independent, church-related, historically black institution. It is affiliated with the United Methodist Church, the United Church of Christ, and the United

Negro College Fund. Huston-Tillotson College is accredited by the Commission on Colleges of the Southern Association of Colleges and Schools to award baccalaureate degrees. The college awards undergraduate, four-year degrees in business, education, the humanities, natural sciences, and social sciences.

Imperial Valley College

Office of Financial Aid
Imperial, CA 92251-0158
619-352-8320
http://www.imperial.cc.ca.us/

Imperial Valley College is a 2-year public community college providing vocational training and transfer preparation for 4-year-college and university-bound students.

Incarnate Word College

4301 Broadway
San Antonio, TX 78209
210-829-6000

Institute of American Indian Arts

P.O. Box 20007
Santa Fe, NM 87504
800-804-6422
http://www.iaiancad.org

The Institute of American Indian and Alaska Native Culture and Arts Development (IAIA) is dedicated to the study, creative application, preservation, and care of Indian Arts and Culture. Since 1962, the IAIA has educated over 3,200 American Indian and Alaska Native students.

Inter-American University of Puerto Rico—Aguadilla

P.O. Box 20000
Aguadilla, PR 00605
787-891-0925
http://www.inter.edu

Inter-American University of Puerto Rico—Arecibo

P.O. Box 4050
Arecibo, PR 00614-4050
787-878-5475
http://www.arecibo.inter.edu

Inter-American University of Puerto Rico—Barranquitas

P.O. Box 517
Barranquitas, PR 00794-0517
787-857-3600
http://www.inter.edu

Inter-American University of Puerto Rico—Bayamon

Carrera 830 #500
Bayamon, PR 00957
787-279-1912

Inter-American University of Puerto Rico—Fajardo

P.O. Box 607003
Fajardo, PR 00738-7003
787-863-2390

Inter-American University of Puerto Rico—Guayama

P.O. Box 10004
Guayama, PR 00785
787-864-2222
http://guayama.inter.edu

Inter-American University of Puerto Rico—Metropolitan

P.O. Box 191293
San Juan, PR 00919-1293
787-766-1912
http://www.metro.inter.edu

Inter-American University of Puerto Rico—Ponce

Carr. 1, Km. 123.2
Interior Mercedita, PR 00715
787-284-1912
http://ponce.inter.edu/

Organizations

Inter-American University of Puerto Rico—San German

P.O. Box 5100
San German, PR 00683
787-264-1912
http://www.sg.inter.edu

Inter-American University of Puerto Rico—School of Law

P.O. Box 70351
San Juan, PR 00936-8351
787-751-1912

Inter-American University—School of Optometry

P.O. Box 191049
San Juan, PR 00919-1049
787-765-1915

Interdenominational Theological Center

671 Beckwith Street
Atlanta, GA 30314
404-527-7700

The center supports research into the integration of African American perspectives on the ministry. With its resources and facilities, the center supports study into theological curriculum and religion.

J. F. Drake Technical College

3421 Meridian Street North
Huntsville, AL 35811
256-539-8161
http://dstc.cc.al.us

Students at Drake College receive training in specialized areas of specific job placement/advancement. The college offers the associate's in applied technology degree in such areas as accounting, computer information, and drafting and design.

Jackson State University

1400 Lynch Street
Jackson, MS 39217
800-848-6817
http://www.jsums.edu

While Jackson State remains proud of its heritage as one of America's leading HBCUs, it has become an increasingly diverse institution offering a myriad of opportunities for personal growth and achievement. The more than 6,200 students enrolled at Jackson State come from every county in Mississippi as well as from across the United States and from numerous foreign countries. The faculty numbers more than 400 talented educators with diverse backgrounds. These teaching and research professionals are drawn to Jackson State from prestigious institutions around the world and 70 percent hold a doctorate or terminal degree in their fields. The student/faculty ratio is 17:1.

Jarvis Christian College

Highway 80 West
P.O. Box 1470
Hawkins, TX 75765-1470
903-769-5700
http://www.jarvis.edu

A private, four-year, accredited, co-educational liberal arts college affiliated with the Christian Church (Disciples of Christ).

Jersey City State College

2039 Kennedy Boulevard
Jersey City, NJ 07305
201-656-2020

John Jay College of Criminal Justice

City University of New York
899 Tenth Avenue
New York, NY 10019
212-237-8000
http://www.jjay.cuny.edu

Founded in 1964, John Jay College of Criminal Justice of the City University of New York, is a liberal arts college which emphasizes as its special mission criminal justice, fire science, and other public service related fields. As such, it is the only one of its kind in the nation. The college serves as a major center for research in criminal justice, law enforcement, and forensic sciences, and as a major training facility for local, state, federal, and international law enforcement agencies, and private security personnel. Its ethnically and culturally diverse student population, in excess of 9,500, includes 25 percent who are members of the uniformed criminal justice and fire service agencies. The majority of the students are civilian preprofessionals who plan careers in public service or already are employed in public service.

Johnson C. Smith University

100 Beatties Ford Road
Charlotte, NC 28216
704-378-1000
http://www.jcsu.edu

Kelsey-Jenney College

7310 Miramar Road, Suite 300
San Diego, CA 92126
619-549-5070

Kentucky State University

400 East Main Street
Frankfort, KY 40601
502-227-6000
http://www.kysu.edu

Kentucky State University offers a comprehensive, liberal studies curriculum, with the lowest student/faculty ratio in the state higher education system. The university has an 80 percent graduate job placement rate. It is 1 of only 17 national 1890 land-grant institutions. Its main campus is located on 309 acres. The university has an internationally recognized Aquaculture Research Center and an $11.5 million Health, Physical Education, and Recreation complex. It also has a $4 million High-Technology Initiative.

Knoxville College

901 College Street, NW
Knoxville, TN 37921
615-524-6511
http://www.knoxvillecollege.edu

Knoxville College is a 4-year liberal arts college (coeducational), organized as a work college. Knoxville College students are focused and committed to achievement in both self and community. They have chosen Knoxville College to re-affirm the importance of their cultural heritage and background and are empowered to take advantage of the college's educational strength. Over 60 percent of the full-time faculty

hold doctoral degrees in their field of study, while 40 percent of the adjunct faculty also have doctoral degrees. Knoxville College offers the College Work Program which guarantees financial resources for all students while preparing them for responsible roles in society. The college partners with neighboring universities and businesses to contribute toward the students' financial well-being while strengthening their work habits and providing hands-on exposure to their chosen professional disciplines.

La Guardia Community College

City University of New York
31-10 Thomson Avenue
Long Island City, NY 11101
718-482-5000
http://www.lagcc.cuny.edu

This branch of the City University of New York serves western Queens and the larger New York metro area, and offers 30 academic majors.

Lac Courte Oreilles Ojibwa Community College

13466 West Trepania Road
Hayward, WI 54843-2186
715-634-4790
http://www.ico-college.edu

The Lac Courte Oreilles Ojibwa Community College provides, within the Indian community, a system of post-secondary and continuing education with an associate degree and certificate granting capabilities.

Lane College

545 Lane Avenue
Jackson, TN 38301
901-426-7500
http://www.lanecollege.edu

Founded in 1882 by a former slave, Lane College is one of the nation's oldest Historically Black Colleges. With strong ties to the Christian Methodist Episcopal Church, the College's mission is to develop the "whole student." That is, in addition to its priority of academic excellence, the college is also concerned about its students' spiritual, social, and ethical development. Consistent with its tradition of providing educational opportunities for those who may not have otherwise attended college, Lane College is committed to preparing students, through its liberal arts curriculum, to assume meaningful positions in their chosen professions, or to pursue graduate studies. The college is supported in part by the United Negro College Fund, and has a legacy of commitment to preparing students to meet the challenges of an ever-changing world. Among its hundreds of renowned graduates is Simon Haley, grandfather of the late historian and author of "Roots," Alex Haley. Located in Jackson, Tennessee, Lane College offers an environment which allows students to grow in a pleasant, caring atmosphere, and at the same time, challenges them to perform their best. Lane College has a student/faculty ratio of approximately 15 to 1.

Laredo Junior College

West End Washington Street
Laredo, TX 78040
956-722-0521
http://www.laredo.cc.tx.us

Lawson State Community College

3060 Wilson Road SW
Birmingham, AL 35221
205-925-2515
http://www.ls.cc.al.us

Lawson State provides education and training programs for diversified employment in industry, business, and government. It also provides university parallel programs, developmental education programs, and programs and facilities for community services and continuing education.

Leech Lake Tribal College

023-2nd Street NW
Cass Lake, MN 56633
218-335-2828

LeMoyne-Owen College

Office of Institutional Advancement
807 Walker Avenue
Memphis, TN 38126
901-774-9090
http://www.lemoyne-owen.edu

The LeMoyne-Owen College in Memphis, Tennessee, is an independent liberal arts institution, related to the United Church of Christ and the Tennessee Baptist Missionary and Education Convention. The college is committed to providing a holistic education for the traditional and non-traditional student and to providing leadership and service to the Memphis and Mid-South community and beyond. The undergraduate academic program at LeMoyne-Owen is carried out under five academic divisions offering majors in 15 areas of study leading to the bachelor's of arts, the bachelor's of science or the bachelor's of business administration degrees. LeMoyne-Owen also offers the master's of science in education degree from its Division of Graduate Studies.

Lewis College of Business

17370 Meyers Road
Detroit, MI 48235
318-862-6300

Lexington College

10840 South Western Avenue
Chicago, IL 60643-3294
773-779-3800

Lincoln University, Missouri

820 Chestnut Street
Jefferson City, MO 65102-0029
800-521-5052
http://www.lincolnu.edu

Lincoln University meets the needs of a diverse student population in terms of age, ethnicity, gender, and socio-economic background. As an historically black institution, particular attention is given to African-American students from both within and outside Missouri. The university also provides academic, personal, and social programs and services to assist the diverse population which it serves. The university provides opportunities for non-traditional students to participate in educational activities held at on- and off-campus sites.

Lincoln University, Pennsylvania

P.O. Box 179
Lincoln University, PA 19352
610-932-8300
http://www.lincoln.edu

Lincoln University is a state-related, 4-year liberal arts institution located in southern Chester County, Pennsylvania. Chartered in 1854, Lincoln is the oldest historically black college/university in the United States. The current undergraduate and graduate enrollment is approximately 2,100 students.

Little Big Horn Community College

P.O. Box 370
Crow Agency, MT 59022-0370
406-638-7211
http://main.lbhc.cc.mt.us/

Little Big Horn College is a public two-year community college chartered by the Crow Tribe of Indians. The college is located in the town of Crow Agency, Montana, the capital of the Crow Indian Reservation in south central Montana. Nine associate of arts degrees are offered. The courses of study offered are directed to the economic and job opportunities in the Crow Indian Reservation area. The student body is comprised of Crow tribal members (90 percent), members of American Indian tribes from around the Intermountain West (8 percent), and residents of the Big Horn County area (2 percent).

Little Priest Tribal College

P.O. Box 270
Winnebago, NE 68071
402-878-2380
http://www.lptc.cc.ne.us

Little Priest Tribal College offers two-year associate degree programs, certificate programs, and community education programs.

Livingstone College

701 West Monroe Street
Salisbury, NC 28144
704-797-1000
http://members.tripod.com/~clandy/livingstone/homef.htm

Livingstone College is a historically black institution. This private, church-supported, coeducational liberal arts college was founded in 1879 by ministers of the African Methodist Episcopal Zion Church. It consists of 2 schools: an undergraduate college of arts and sciences, and a graduate school of theology. Livingstone College is accredited by the Southern Association of Colleges and Schools.

Long Beach City College

4901 E. Carson Street
Long Beach, CA 90808
562-938-4111
http://www.lbcc.cc.ca.us

Los Angeles City College

855 North Vermont Avenue
Los Angeles, CA 90029
323-953-4000
http://citywww.lacc.cc.ca.us

Among the educational programs at Los Angeles City College is a transfer program that enables the student who completes two years of study to continue upper division (third-year) work at accredited four-year colleges and universities. The college also has an occupational education program, associate degree programs, remedial and basic skills education, and continuing education.

Los Angeles County Medical Center School of Nursing

1200 North State Street
Los Angeles, CA 90033-1083
213-226-4911

Los Angeles Harbor College

1111 Figueroa Place
Wilmington, CA 90744-2397
310-522-8200
http://www.lahc.cc.ca.us

Los Angeles Mission College

13356 Eldridge Avenue
Sylmar, CA 91342
818-364-7600
http://www.lamission.cc.ca.us

Organizations

L.A. Mission has been providing academic, vocational, and occupational training to the Northeast San Fernando Valley since 1975. For the college to stay current it has formed partnerships with local industry to get insight into future trends, emerging technologies, potential internships, and job placement opportunities for its students. The Library/Learning Resources Center houses over 350 computers, with the latest programs, Internet access, and email for students.

Los Angeles Trade-Technical College
400 West Washington Boulevard
Los Angeles, CA 90015
213-744-9058
http://www.lattc.cc.ca.us

Los Angeles Training Technical College
400 West Washington Boulevard
Los Angeles, CA 90015-4181
213-744-7058
http://www.lattc.cc.ca.us

Founded in 1925 as the Frank Wiggins Trade School, Trade-Tech is the oldest of the nine, public two-year colleges in the Los Angeles Community College District. Nearly half of all Trade-Tech students work more than 30 hours per week and approximately this same percentage indicate that they are attending the college for job preparation. The degrees granted are the associate in arts and associate in science as well as certificates of completion in any one of many vocational programs. All academic courses required for transfer to a four-year college or university are offered, as well as nearly 90 different occupational programs, some of which can be completed in as little as one year.

Los Angeles Valley College
5800 Fulton Avenue
Van Nuys, CA 91401-4096
818-781-1200
http://www.lavc.cc.ca.us

Luna Vocational Technical Institute
P.O. Box 1510
Hot Springs Boulevard
Las Vegas, NM 87701
505-454-2500
http://www.lvti.cc.nm.us

Luna Vocational Technical Institute is the only vocational technical community college in northeastern New Mexico. As a two-year institution of higher education, LVTI offers over 30 areas of study.

MacCormac College
506 South Wabash
Chicago, IL 60605
312-922-1884
http://www.maccormac.edu

The college offers an 18-month associate degree in accounting, court reporting, international business, legal assistant, legal secretarial, medical transcription, office systems management, and tourism management. It also offers a 9 month diploma in the areas of computer software specialist, executive assistant, medical transcription, and travel consultant.

Manhattan Community College
City University of New York
199 Chambers Street
New York, NY 10007
212-346-8100
http://www.bmcc.cuny.edu

BMCC offers a wide range of degree programs, including accounting, allied health sciences, business administration, business Management, computer programming and computer operations, computer science,corporate and cable communications, early childhood education, engineering science, human services, liberal arts, mathematics, nursing, office automation, and office operations, science and small business entrepreneurship, as well as many non-degree programs in adult and continuing education.

Martin University

2171 Avondale Place
Indianapolis, IN 46218
317-543-3256
http://www.martin.edu

Martin University is a private, not-for-profit, non-denominational institution dedicated to the higher education of adult learners, low-income persons, minorities, the elderly, and prison inmates. The main campus is comprised of 9 buildings, including the Bernice Fraction Center for Performing Arts; the Martin University Health Education Center, which conducts addiction and counseling programs; and classroom and administrative buildings, which house offices for academic staff, financial aid staff, and student services. Martin University also offers master's degrees in community psychology and urban ministry.

Mary Holmes College

Highway 50 West
P.O. Drawer 1257
West Point, MS 39773-1257
662-494-6820
http://www.maryholmes.edu

Mary Holmes College is an open admission, two-year, historically black, coeducational, primarily residential institution related to the Presbyterian Church (USA) and located in West Point, Mississippi. Its mission is to serve a student population from the Southeast region of the United States which is primarily underserved and economically disadvantaged. The college has made it possible for many without opportunity to achieve success in such diverse fields as religion, education, law, and medicine.

Marygrove College

8425 West McNichols Road
Detroit, MI 48221-2599
313-927-1200
http://www.marygrove.edu

This is a four-year and master's degree college with a predominantly black enrollment. At Marygrove students prepare for specific contemporary careers and, through liberal arts studies, develop skills of critical thinking, communication, and ethical decision-making skills necessary for career effectiveness and flexibility. As an intentionally small college, Marygrove places a high priority on the development of leadership skills through curricular and extra-curricular experiences including student government, performing arts, peer tutoring, community service, and college-wide committee work. Marygrove faculty members offer excellent instruction, careful attention to individual student needs, and thorough academic advising. Marygrove places a high value on its diverse student body—women and men of all ages with various cultural, ethnic, and political backgrounds. Serious attempts are made to recruit faculty and staff who will serve as excellent role models for students.

Maryland, University of, Eastern Shore

Backbone Road
Princess Anne, MD 21853
410-651-2200
http://www.umes.umd.edu

A historically black university on the rural Eastern Shore, UMES grants degrees in the arts and sciences, agriculture, and business. True to its land-grant mission, the campus offers a number of unique programs geared to the needs of the region, including construction management, airway science, criminal justice, and hotel and restaurant management. Pre-professional training is offered in 9 fields. The university's 10 graduate offerings include doctoral programs in toxicology and marine-estuarine-environmental sciences.

Mashantucket Pequot Academy

P.O. Box 3057
Mashantucket, CT 06339-3057
860-312-1030
http://www.pequotacademy.com

The academy serves the Mashantucket Pequot Tribal Nation through business-driven educational development.

Organizations

Medgar Evers College

City University of New York
1150 Carroll Street
Brooklyn, NY 11225
718-270-4900

Medgar Evers offers outstanding programs, including marketing, nursing, business, liberal arts, science, public administration, elementary education, computer applications, and several certificate programs. The college offers both baccalaureate and associate degrees. The School of Continuing Education offers extensive programs that address the needs of students seeking specialized training or career advancement.

Meharry Medical College

1005 Todd Boulevard
Nashville, TN 37208
615-327-6223
http://www.mmc.edu

Meharry Medical College is the largest private historically black institution exclusively dedicated to educating health care professionals and biomedical scientists in the United States. The college strives to maintain a nationally recognized center of excellence for the practice and delivery of community-oriented health care services, health promotion and disease prevention, quality primary care training, and the conduct of basic, clinical, and applied research with special emphasis on diseases and health conditions that disproportionately affect ethnic minority populations.

Merced College

3600 M Street
Merced, CA 95348-2898
209-384-6000

Mercy College

555 Broadway
Dobbs Ferry, NY 10522
800-MERCY-NY
http://www.mercynet.edu

Mercy College offers a curriculum of liberal arts and sciences, as well as pre-professional programs. Mercy attracts students from primarily the New York/New Jersey metropolitan area as

well as from around the United States and 67 other countries.

Miami, University of

Coral Gables, FL 33124
305-284-2211
http://www.miami.edu

The University of Miami has been described as a major research university set in a tropical garden. One of only 26 private research universities to operate both a law and medical school, the University of Miami comprises 14 schools and colleges devoted to various fields of study from architecture to international studies.

Miami-Dade Community College, Wolfson

300 NE Second Street
Miami, FL 33132
305-237-3035
http://www.mdcc.edu

The college offers programs in banking, business, microcomputers, paralegal studies, architecture, economics, hospitality management, engineering, the arts, humanities, and the social sciences.

Miles College

P.O. Box 3800
Birmingham, AL 35208
205-929-1000
http://www.miles.edu

Miles College is a 4-year, fully accredited liberal arts college, and a member of the United Negro College Fund.

Mississippi Valley State University

Itta Bena, MS 38941
601-254-9041
http://www.mvsu.edu

Mississippi Valley State University is a regional institution responding to the needs of the delta region of the State of Mississippi for accessible, relevant, and quality undergraduate programs as well as some graduate and public service programs. The academic programs of the university offer opportunities for concentrated study in the arts, humanities, sciences, technology, and professional fields of business, education, special services, and pre-professional health services. Enrichment programs and support services enhance the university experience, help students achieve their personal and professional goals, and promote life-long learning.

Morehouse College

830 Westview Drive, SW
Atlanta, GA 30314
404-681-2800
http://www.morehouse.edu

Morehouse College was founded in 1867 and is the nation's only private, 4-year liberal arts institution for African American men. Degrees can be obtained through the bachelor's level.

Morehouse School of Medicine

720 Westview Drive, SW
Atlanta, GA 30310
404-752-1650
http://www.msm.edu

The Morehouse School of Medicine is an historically black institution established to recruit and train minority and other students as physicians and biomedical scientists committed to the primary health care needs of the underserved.

Morgan State University

1700 East Cold Spring Lane
Baltimore, MD 21251
443-885-3333
http://www.morgan.edu

The university awards more bachelor's degrees to African-American students than any campus in Maryland. In many fields, but particularly in engineering and the sciences, Morgan accounts for large percentages of the degrees received by African Americans from Maryland institutions. An above-average percentage of Morgan graduates enter graduate and professional school. Historically, the university has ranked among the top public campuses nationally in the number of black graduates subsequently receiving doctorates from U.S. universities.

Morris Brown College

643 Martin Luther King, Jr. Drive
Atlanta, GA 30314
404-752-1725
http://www.morrisbrown.edu

Morris Brown College is fully accredited by the Southern Association of Colleges and Schools with majors offered in more than 40 areas of study including business sciences, computer science, chemistry, biology and hospitality administration.

Morris College

100 West College Street
Sumter, SC 29150
803-934-3200
http://www.icusc.org/morris/mchome.htm

Morris College is an historically black, coeducational, liberal arts college, operated by the Baptist Educational and Missionary Convention of South Carolina. The college is accredited by the Commission on Colleges of the Southern Association of Colleges and Schools to award bachelor's degrees and is committed to promoting the intellectual and personal development of every one of its students. The college offers degrees in biology, business administration, broadcast media, Christian education, criminal justice, early childhood education, elementary education, English, health science, history, journalism, liberal studies, mathematics, organizational management, pastoral ministry, political science, recreation administration, and sociology, and it offers teacher preparatory certification in biology, English, history, mathematics, and social studies.

Morton College

3801 South Central Avenue
Cicero, IL 60804
708-656-8000
http://www.morton.cc.il.us

Besides its highly rated university transfer program, the college provides programs in vo-tech education, liberal studies, continuing education, and community service.

Organizations

Mount St. Mary's College

12001 Chalon Road
Los Angeles, CA 90049-1599
310-954-4000
http://www.msmc.la.edu

Mount St. Mary's College, Los Angeles, is an independent, Catholic, liberal arts college primarily for women. Baccalaureate degree programs, including a Weekend College for working adults, are offered on the Chalon Campus in West Los Angeles, while associate and graduate degree programs are offered at the Doheny Campus in downtown Los Angeles. Mount St. Mary's is committed to providing educational opportunities to underserved women. More than 58 percent of students are first-generation college students, and about 69 percent of undergraduate students are minorities.

Mountain View College

4849 West Illinois Avenue
Dallas, TX 75211
214-860-8600
http://www.mvc.dcccd.edu

Mt. San Antonio College

1100 North Grand
Walnut, CA 91789
909-594-5611
http://www.mtsac.edu

Mt. SAC offers the associate in arts degree and majors leading to associate in science degrees to meet the transfer requirements of virtually every baccalaureate level program offered by the California State University and University of California systems. Mt. SAC also offers many occupational certificate programs, community education classes, and a wide variety of student services.

Native American Educational Services

2838 West Peterson
Chicago, IL 60659
773-761-5000
http://NAES.indian.com/

This school is the only private Native-controlled college in the nation offering a BA degree in community studies and offering a variety of other educational programs designed to serve elementary, secondary, and adult Native American students.

Native American Multicultural Education School

3600 Morrison Road
Denver, CO 80219
303-934-8086
http://www.alphacdc.com/names/

The school offers adult basic education, the GED, and computer training.

Nebraska Indian Community College

P.O. Box 428
Macy, NE 68039
402-837-5078

This is a two-year college established to meet the unique education needs of the state's Native American community. The college is located on the Omaha and Santee Sioux reservations and also includes the Yankton Sioux Tribe of Marty. Admissions policy is open, with courses accredited and applied toward an associate of arts degree.

New Mexico Highlands University

P.O. Box 9000
Las Vegas, NM 87701-9000
505-454-7511
http://www.nmhu.edu

First established as New Mexico Normal School, the school has expanded beyond teacher education and became New Mexico Highlands University in 1941. Today, NMHU in Las Vegas offers graduate and undergraduate programs in arts and sciences, business, education, and social work. Through distance education and the Internet, NMHU also offers classes around the state, as well as with on-site faculty in Rio Rancho, Santa Fe, Espanola, Farmington, Tucumcari, and Hobbs. As part of its mission to serve the individual student through personal attention, Highlands maintains an open enrollment, small classes, and low tuition. The university is known for its research activities, student and faculty achievement, and opportunities for students to combine study with real-world experience. NMHU is accredited by the North Central Association of Schools and Colleges and is a member of the Rocky Mountain Athletic Conference, NCAA Division II.

New Mexico Junior College

5317 Lovington Highway
Hobbs, NM 88240
505-392-4510

New Mexico State University, Carlsbad

La Cruces, NM 88003-8001
505-646-0111
http://www.nmsu.edu

New Mexico State University, which began in 1888 as an agricultural college and preparatory school, is a comprehensive institution dedicated to teaching, research, and service. The university is in the southern New Mexico city of Las Cruces, which has a population of about 78,000. The region features desert mesas, the farmlands of the Rio Grande Valley, and the Organ Mountains, an extension of the Rocky Mountain chain. Total fall 1999 enrollment for NMSU main campus and branch campuses was 23,818. The main campus enrollment was 15,449; branch campuses totalled 8,217; and the Las Cruces Extension courses, 152. Minority enrollment is about 46 percent (39 percent Hispanic, 3 percent American Indian, 2 percent African-American, and 2 percent Asian-American). The University offers 43 bachelor's programs, 51 master's programs, 4 specialist in education, and 24 doctoral.

New Mexico State University, Dona Ana

3400 S. Espina MSC3DA
P.O. Box 30001
Las Cruces, NM 88003
505-527-7500
http://www.nmsu.edu

New Mexico State University, Grants

1500 Third Street
Grants, NM 87020
505-287-NMSU
http://www.grants.nmsu.edu

NMSU—Grants Campus is located in the city of Grants, New Mexico. Grants is located in the northwest corner of New Mexico about 75 miles west of Albuquerque. NMSU—Grants was established as a branch of New Mexico State University in 1968 through the cooperative efforts of New Mexico State University and Grants Municipal Schools.

New Mexico, University of (Los Alamos)

4000 University Drive
Los Alamos, NM 87544
505-662-5919
http://www.la.unm.edu:8001

New Mexico, University of (Main Campus)

Albuquerque, NM 87131-0001
505-277-0111
http://www.unm.edu

New Mexico, University of (Taos Education Center)

115 Civic Plaza Drive
Taos, NM 87571
505-758-7667
http://www.unm.edu/~taos

New Mexico, University of, at Valencia

280 La Entrada
Los Lunas, NM 87051-7633
505-925-8500
http://www.unm.edu.~unmvc

The University of New Mexico at Valencia is a 2-year community college offering academic transfer programs and vocational training. The campus occupies 150 acres of rural land overlooking the Rio Grande Valley to the west, the Manzano Mountains to the east, and historic Tome Hill to the north. As a branch college of the University of New Mexico, UNM Valencia Campus is fully accredited by the North Central Association of Colleges and Secondary Schools.

Organizations

New York City Technical College

City University of New York
300 Jay Street
Brooklyn, NY 11201
718-260-5000

The college offers 40 career-specific baccalaureate, associate, and specialized certificate programs in a diverse range of art and design, business, communications, entertainment, healthcare, human services, law, and engineering-related technologies deriving from or strongly influenced by the basic and applied sciences. Unique baccalaureate degree programs include electromechanical engineering technology, graphic arts and advertising production management, hospitality management, human services, legal assistant studies, occupational/technology teacher education, stage technology, and telecommunications technology. These programs and those at the associate's degree level combine state-of-the-art technical education with a solid theoretical foundation in the arts and sciences. Through special academic initiatives such as the CUNY-wide Alliance for Minority Participation (AMP) Program, students interested in careers in science and mathematics can participate in specialized workshops and research assistantships.

Norfolk State University

700 Park Avenue
Norfolk, VA 23504
757-823-8600
http://www.nsu.edu

NSU is a four-year, coeducational, state assisted public institution. The university offers 39 bachelors, 14 master's, and 2 doctoral degrees to its 7,300 students recruited from some 38 countries and territories. NSU is regionally as well as nationally accredited and employs approximately 950 individuals.

North Carolina Agricultural and Technical State University

Student Financial Aid Office
Greensboro, NC 27411
919-334-7973
http://www.ncat.edu

North Carolina A&T State University is comprised of 6 schools and 2 colleges. Among them: the School of Agriculture, the School of Business and Economics, the College of Engineering, and the School of Technology.

North Carolina Central University

School of Library and Information Science
P.O. Box 19586
Durham, NC 27707
919-560-6100
http://www.nccu.edu

North Carolina Central University is a comprehensive university offering programs at the undergraduate and graduate levels. It is the nation's first public liberal arts institution founded for African Americans.

Northeastern Illinois University

5500 North Saint Louis Avenue
Chicago, IL 60625-4699
773-583-4050

Northern New Mexico Community College

1002 North Onate Street
Espanola, NM 87532
505-747-2111
http://nnm.cc.nm.us

Nearly 65 certificate and degree programs are offered on the Española campus including: accounting, business administration, computer science, design foundation, computer aided drafting, early childhood education, fine arts, human services, library technology, micro electronics, management information systems, nursing, radiography, science, substance abuse counselor, and welding technology.

Northwest Indian College

2522 Kwina Road
Bellingham, WA 98226
360-676-2772
http://www.nwic.edu

Northwest Indian College provides post-secondary educational opportunities for Northwest Indian people. The college curriculum includes academic, vocational, continuing, cultural, community service, and adult basic education.

Oakwood College

7000 Adventist Boulevard
Huntsville, AL 35896
256-726-7030
http://www.oakwood.edu

Founded in 1896, Oakwood College is a historically black, primarily liberal arts four-year co-educational Seventh-Day Adventist institution. Located in Huntsville, Alabama, a city of more than 160,000, Oakwood is recognized nationwide as one of America's premier colleges in the preparation of African-Americans for medical school and health science careers. The college offers a total of 52 majors. Its student body and faculty consist of individuals from 39 states and 22 foreign countries and territories.

Odessa College

201 West University
Odessa, TX 79764
915-335-6432
http://coyote.odessa.edu

At Odessa College, students can enroll in adult basic education, continuing education, or community recreation courses. Many university-parallel courses are offered for students planning to complete four-year degrees at senior colleges or universities and are freely transferable. More than 30 occupational/technical programs also are offered.

Oglala Lakota College

P.O. Box 490
Kyle, SD 57752
605-455-2321
http://www.olc.edu

Oglala Lakota College was one of the first tribally controlled colleges in the United States. From its initial status as a community college, Oglala Lakota has grown to offer baccalaureate degrees and a master's degree in Lakota Leadership along with certificates and A.A. degrees. The enrollment is around 1,000 students with a full time equivalency of 650-700 students per semester. Oglala Lakota College is a North

Central accredited college, and its credits transfer to any college depending on each institution's particular method of how it accepts transfer credit.

Otero Junior College

1802 Colorado Avenue
La Junta, CO 81050
719-384-6831
http://www.ojc.cccoes.edu

Our Lady of the Lake University

411 Southwest 24th Street
San Antonio, TX 78207-4689
210-434-6711

Our Lady of the Lake University was established in 1895 by the Congregation of Divine Providence. The congregation continues as its sponsoring organization. The university is an independent, Catholic coeducational institution offering 56 undergraduate areas of study, 22 psychology, and one in leadership studies. The Lake holds classes at its main campus in San Antonio and at campuses in Houston and Dallas.The university's popular Weekend College, designed for working adults, offers classes on Saturdays and Sundays. The weekend format enrolls students in bachelor's degree programs from business to liberal arts and offers a master's of business administration program which enables managers to grow professionally and enhance their competitive position without interrupting their careers.Recent new degrees at The Lake include the bachelor's degree in environmental science, the bachelor's degree in electronic commerce, the M.B.A. in electronic commerce management, and the Ph.D. in leadership studies. The university also has extensive articulation agreements with community colleges around Texas, academic exchange programs with institutions in Kumamoto, Japan, in addition to Merida and Queretaro, Mexico, and business study tours in Australia.

Oxnard College

4000 South Rose Avenue
Oxnard, CA 93033
805-986-5800
http://www.oxnard.cc.ca.us

Organizations

Oxnard College provides studies leading to associate degrees and certificates of achievement in transfer programs and occupational/professional fields. In addition, the college works closely with local business and governmental agencies to provide specific and specialized training to help meet the needs of the community. Oxnard also offers many services that provide students help and support including: counseling, job placement/career center, health center, financial aid, and services for international students.

Paine College
1235 15th Street
Augusta, GA 30901
800-476-7703
http://www.paine.edu

The liberal arts curriculum offers 13 majors leading to the bachelor of arts or bachelor of science degree. Minors and concentrations are offered in a variety of areas.

Palo Alto College
1400 West Villaret
San Antonio, TX 78224
210-921-5000
http://www.accd.edu/pac

As one of the four colleges of the Alamo Community College District, Palo Alto College is an open admission, public, two-year college dedicated to the pursuit of excellence in its educational programs and services. Programs include lower-division preparation for college/university transfer; technical and vocational preparation for entry into the current job market; and continuing education activities to upgrade and retrain business and industrial workers.

Palo Verde College
811 West Chanslorway
Blythe, CA 92225
760-922-6168
http://www.paloverde.cc.ca.us

Pasadena City College
1570 E. Colorado Boulevard
Pasadena, CA 91106
626-585-7123

Passaic County Community College
One College Boulevard
Paterson, NJ 07505
973-684-6868
http://www.pccc.cc.nj.us

PCCC is a public community college serving Passaic County residents. In addition to the degree programs, the college offers: cooperative education; educational opportunity fund; honors program; continuing education; corporate & customized training; and transfer programs.

Paul Quinn College
3837 Simpson-Stuart Road
Dallas, TX 75241
800-237-2648
http://www.pqc.edu

Founded in 1872, Paul Quinn College is the oldest liberal arts college for African Americans in Texas and west of the Mississippi River. Paul Quinn's faculty and staff is a large diverse group of exceptional Christian scholars and teachers. Student to teacher radio is 18 to 1.

Philander Smith College
812 West 13th Street
Little Rock, AR 72202-3718
501-375-9845
http://www.philander.edu

Philander Smith College, founded in 1877, is a small, privately supported, historically black, 4-year liberal arts, career-oriented college, related to the board of higher education and ministry of the United Methodist Church. In fall 1998, enrollment was 918. Accredited by the North Central Association of Colleges and Universities, the Association for Collegiate and Business School Programs, and the National Council for the Accreditation of Teacher Education.

Pima Community College

4905C East Broadway
Tucson, AZ 85709-1005
520-206-4666
http://www.pima.edu

Pima Community College is a two-year institution that serves residents of Pima and Santa Cruz counties. Each year, the college opens its doors to more than 53,000 credit and noncredit students. Pima has five campuses that offer university transfer programs, occupational and developmental education, and general studies courses. Classes, workshops, and seminars are held at more than 100 off-campus locations in Tucson, Green Valley, and Nogales.

Ponce School of Medicine

P.O. Box 7004
Ponce, PR 00732-7004
787-840-2575

Pontifical Catholic University of Puerto Rico—Arecibo

Call Box 144045
Arecibo, PR 00614-4045
787-881-1212
http://www.pucpr.edu

Pontifical Catholic University of Puerto Rico—Guayama

5 S Palmer Street
Guayama, PR 00784
787-864-0550
http://www.pucpr.edu

Pontifical Catholic University of Puerto Rico—Mayaguez

Apartado 1326
Mayaguez, PR 00681
787-834-5151
http://www.pucpr.edu

Pontifical Catholic University of Puerto Rico—Ponce

2250 Avenue Las Americas, Suite 564
Ponce, PR 00731-6382
787-848-0854
http://www.pucpr.edu

Porterville College

100 East College
Porterville, CA 93257
209-791-2200
http://www.pc.cc.ca.us

Prairie View A&M University

P.O. Box 4019
Prairie View, TX 77446-4019
409-857-3311
http://www.pvamu.edu

Prairie View A&M University is part of the Texas A&M University System. The main campus is located approximately 40 miles northwest of Houston, Texas. The university offers a broad range of academic programs through six colleges and two schools: College of Agriculture and Human Sciences; College of Arts and Sciences; College of Business; College of Education; College of Engineering; College of Nursing; School of Architecture; and School of Juvenile Justice. One additional school, the Graduate School, offers programs through these colleges.

Pueblo Community College

900 West Oman Avenue
Pueblo, CO 81004-1499
719-549-3200
http://www.pcc.cccoes.edu

Pueblo Community College, located in Pueblo, Colorado, is a public, non-denominational, co-educational, two-year institution that was founded in 1933 and is currently operating on the semester system. PCC constantly strives to provide students with modern facilities, state-of-the-art equipment, and comprehensive technical and transfer programs that will prepare students either for the job market or for transferring to four-year institutions. Students have access to a wide range of academic support services, counseling and advising services, and student activities.

Puerto Rico, University of (Aguadilla)

P.O. Box 25160
Aguadilla, PR 00604
787-891-4519
http://www.upr.edu

Organizations

Puerto Rico, University of (Arecibo)
P.O. Box 4010
Arecibo, PR 00613
787-878-2831
http://www.arecibo.inter.edu

Puerto Rico, University of (Carolina)
P.O. Box 4800
Carolina, PR 00984
787-276-0226
http://www.upr.clu.edu

Puerto Rico, University of (Bayamon)
Carretera
174 Parque Industrial Minillas
Bayamon, PR 00959
787-786-2885
http://wwwcutb.upr.clu.edu

Puerto Rico, University of (Cayey)
Avenida Antonio R. Barcelo
Cayey, PR 00736
787-738-2160
http://wwwcuc.upr.clu.edu

Puerto Rico, University of (Humacao)
100 Carretera 908 CUH Station
Humacao, PR 00791-4300
787-850-0000
http://cuhwww.upr.clu.edu

Puerto Rico, University of (La Montana)
P.O. Box 2500
Utuado, PR 00641-2500
787-894-2828
http://www.upr.edu

Puerto Rico, University of (Mayaguez)
P.O. Box 9000 College Station
Mayaguez, PR 00681
787-832-4040

Puerto Rico, University of (Medical Sciences Campus)
G.P.O. Box 365067
San Juan, PR 00936-5067
787-758-2525
http://wwwrcm.upr.clu.edu

Puerto Rico, University of (Ponce)
P.O. Box 7186
Ponce, PR 00732
787-844-8959
http://www.upr.edu

Puerto Rico, University of (Rio Piedras)
University Station, P.O. Box 23300
San Juan, PR 00931-3300
787-764-0000
http://www.upr.edu

Rancho Santiago Community College
1530 W. 17th Street
Santa Ana, CA 92706
714-564-6000
http://www.rancho.cc.ca.us

Reedley College
995 North Reed Avenue
Reedley, CA 93564
209-638-3641
http://www.scccd.cc.ca.us

Rio Hondo College
3600 Workman Mill Road
Whittier, CA 90601
562-692-0921
http://www.rh.cc.ca.us

Rio Hondo College enrolls close to 20,000 students per semester in educational programs which include: transfer to 4-year colleges, general education courses, vocational training, and courses to improve academic performance to succeed in higher education.

Riverside Community College
4800 Magnolia Avenue
Riverside, CA 92506
909-222-8000
http://www.rccd.cc.ca.us

Rust College
150 Rust Avenue
Holly Springs, MS 38635
662-252-8000
http://www.rustcollege.edu

This private, historically black, 4-year institution consists of 5 major areas: humanities, social science, science and mathematics, business and education. Preprofessional programs are also available in nursing, engineering, medical technology, medicine, and law.

Saint Augustine Community College

1333-45 West Argyle
Chicago, IL 60640
773-878-8756
http://www.staugustinecollege.edu

A member of the Association of Episcopal Colleges and the Hispanic Association of Colleges and Universities, St. Augustine College is the only bilingual (English/Spanish) institution of higher education in the Midwest that has North Central Association of Colleges and Schools accreditation. The college offers 13 academic and 3 occupational programs, as well as pre-college programs.

Saint Augustine's College

1315 Oakwood Avenue
Raleigh, NC 27610
919-516-4000
http://www.st-aug.edu/index.htm

Saint Augustine's College provides a liberal arts education as a base for all of its students and, at the same time, insures sufficient flexibility that will enable students to make certain educational and vocational choices. The college serves a multi-ethnic student body of which one-tenth are of different national backgrounds.

Saint John's Seminary College

5118 Seminary Road
Camarillo, CA 93012-2598
805-482-2755
http://www.west.net/~sjsc

Saint John's Seminary College is a 4-year, private, undergraduate institution for young men preparing for the Roman Catholic priesthood. It offers a liberal arts education.

Saint Paul's College

406 Windsor Avenue
Lawrenceville, VA 23868
804-848-3111
http://www.utoledo.edu/~wfraker/stpaul.html

Majors of study offered at Saint Paul's College include English, political science, business administration, and computer science.

Saint Peter's College

2641 Kennedy Boulevard
Jersey City, NJ 07306
888-SPC-9933
http://www.spc.edu

Saint Peter's College, founded in 1872, is a Jesuit, Catholic, coeducational, liberal arts college in an urban setting which seeks to develop the whole person in preparation for a lifetime of learning, leadership, and service in a diverse and global society. Committed to academic excellence and individual attention, Saint Peter's College provides education, informed by values, primarily in degree-granting programs in the arts, sciences, and business, to resident and commuting students from a variety of backgrounds.

Saint Philip's College

1801 Martin Luther King Drive
San Antonio, TX 78203
210-531-3200
http://www.accd.edu/spc/spcmain/spc.htm

St. Philip's College is an Historically Black and Hispanic Serving Institution located just east of downtown San Antonio.

Saint Thomas University

16400 NW 32nd Avenue
Miami, FL 33054-6459
800-367-9010
http://www.stu.edu

Saint Thomas University offers undergraduate, graduate, and professional studies programs, enrolling more than 2,100 students. Saint Thomas is the only Catholic Archdiocesan sponsored university in Florida, but welcomes students of all faiths.

Organizations

Salish Kootenai College
P.O. Box 117
Pablo, MT 59855
406-675-4800

Salish Kootenai College is one of 32 tribal colleges in the United States. It is a fully accredited institution providing opportunities for one, two, and four-year degrees. The school is located on the Flathead Indian Reservation in northwest Montana and has a current annual enrollment of just over 1000. Since its inception more than 20 years ago, the college has sought to develop an academic program that reflects traditional native values while preparing graduates for success in a modern world. Key degree areas include Native American studies, nursing, human services, enviornmental science, computer science, office education, business, education, dental, building trades, heavy equipment operation and medical records. Salish Kootenai College has a diverse population and is open to all.

San Antonio College
1300 San Pedro Avenue
San Antonio, TX 78214
210-733-2000
http://www.accd.edu/sac

San Antonio College is a public community college which provides for and supports the educational and lifelong learning needs of a multicultural community. Among its programs: transfer education designed to provide students with the first two years of the bachelor's degree; general education courses in the liberal arts and sciences to support all college degree programs; career preparation provided through a wide range of programs to prepare students for immediate employment; developmental studies for students needing to bring their basic skills to a level appropriate for college work; continuing education to offer a variety of training, licensure, and professional programs; academic support services that include a comprehensive learning resource center and basic skills activities that complement instruction; and student support services to provide assessment, advising, counseling, tutoring, financial assistance, and social and cultural activities for all students, including those with special needs.

San Bernardino Valley College
701 S. Mt. Vernon Avenue
San Bernardino, CA 92401
909-888-6511
http://www.sbccd.cc.ca.us/sbvc

San Diego State University
5500 Campanile Drive
San Diego, CA 92182
619-594-5200
http://www.sdsu.edu

Santa Fe Community College
P.O. Box 4187
Santa Fe, NM 87502
505-471-8200
http://www.santa-fe.cc.nm.us/

Santa Fe, College of
1600 Saint Michaels Drive
Santa Fe, NM 87505
505-473-6011
http://www.csf.edu

The College of Santa Fe is an independent college in the Lasallian Catholic tradition with academic emphases on the arts, business, and education.

Savannah State University
State College Branch
Savannah, GA 31404
912-356-2186
http://www.savstate.edu

Savannah State University, established in 1890, is the oldest public historically black university in the state of Georgia. SSU offers 25 undergraduate and 3 graduate degree programs in 3 colleges: Business Administration, Liberal Arts and Social Sciences, and Sciences and Technology. While many of the 2,500 students enrolled at the university are from Georgia, a growing number hail from other states throughout the United States and abroad. The 165-acre verdant campus is located next to a salt-marsh estuary, which makes the location ideal for marine science majors to study marine life and the ecosystem. In conjunction with Georgia Tech, SSU offers 2 degree programs in engineering: civil and computer engineering. Students can complete the degree requirements on the SSU campus and receive a Georgia Tech degree at graduation.

Scottsdale Community College

American Indian Programs
9000 East Chaparral Road
Scottsdale, AZ 85256-2614
480-423-6531
http://www.sc.maricopa.edu/aip/index

Scottsdale Community College is located on the Salt River Pima-Maricopa Community and offers a Tribal Development and American Indian Studies Program, which awards a certificate of completion and AAS degree. SCC also offers a Gaming Institute, which awards a certificate of completion and AAS degree. American Indian Programs is a comprehensive support service program that provides counseling, advisement, registration, financial aid advisement, recruitment, retention, and other support services for American Indian students.

Selma University

1501 Lapsley Street
Selma, AL 36701
205-872-2533

Shaw University

118 East South Street
Raleigh, NC 27611
919-546-8200

Sinte Gleska University

P.O. Box 490
Rosebud, SD 57570
605-698-3966
http://sinte.indian.com

Sinte Gleska University is located on the Rosebud Sioux Indian Reservation. Its academic programs include a computer science program, and a master's in education program. The university is also the home of the Native American Mathematics and Science Educational Leadership Program.

Sisseton-Wahpeton Community College

P.O. Box 689
Agency Village, SD 57262-0689
605-698-3966
http://swcc.cc.sd.us/cc.htm

SWCC was chartered by the Sisseton Wahpeton Sioux Tribe in 1979 and provides associate of arts and associate of science degrees in selected fields of study. SWCC is a member of the American Indian Higher Education Consortium and is accredited by the North Central Association of Schools and Colleges. Credits received at SWCC are accepted by member institutions and/or other accredited institutions of higher education throughout the United States and foreign countries.

Sitting Bull College

HC1 Box 4
Fort Yates, ND 58538

South Carolina State University

1890 Research and Extension
Orangeburg, SC 29115
803-536-7000
http://www.orangenet.edu/scsu/state.htm

South Mountain Community College

750 South 24th Street
Phoenix, AZ 85040
602-243-8000
http://www.smc.maricopa.edu

South Mountain Community College offers degree and certificate progrms in many areas, including art, business administration, chemistry, political science, pre-engineering, and teleservices technology.

South Plains College

Levelland, TX 79336
806-894-9611
http://www.spc.cc.tx.us

South Plains College is a community college offering 2-year academic programs that allow for transfer to a major university; it also offers technical programs and associate degrees.

Organizations

South Texas Community College

P.O. Box 9701
McAllen, TX 78502
956-631-4922
http://www.stcc.cc.tx.us

Southern University and Agriculture and Mechanical College System at Baton Rouge (Main)

Baton Rouge, LA 70813
225-771-4500
http://www.subr.edu

Southern University consists of 3 campuses (of over 17,000 students), and is the nation's only historically black university system. The university offers programs of study ranging from associate degree to doctoral and professional degrees. Southern University provides opportunities for internships in industry and with the federal government. Southern provides advantages for intellectual and personal growth through training by the division of Military Science (Army ROTC) and Naval Science (Navy and Marine ROTC).

Southern University, New Orleans

6400 Press Drive
New Orleans, LA 70126
504-286-5000
http://www.suno.edu

Southern University of New Orleans is an open-enrollment university, serving Louisiana, southern Mississippi, and the Greater New Orleans area. It is also an HBCU, and so was created to serve the needs of the African American community. SUNO averages about 4,000 undergraduates, and is striving to establish several graduate programs in addition to its well-known MSW program.

Southern University, Shreveport— Bossier City

3050 Martin Luther King Drive
Shreveport, LA 71107
318-674-3300

Southwest Indian Polytechnic Institute

9169 Coors Road, NW
P.O. Box 10146
Albuquerque, NM 87196
505-766-3189
http://kafka.sipi.tec.nm.us

The Southwest Indian Polytechnic Institute offers programs of study in environmental science and industrial hygiene, graphic arts technology, liberal arts, natural resources technology, and optical technologies.

Southwest Texas Junior College

2401 Garnerfield Road
Uvalde, TX 78801
830-278-4401
http://www.swtjc.cc.tx.us

Southwest Texas Junior College has four campuses: the main campus located in Uvalde, as well as Outreach Centers located in Del Rio, Eagle Pass, and Crystal City. SWTJC's service area includes 11 counties. The college has over 75 full-time faculty and 93 part-time faculty. The college offers the first two years of regular college work leading to higher degrees in liberal arts colleges and professional schools. This work is performed under conditions that are conducive to better learning, better grades, and fewer failures. Students who do not plan to go beyond the first two years of college may take a two-year course in agriculture, business training, or in other vocations or semi-professional careers without having to satisfy the requirements of the senior colleges.

Southwestern College

900 Otay Lakes Road
Chula Vista, CA 91910
619-421-6700
http://swc.cc.ca.us

One of California's 106 public community colleges, Southwestern is the only postsecondary educational institution in South San Diego County. It serves students pursuing the first 2 years of a traditional 4-year college education; earning AA degrees in preparation to enter technical and occupational careers; learning new languages, studying art, or acquiring skills in the pursuit of personal development and job enhancement; and acquiring new occupational skills to meet the challenges and opportunities of an ever changing workplace.

Spelman College

Office of Financial Aid
350 Spelman Lane, SW
Atlanta, GA 30314-4399
404-681-3643
http://www.spelman.edu

This predominately residential college is a member of the Atlanta University Center (AUC) and the University Center in Georgia. Membership in these consortia benefits students by giving them access to the resources of the participating institutions while allowing them to retain all the advantages of a small college.

Stillman College

3600 Stillman Boulevard
Tuscaloosa, AL 35403
205-349-4240
http://www.stillman.edu

Stillman College is a four-year liberal arts college offering the bachelor of arts and bachelor of science degrees. Stillman offers majors in 16 areas including business, computer science, music, and international studies. Stillman also has pre-professional programs in engineering, law, medicine, ministry, and social work. Stillman offers cooperative programs with colleges and universities in Alabama, Tennessee, New York, Michigan, Ohio, and Washington.

Stone Child College

Rural Route 1, Box 1082
Box Elder, MT 59521
406-395-4313
http://www.montana.edu/~wwwscc.html

Strayer College

1025 15th Street, NW
Washington, DC 20005
202-408-2400
http://www.strayer.edu

Strayer University is a private university specializing in information technology and business-oriented education. Undergraduate and graduate programs are available at 13 campuses in Washington, D.C., Maryland, and Virginia, as well as online. Classes are available seven days and nights a week.

Sul Ross State University

P.O. Box C-119
Alpine, TX 79832
916-837-8432
http://www.sulross.edu

Sul Ross State University is accredited by the Commission on Colleges of the Southern Association of Colleges and Schools to award associate, bachelor's, and master's degrees. The Teacher Education program offered at Sul Ross State University is approved by the Texas Education Agency. The Animal Health Technology program is accredited by the Committee on Animal Technician's Activities and Training of the American Veterinary Medical Association. Sul Ross State University, through its Department of Business Administration, is nationally accredited by the Association of Collegiate Business Schools and Programs to offer the bachelor of business adminstration (BBA) with majors in accounting, business management, and office systems, and The master of business administration (MBA).

Talladega College

627 West Battle Street
Talladega, AL 35160
256-362-0206
http://www.talladega.edu

Tennessee State University

3500 John Merritt Boulevard
Nashville, TN 37209
615-963-5000
http://www.tnstate.edu

As an 1890 land grant institution, Tennessee State University provides instructional programs, state-wide cooperative extension services, cooperative agricultural research, and food and agricultural programs of an international dimension. As a comprehensive institution,

Organizations

Tennessee State University provides programming in agriculture, allied health, arts and sciences, business, education, engineering and technology, home economics, human services, nursing, and public administration. The institution is broadly comprehensive at the baccalaureate and master's levels. While doctoral programs are focused in education and public administration, future doctoral programs will continue to address the needs of an urban population. As a major urban institution, located in the capital city, Tennessee State University provides both degree and non-degree programs (day, evening, weekend, and at off-campus sites) that are appropriate and accessible to a working urban population.

Texas A&M International University

5201 University Boulevard
Laredo, TX 78041-1900
956-326-2320
http://www.tamiu.edu

Texas A&M International University is poised at the gateway to Mexico and serves as the intellectual center of a vibrant bilingual and bicultural community. The university offers baccalaureate and master's programs in the arts; humanities; business; education; physical, biological, and social sciences; and health professions with authority for select doctoral programs. Programs focus on developing undergraduate and graduate offerings and progressive agenda for global study and understanding across all disciplines.

Texas A&M University, Kingsville

P.O. Box 115 Station 1
Kingsville, TX 78363
361-593-3911
http://www.tamuk.edu

Texas A&M University—Kingsville offers 56 undergraduate degrees in 52 areas of study, 55 master's degrees in 38 areas of study, and three doctoral degrees in three areas of study, including two in education and one in wildlife science. Texas A&M is a four-year public university, with a student population of 6,000.

Texas College

2404 North Grand Avenue
Tyler, TX 75702-1962
903-593-8311

Texas Southern University

3100 Cleburne
Houston, TX 77004
713-313-7011
http://www.tsu.edu

The university's academic programs include colleges of arts and sciences, education, pharmacy, business, and technology. The university also has a graduate school and a school of law.

Texas Southmost College/University of Texas, Brownsville

80 Fort Brown Street
Brownsville, TX 78520
956-544-8200
http://www.utb.edu

The University of Texas at Brownsville and Texas Southmost College Partnership offers certificate, Associate, baccalaureate, and master's degrees in liberal arts and sciences, and in professional programs designed to meet student demand and regional needs. UTB/TSC also supports the delivery of doctoral programs through cooperative agreements with doctoral degree-granting institutions.

Texas State Technical College

2424 Boxwood Street
Harlingen, TX 78550-3697
956-364-4000
http://www.harlingen.tstc.edu

Texas State Technical College Harlingen offers certificates of completion and associate of applied science (AAS) degrees in 32 technical areas of study. Some areas offer both an AAS degree and a certificate-level option. A total of 23 two-year associate of applied science degree programs and 22 one-year or less certificate options are available. TSTC Harlingen offers adult continuing education courses and provides contract training for business and industry to enhance on-the-job skills of current employees and to train area residents for jobs in new incoming industries.

Texas, University of (Brownsville)

80 Fort Brown
Brownsville, TX 78520
956-544-8200
http://www.utb.edu

Texas, University of (of the Permian Basin)

4901 East University
Odessa, TX 79762-0001
915-552-2020
http://www.utpb.edu

Texas, University of, El Paso

El Paso, TX 79968
915-747-5000
http://www.utep.edu

UTEP offers 60 bachelor's and 53 master's degrees in a broad range of academic fields, and doctoral degrees in geological sciences, computer engineering, pathobiology, materials science and engineering, psychology, environmental science and engineering, and educational leadership and administration.

Texas, University of, Pan American

1201 West University Drive
Edinburg, TX 78539-2999
956-381-2011
http://www.panam.edu

UT Pan American's 6 academic colleges—Arts and Humanities, Business Administration, Education, Health Sciences and Human Services, Liberal and Performing Arts, Science and Engineering, and Social and Behavioral Sciences—offer a wide range of degree options encompassing a comprehensive series of academic concentrations and selected areas of professional study. The university offers the associate's, bachelor's, master's and doctoral degrees.

Texas, University of, San Antonio

6900 North Loop 1604 West
San Antonio, TX 78249-0619
210-691-4011
http://www.utsa.edu

UTSA is a comprehensive public university with 52 bachelor's, 36 master's, and three doctoral degree programs. More than 50 percent of UTSA's students come from groups underrepresented in higher education, and more than 42 percent are Hispanic. UTSA is ranked fifth among all U.S. universities in the number of bachelor's degrees granted to Hispanic students. In addition to two academic campuses, UTSA includes the Centers for Economic Development and the Institute of Texan Cultures, both located in downtown San Antonio. Community outreach efforts include UTSA's Office of Extended Education, the Metropolitan Research and Policy Institute, the Alliance for Education, and the Center for Professional Excellence.

Tougaloo College

500 County Line Road
Tougaloo, MS 39174
601-799-7700
http://www.tougaloo.edu

Tougaloo College is an historically African American, private, coeducational, church-related, four-year, liberal arts institution located at the northern edge of Jackson, Mississippi. Founded in 1869 by the American Missionary Association, Tougaloo retains and respects its traditions, remains dedicated to the equality of all people, and continues to be a value-centered community where students, guided by a concerned faculty and staff, apply current knowledge and prepare for lifelong education related to new information and technologies, as well as humane standards in the changing world. Tougaloo College offers an undergraduate curriculum designed to encourage students to apply critical thought to all areas of life; to acquire a basic knowledge of the humanities, the natural sciences, and social sciences; to develop entry-level skills required in selected professions; and to provide leadership in a democratic society.

273

Organizations

Trenholm State Technical College
1225 Air Base Boulevard
Montgomery, AL 36108
334-832-9000
http://www.tstc.cc.al.us/

As a member of the Alabama College System, Trenholm State Technical College is dedicated to meeting the postsecondary educational needs of the residents of its service area by providing opportunities in general education, occupational education, and community services. These opportunities are offered at a moderate tuition rate through an "open door" admission policy, a policy which does not limit education to the financially, socially, or intellectually elite.

Trinidad State Junior College
600 Prospect Street
Trinidad, CO 81082
800-621-8752

Fully accredited by the Commission on Institutions of Higher Education of the North Central Association of Colleges and Schools, TSJC offers instruction in liberal arts transfer programs and vocational technical areas. These programs lead to the degrees of associate of arts, associate of science, associate of general studies, associate of applied science and various certificates.

Trinity International University
500 NE 1st Avenue
Miami, FL 33132-1196
305-577-4600
http://www.trin.edu

Turtle Mountain Community College
P.O. Box 340
Belcourt, ND 58316
701-477-5605
http://www.turtle-mountain.cc.nd.us

The Turtle Mountain Community College consists of four academic departments: the department of math and science; department of arts, humanities, and social science; department of adult/continuing education; and the department of vocational education.

Tuskegee University
School of Education Scholarships
Office of Financial Aid
Tuskegee, AL 36088
800-622-6531
http://www.tusk.edu

Among Tuskegee University's points of distinction: the university is the number one producer of African American aerospace science engineers in the nation, and the number two producer of African-American engineering graduates in three other engineering fields in the country; it's the only Historically Black College and University approved to offer the doctor of philosophy (Ph.D.) in materials science and engineering, which began in the fall of 1998; it offers one of the oldest baccalaureate programs in nursing in the country; and it's the largest producer of African Americans with baccalaureate degrees in math, science, and engineering in Alabama.

United Tribes Technical College
3315 University Drive
Bismarck, ND 58501
701-255-3285
http://www.united-tribes.tec.nd.us

The college was founded to provide opportunities through which American Indians can obtain a technical education and become self-sufficient. It provides not only occupational education and training, but also a comprehensive set of support services to the adults and their children. The college has an American Indian families focus. There are two day care centers and a K-8 elementary school on campus.

Universidad Adventista de las Antillas
P.O. Box 118
Mayaguez, PR 00681-0118
787-834-9595
http://www.uaa.edu

Universidad Central del Caribe
Call Box 60-327
Bayamon, PR 00960-6032
787-798-3001

Universidad del Turabo

Estacion Universidad, Apartado 3030
Gurabo, PR 00778
787-743-7979

Universidad Metropolitana

P.O. Box 21150
San Juan, PR 00928-1150
787-766-1717
http://umet_mie.suagm.edu

Universidad Politecnica de Puerto Rico

P.O. Box 192017
San Juan, PR 00919-2017
787-754-8000
http://www.pupr.edu

University of Laverne

1950 Third Street
Laverne, CA 91750
909-593-3511
http://www.ulaverne.edu

University of the Sacred Heart

P.O. Box 12383
San Juan, PR 00914-0383
787-728-1515
http://www.usc.clu.edu

Ventura College

4667 Telegraph Road
Ventura, CA 93003
805-654-6400
http://vcss.k12.ca.us/vcccd/

Victoria College

2200 East Red River
Victoria, TX 77901
512-573-3291
http://www.vc.cc.tx.us

Virgin Islands, University of

2 John Brewers Bay
St. Thomas, VI 00802-9990
340-776-9200
http://www.uvi.edu/pub-relations/uvi.htm

The University of the Virgin Islands is the only HBCU outside of the continental United States. UVI enrolls approximately 3,200 full-time and part-time students on its two campuses. It offers a high quality, affordable liberal arts education in a culturally diverse environment, with academic areas in business administration, education, humanities, nursing, science and mathematics, and social sciences. UVI has campuses on St. Thomas and St. Croix, and an ecological research station on St. John.

Virginia State University

Office of Admissions
Petersburg, VA 23806
800-524-5000
http://www.vsu.edu

Virginia State University, America's first fully state supported four-year institution of higher learning for blacks, is a comprehensive university and one of two land-grant institutions in the Commonwealth of Virginia. Virginia State University is accredited by the Commission on Colleges of the Southern Association of Colleges and Schools to award bachelor's and master's degrees and a certificate of advanced graduate study.

Virginia Union University

1500 North Lombardy Street
Richmond, VA 23220
800-368-3227
http://www.vuu.edu

VUU is a charter member of The College Fund/UNCF, a consortium of select HBCUs across the nation. Today the university opens its doors to all qualified students and welcomes diversity among faculty and staff as well as the student body. As a liberal arts institution, Virginia Union University requires that all students complete a core curriculum of courses from the humanities, natural sciences, mathematics, and social sciences. The student-to-faculty ratio is15:1. There are also many educational opportunities outside of the classroom, such as internships with community organizations and businesses, and a cooperative educational program that allows students to gain work experience, credit hours, and funds to assist with their college expenses.

Organizations

Vorhees College
1411 Vorhees Road
Denmark, SC 29042
800-446-6250
http://www.voorhees.edu

Vorhees College is a 4-year private, liberal arts college with 16 degree programs, and an excellent faculty and facilities. Financial aid is available, as well as a special program for single mothers to earn a college degree.

West Hills Commercial College
300 Cherry Lane
Coalinga, CA 93210
800-266-1114
http://www.westhills.cc.ca.us

West Hills College provides collegiate transfer, occupational, non-credit, and basic skills education. The Distance Learning Center offers a variety of college credit courses for students interested in learning on an independent basis.

West Virginia State College
P.O. Box 1000
Institute, WV 25112-1000
800-987-2112
http://www.wvsc.edu

West Virginia State College is the largest institution of higher education in the Kanawha Valley and serves as a major resource center for the metropolitan area. The college provides a broad spectrum of undergraduate degree programs, both baccalaureate and associate, for residential and commuting students, and offers a comprehensive schedule of classes to an exceptionally large population of evening students. The institution continuously strives to meet the special educational and training needs of its service area. The needs are met through comprehensive transfer programs, career-technical programs, employee training, continuing education, developmental education, and community service activities.

Western Carolina University
Student Affairs, Multi-Cultural Office
Cullowhee, NC 28723
828-227-7231
http://www.wcu.edu

The university has operated a number of courses for Native Americans at Cherokee, N.C. It also offers a minor in Cherokee studies. Contact Jim Farris at 704-227-7170 or 704-497-7920.

Western New Mexico University
1000 West College Avenue
Silver City, NM 88062
505-538-6336
http://www.wnmu.edu

Western New Mexico University serves the people of the state of New Mexico and its surrounding areas as a comprehensive, regional, rural, public, coeducational university. Its student body is diverse in age, culture, language, and ethnic background. Teacher education continues to provide the basic foundation of WNMU's programs. That focus has broadened to include a range of certificate, associate, baccalaureate, and several graduate programs which also meet the needs of students in allied health, arts and sciences, business, and vocational education. All undergraduate degree programs include a strong comprehensive general education requirement.

White Earth Tribal and Community College
210 Main Street South
P.O. Box 478
Mahnomen, MN 56557

Whittier College
P.O. Box 634
Whittier, CA 90608
562-907-4200
http://www.whittier.edu

Wilberforce University

1055 North Bickett Road
Wilberforce, OH 45384
937-376-2911
http://www.wilberforce.edu

Wilberforce University is the oldest, private, historically black, liberal arts school in the nation. Since 1856, our mission has been to educate students of all colors, creeds, and religious denominations. Wilberforce is affiliated with the African Methodist Episcopal Church and accredited by the North Central Association of Colleges and Schools. Wilberforce University is an Ohio education resource.

Wiley College

711 Wiley Avenue
Marshall, TX 75670
903-927-3300
http://www.wileyc.edu

Wiley College is a 4-year, co-educational, liberal arts, private institution. The college is affiliated with the United Methodist Church and was the first accredited historically black college west of the Mississippi. Wiley is accredited by the Southern Association of Colleges and Schools. Average enrollment is 650 students with many attending from Texas, western Louisiana, southeastern Oklahoma, and western Arkansas.

Winston-Salem State University

601 Martin Luther King Jr. Drive
Winston-Salem, NC 27110-0003
336-750-2000
http://www.wssu.edu

Winston-Salem State University is a public university whose primary mission is to offer high quality educational programs at the baccalaureate level for diverse and motivated students. Master's and intermediate level programs for professional study are also available in the Winston-Salem State University Graduate Center through inter-institutional agreements.

Woodbury University

7500 Glen Oaks Boulevard
Burbank, CA 91510
818-767-0888

Xavier University of Louisiana

7325 Palmetto
New Orleans, LA 70125
504-486-7411
http://www.xula.edu

Xavier University is the nation's only institution of higher learning that is both historically black and Catholic. Xavier offers preparation in three dozen majors on the undergraduate, graduate, and professional degree levels. According to the U.S. Department of Education, Xavier continues to rank first nationally in the number of African American students earning undergraduate degrees in biology, physics, and the physical sciences overall. Xavier was recently selected for funding by the National Science Foundation to participate in the program for Model Institutions for Excellence in Science, Engineering, and Mathematics—one of only six chosen in a national competition among sixty-nine eligible schools.

York College

City University of New York
9420 Brewer Boulevard
Jamaica, NY 11451
718-262-2000
http://www.york.cuny.edu

York College, a senior college of The City University of New York, opened its doors in the fall of 1967, offering professional degree programs and more than 40 baccalaureate options. With a steadily growing community of 6,000 students who represent a wide cross section of nationalities, York blends traditional academic disciplines in the liberal arts with career and professional preparation. Multicultural and international education have long been integral themes for all the college's programs, which have helped more than 12,000 students enter the mainstream of the economy. The college is distinguished for bringing professional programs in business, accounting, and the health sciences to traditionally underserved populations of all ages. York has the only social work program and upper level RN-BSN nursing program in Queens as well as the only gerontology program in the university. In addition, the college's close ties to its community enable students to conduct valuable fieldwork and internships in the subject areas of community health education, gerontology, occupational therapy, political science, psychology, and social work.Through the curricula of major courses of study and through faculty-guided research projects, York provides an environment for undergraduates to prepare for graduate or professional school. In the spring of 2000, a new physician's assistant program began, and a new U.S. Food and Drug Administration laboratory and office building opened on campus. Locating the federal facility on York's campus enhances the college's already strong biotechnical programs with collaborative efforts of the FDA in its largest site out of Washington, DC. Projects in this facility will complement existing research opportunities in the college's other areas of study.

Fraternities and Sororities

Alpha Delta Kappa Sorority
University of Southern California
Los Angeles, CA 90089
http://www.geocities.com/CollegePark/
Campus/3588/

Alpha Kappa Delta Phi Sorority
http://www.akdphi.org/national/

Alpha Phi Alpha Fraternity
2313 St. Paul Street
Baltimore, MD 28218-5234
410-554-0040
http://www.apa1906.org

Alpha Phi Gamma Sorority
3801 West Temple Avenue #26
Pomona, CA 91768
http://www.alphaphigamma.8m.com

Alpha Rho Lambda Sorority
30 Silver Hill Lane #5
Natick, MA 01760
http://www.cs.tufts.edu/~wvargas/anim.html

Alpha Sigma Lambda Fraternity
3801 West Temple Avenue
Pomona, CA 91768
http://www.welcome.to/alpha.sigma.lambda

Chi Alpha Delta Sorority UCLA
Los Angeles, CA 90024
http://www.geocities.com/CollegePark/Square/
3942/

Delta Psi Epsilon Sorority
http://www.angelfire.com/ca2/deltaepsilon/

Delta Sigma Theta Sorority
1707 New Hampshire Avenue, NW
Washington, DC 20009
202-986-2400
http://www.dist1913.org

Delta Xi Phi Sorority
http://www.geocities.com/~deltaxiphi/

Educational Advancement Foundation
5656 South Stony Island Avenue
Chicago, IL 60637
http://www.aka1908.com

Gamma Phi Eta Fraternity
P.O. Box 17793
Statesboro, GA 30460
912-681-9252
http://www.angelfire.com/ga/GAMMAPIETA/
page.html

Gamma Phi Omega Sorority
3329 South Western
Chicago, IL 60608
http://www2.uic.edu/stud_orgs/greek/gpo/

Gamma Phi Sigma Fraternity
http://www.g-phi.org

Gamma Zeta Alpha Fraternity
385 East San Fernando Street
San Jose, CA 95112
800-858-2036
http://www.gammas.org

Iota Phi Lambda Sorority
800-982-IOATA
http://www.iota1929.org

A business and professional national organization.

Iota Phi Theta Fraternity
22842 South Lake Shore Drive
Richton Park, IL 60471
708-503-0739
http://www.iotaphitheta.org

Kappa Alpha Psi Fraternity
2322-24 North Broad Street
Philadelphia, PA 19132-4590
215-228-7184
http://www.kapsi.org

Kappa Phi Iota Sorority
http://www.angelfire.com/nj/kappaphiiota/

Kappa Phi Lambda Sorority
http://www.geocities.com/Tokyo/Towers/9059/

Lambda Alpha Upsilon Fraternity
P.O. Box 1767
New York, NY 10156-0609
http://www.lambdas.com

Lambda Phi Epsilon Fraternity
http://www.lambdaphiepsilon.com

Lambda Psi Delta Sorority
P.O. Box 200009
New Haven, CT 06520
http://www.lambdapsidelta.org

A multicultural sorority.

Lambda Theta Nu Sorority
P.O. Box 231906
Sacramento, CA 95823
http://www.lambdathetanu.org

Lambda Upsilon Lambda Fraternity
PMB #39, 511 6th Avenue
New York, NY 10011
http://www.launidadlatina.org

National Pen-Hellenic Council
Memorial Hall West, Room 111
Bloomington, IN 47405
812-855-8820
http://www.nphc.org

The coordinating agent of 9 African American fraternities and sororities.

Nu Alpha Kappa Fraternity
Student Life and Activities
Box #96
California Polytechnic State University
San Luis Obispo, CA 93401
http://www.naknet.org

Omega Delta Phi Fraternity
http://www.omegadeltaphi.com

Omega Phi Beta Sorority
University at Albany
State University of New York
1400 Washington Avenue
Albany, NY 12222
http://www.albany.edu/~opbsi/

Organizations

Omega Psi Phi Fraternity
3951 Snapfinger Parkway, Suite 330
Decatur, GA 30035
404-284-5533
http://www.omegapsiphifraternity.org

Omega Xi Delta Fraternity
Student Life and Activities
P.O. Box 65
Cal Poly
San Luis Obispo, CA 93403
http://www.calpoly.edu/~dfong/omega.html

Phi Beta Sigma Fraternity
145 Kennedy Street, NW
Washington, DC 20011
202-726-5434
http://pbs1914.org

Phi Delta Psi Fraternity
P.O. Box 19963
Kalamazoo, MI 49019
http://members.tripod.com/~PHIMAN/

Phi Iota Alpha Fraternity
P.O. Box 1102
Grand Central Station
New York, NY 10163
212-642-1087
http://www.oswego.edu/~fia

Phi Rho Eta Fraternity
http://www.phirhoeta.org

Pi Delta Psi Fraternity
http://www.pideltapis.org

Pi Psi Fraternity
7610 Penn Avenue South #23
Minneapolis, MN 55423
http://www.pipsi.org

Sigma Gamma Rho Sorority
8800 South Stony Island Avenue
Chicago, IL 60617
773-873-9000
http://www.sgr1922.org

Sigma Iota Alpha Sorority
P.O. Box 237
Prince Street Station
New York, NY 10012
http://www.hermandad-sia.org

Sigma Lambda Gamma Sorority
Room 145 Iowa Memorial Union
Iowa City, IA 52242-1317
319-335-2828
http://www.kcnet.com/~taina/Gammas/

Sigma Lambda Upsilon Sorority
P.O. Box 4170
Grand Central Station
New York, NY 10163
http://www.brown.edu/students/
sigma_lambda_upsilon/

Sigma Psi Zeta Sorority
http://www.sigmapsizeta.org

Sigma Theta Psi Sorority
San Diego State University
San Diego, CA 92182
http://www-rohan.sdsu.edu/dept/sigma/

A multicultural sorority.

Sigma Theta Psi Sorority
San Diego State University
San Diego, CA 92182
http://www.betaomegaphi.com

Tau Beta Sigma Sorority
P.O. Box 849
Stillwater, OK 74076-0849
800-543-6505
http://www.kkytbs.org

A national honorary band sorority.

Zeta Chi Epsilon Fraternity
San Francisco State University
San Francisco, CA 94132
http://members.aol.com/zzxe4life/

Zeta Epsilon Tau Fraternity

California State University
Long Beach, CA 90802

Zeta Phi Beta Sorority

Scholarship Chairperson
1827 17th Avenue
Washington, DC 20009
202-387-3103
http://www.zpb1920.org

Section C
Additional Information

This section lists publications (magazines, journals, newspapers), directories, and Web sites of relevance to minorities looking to develop their careers.

Publications

A. Magazine
131 West 1st Street
Duluth, MN 55802
800-346-0085
http://www.amagazine.com

A magazine for young Asian Americans; Web site features articles from the print publication.

American Indian Report
Falmouth Institute
3702 Pender Drive, Suite 300
Fairfax, VA 22030
800-992-4489
http://www.falmouthinst.com

The leading news source for the nation's tribal leaders and legislators, educators, business leaders, and environmentalists.

Asian Enterprise
P.O. Box 2135
Walnut, CA 91788
http://www.asianenterprise.com

Asian Enterprise is a publication focusing on small business enterprises of Asian Pacific Americans nationwide. On a monthly basis, AE provides important information to a growing number of Asian Pacific American entrepreneurs, addressing issues that impact the Asian Pacific American business community.

Black Business Journal
8303 Southwest Freeway, Suite 100
Houston, TX 77074
713-270-6500
http://www.bbjonline.com

A newspaper for African Americans; covers business news and markets.

Black Collegian
140 Carondelet Street
New Orleans, LA 70130
http://www.blackcollegian.com

A national career opportunities magazine; general feature articles and career planning/job search information. Free in your college's career office, or access articles via the Web site.

Additional Information

Black Congressional Monitor
Len Mor Publications
PO Box 75035
Washington, DC 20013
202-488-8879

The Monitor is a twice-monthly report of federal government news by and about, and of interest and benefit to African Americans. It presents information on available grant awards, contract and subcontract opportunities, public meetings, public notices, publications, and other public policy documents. In addition, it reports on the legislative initiatives of African Americans in the U.S. Congress, e.g., public laws enacted, bills and resolutions introduced, hearings held, reports to and by Congress, statements made on the House and Senate floors, and thoughts about Congressional intent.

Black Enterprise
130 5th Avenue, 10th Floor
New York, NY 10011-4399
212-242-8000
http://www.blackenterprise.com

The leading publication covering the world of African American businesses and corporations.

Black Issues in Higher Education
10520 Warwick Avenue, Suite B-8
Fairfax, VA 22030
800-783-3199
http://www.blackissues.com

Black Issues in Higher Education is the nation's only news magazine dedicated exclusively to minority issues in higher education.

Black Philanthropy
The Corporation for Philanthropy
PO Box 3092
Oakton, VA 22124-9092
703-255-2447

This bimonthly report offers information about black philanthropists, foundation and corporate givers, fund-raisers, interesting fund-raising strategies, innovative programs, new appointments, promotions, and upcoming events.

Black Scholar
PO Box 2869
Oakland, CA 94609
510-547-6633

This journal of African American studies and research publishes criticism and interviews by scholars and other writers.

Black Talent News
PO Box 7374
Culver City, CA 90233-7374
213-960-3991

The *Black Talent News* is the national trade publication for African Americans in the entertainment industry.

Callaloo
Department of English
322 Bryan Hall
University of Virginia
P.O. Box 400121
Charlottesville, VA 22904-4121
http://muse.jhu.edu/journals/callaloo

An African and African American literary journal featuring original works by and critical studies of black writers worldwide.

CD Publications
8204 Fenton Street
Silver Spring, MD 20910
301-588-6380
http://www.cdpublications.com

This small press publishes a variety of newsletters, including newsletters focused on issues of minority business.

Conduit, The
857 Crompton Road
Redwood City, CA 94061
http://www.theconduit.com

A technology Web site and newsletter for African Americans.

Cultural Diversity at Work

13751 Lake City Way NE, Suite 210
Seattle, WA 98125-8612
206-362-0336
http://www.diversityhotwire.com

This journal deals with managing cultural diversity in the workplace and the business world.

Dow Jones Newspaper Fund

P.O. Box 300
Princeton, NJ 08543-0300
800-DOW-FUND
http://www.dj.com/newsfund

"Newspapers, Diversity & You," a free journalism career guide for minority students, provides information on grants, scholarships, and internships as well as articles written by professional journalists of color who tell why they chose their careers and offer advice.

Equal Opportunity

Equal Opportunity Publications
1160 East Jericho Turnpike, Suite 200
Huntington, NY 11743
516-421-9421
http://www.eop.com

A career guidance and recruitment magazine distributed free of charge to minority college students and professionals in all fields.

Hispanic Business

425 Pine Avenue
Santa Barbara, CA 93117-3709
http://www.hispanicbusiness.com

A magazine for Hispanic professionals; features the latest business news and its effect on the Hispanic community.

Hispanic Magazine

999 Ponce de Leon, Suite 600
Coral Gables, FL 33134
305-442-2462
http://www.hisp.com

A magazine and online service for the general interests of the Hispanic community.

Indian Country

P.O. Box 4250
1920 Lombardy Drive
Rapid City, SD 57703
http://www.indiancountry.com

A nationwide newspaper covering stories and issues relevant to Native Americans; serves as a major source of information for Native American schools and colleges.

Minority Business Entrepreneur Magazine

3528 Torrance Boulevard, Suite 101
Torrance, CA 90503
310-540-9398
http://www.mbemag.com

A bimonthly publication for and about minority and women business owners.

Minority Engineer

Equal Opportunity Publications
1160 East Jericho Turnpike, Suite 200
Huntington, NY 11743
516-421-9421
http://www.eop.com

A free publication for qualified engineering, computer science, and information technology professionals who are African American, Hispanic, Native American, or Asian American.

Mosaic Literary Magazine

314 West 231st Street, #470
Bronx, NY 10463
603-761-8150
http://www.mosaicbooks.com

A literary magazine featuring original fiction, poetry, and reviews by African American writers.

Multicultural Education

3145 Geary Boulevard, Suite 275
San Francisco, CA 94118
415-750-9978

The magazine features articles, reviews, and listings of resources to assist with multicultural education programs in schools.

Additional Information

National Black Law Journal

Columbia University Law School
New York, NY 10019
212-854-3318

This journal publishes scholarly studies of law and the African American community.

National Minority Business Council

235 East 42nd Street
New York, NY 10017
212-573-2385
http://www.nmbc.org

The council's publications include "The Business Person's Guide to Africa," "The African American Market," and "NMBC Vendor Directory."

Native American Law Digest

Falmouth Institute
3702 Pender Drive, Suite 300
Fairfax, VA 22030
800-992-4489
http://www.falmouthinst.com

A monthly summary of all legal decisions significant to the American Indian community.

Native Peoples Magazine

5333 North Seventh Street, Suite C-224
Phoenix, AZ 85014
602-252-2236
http://www.nativepeoples.com

This magazine covers the art and lifestyle of Native Americans, and features the work of freelance writers and photographers.

Network Journal: Black Professional and Small Professional News

139 Fulton Street, Suite 407
New York, NY 10038
212-962-3791
http://www.tnj.com

Features business and trade news of interest to the African American and Caribbean American community.

Onyx Woman

P.O. Box 91362
Pittsburgh, PA 15221
http://www.onyxwoman.com

A career and entrepreneur development magazine for women of color

SuperOnda

425 Pine Avenue
Santa Barbara, CA 93117
http://www.superonda.com

A newspaper for young Hispanics; features career information, and scholarship and education guides.

Tribal College Journal

PO Box 720
Mancos, CO 81328
970-533-9170
http://tribalcollegejournal.org

The Journal provides information about American Indian higher education.

Try Us Resources

2105 Central Avenue NE
Minneapolis, MN 55418
612-781-6819
http://www.tryusdir.com

Try Us Resources is a company that publishes information resources for the development of minority businesses. Its titles include "The Try Us National Minority Business Directory" and "The Minority Business Information Resources Directory."

Upscale Magazine

2141 Powers Ferry Road
Marietta, GA 30067
770-988-0015
http://www.upscalemagazine.com

A magazine for African American professionals; features articles on business, technology, entertainment, and travel.

Workforce Diversity for Engineering and IT Professionals

Equal Opportunity Publications
1160 East Jericho Turnpike, Suite 200
Huntington, NY 11743
516-421-9421
http://www.eop.com

A magazine distributed free to the professional, diversified, high-tech workforce.

Directories

Bilingual Education and Migrant Immigrant Assistance

Government Information Services
4301 North Fairfax Drive
Arlington, VA 22203-1627
800-876-0226

This directory describes 13 federal grant programs designed to enable limited English-proficient students to become proficient in English and to meet the same challenging state content requirements and student performance standards that are expected of all children and youth. Included among the program descriptions are: bilingual and education program development and implementation grants; the emergency immigrant education assistance program; refugee assistance programs; and bilingual education comprehensive school grants.

Church Philanthropy for Native Americans and Other Minorities: A Guide for Multicultural Funding from Religious Sources

CRC Publishing-Eaglerock Books
PO Box 22583
Kansas City, MO 64113-2583
800-268-2059
http://www.crcpub.com

This publication helps grant seekers to obtain

church dollars earmarked for issues of self-determination, social justice, economic development, and the preservation of indigenous and ethnic cultures.

Daimler Chrysler Hispanic Scholarship Guide: College Financial Assistance Opportunities

Montemayor y Asociados
70 NE Loop 410
San Antonio, TX 78216

This annual publication lists sources of financial assistance available from the federal government, colleges and universities, and private institutions, giving particular emphasis to major organizations that offer specialized programs for Hispanics, in specialized fields of study. These fields include arts and humanities, business and public administration, communications, education, federal programs, health sciences, law, science, mathematics and engineering, and social and behavioral sciences. At the end of the book is a bibliography containing a list of other sources.

Directory of Grant Support and Technical Assistance for Native American Initiatives

Center for Economic Development Research and Assistance
PO Box 30001
Department 3CR
Las Cruces, NM 88003-0001
505-646-1434

The directory lists sources of financial and technical assistance available to American Indians and Native Alaskans. It includes descriptions, contact names, and addresses, and is divided into program ideas.

Financial Aid for African Americans

Reference Service Press
5000 Windplay Drive, Suite 4
El Dorado Hills, CA 95762
916-939-9620

This directory provides detailed descriptions of scholarships, fellowships, loans, grants, awards,

Additional Information

and internships available to African Americans at any level (from high school through professional and postdoctoral). Entries are arranged by program type and indexed by sponsor, title, geographic coverage, subject, and deadline.

Financial Aid for Asian Americans

Reference Service Press
5000 Windplay Drive, Suite 4
El Dorado Hills, CA 95762
916-939-9620

This publication contains detailed descriptions of funding opportunities open to Chinese Americans, Japanese Americans, Korean Americans, Vietnamese Americans, Filipinos, and other Americans of Asian ancestry. Entries are arranged by program type and indexed by sponsor, title, geographic coverage, and subject.

Financial Aid for Hispanic Americans

Reference Service Press
5000 Windplay Drive, Suite 4
El Dorado Hills, CA 95762
916-939-9620

This publication contains detailed descriptions of scholarships, fellowships, loans, grants, awards, and internships available to Hispanic Americans, including Mexican Americans, Puerto Ricans, Cuban Americans, and others of Latin American origin. Entries are arranged by program type and indexed by sponsor, title, geographic coverage, subject, and deadline.

Financial Aid for Native Americans

Reference Service Press
5000 Windplay Drive, Suite 4
El Dorado Hills, CA 95762
916-939-9620

This publication lists funding opportunities open to American Indians, Native Alaskans, and Native Pacific Islanders (including Native Hawaiians and Samoans). Entries are arranged by program type and indexed by sponsor, title, geographic coverage, subject, and deadline.

Grants for Minorities

The Foundation Center
79 Fifth Avenue
New York, NY 10003-3076
212-807-3677

This publication lists grants of $10,000 or more recently awarded to programs for minority populations, such as blacks, Hispanics, Asian Americans, American Indians, gay men, lesbians, immigrants, and refugees. Information is indexed by the type of organization receiving the grant, and the geographic area in which the program is located.

The Higher Education MoneyBook for Minorities and Women: A Directory of Scholarships, Fellowships, Internships, Grants and Loans

Young Enterprises Inc.
5937 16th Street, NW
Washington, DC 20011
http://www.moneybook.com

This directory contains listings for undergraduate, graduate, and postgraduate students. Each listing includes a description of the program, name, address, telephone and fax number of the contact person, the amount of the award, and the deadline date.

Hispanic Scholarship Directory

National Association of Hispanic Publications
652 National Press Building
Washington, DC 20045
202-662-7250

This directory lists scholarships that are available to Hispanic students.

Hispanic Scholarship Guide

Chrysler/VISTA Hispanic Scholarship Guide
PO Box 3315
Livonia, MI 48151-3315
800-521-0953

This publication lists scholarships, grants, and other financial aid programs for Hispanics. It includes assistance from the federal government, college and universities, and private institutions for all fields of study.

National Directory of Foundation Grants for Native Americans

CRC Publishing Co.; Eaglerock Books
PO Box 222583
Kansas City, MO 64113-2583
800-268-2059
http://www.crcpub.com

This publication profiles the philanthropy of 56 private foundations considered to be the most prominent funders of Native American programs. Mainstream foundations who target American Indian communities and those that earmark Native American studies and education programs are featured.

Nestle Minority Scholarship Database

Community Affairs
800 North Brand Boulevard
Glendale, CA 91203

The Minority Scholarship Database gives free information on financial aid available to minority students nationwide. It lists more than 600 scholarships in a variety of fields, including business, engineering, and the sciences. In addition to assisting students seeking financial information, the database can also help students find sources of fellowships and summer internship programs. Students can access the database by writing to Nestle for an application.

Web Sites

Affiliated Tribes of Northwest Indians

222 Northwest Davis, Suite 403
Portland, OR 97209
503-241-0070
http://www.atni.org

ATNI is a nonprofit organization representing 43 Northwest tribal governments from Oregon, Idaho, Washington, southeast Alaska, Northern California, and western Montana. The Web site includes a calendar of events, lists of powwows and cultural gatherings, and information from committees on economic development, education, health, and other issues.

Africa Online

http://www.africaonline.com

An online connection to the countries of Africa.

African American Business Directory

http://www.sablenet.com

This site features career resources (job and resume posting), a directory of businesses, free email accounts, and a business center with information for the entrepreneur.

African American Business Link

http://www.aabl.com

Offers a business directory and information about promoting your business online.

African American Chemist

http://members.tripod.com/~chem89/index-2.html

This is an online networking group of individuals in the field of chemistry. The group corresponds via emails and bi-monthly chat sessions. Students and aspiring chemists are invited to join.

African American Internetwork

http://www.afamnet.com

This Web site for the African American community features information about jobs, technology, and education.

African American Online

http://www.proto-vision.com/aaol/

African American Online provides information to the African American community. Featured services include African American news, photography, a shopping mall, and radio stations.

Additional Information

African American Psychology Network
http://pages.hotbot.com/careers/talyre/index.html

This site provides African American students and those in the mental health profession with support and dialogue.

African American Shopping Mall
http://www.aasm.com

The Shopping Mall is a directory of links to products and services of interest to the African American community. It allows African American merchants to showcase their wares.

African American Web Connection
http://www.aawc.com

An African American Web directory of organizations, business sites, and publications online.

Afrika.com
http://www.afrika.com

An Internet site focusing on Afrocentric business and information.

Afrisearch
http://www.afrisearch.com

An African American Web directory and search engine.

Afrocentric Resources Centre
http://www.jazm.com

A directory of Web sites by and for African Americans; includes sections on careers and jobs, college, and organizations.

Afronet
http://www.afronet.com

An Internet service offering free Internet access, message boards, chat, and departments focusing on such subjects as business and technology.

American Visions Society
http://www.americanvisions.com

This African American online community features information on education, careers, finance, and health.

Artists' Corner
http://victorian.fortunecity.com/benjamin/187/

The Artists' Corner is a Web site where artists of all genres can share their work and participate in an online community.

Asia Vision
http://asia-vision.com

This Web site provides university information, chat rooms, feature articles, and job preparation.

Asian Avenue
http://www.communityconnect.com/AsianAvenue.html

Asian Avenue is the largest online community for Asian Americans. Membership entitles you to chat room access, personal pages, and career information.

Asian-Net
http://www.asia-net.com

This online job database serves the Asia/Pacific-Rim business community by providing career information to professionals, and assisting companies in recruitment.

Asian Web
http://www.asianweb.net

Asian Web is an Internet carrier that provides Internet service solutions for businesses and individuals. The site hosts an Asian Community Bulletin Board.

AsiaWired.com
http://www.asiawired.com

This Internet company offers media, conference services, market research, and interactive services.

Ask Recy
http://www.askrecy.com

An online question-and-answer column with advice for minority business owners.

Black College Experience
http://www.blackcollegeexperience.com

Black College Experience is an online magazine for college students.

Black College Sports Online
http://www.onnidan.com

This online magazine provides news and conference reports on college sports.

Black Health Net
http://www.blackhealthnet.com

This online health source for African Americans features informative articles, a doctor search, a medical q&a, and other free services.

Black Informed Professionals
http://firms.findlaw.com/bipinc/

This is an online network joining African American professionals. It allows you to network and to exchange information about your career.

Black Voices
http://www.blackvoices.com

This online community for African Americans features a career center with job and resume postings.

Black Vue
http://www.blackvue.com

An African American Web site directory with links to organizations, reference, and business and education information.

Black World Today
http://www.tbwt.com

The Black World Today is an online collective of African American journalists, writers, artists, communicators, and entrepreneurs.

BlackAthlete.com
http://blackathlete.com

An online magazine covering the sports industry and the concerns of African American athletes.

Blackcollege.com
http://www.blackcollege.com

This site features articles about campus life and provides extensive information about the college experience for African American students. Also features a directory of historically black colleges and universities.

Blackworld
http://www.blackworld.com

This Internet directory of resources for African Americans links to arts and culture, business, education, finance, and government sites, and many others.

BPNetwork
http://www.bpnetwork.com

BPNetwork provides business services and resources for African American professionals. On the site, you can browse company Web pages, job listings, lists of mutual funds, and discussion groups.

Additional Information

Click 2 Asia
http://www.click2asia.com

This online community gives members access to forums, clubs, chat, and news.

Creative Invest Research
http://www.creativeinvest.com

This investment research and management company provides information online about minority and women-owned financial institutions.

CVLatino.com
http://www.cvlatino.com

This site allows Hispanic professionals to share their curriculum vitae with other professionals and global companies. The site features many job listings for individuals who speak Spanish, Portuguese, and English.

DiversiLink Employment Web Site
http://www.diversilink.com

Sponsored by The Society of Hispanic Professional Engineers, DiversiLink is an online database of jobs and resumes.

Diversity Employment
http://www.diversityemployment.com

Diversity Employment is a multicultural employment resource offering a job and resume database, and advertising opportunities.

Diversity/Careers in Engineering and Information Technology
http://www.diversitycareers.com

This online magazine covers the rapidly growing IT industry, and focuses on companies with diversity initiatives. The magazine publishes feature articles, provides access to back issues, and features an annual college issue. The Web site hosts a resume database.

DiversityDirect
http://www.diversitydirect.com

A free service for job seekers, the site allows you to search through the extensive database by employer, industry, job title, and geographic location.

DiversityInc.com
http://www.diversityinc.com

This Web site promotes diversity in the workplace and in business relations. It consists of 4 departments of information: workforce, suppliers, customers, and investors.

Everythingblack.com
http://www.everythingblack.com

In addition to hundreds of links to Web sites of interest to African Americans, Everythingblack.com features discussion boards, free email, and stock quotes.

Hispanic Scholarship Fund Online
http://www.hsf.net

The Hispanic Scholarship Fund offers its own scholarship programs as well as lists updated scholarship information and internship opportunities.

Hispanicareers.com
http://www.hispanicareers.com

A database of companies committed to diversity; a free career search engine.

Homecoming: The Networking Magazine for Black Graduates
http://www.homecoming.com

This online site features free information for graduates and students affiliated with the nation's Historically Black Colleges and Universities.

I Love China

http://www.iLoveChina.net

This Web directory offers a message board, free classifieds, an index of Chinese news, and links to organizations and churches.

ihispano.com

http://www.ihispano.com

This Web site serves as a career information resource for Hispanics; it allows you to create a profile and to search for jobs.

INDIANnet

http://indiannet.indian.com

This Indian owned and operated network is dedicated to establishing and developing affordable public access, computerized information, and communication services for American Indians and Alaskan Natives.

International Black Index

http://www.blackindex.com

A Web site directory divided into 4 sections: business, culture, entertainment, and life.

Job Latino

http://www.joblatino.com

This free online database of resumes also features listings of many organizations, job training programs, and scholarships and fellowships.

Komericans.com

http://www.komericans.com

A Web resource for Korean Americans. Features links to Korean news, community information, education sites, and other Internet sources.

Latino Link

http://www.latinolink.com

Latino Link is an online community offering free email, chat, bulletin boards, a job bank, and links to resources for students and entrepreneurs.

Latino Medicine

http://www.latinomed.com

A Web site featuring information of interest to Hispanic health care professionals and students. Includes information on education, research, and scholarships.

Latino Net Pages

http://www.latinonetpages.com

A directory of Latino businesses and organizations on the Web.

LatinoNet

2601 Mission Street, Suite 707
San Francisco, CA 94110-3111
415-550-2493
http://thecity.sfsu.edu/users/LatinoNet/

This online computer network offers information on scholarships, naturalization issues, grant-making opportunities, Latino nonprofit agencies, news briefs, job openings, Latino community events, resource sharing, demographics, etc. Individuals must subscribe to America Online.

LatPro Professional Network

http://www.LatPro.com

The network assists Spanish and Portuguese bilingual professionals in meeting industry recruiters. The site also features news and forums for commentary.

MBNet.com

http://www.mbnet.com

MBNet.com is a business information and resource service. It provides opportunities for minorities to market and expand their businesses.

Additional Information

Minorities' Job Bank
http://www.minorities-jb.com

The job bank allows you to search the job listings, post resumes, and access employer profiles. You can also visit a special section on career development.

Minority Business and Professional Yellow Pages
http://www.minoritybusiness.com

The online Yellow Pages lists minority businesses and professionals; the site also includes links to a variety of minority resources.

Minority Business Network Global
http://www.mbnglobal.com

An online site dedicated to covering diversity in the business world.

Minority Career Connection
http://www.minority2career.com

An online professional minority job placement service.

Minority Career Network
http://www.minoritycareernet.com

This online employment service offers free access to thousands of positions nationwide.

MinorityFinance.com
http://www.minorityfinance.com

This site serves as a resource to minorities seeking business financing.

MOLIS Scholarships/Fellowships
http://www.fie.com/molis/scholar.htm

This search service provides information about scholarship opportunities for minorities.

Multicultural Publishing and Education Catalog
http://www.mpec.org

The MPEC is a national network for independent publishers, authors, educators, and librarians committed to multicultural books and materials.

National Diversity Newspaper Job Bank
http://www.newsjobs.com

This job bank promotes diversity in the newspaper industry and allows you to view or post jobs, submit a resume, and link to job Web sites.

Native Web
http://www.nativeweb.org

Contains listings of resources for indigenous cultures around the world. Features news features, message boards, job listings, and links to Web sites.

NativeTech
http://www.nativetech.org

This educational Web site covers topics of Native American technology and art.

Netnoir
http://www.netnoir.com

Netnoir: The Black Network features articles, links, and online communities (under the topics of education, spirituality, life, and health), along with separate channels on travel, technology, finance, and black issues.

Netstudent.com
http://www.netstudent.com

This site on student life offers feature articles, links to resources such as financial aid and other services, job listings, and news.

Network of African American GIS Professionals

http://clubs.yahoo.com/clubs/naagisp

The goal of NAAGISP is to promote networking between African American professionals and students involved in the implementation, study, or use of Geographic Information Systems. GIS is a relatively new and rapidly expanding information technology. It employs geographers, planners, computer Scientists, programmers, analysts, as well as other spatial information professionals.

Northern Cherokee Cultural Association

http://clubs.yahoo.com/clubs/northerncherokeeculturalassn

The site serves as a forum for people of Cherokee heritage to discuss history, culture, news, and current events.

Nubian Network

http://www.nubian.net

This site offers an Internet networking community for African American businesses.

Red Ibis

http://www.redibis.com

Red Ibis connects Internet industry professionals of color. The site contains message boards, mailing lists, and an educational center.

San Diego BLAACK Pages

http://www.sdbp.com

A Web directory with links to pages on black history, education, organizations, classifieds, and discussion forums.

TodoLatino

http://www.todolatino.com

The site features recent news and a links directory with a variety of categories including careers, culture, education, and organizations.

United States Black Online

http://www.usbol.com

USBOL is the largest African American Internet services provider in the country, offering networking services to individuals, businesses, and organizations.

Universal Black Pages

http://www.ubp.com

A directory of educational opportunities, professional and student organizations, and other resources online.

Yolk Magazine

http://www.yolk.com

Yolk is an electronic magazine about Asian American pop culture and experience for young Asian Americans. The magazine accepts article submissions.

Institution and Financial Aid Name Index

This index lists the names of all the institutions, organizations, publications, Web sites, and financial aid (fellowships, grants, scholarships, awards, loans, internships) that appear in this directory.

Indexes

Indexes

Indexes

Indexes

Indexes

Indexes

Indexes

Indexes

Indexes

Indexes

Indexes

Strayer College 271
Studio Art Centers International 165
      International Incentive Awards 165
      Scholarship 165
Studio Museum in Harlem 97, 230
      Grants 97
Substance Abuse and Mental Health Services
   Administration 84
      Fellowships 84
Sul Ross State University 271
Sumitomo Bank of California Scholarships 136
Sundance Institute 85
      Native American Program 85
SUNY Empire State/Brockport College
   Foundation Minority Honors Scholarship
   164
SuperOnda 286
Sylvia L. Wilson Memorial Scholarship 152
Synod of the Covenant 165
      Scholarship 165

T

Talento Bilingue de Houston 230
Talladega College 271
Tau Beta Sigma Sorority 280
Teach for America 230
TELACU Education Foundation 165
TELACU Education Foundation's Scholarship
   Program 165
Tenneco Scholarship 176
Tennessee African American Graduate
   Fellowship 64
Tennessee State University 271
Tennessee Student Assistance Corporation 85
      Minority Teaching Fellows Program 85
Tennessee Technological University 165
      Scholarships 165
Tennessee, University of, Knoxville 165
      Minority Undergraduate Scholarship
      165
      Scholarship 165
Texas A&M International University 272
Texas A&M University, College Station 165
      Scholarships 166
Texas A&M University, Kingsville 272
Texas College 272
Texas Southern University 273

Texas Southmost College/University of Texas,
   Brownsville 273
Texas State Technical College 272
Texas, University of (Brownsville) 273
Texas, University of (of the Permian Basin) 273
Texas, University of, El Paso 273
Texas, University of, Pan American 273
Texas, University of, San Antonio 273
Theodore Ward Prize 100
Thomas P. Papandrew Scholarship 138
Thornton (Ann C.) Memorial Fund Scholarship
   166
Thunderbird: The American School of
   International Management 166
      Scholarships 166
Thurgood Marshall Dissertation Fellowship 69
Thurgood Marshall Scholarship Fund 230
Tlingit and Haida Indian Tribes of Alaska 230
TodoLatino 295
Tonkawa Tribe of Oklahoma 166
      Financial Aid 166
Tougaloo College 273
Trenholm State Technical College 274
Tribal College Journal 286
Trinidad State Junior College 274
Trinity College, Hartford 85
Trinity International University 274
Try Us Resources 286
Tulalip Tribe 166
      Scholarship 166
Turtle Mountain Community College 274
Tuskegee University 166, 274
      Awards 166
      Scholarship 166
Twenty-first Century Foundation 230

U

U.S. Bureau of Indian Affairs 97
      Higher Education Grants 98
U.S. Department of Agriculture 98, 166
      Higher Education Multicultural Scholars
      Program 98
      National Scholars Program 166
U.S. Department of Education 85
      Indian Fellowship Program 85
U.S. Department of Energy 166
      Minority Honors Training and Industrial
      Assistance Program 166

Indexes

State Index

This index lists financial aid (fellowships, grants, scholarships, awards, loans, internships) by state.

Alabama

Fellowships

Alabama A&M University 2, 57
Auburn University 2, 64

Minority Colleges

Alabama State University, 233
Bishop State Community College, 237
Faulkner University, 246
J.F. Drake Technical College, 252
Lawson State Community College, 254
Miles College, 258
Oakwood College, 263
Selma University, 269
Stillman College, 271
Talladega College, 271
Trenholm State Technical College, 274
Tuskegee University, 274

Scholarships

Baptist Health System, 113
Bishop State Community College, 114
Tuskegee University, 166, 172

Alaska

Grants

Alaska Native Health Career Program, 87, 104
Alaska State Council on the Arts, 87

Scholarships

Alaska Native Health Career Program, 87, 104
Sitka Tribe of Alaska Higher Education Program, 162

Arizona

Fellowships

Arizona State University, 62, 138
Arizona, University of, Tucson, 62

Grants

Hopi Tribe Grants and Scholarship Program, 91, 134

Internships

Arizona State University 62, 138
Environmental Education Outreach Program, 178
Northern Arizona University, 178

Minority Colleges

American Indian College of the Assemblies of God, 234
Arizona Institute of Business and Technical-Phoenix, 234
Arizona Institute of Business and Technology, 235
Arizona Western College, 234
Central Arizona College, 239
Diné College, 244

Internships

Minority Colleges

Scholarships

Indexes

Colorado

Grants

Minority Colleges

Scholarships

Connecticut

Fellowships

Mystic Seaport Museum, 75
Trinity College, Hartford, 85

Internships

Hispanic Health Council, 179

Minority Colleges

Mashantucket Pequot Academy, 257

Scholarships

American Institute for Foreign Study, 108
Connecticut, University of, West Hartford, 123
Hartford Courant Foundation, Inc., 131
Quinnipiac College, 159

Delaware

Minority Colleges

Delaware State University, 243

Scholarships

Delaware, University of, 125

District of Columbia

Awards

American College Theater Festival, 99
National Association of Black Women Attorneys, 101
National Black Law Students Association, 102

Fellowships

Academy for Educational Development, 57
American Academy of Child and Adolescent Psychiatry, 58
American Association of Health Plans, 58
American Association of University Women, 58
American Nurses Association, Inc., 60, 88

American Planning Association, 60, 110
American Political Science Association, 60
American Psychiatric Association, 61
American Psychological Association, 61
American Society for Microbiology, 61
American Sociological Association, 62
Congressional Black Caucus Foundation, 68, 123
Congressional Hispanic Caucus Institute, 68, 123
Hispanic Bar Association, 71
Hispanic Link Journalism Foundation, 71, 133
Hispanic-Serving Health Professions Schools, 71
Howard University College of Medicine, 72
Institute for the Study of World Politics, 73
National Academy of Sciences, 76
National Asian Pacific American Bar Association, 77, 144
National Council of La Raza, 78
National Organization for the Professional Advancement of Black Chemists and, 79, 149
Chemical Engineers, 79, 108, 149
National Puerto Rican Coalition, 79
Radio and Television News Directors Foundation, 82, 159
Smithsonian Institution, 83, 97
U.S. Department of Education, 85
U.S. National Endowment for the Humanities, 85
U.S. National Research Council, 86

Grants

Administration for Native Americans, 87
American Association of State Colleges and Universities, 87
American Nurses Association, Inc., 60, 88
American Society of Mechanical Engineers, 61, 88
Business and Professional Women's Foundation, 89
Margaret McNamara Memorial Fund, 92
Office of Indian Education, 95, 98
Smithsonian Institution, 83, 97
U.S. Bureau of Indian Affairs, 97
U.S. Department of Agriculture, 98, 166
U.S. General Accounting Office, 98
U.S. National Park Service, 98
Zeta Phi Beta Sorority, Washington, 171

Indexes

Florida

Grants

Inter American Press Association, 92
National Hispanic Corporate Achievers, 94

Minority Colleges

Barry University, 235
Bethune-Cookman College, 236
Caribbean Center for Advanced Studies-Miami, 239
Edward Waters College, 245
Florida Agricultural and Mechanical University, 246
Florida International University, University Park, 247
Florida Memorial College, 247
Miami, University of, 258
Miami-Dade Community College, Wolfson, 258
Saint Thomas University, 267
Trinity International University, 274

Scholarships

Bethune-Cookman College, 114, 173
Central Florida, University of, 118
Community Foundation for Palm Beach and Martin Counties, 122
Florida Department of Education, 127
Florida Education Fund, 70, 128
PCP Bar Association, 157
Pinellas County Education Foundation, 157
Seminole Tribe of Florida, 161
Stetson University, Gulfport, 164

Georgia

Fellowships

Atlanta History Center: Headquarters for the National Museum Fellows Program, 63
Clark Atlanta University, 67, 172-173
Emory University, 69
Fund for Theological Education, 70
Omega Psi Phi Fraternity, 81, 155

Minority Colleges

Albany State College, 233

Clark-Atlanta University, 241
Fort Valley State University, 248
Interdenominational Theological Center, 252
Morehouse College, 259
Morehouse School of Medicine, 259
Morris Brown College, 259
Paine College, 264
Savannah State University, 268
Spelman College, 271

Scholarships

Black Caucus of the American Library Association, 114
Cox Minority Journalism Scholarship
Eddie G. Robinson Foundation, 127
Institute of Industrial Engineers, 135
Omega Psi Phi Fraternity, 81, 155
Spelman College, 138, 164, 172

Hawaii

Fellowships

American Association of University Women, Hawaii, 58
East-West Center, 69

Grants

Pacific Islanders in Communications, 96

Scholarships

Fukunaga Scholarship Foundation, 129
Hawaii Community Foundation, 132

Idaho

Scholarships

Albertson College of Idaho, 105
Nez Perce Tribe, 153

National Consortium for Graduate Degrees for Minorities in Engineering, Inc., 78
Purdue University, 72, 82, 100

Internships

National Collegiate Athletic Association, 147
Notre Dame, University of
Purdue University, 72, 82, 100

Loans

Disciples of Christ (Christian Church), 104, 126

Minority Colleges

Martin University, 257

Scholarships

American College of Sports Medicine, 106
Ball State University, 113
Disciples of Christ (Christian Church), 104, 126
Evansville, University of, 127
Future Farmers of America, 129
Huntington College, 134
Indiana State Student Assistance Commission, 135
National Collegiate Athletic Association, 147
Spokane Tribe, 137, 164
State Student Assistance Commission of Indiana, 164

Iowa

Fellowships

Iowa, University of, 72-73, 92, 100, 136

Grants

Iowa, University of, 72-73, 92, 100, 136

Scholarships

Briar Cliff College, 115
Des Moines Register, 126
Iowa, University of, 72-73, 92, 100, 136
Morris Scholarship Fund, 143

Kansas

Grants

Bethel College, 88

Minority Colleges

Dodge City Community College, 244

Scholarships

Garden City Community College Endowment Association, 129
Haskell Indian Nations University, 131
Kansas Board of Regents, 137
Kansas, University of Lawrence, 137

Kentucky

Fellowships

Kentucky, University of, 74

Grants

Presbyterian Church, 96, 153, 157-158

Minority Colleges

Kentucky State University, 253

Scholarships

Asbury College, 111
Presbyterian Church, 96, 153, 157-158
Western Kentucky University, 170

Louisiana

Fellowships

Zeta Phi Beta Sorority, 87, 99, 171

Minority Colleges

Dillard University, 244
Grambling State University, 248

Indexes

Maine

Scholarships

Maryland

Awards

Fellowships

Grants

Loans

Minority Colleges

Scholarships

Massachusetts

Fellowships

Internships

Scholarships

Michigan

Awards

Fellowships

Grants

Internships

Minority Colleges

Scholarships

Minnesota

Fellowships

Grants

Indexes

Internships

Minority Colleges

Scholarships

Mississippi

Minority Colleges

Missouri

Fellowships

Internships

Loans

Minority Colleges

Scholarships

Montana

Grants

Minority Colleges

Scholarships

Nebraska

Awards

Indexes

Scholarships

New York

Awards

Fellowships

Grants

Internships

Loans

Minority Colleges

North Carolina

North Dakota

South Dakota

Fellowships

Tennessee

Fellowships

Scholarships

Texas

Fellowships

Indexes

Minority Colleges

Scholarships

Washington

Fellowships

Grants

Internships

Minority Colleges

Scholarships

West Virginia

Minority Colleges

Scholarships

Wisconsin

Fellowships

Grants

Minority Colleges

Scholarships

Wyoming

Academic Index

This index lists financial aid (fellowships, grants, scholarships, awards, loans, internships) by academic subject.

Indexes

Athletics

Scholarships

Business

Fellowships

Grants

Internships

Loans

Scholarships

Indexes

Business, Computer Science

Scholarships

Business, Education

Fellowships

Business, Education, Engineering, Health, Law

Scholarships

Business, Engineering

Scholarships

Business, Engineering, Computer Science

Scholarships

Indexes

National Action Council for Minorities in
    Engineering, 76, 101, 143
Oak Ridge Associated Universities, 81, 155
U.S. National Research Council, 86

Grants

American Society of Mechanical Engineers, 61,
    88

Internships

American Society of Mechanical Engineers, 61,
    88

Scholarships

American Institute of Architects/American
    Architectural Foundation, 108
American Institute of Chemical Engineers, 108
American Nuclear Society, 109
American Water Works Association, 111
Amoco Foundation, Inc., 111
Bay Area Urban League, 114
Chicago Urban League, 119
Chinese American Engineers and Scientists
    Association of Southern California,120
COMTO National Scholarship Awards Program
General Motors Engineering Excellence Awards,
    173
Institute of Industrial Engineers, 135
Kansas, University of Lawrence, 137
League of United Latin American Citizens, 139
Malcolm Pirnie Scholars Program, 174
Maryland, University of, College Park, 140
National Action Council for Minorities in
    Engineering, 76, 101, 143
National Society of Black Engineers, 149-150
National Technical Association, 151
Oak Ridge Associated Universities, 81, 155
Society of Hispanic Professional Engineers
    Foundation, 162
Society of Women Engineers, 162
Tuskegee University, 166, 172
Xerox Technical Minority Scholarship Program,
    170

Engineering, Humanities, Science

Fellowships

National Academy of Sciences, 76

Scholarships

George Bird Grinnell American Indian
    Children's Fund, 129

Engineering, Science

Fellowships

Argonne National Laboratory, 62
California Institute of Technology, 65
Southern Illinois University, Carbondale, 84, 97

Grants

National Science Foundation, 81, 95

Internships

Korean-American Scientists and Engineers
    Association, 138

Scholarships

AT&T Bell Laboratories, Holmdel, 113
Council of Energy Resource Tribes, 124
Development Fund for Black Students in
    Science and Technology, 126
Falu Foundation, 127
Korean-American Scientists and Engineers
    Association, 138
Society of Mexican American Engineers and
    Scientists, 162

Engineering/Science

Fellowships

National Consortium for Graduate Degrees for
    Minorities in Engineering, Inc., 78

Health: Doctors

Awards

National Medical Fellowships, 78-79, 102, 148, 180

Fellowships

American Psychiatric Association, 61
American Psychological Association, 61
Bristol-Myers Squibb Foundation, 64
Center of American Indian and Minority Health, 67
Fred Hutchinson Cancer Research Center, 70
National Heart, Lung, and Blood Institute, 78, 93, 179
National Institute of Allergy and Infectious Disease, 78
National Institute of General Medical Sciences, 79, 95
National Medical Fellowships, 78-79, 102, 148, 180
Sealy Center on Aging, 83

Grants

Alaska Native Health Career Program, 87, 104
American Digestive Health Foundation, 88
Center for AIDS Prevention Studies, 90
Medical College of Pennsylvania, 93
National Cancer Institute, 93
National Heart, Lung, and Blood Institute, 78, 93, 179
National Institute of Arthritis and Musculoskeletal and Skin Diseases, 94
National Institute of Mental Health, 62, 69, 90, 94
National Institute on Aging, 94
Zeta Phi Beta Sorority, Washington, 171

Internships

Case Western Reserve University, School of Medicine, 178

Loans

Missouri Department of Health, 104

Scholarships

American Dental Association, 106
American Respiratory Care Foundation, 110
BECA Foundation, 114
California Chicano/Latino Medical Student Association, 116
Dr. Rosa Minoka Hill Fund, 126
Harry C. Jaecker Scholarship, 173
Higgins Scholarship, 173
National Medical Fellowships, 78-79, 102, 148, 180
Spelman College, 138, 164, 172
U.S. Department of Health and Human Services, Rockville, 167

Health: General/Other

Awards

National Association of Health Services Executives, 102, 145

Fellowships

American Academy of Allergy and Immunology, 57
American Academy of Child and Adolescent Psychiatry, 58
American Association of Health Plans, 58
American Speech-Language-Hearing Association Foundation, 62
Columbia University, 67-68, 82, 148
Congressional Hispanic Caucus Institute, 68, 123
Harvard Medical School, 70
Hispanic-Serving Health Professions Schools, 71
Kaiser Family Foundation, 74, 179
Native American Center of Excellence, 80
Substance Abuse and Mental Health Services Administration, 69, 84

Grants

Health Resources and Services Administration, 91
Iowa, University of, 72-73, 92, 100, 136
National Institute on Deafness and Other Communication Disorders, 94

Health: General/Other, Law

Scholarships

Health: Nurses

Fellowships

Grants

Scholarships

Humanities

Awards

Fellowships

Grants

Internships

Scholarships

Indexes

Journalism, Law

Scholarships

Law

Awards

Fellowships

Internships

National Conference of Black Lawyers

Scholarships

Law, Social Science

Fellowships

Performing and Visual Arts

Fellowships

Grants

Internships

Scholarships

Religion

Awards

Fellowships

Grants

Loans

Scholarships

Science

Fellowships

Grants

Internships

Scholarships

Skilled Trades

Scholarships

Social Sciences

Fellowships

Grants

Internships

Scholarships

Minority Index

This index lists financial aid (fellowships, grants, scholarships, awards, loans, internships) by type of minority.

African American

Indexes

Indexes

Asian American

Awards

Fellowships

Grants

Internships

Scholarships

Hispanic American

Awards

Avon Latina Model of the Year, 99

California Chicano News Media Association, 99, 116

Chicano/Latino Literary Prize, 100

Hispanic Association of AT&T Employees, New Jersey, 101, 132

Inner City Cultural Center, 101

Fellowships

Arts International, 63

Columbia University, 67-68, 82, 148

Congressional Hispanic Caucus Institute, 68, 123

Hispanic Link Journalism Foundation, 71, 133

Hispanic-Serving Health Professions Schools, 71

NALEO Educational Fund, 76

National Council of La Raza, 78

National Puerto Rican Coalition, 79

Grants

Business and Professional Women's Foundation, 89

Hispanic Theological Initiative, 91

Inter American Press Association, 92

National Hispanic Corporate Achievers, 94

National Latino Communication Center, 95

Youth Opportunities Foundation, 99

Internships

Congressional Hispanic Caucus Institute, 68, 123

Hispanic Alliance for Career Enhancement, 132

Hispanic Health Council, 179

NALEO Educational Fund, 76

National Association of Hispanic Journalists, 145

TELACU Education Foundation, 165

U.S. Hispanic Chamber of Commerce, 167

Scholarships

American Association of Hispanic Certified Public Accountants, 105

Northern California Chapter, 105

American G.I. Forum, 106-107

Amigos Scholarship Foundation, 111

Amoco Foundation, Inc., 111

Arizona, University of, Phoenix, 111

Association for the Advancement of Mexican-American Students, 112

BECA Foundation, 114

California Chicano News Media Association, 99, 116

California Chicano/Latino Medical Student Association, 116

Carnegie Mellon University, 118

Central Florida, University of, 118

Chevrolet Excellence in Education Award, 119

Chicana Latina Foundation, 119

Congressional Hispanic Caucus Institute, 68, 123

Cuban American Scholarship Fund, 125

Cuban American Teachers' Association, 125

Disciples of Christ (Christian Church), 104, 126

Falu Foundation, 127

Florida Department of Education, 127

Garden City Community College Endowment Association, 129

Hartford Courant Foundation, Inc., 131

Hispanic Alliance for Career Enhancement, 132

Hispanic Association of AT&T Employees, New Jersey, 101, 132

Hispanic College Fund Scholarships, 132

Hispanic Dental Association, 133

Hispanic Designers, Inc., 133

Hispanic Link Journalism Foundation, 71, 133

Hispanic Outlook Scholarship Fund, 133

Hispanic Scholarship Fund, 133

Hispanic Women's Council, 134

Hispanic Women's Council Scholarship Program, 134

Jesse Arias Scholarship Fund, 137

Kansas, University of, Lawrence, 137

Lambda Theta Phi, 138

Latin American Educational Foundation, 139

Latin Business Foundation, 139

League of United Latin American Citizens, 139

McDonald's, 140

Mexican American Business and Professional Scholarship Association, 141

Mexican American Grocers Association, 141

Indexes

Mexican American Legal Defense and Educational Fund, 141
National Association of Hispanic Journalists, 145
National Association of Hispanic Nurses, 145
National Hispanic Foundation for the Arts, 148
National Society of Hispanic MBAs, 151
Professional Hispanics in Energy, 158
Project Cambio Foundation, 158
Reforma, 159
Sacramento Hispanic Chamber of Commerce, 160
Society of Hispanic Professional Engineers Foundation, 162
Society of Mexican American Engineers and Scientists, 162
Southwestern University, School of Law, 163
TELACU Education Foundation, 165
U.S. Hispanic Chamber of Commerce, 167
Vikki Carr Scholarship Foundation, 168
Washington University, St.Louis, 86, 169

Scholarships, Internships

National Association of Hispanic Journalists, 145

More than one minority group

Awards

Calvin Theological Seminary, 100, 117
Committee on Institutional Cooperation, 72, 100
National Action Council for Minorities in Engineering, 76, 101, 143
National Medical Fellowships, 78-79, 102, 148, 180
Organization of American Historians, 103

Fellowships

Academy for Educational Development, 57
Alabama A&M University, 57
American Academy of Allergy and Immunology, 57
American Academy of Child and Adolescent Psychiatry, 58

American Association of Family and Consumer Sciences, 58
American Association of Health Plans, 58

This book is to help meh get smarter by the time Im in 7th grade and I also want to be a doctor when I grow up so this will help meh

LaTavia Parke

Association Foundation, 62
American Vocational Association, 62
Argonne National Laboratory, 62
Arizona, University of, Tucson, 62
Arkansas Department of Higher Education, 62, 88, 111
Atlanta History Center: Headquarters for the National Museum Fellows Program, 63
Bristol-Myers Squibb Foundation, 64
Brown University, 65
Buffalo, University at, 65
California Institute of Technology, 65
California State University, Northridge, 65
California Student Aid Commission, 65, 89-90
California, University of, Berkeley, 65
California, University of, Los Angeles, 66, 117
Carleton College, 66, 118
Chicago, University of, 67, 72, 100
City University of New York, New York, 67
Clark Atlanta University, 67, 172-173
Columbia University, 67-68, 82, 148
Congressional Black Caucus Foundation, 68, 123
Consortium for Graduate Study in Management, 68
Council on Social Work Education, 68
Dartmouth College, 69
Earthwatch Institute, 69
Emory University, 69
Entomological Society of America, 70

Grants

Indexes

Internships

Loans

Scholarships

Indexes

Native American

Awards

Fellowships

Grants

Internships

Loans

Scholarships

Indexes